DECLINE OF HONOR

AVRI EL-AD

with James Creech III

Henry Regnery Company · Chicago

Library of Congress Cataloging in Publication Data

El-Ad, Avri, 1925-
  Decline of honor.

  Autobiographical.
  1. Espionage, Israeli—Egypt. 2. Spies—Personal
narratives. 3. El-Ad, Avri, 1925-   I. Creech,
James, joint author. II. Title.
DS119.8.E3E4   327′.12′0924 [B]   75-32959
ISBN 0-8092-8116-3

Published by Henry Regnery Company
180 North Michigan Avenue, Chicago, Illinois 60601
Manufactured in the United States of America
Library of Congress Catalog Card Number: 75-32959
International Standard Book Number: 0-8092-8116-3

Published simultaneously in Canada by
Beaverbooks
953 Dillingham Road
Pickering, Ontario L1W 1Z7
Canada

This book is dedicated to my son, Harel,
my family, and all my friends
who stood beside me in the darkest hours of my life.

Preface

The material contained in my story, *Decline of Honor*, is drawn from memory, public records, and documentation. The portrayals are true, as I experienced them.

The contents of Books I, II, and III are documented in secret field reports I wrote as an operative of Israel's Military Intelligence Corps, field reports once known in intelligence circles as "El-Ad Sarchi's volumes."

Book IV is also documented in secret archives. My interrogation transcript is an integral part of my *in camera* trial transcript, as is my appeal, after conviction, to the Supreme Court. None of the "secret material" has been made available to me. A concerted governmental effort has long guaranteed its inaccessibility.

My country, Israel, has yet to admit its complicity in this story, which remains censored to this day, more than twenty years after its onset, holding to the theory that "what is best for the State's world image must be."

The world slate, for the most part, has been left clean in the scandals known as the security mishap and the Lavon affair. Yet this successful suppression has also kept them in the realm of the arcane, a mystery with a missing link. My story supplies this missing link.

There will be those who will question the clarity of recall of details that are recorded here. To those readers I say only this: When one is young, in love with life, and threatened with losing it at any moment, his awareness is indescribably heightened. Once recorded, the memory endures. This, then, is the way it happened, the way it was.

Avri (Seidenwerg) El-Ad

Introduction

The end of World War II created a forum for a strange and different kind of conflict: the cold war. The teams were clearly marked, and the players were easily recognizable: capitalists, Communists. The cold war divided most of the world into the East and West supercamps.

However, a new, equally fervent, philosophy had arisen in the Middle East: nationalism. By the early 1950s, it was synonymous with David Ben-Gurion's Israel and Gamal Abdul Nasser's Egypt, the prime impetus for all Arab nationalism.

As capitalism and communism focused on the Middle East, nationalism was to eclipse the West's game plan—but this was not to be fully realized until late 1955, when Nasser dramatically announced to the world his "cotton for arms" agreement with the Soviet Union's "salesmen," the Czechs. Russia's Middle East ambitions, dating back to czarist times, would finally be fact: They would have a political and military foothold in the area. All of this because of one man's narrowed vision, forcing a small country into desperation.

January, 1953, was a turning point in America's foreign policy: Harry S Truman passed the presidency to Dwight D. Eisenhower (and Eisenhower's secretary of state, John Foster Dulles, took over).

Truman almost unqualifiedly a supporter of Israel since her creation[1],

---

1. Upon vacating Washington, Truman said at a testimonial dinner in Independence, Missouri: "6:12 P.M. on Friday, May 14, 1948, when I recognized Israel, was the proudest moment of my life."

had enjoyed the general approval of the American constituency on Middle East policy. To the American the Israeli was young, eager, and determined; the Arab was old, corrupt, and resigned.

Under Truman, Israel enjoyed overwhelming "favoritism" as compared to the emerging Arab countries, which were experiencing the hangover of European colonialism but were afire with nationalism. One of the few concessions Truman had not made to Israel was the delivery of offensive armaments. Earlier, in the tripartite Declaration of 1950, the United States, England, and France—the major arms exporters—had agreed to limit the sale of arms to the Middle East belligerents to strictly defensive weapons.

On July 23, 1952, six months prior to Eisenhower's inauguration, a military junta led by Lt. Colonel Gamal Abdul Nasser overthrew the Egyptian despot, King Farouk. Colonel Nasser's request to Truman for aid and arms was ill-timed; only weeks remained of Truman's incumbency. Neither government was sufficiently prepared to finalize the secret talks; negotiation doors were left open for the incoming administration.

Beginning in January 1953, Secretary of State Dulles would almost single-handedly direct American foreign policy. After a whirlwind assessment of America's political posture in the Middle East, Dulles embarked on a course of "friendly impartiality," making it clear that the bias of the previous administration would be corrected. The United States would henceforth strive to help all peoples in the area, without prejudice, without favoritism.

Accompanied by Harold E. Stassen, mutual security director, who had previously urged Congress to give special help to Egypt, Dulles had found on his 21-day tour of Arab countries (and Israel) a picture to gladden his puritanical, anti-Communist heart. Arab nationalism, epitomized in Nasser's regime in Egypt, presented a portrait of staunch anti-communism. Dulles envisioned Egypt as the Arab cornerstone of a Middle East alliance aimed at ringing Russia in the cold war.

Dulles's next move was clear. To win Nasser's allegiance he began pressuring England to remove her eighty-thousand-man garrison based along the Suez Canal and to quit Egyptian soil altogether. (After seven decades of British hegemony, this was the primary goal of every Egyptian nationalist.) Dulles's direction was furthered by his assistant secretary of state on Middle East affairs, Henry A. Byroade, who said in July, six months after Dulles took over the State Department, that arming the Arabs was more important than arming Israel. Dulles had already announced that he was deeply shocked by the Israeli plan for the immigration of three or four million Jews to Israel—making gain with Nasser, who, like all Middle East Arabs, feared the Jewish influx.

In September, pressured by Dulles and Nasser-backed Arab vehemence, London announced a *near* agreement with Egypt for the evacuation of all British troops from the Suez Canal.

In October a test of Dulles's impartiality occurred after the Israeli Kibya incident. Reacting to only one of hundreds of border skirmishes with Arab guerrillas, an Israeli force crossed into Jordan and carried out a reprisal raid on the village of Kibya that left scores of dead or maimed Arabs and much destruction. Dulles's reaction was immediate: He demanded that the United Nations condemn Israel and, as a personal sanction (but attributed to unrelated circumstances), he announced that $26 million in economic aid to Israel would be withheld. Eisenhower at first supported Dulles's decision but quickly rescinded, succumbing to powerful Jewish lobbying.

Relations between world Zionists and Eisenhower's administration became further strained in the spring of 1954 with Byroade's sensational announcement that Israel should halt its belligerency, cease immigration, stop regarding herself as the Jewish bastion against the world, and make the effort to assimilate herself into the community of the Middle East. Byroade added that aid to Israel would be decreased and aid to the Arabs increased.

Dulles proceeded rigidly on his course of new politics despite the warnings of Prime Minister Winston Churchill, who was more familiar with the will-o'-the-wisp Arab. Dulles was adamantly committed to curbing Communist expansion by establishing a military alliance with Egypt and the northern-tier Moslem countries; he was determined to see peace between the Arabs and Jews, on his own grounds, even if it killed them. To this task he dedicated himself and the United States.

It is fatefully ironic that every move he made led not to peace but inexorably toward the Sinai Campaign of 1956 and the polarization of the Middle East political scene, which continues to this writing.

The subtleties of Dulles's "friendly impartiality" were lost on Israel. His retreat from Truman's direction smelled of a sellout. Israel had no illusions about who was threatening her fragile security.

In December 1953, Prime Minister David Ben-Gurion resigned in protest, his policies of hitting the Arab menace hard unacceptable to his cabinet and other powerful figures, who now preferred to live in Dulles's turbulent wind. Ben-Gurion, a warrior, had found himself saddled with a dovish, recalcitrant government. He retired to the desert, having appointed a triumvirate to the three most important positions in the Israeli political-military complex.

By May 1954, tension in Israel had reached crisis level: The government could not agree on policy; her "magic carpet" policy of ingathering the

Oriental Jews had swamped her economically; inflation was rampant; the economy neared collapse, and morale was frightfully low. (Contrary to the State Department's call for Israel to cease immigration, that country actually lost, through emigration, more citizens than it gained through immigration during the years 1952-53.)

Even more devastating to Israel, she appeared to have been abandoned by her benefactor, the United States. Dulles was promising to rearm the Arabs; and if the British evacuated the Suez Canal, it would be forever closed to Israeli shipping (as it had already been for several years). With the British gone from the canal, Egypt would have a clear field across the Sinai Desert to harass or attack Israel at will. Armed Arab border infiltration was again on the rise. Lastly there was the growing threat of a unified Arab world—multitudes against a few.

Israel's future loomed ominous. In the near-traumatic state of anxiety over the United States' clearly indicated intentions, she had to act. These things she had to do: (1) keep the British buffer garrison on the Suez Canal, thus denying Egypt hegemony over it; (2) deny Egypt the wealth of military bases and hardware the British would leave behind (thirty-eight years of British military build-up); (3) most important, she had to break up America's courtship of the Arabs, especially of Nasser's Egypt.

It was into this political maelstrom that I was recruited as an operative of Israel's Military Intelligence Corps.

DECLINE OF HONOR

Book 1

Chapter 1

A blustering fall day, 1952. Israel.

'Avri! *Avri Seidenwerg!*"

Hearing my name meant nothing more than someone trying to catch up with me on a gusty Haifa street. I had no warning, no premonition that this simple everyday summons would ignite a chain of events that would reshape the course of my life.

I was glad to see Chaim Kandel as he broke through the crowd. Until two years ago, we hadn't seen each other since serving together in Italy during World War II, as part of the (Jewish) Palestinian Unit, General Transport Company 462, British Army. Chaim's enthusiastic handclasp gave me a warm feeling of acceptance. He had no idea how much I needed that feeling this day.

Angling toward a small café, we passed a truck loaded high with lumber, its red danger flags snapping in the wind. We eyed the raw wood, our minds tracking simultaneously.

"Shall we give it a go?" asked Chaim, his eyes twinkling. He was referring to a stickup that he and I had carried out against black-marketeering of lumber near the close of the Italian campaign.

In those days of chaos, thousands of refugees were pouring down from the body of Europe into Italy, fleeing the horrors of Hitler's insanity and the desperate but futile struggles of the German superman, as he clawed at territories slipping fast from the projected enclave of his Thousand-Year

Reich. This mass of shocked, miserable humanity had to be fed, clothed, and housed. Moving quickly to their aid, Palestinian volunteers, most of us veterans of the Haganah,[1] established camps exclusively for Jewish survivors who had miraculously made their way out of the holocaust. They came not en masse, but in trickles, looking as if they would never survive the journey to the prophesied State of Israel, then several years in the future.

This was where Chaim and I came in. Our truckload of contraband lumber, worth its weight in gold to Italy's decimated economy, was sold, and the money was given to the Jewish refugee camps we helped maintain.

Thinking back, I hadn't answered him. Now I did, laughing.

"Not again! The war is over."

"But this time it's for our *own* pockets!" Chaim protested.

We were still laughing when we arrived at the patio café offering the best cake in town. Chaim rattled on while I ordered for us. Watching, half listening, I dreaded his asking why I was in mufti. Chaim had only known me in uniform.

But I hid my shame. Chaim did not know of my court-martial a year ago, nor of my demotion from major to private for "behavior unbefitting an officer."

"I've been doing all the talking, Avri," he said finally. "What's with you?"

Just the effort of trying not to think of the turmoil of the past year was exhausting. An outline for Chaim would do; it fitted his style.

"It's been the lousiest year on record. A few weeks ago I left a good job. Good but dull." I chuckled cynically. "The third good but dull job I've had this year!" I hesitated, feeling the weight of my recollections. "I also got divorced this past summer. But Shula and I still live together. . . ."

What I could not reveal to him, or to anyone, was the anguish this unconventional arrangement had heaped on Shula and me. To say that we still lived under the same roof, slept in the same bed, and occasionally were intimate, was to credit ourselves with vastly more maturity than we actually possessed. Circumstances had forced the situation on us, and we were helpless to undo it.

Shula had our three-year-old son, Harel, and her secretarial job, which paid too little to allow her independence. I had no job, no money, no hopeful future.

All we had left were rare moments. However, we knew when our lovemaking began that the aftermath would be the same. Strangers occupied

---

1. HAGANAH. The Jewish Palestinian underground defense forces during British Mandate in Palestine. This clandestine organization was the military arm of the Jewish community.

our bed, took advantage of our fears and desires, used us, yet refused to leave. We stayed on, with the pain.

By the time we parted, Chaim knew only that I was drifting aimlessly in my confusion. We said goodbye, and he walked out of sight on Herzl Street and out of mind. I went back to our tiny one-room flat. I still had no premonition.

Again unexpectedly, I saw Chaim shortly afterward; he sought me out to tell me that someone might have a job for me. The man was waiting for us in a dark corner of a tiny café on a Haifa side street.

Avraham Dar was not the most likable character I'd ever met. His aggressive handshake and his overly confident smile were too perfect to be genuine. However, I settled at his table in the bleary light, determined to hear him out.

Immediately he launched into an explanation of why I should not expect too much information from this meeting. He was military but would say no more. Listening to him, a feeling of familiarity deepened. Where had I seen this physical mixture of Russian and Yemenite before? Then I remembered encountering him prior to our 1948 War of Independence when we were both in the Palmach.[2]

"One thing I want to impress on you," he was saying. "Don't mention this meeting to anyone."

I understood the terms. But not the reasons.

"You have been in the army," he said. "What branch?"

"Infantry and paratroop."

"Your last rank?"

"Major."

"Do you speak Arabic?"

"I studied two years in school at Ben-Shemen. I speak very little but understand it when spoken."

"What about English and German?"

"I'm fluent in German. My English is about as good, or bad, as my Arabic."

"I know you were in Shimon Koch's German Platoon.[3] I used to get up to your training area and watch you people trotting around, playing German. Tell me, Avri, after being so long away from your Austrian background, did you find it difficult adjusting yourself to the regimen of a German soldier?"

---

2. PALMACH. The elite shock troops of the Haganah underground.

3. Created in 1943 in Palestine, of Palestinian Jews of German and Austrian origin, for behind-the-lines activity. Many were activated in the European Theater, others in the North African campaign against Field Marshal Rommel's Afrika Korps.

"Not very. I was sent out of Austria at thirteen, in 1939. I remembered pretty well!" More meaning went into the words than was intended. I didn't know if Dar or Chaim were aware that my mother had disappeared in a German concentration camp. But then so many of our mothers had. "The language came back to me very quickly," I said.

"Could you pose as a German today, live among them convincingly?"

Dar's interest in me was beginning to take shape. If I had the slightest chance to prove myself, then I'd better be certain of my claims.

The language was no problem, even taking into account my not having spoken it routinely in thirteen years. A cram course in new terminology and idiomatic German should bring me completely up to date.

As for posing as a German, in the German Platoon I'd had no real trouble making myself into a believable German soldier.

"I believe I could," I said at length.

"Are you married?" he asked.

I studied Chaim's face, then Dar's. They were noncommittal. "We're divorced," I said, suspecting that Chaim had told him that part of it, too.

"Do you have children?"

"A son, three years old."

"Could you be absent from home for extended periods without complicating your personal situation?"

It suddenly dawned on me that time and distance just might be the key to salvaging my disastrous marriage. Without the emotions, Shula and I might have a chance after all.

"Yes," I said emphatically.

Dar seemed to be driving at something to do with Arabs, Germans, and me.

"Can you tell me what this is all about?" I asked, curious as to whether Chaim's presence precluded mentioning my army court-martial.

"Not this time." Dar flashed his trust-me smile. "I hope you understand."

I didn't but answered to the contrary. After agreeing to a meeting two weeks hence, I rose. Chaim gave no indication of leaving with me. "*Shalom,* Chaim. I'll see you."

I walked home, partly relieved, partly disturbed, but deeply engrossed. My imagination probed at the job I might be called upon to perform—a job with a smell of risk about it, the passing as a German. For what? But the likelihood of danger in no way concerned me.

As I weighed the possibility of my extended absence from home, I became more convinced that such an opportunity might offer a solution for Shula and me. Dar had no way of knowing that my home arrangement was slowly eating my guts out. To go, to leave, was the answer.

6

My next rendezvous with Dar was on a breezy, crisp morning with a sky clear blue as far as one's eye could see from Mount Carmel's upper slope. In spite of it, the day was souring. Dar was late. I was ready to return to my flat when a green Land Rover braked at the curb. Avraham Dar was wearing the uniform of a major and the crested-sword emblem of Modiin[4] on his olive green beret. Somehow I wasn't surprised, only curious.

We headed south toward Tel Aviv. Dar made only small talk. As the two-hour ride progressed, I found myself giving less attention to him and more to the lucid green Mediterranean far off to our right. Dar's seemingly endless supply of risqué stories (of which he was always the central figure) grew increasingly tiring. Giving him my undivided attention was tantamount to giving matches to a pyromaniac.

But in Tel Aviv he confided to me the purpose of our trip: I was to be interviewed by his superior, for whom Dar's contempt was so blatant that I found myself growing eager to meet the man.

Driving from modern Tel Aviv into the ancient port city of Jaffa was like taking a giant step backward into the Bible. Though little distance separated the two, the contrast was stark. Tel Aviv's streets began to squeeze inward until, at Jaffa's periphery, it seemed that the curbs would close together. We passed unencumbered through empty morning streets of cramped stagnation that reflected my own feeling.

I had suspected that our destination was Modiin headquarters, but Dar unexpectedly halted us in a narrow, littered alley. Leaving the vehicle, we picked a path through the refuse, and several alleys later we reached the porch of a bleak two-story stone house, its skin of faded blue paint shredding in painful strips. Like everything in Jaffa, the house had once been an Arab's home. Now it was officially abandoned Arab property—spoils of war. Perfect for anything needing isolation.

"Don't pay any attention to what is said to you," Dar cautioned *sotto voce*. "Just remember, when you are out in the field, you are your own boss, your own commander."

This was a little unsettling. Dar already had me out in the field, and I had only a vague idea of what this was all about. Up a shaky flight of stairs, we stopped at a formidable wooden door totally incompatible with its surroundings. Dar pressed a button and a small, solid wooden panel opened. A provocative pair of dark female eyes stared out at us, short brown hair framing the square, pretty face.

"*Shalom*, Henja," Dar greeted her.

"*Shalom*, Avraham." Henja threw me a curious, friendly glance. "Who're you?"

---

4. MODIIN. Israel's Military Intelligence Corps.

Before I could identify myself, Dar said shortly, "He's with me. The boss is going to see him."

Henja flashed anger. "I'm supposed to ask, Avraham." The panel closed, the door opened. We passed the threshold. Dar disappeared down a short hall. As quickly, he came back. "Come with me."

At the last door off the drab hall, he ushered me inside. The door closed; Dar remained outside. As the house wasn't much of a house, neither was the office much of an office. Behind the battered desk a hulking, uniformed body leaned forward and peered at me; I recalled a childhood memory: " 'Come into my parlor,' said the spider to the fly. . . ."

Facing me was Lt. Colonel Mordechai "Motke" Ben Zur, a former platoon commander in the Palmach and, in the War of Independence, an assistant to the field intelligence officer of the Palmach's Harel Brigade. He was an old acquaintance of mine. At one time he had been my subordinate in the chain of command. I felt embarrassed remembering it.

Waving me into an armchair, Motke asked: "How have things been going, Avri?"

My service record was partly obscured by his arm. His question was inane as hell; he knew the answer.

"Oh, you know! The usual, like everybody else." As I sat, Motke's slow grin showed he understood my empty retort. It helped.

I looked at the old, worn furniture dispersed pathetically about the office, quite a demeaning sight for an officer of his rank. But then there was a feeling of irregularity about the whole picture.

Dismissing the state of his office, Motke said, "I understand you might be willing to join the club. I'm in no position to go into details, but I can tell you that this is a secret unit dealing in unorthodox operations." He paused. "If you know what I mean."

I had better than a fair idea of what he meant—as Motke knew. Two years ago, while still in the army, I had participated in a one-year course for regimental commanders and had written a thesis on unorthodox operations behind enemy lines.

"From what I know about you, Avri," Motke was saying in his slow, purposeful manner, "your experience, your record, maybe even your present personal plight, as well—I think you might fit in with this particular kind of work. I want you to fill out a questionnaire and leave it with my secretary. I'm sorry I can't stay but I have to rush off to a meeting. I'm already late." From his desk drawer he took out a thick questionnaire and handed it to me.

Motke rounded his desk and held the door for me. I went out, pausing while he carefully locked his office. In the waiting room he was half out the door when he turned to me.

"Call me in ten days. *Shalom*." And he was gone.

"Would you like a cup of coffee?" Henja asked.

"Please," I said. She disappeared down the hall, returning promptly with a cup of strong Arabic coffee and a pencil.

"Thanks, Henja." I watched her go. Nice.

I stared at the questionnaire, completely open to it. It meant my very life. It could mean the restoration of everything that had been snatched away this past year with the loss of my family and the disgrace of the court-martial. Even more, it could mean a new horizon. I was prepared to go wherever it led.

Slowly, eagerly, I glanced through it. Its probing spared nothing, missed nothing; yet it limited my qualifying certain personal details I feared might preclude my acceptance into Modiin.

I hesitated over the marital status section because of the divorce. The military section was a far more serious subject. My court-martial and demotion from major to reserve private was the blackest stigma any Israeli could carry. But a nagging thought cropped up; an old adage, "If you want to catch a thief, hire a thief." It cut deeply to think my inclusion into Modiin might, to some degree, be an extension of that philosophy. I took up the pencil and started.

1 —*PERSONAL*

NAME: *Avraham (Avri) Seidenwerg*   AGE: *26*

RESIDENCE: *Simtat Schmuel 6*
        Hadar-Hacarmel
        Haifa

BIRTH   DATE: *February 19, 1925* BIRTHPLACE: *Vienna, Austria*

RELIGION: *Jew*

SEX: *Male* HGT: *6'2"* WGT: *183* EYES: *Blue*

HAIR: *Brown*

2 —*IMMIGRATION DATA (IF APPLICABLE)*

PLACE OF EMIGRATION: *Vienna, Austria*

DATE OF IMMIGRATION: *April, 1939*

REASON FOR IMMIGRATION:

> *Hitler! My father was in a concentration camp. My sister had already come to Palestine. As a member of the Zionist Youth Movement, I was included in the immigration quota.*

3   —*EDUCATION*
LIST ALL SCHOOLS, COLLEGES, TRADE AND BUSI-
NESS SCHOOLS ATTENDED:
> *Up to my immigration, the Vienna public schools. Then Ben-
> Shemen Agricultural School (technical-mechanical branch)
> until graduation in 1942.*

ADVANCED DEGREES, SPECIAL SKILLS, ETC.:
> *No advanced degrees. Finished technical studies of Max Fine
> School in Ben-Shemen. (See Military Section for special
> skills.)*

LANGUAGES:
> *Hebrew and German fluently. Studied Arabic two years in
> Ben-Shemen. Limited English, Italian and French.*

4   —*FINANCIAL*
ARE YOU A MEMBER OF KEREN MIVTAHIM (THE
SOCIAL SECURITY FUND):
> *Yes.*

PRESENT EMPLOYER (GIVE NAME AND ADDRESS):
> *None.*

PRESENT INCOME:
> *None. Unemployed.*

DO YOU HAVE ANY CASH OR SAVINGS ACCOUNTS:
> *No, neither.*

DO YOU OWN YOUR HOME OR APARTMENT:
> *No.*

IF YOU RENT, HOW MUCH PER MONTH:
> *18 I£ per month.*[5]

LIST ALL ASSETS OTHER THAN PERSONAL AND
HOUSEHOLD ITEMS:
> *None.*

LIST ALL DEBTS. INCLUDE PERSONAL:
> *None.*

5   —*MARITAL STATUS. CIRCLE ONE:*
SINGLE - MARRIED - WIDOWED - SEPARATED -
DIVORCED.

I caught myself, the pen hovering. Instinctively, I'd begun to respond as
if the divorce had not happened six long months ago. It made me keenly

---

5. Official rate: $1 = 1.80 I£ in 1954.

aware that the divorce ceremony had not affected my emotions, only my vows. What they needed, I thought angrily, was a new category; divorced but still living together. As quickly as the anger came, it fled. For Israel her civil laws lockstepped with the religious laws; our arrangement was dishonorable enough without the jokes.

I bypassed Marital Status for the moment. What the devil—Motke knew anyhow. Hadn't he referred to my personal situation?

MARRIAGE DATE: *July 7, 1948*
PLACE OF MARRIAGE: *Jerusalem*
NUMBER OF DEPENDENTS: *2*
IF DIVORCED, NAME OF FORMER SPOUSE:

Again I hesitated. To blatantly answer these questions meant to write off Shula and myself; we would no longer exist for each other. To state our situation this coldly seemed the last disloyalty to whatever feeling lingered between us. Shula was not to be dismissed as just a former spouse. But that was my concern, no one else's.

DATE OF DIVORCE: *May 7, 1952.* PLACE: *Rabbinical Court, Haifa*
REASON: *Incompatibility.*

I wanted badly to qualify incompatibility. I could have said a great deal about myself as the stubborn, dedicated, fiery young chauvinist who believed vehemently that country and duty came before family. And I could have said much about Shula as the lovely, young, fun-loving woman and mother who wanted a faster, more comfortable, more materialistic life than we in Israel had yet to realize. I hadn't seen it her way. The task of creating Israel as a viable state was not yet finished. Zahal[6] was my life.

6 —*MEDICAL HISTORY*
GIVE NATURE AND EXTENT OF ANY ILLNESS OR INJURY REQUIRING HOSPITALIZATION DURING THE PAST FIVE YEARS: Compound fracture of right ankle in late 1950.
HAVE YOU ANY KNOWN HEALTH DEFECTS: *No.*
DO YOU USE INTOXICATING BEVERAGES: *An occasional drink.*
DO YOU USE NARCOTICS: *No.*

---

6. ZAHAL: Israel Defense Forces.

HAVE YOU EVER HAD ANY OF THE FOLLOWING:

Tuberculosis	*no*	Rheumatism	*no*
Syphilis	*no*	Asthma	*no*
Diabetes	*no*	Epilepsy	*no*
Heart trouble	*no*	Drug addiction	*no*
Alcoholic	*no*	Depressions	*no*
Stomach ulcers	*no*	Suicide attempts	

Suicide!

It leaped out at me.

I could not answer this question truthfully and survive. Modiin would not trust me with critical assignments if they learned I'd once put a gun against my head and had pulled the trigger, meaning to die. Of the thousands of rounds I had fired during my life, it seemed incredible that the last shell—the bullet my hand had intended for my head—would misfire.

No amount of persuasion could make them see that terrible moment in my life, broken in rank and spirit, as an isolated, desperate act totally unconnected to the man now making application. Stability was too great a factor.

Answering the question with a no, I moved on.

7 —*LEGAL*

DRIVER'S LICENSE NO: *505971* TYPE OF LICENSE: *Class A+C*

WHEN WAS FIRST LICENSE ISSUED: *1946 (under the British mandate)*

LIST THE VEHICLES YOU OPERATE:

   Automobiles, motorcycles, tractor. All army vehicles and all civilian vehicles up to 10 tons.

HAVE YOU BEEN INVOLVED IN A TRAFFIC ACCIDENT: *No.*

HAVE YOU EVER BEEN ARRESTED, DETAINED FOR INVESTIGATION, QUESTIONED, FINGERPRINTED BY ANY LAW ENFORCEMENT AGENCY? IF YES, ANSWER BELOW:

   See military section.

8 —MILITARY BACKGROUND: INCLUDE UNDERGROUND ACTIVITY UNDER THE BRITISH MANDATE, IF ANY:

   a—*Haganah. I took the oath[7] of the Haganah the same year of immigration, while in school at Ben-Shemen, 1939.*

---

7. *Oath of the Haganah:* I hereby declare that, freely and voluntarily, I join the Hebrew Defense Organization in the land of Israel. I hereby swear that I shall remain faithful all the

b—Palmach. I took the oath[8] of the Palmach in 1942; training was primarily commando tactics. Then transferred to the German Platoon (7th Company).

c—British Army: Volunteered in 1943. Basic infantry, driver-mechanic, motorcycle training in Palestine and Egypt. Volunteered for basic parachute training and trained at RD (Ramat-David). Advanced parachute training at Genifa Training Depot (near Bitter Lake in Egypt). Transferred to the Italian Front after volunteering for the commandos.
In Italy, I joined one of the Palestinian Units (462 Company, RASC).
Released from the British Army in early 1946.

d—Late 1946, I became a permanent staff member of the Haganah.

e—At the outbreak of hostilities with the Arabs in 1948, I was adjutant to Maccabi Mozerie (later killed while accompanying a convoy to Jerusalem). Our area of responsibility was the protection of convoys on the road to Jerusalem.

f—At the outbreak of War of Independence, I was intelligence officer of the Palmach 6th Battalion.

g—Later, HQ company commander of the Harel Brigade in the besieged Jerusalem. Also logistics officer of the brigade.

THE FOLLOWING DATA ON YOUR MILITARY SERVICE IS APPLICABLE ONLY AFTER THE CREATION OF THE STATE OF ISRAEL, AND AFTER THE FORMATION OF ZAHAL:

ENLISTMENT DATE: *With the creation of Zahal.*
ARMY NUMBER: *K/118623.*
BRANCH OF SERVICE: *Infantry and Paratroops.*
LAST RANK: *Major*
BRIEFLY DETAIL YOUR DUTIES AND AREAS OF SERVICE:
    a—co-founded and instructed the first Parachute Battalion in Israel.

---

days of my life to the Haganah, to its code of law and its orders as defined in its foundations by its High Command. I swear that I am at the service of the Defense Organization all the days of my life, that I shall accept its discipline unconditionally, that I will obey its call to active duty anywhere and at any time, and that I submit to all its commands and fulfill all its instruction. I hereby swear that I will dedicate all my strength, and if necessary, give my life for the defense of my people and my homeland for the freedom of Israel and redemption of Zion.

8. *Oath of the Palmach:* With this weapon, which has been entrusted to me by the Haganah, in the Land of Israel, I shall fight against the enemies of my people, for my country, without surrendering, without flinching, and with complete dedication.

b—In January 1950, assigned as commander of Battalion 128 attached to the Haifa Area Command. Remained with the Battalion until its disbanding.

c—Zevet Hahafala. Selected along with 30 to 40 other officers, we spent four months as the "put-into-operation team." Task of this group was to introduce the doctrine of the "Self-Sustaining Combat Regiment" to Zahal.

d—From October 1950 to August 1951, in the Battalion and Regimental Commanders Course.

e—Five months as chief instructor at the 10th Regiment Infantry School.

f—

Again I laid the pen aside. There was nothing more to explain; nothing but my court-martial and my release from the army.

For the form I wrote:

Court-martialed, charged with theft of military property. The military high court dismissed the charge of theft. However, the court's verdict read: Guilty of behavior unfitting an officer, and dismissal from the army.

How could I explain that "theft of military property" meant no more than a simple exchange of my refrigerator for another of questionable better quality, one that was not military property but spoils of war, classified as "abandoned Arab property." The exchange had lasted exactly one day before I thought better of what I'd done, but I hadn't counted on a senior officer of mine who had it in for me. He had seized on the opportunity to ruin me. Motke would be asking about that for sure.

I read my answer over several times, trying to find some way to reduce its harshness. After a while, I said aloud: "To hell with it!"

RESERVE RANK: *Private.*

I wrote in my reserve rank, underlining it twice, hoping my disgust would not go undetected. I worked my way through the questionnaire.

9 *—FAMILY HISTORY*
  I—SPOUSE
    a—SPOUSE'S NAME: *Shulamit "Shula" (Landshut) Seidenwerg.*
  RESIDENCE: *See my address.* TELEPHONE: *None.*
  DATE OF BIRTH: *25, May 1928* PLACE OF BIRTH: *Deutsch Eilau, Germany*

RELIGION: *Jew*

OCCUPATION: *Secretary (presently with Solel Boneh Industrial).*

EDUCATION: *Schooled in Germany until age 8. A 1942 graduate of Ben-Shemen Agricultural School.*

POLITICAL AFFILIATIONS: *None.*

LANGUAGES: *German and Hebrew. English fluently.*
Studied Arabic at Ben-Shemen.

DATE OF IMMIGRATION: *1936.*

b—MILITARY BACKGROUND (IF ANY):
8 years membership in the Haganah. Volunteered for the Royal Air Force (WAAF), trained in radar plotting. Served from 1942 till 1945.

c—BRIEF BACKGROUND:
After the war in 1945, as stated above, she worked for the British government at the request of the Haganah. Her position required her to handle certain valuable and secret information. During the War of Independence, on July 7, 1948, we were married in Jerusalem. After a brief move to Tel Aviv, we went to Haifa. Shula began secretarial work for the Immigration Department. In August, 1949, our son, Harel, was born. Early in 1950, Shula commenced work with Solel Boneh as secretary and is still with them.

d—SPECIAL REMARKS:
My wife and I have been divorced since May of this year.

II—FATHER

a—FATHER'S NAME: *Siegmund Seidenwerg.*

RESIDENCE: *Vienna, Austria.*

DATE OF BIRTH: *February 12, 1890.* PLACE OF BIRTH: *Austria.*

RELIGION: *Jew.*

OCCUPATION/PROFESSION: *Trade union functionary in Austria.*

EDUCATION: *Schooled in Austria.*

POLITICAL AFFILIATIONS: *Austrian Socialist Democratic Party.*

LANGUAGES: *German and English.*

b—MILITARY BACKGROUND (IF ANY): *Served in World War I.*

c—BRIEF BACKGROUND:
Born in that part of Austria annexed by Poland after WWI, he became active in the Revolutionary Socialist Movement. In

1935, he spent 3 years in Stein a/d Donau and Woellersdorf Prison as a political prisoner. After the Anschluss in 1938, a general amnesty was declared on all political prisoners. On gaining his release, the Nazis rearrested him for being a Jew and was sent to Dachau, later transferred to Buchenwald. His Socialist friends clandestinely maneuvered his release. He escaped to England in 1940, where he was held one year in an internment camp as a suspicious alien. Released in 1941, he went into retail fur business with his brother, Leo, who had been in London since the late 1920s. At the end of World War II, my father returned to Vienna.

d—RELATIVES OF FATHER RESIDING IN ISRAEL:
None (save my sister).

e—SPECIAL REMARKS:
In 1949, assured of my mother's death, father remarried; an Austrian woman he had met in England during the war. Olga Kupferstein was born in Austria, some time in 1905. She is an accountant for the Arbeiter Zeitung, the well-known newspaper in Vienna. She is also highly active in the Socialist Party.

III—MOTHER
a—MOTHER'S NAME: Cilli (Kober) Seidenwerg.
RESIDENCE: (My mother is assumed dead).
DATE OF BIRTH: September 10, 1900. PLACE OF BIRTH: Galizia.
RELIGION: Jew.
OCCUPATION/PROFESSION: Housewife.

c—BRIEF BACKGROUND:
When father escaped to England, a work permit was issued to my mother so she could emigrate to this country. Well-intended friends in the Jewish Community Center (Kultusgemeinde) gave the permit to someone else. Their reason: as the wife of a rising Socialist, she was too good to accept a work permit for a domestic.

d—RELATIVES OF MOTHER RESIDING IN ISRAEL:
None.

IV—SISTER
a—SISTER'S NAME: Edith Ruth (Seidenwerg) Swet.
RESIDENCE: Tel Aviv.
DATE OF BIRTH: February 24, 1923. PLACE OF BIRTH: Vienna, Austria.

RELIGION: *Jew.*
OCCUPATION/PROFESSION: *Nurse.*
EDUCATION: *Vienna public and high schools.*
POLITICAL AFFILIATIONS: *None that I know of.*
LANGUAGES: *German, Hebrew, English, Studied Latin.*
DATE OF IMMIGRATION: *1938.*

   b—MILITARY BACKGROUND (IF ANY):
   *Several years in the Haganah. She served 4 years in the British
   Army (ATS) as a nurse. Last rank: Sergeant. Served in
   Palestine and Egypt.*

   c—BRIEF BACKGROUND:
   *In 1946, while nursing rehabilitees, she met and married Zvi
   Swet (a dual amputee wounded in Italy). Zvi served in the
   British Army.*

   d—RELATIVES OF SISTER RESIDING IN ISRAEL:
   Only me, her husband and their 5 small children.

   e—SPECIAL REMARKS:
   *My sister's husband, Zvi Swet, immigrated from Latvia to
   Palestine in the late 1930s. He was a member of the Lechi
   (Stern) underground, before and after World War II. Zvi spent
   4-1/2 years in the British Army and served in a commando
   unit. A dual amputee: 100% invalid according to medical regulations. However, he alternates between farming and driving
   his taxi.*

I signed the questionnaire, drained of energy. The damned form had dug
deeper into my soul than it deserved. Strangely tranquil, I felt an inner
peace seeping slowly into my veins. Suddenly the room became softly vi-
brant with the faint drift of Arabic music beneath an occasional ping of a
typewriter carriage. Now I listened, staring blankly at the wall behind
which Henja busied herself. The door implied *verboten.* The aura of
secrecy was strong.

Thinking of secrecy dragged my attention back to the questionnaire's
request for a recent picture of me. I had several old ones stuck away in my
wallet. Getting them out, I spread them down the length of my thighs.

There were pictures I'd almost forgotten, fraying at the edges: snapshots
of friends and fellow underground soldiers—taken during our push to free
Jerusalem of the stranglehold of the Arabs. Staring at the laughing, dirty,
exhausted, happy faces, I remembered again that not all of them were
alive.

The three pictures of Shula and me had been taken in the summer of
1948, during the War of Independence and near the time of our marriage.

I saw laughing faces of mere youths, not yet tainted by the death around us. I was unable to detect in our eyes the fatalism I remembered vividly in other eyes, in other faces. Our fatalism would come later, with the disillusionment of our marriage. I looked again at the pictures, at happy faces of love, wondering where it had all gone.

I ripped one of the pictures in half. Odd, it struck me, that torn lives tend to be like torn pictures: ragged on the edges. I placed the half with my picture on it on the last page of the questionnaire, replaced the snapshots in my wallet, gathered together the questionnaire, and stood up. The important questions had been covered. I was finished.

Chapter 2

Ten days later, Motke and I met at Gan Tamar, an Arab restaurant near his headquarters. All the way from Haifa to Jaffa, my anxiety had ridden me hard. Had my court-martial eliminated me?

Upon his arrival, Motke said without preamble, "There's been no clearance yet, Avri. Nevertheless bring your belongings tomorrow. Be prepared to spend some time with us. Whatever happens, there's no time to lose."

He hitched his chair closer to the table, and I breathed my first sigh of relief. "There's one thing I want to hear from you," he continued, "the circumstances of your court-martial. I read the transcript, but I'd like to hear it from you."

This was no time to let my embarrassment come into play. I had to give Motke the facts freely.

I told him that the events leading to the court-martial began when I left the parachute unit and took over Battalion 128 in Haifa; the sole duties of the battalion were antiaircraft defense of the city and the guarding of munitions caches for the Northern Command. But in January 1950, the unit was guarding empty skies—independence was a fact; the Arabs had departed, and the State of Israel existed. Morale was low because of two main personnel factions within the unit: the soldiers who wanted to go home to their families and civilian life; and the malcontents, many of whom had been transferred to the unit from detention camps, in the wake of an amnesty called after the establishment of Israel's first Knesset (parliament) in two thousand years. Another problem was the overlapping of its duties with the Northern Command forces. In my mind Battalion 128 did not justify its own existence.

I recommended disbanding the battalion to Lt. Colonel Lublini, head of District-Command Haifa. I was fully aware that the subject was under discussion in higher quarters. Lublini was outraged; disbanding the 128th would make him a field commander without a command. But I took the matter to the Department of Manpower, GHQ. Two weeks later the order for disbanding came down, and I was put in charge.

During all this my sergeant major told me of an abandoned refrigerator and suggested casually that I exchange it for the one in my home. Finding the refrigerator unlisted on any of the battalion books, I made the swap.

When he learned of this, Lt. Ami Hadani, my transportation officer and friend, gave me hell for having done it. Didn't I know that the sergeant major was Lublini's man? Didn't I realize that Lublini probably blamed me for the disbanding of the 128th? Lublini now had the rope he needed to hang me; and even though I immediately returned the refrigerator to the return depot, Lublini had already set the trap. He ordered two successive investigators to investigate the case of the missing refrigerator; each quickly cleared me. I assumed that the matter was finished.

However, Lublini ordered me to appear before court-martial; the charge was theft of military property. In two hearings the file of the missing refrigerator was closed, grounds unknown. Again I had underestimated Lublini.

"From the disbanding of the 128th," I told Motke, "I went to the Zevet Hahafala, a team of some forty officers assembled for specialized and advanced training. We received the total command functions of various formations up to regimental size."

"Then you spent a year in the battalion commanders' course," Motke observed.

Up to now my voice had sounded flat and factual, but as I remembered that year I felt energy pouring into me. "I don't mind telling you," I added, "it was a tremendous experience. All the real fighters were there."

Then came reassignment to the infantry school *and* an order to appear in Nazareth at the seat of Northern Command. For two years the file on the missing refrigerator had been closed, yet I found myself again facing court-martial on the same charge before the panel of three military judges!

Again Nachum Segal defended me. Over his objections to the panel's decision to read the old transcript instead of calling the witnesses, I was found guilty of unlawfully taking army property and of conduct unbefitting an officer of my rank. Sentence: *18 months' imprisonment and revocation of my rank of major.*

All my dedication and service to my country and her army had ended in disgrace. My place as an officer in Zahal, the very reason for my being, had been denied me, and my 26 years of life were blackened with dismissal from our proud army.

I recounted the rest of the facts to Motke. Shula and my sister had engaged a lawyer despite my protestations, and he appealed my case to a higher court. At the end the charge of theft was dropped, but I was stripped of my rank. I had behaved improperly as a Zahal officer.

I finished, brooding. Motke sat staring into my eyes. I waited for his judgment. He stood. I rose with him.

"I've heard enough," he said heavily. "Come, I'll show you to your quarters." I followed him out, feeling as if the weight of the world had been lifted from my shoulders.

Had I been able to foresee where my first step toward Modiin Unit 131[1] was to take me, I would have avoided the journey. What lay ahead would demand of me the best part of my life. But I was not equipped with clairvoyance on that warm November day in 1952; I have no such powers now. My wisdom, these twenty-odd years later, is the result of experience and hindsight.

As yet the journey is not over; nor do I see an end beyond this writing.

The ride back to Haifa gave me time to ponder how I would explain to Shula. Very likely I would not be seeing her or my son for a long time. Though I had so far only a hint of what my involvement in Modiin might entail, I knew that in a short while I could be anywhere, even dead. Intelligence units whose function is unorthodox operations do not give guarantees of safety. But I had to go with Modiin. I had to do this for myself—*just* for myself, whatever the price. I had to capture something I'd lost along the way: my pride.

With a pounding heart I watched town center coming up. Soon I stood clutching the doorknob of the flat. A wave of relief swept over me as I realized that Shula was out with the boy. Only then did I sense the enormity of the tension gripping me.

Inside, nostalgia slowed my packing, not that there was much to pack. One suitcase held everything: my few shirts and trousers, trivial personal things, shaving gear, a jacket. All I owned except a closetful of obsolete military clothing. When I was ready to leave, my eyes nervously roamed about the one-room flat. It struck me that I could remain with Shula and Harel another night and leave for Tel Aviv early the next morning. But it was better to go now, to leave without trying to explain what I was not allowed to explain. Yet I had to say something to her, whether I said it well or not. I sat down with pencil and paper.

---

1. UNIT 131. A secret unit of military intelligence organized for unorthodox operations.

Dearest Shula,

As you can see, I am doing what we both have wanted for two years. I think it's better this way.

I can't explain my whereabouts, or what I'm doing, but somebody will be in contact with you soon. All I can say is that I hope the step I've taken is the right one; it's so very important to me. Please try to understand I can say no more for now.

In spite of all that's happened to us, you know in your heart that nothing will erase my feelings for you and the boy.

Be blessed.

Avri

Putting my keys atop the note, I realized that the two together represented the surrender of my past life. I grabbed my suitcase and stepped outside, moving quickly. I couldn't look backward.

My first visitor at my temporary quarters in Jaffa's wasteland of anonymity was Martin Hauser, who was attending to the administrative details of my employment with Modiin. I stared at his bald, egg-shaped head, his deep blue eyes, his lean tanned face, while he pointed out my probationer status. "Until you complete training, you won't receive the usual full payment," he said. Watching for my reaction, he added, "Don't worry, Avri, it will cover your expenses."

"My responsibility is to the upkeep of my boy who lives with his mother. My own needs are simple," I told him.

"How much are you required to pay?"

"According to the Rabbinical Court, only forty pounds a month." From his look Martin seemed to be suggesting something less than that figure. "For the time being," I said, "I need at least a hundred pounds for her. A pound a day will do for me."

"Come now. One pound a day!"

I pointed out that my lodging was taken care of by "the club." "Besides, breakfast costs a half-pound. The rest will see me through. There's no problem."

Martin laughed. "I only wish the others were like you. OK, we'll work something out. Who's your next of kin, in case——"

"Shula, of course." Hauser's eyebrows lifted quizzically. "Shula is the legal guardian of my son."

"All right then, the matter is settled."

Motke came with an armload of books. "Read these and write a summary of their contents . . . as well as your own interpretations."

I quickly leafed through each of the books: *The Islam, Ancient and New*

Egypt, others of related topics. *From Cairo to Damascus* by Roy Carlson caught my attention.

I had met Roy Carlson during the Siege of Jerusalem in the summer of 1948. He had slipped from the Jordanian sector of Jerusalem into our lines, where he was picked up. He volunteered information on the Arabs' preparations to use heavy guns against our positions in the corridor leading into the city. Command was skeptical. Unfortunately his information proved to be accurate. Only hours had elapsed before Naveh Ilan, a kibbutz stronghold in the Judean Hills, was heavily shelled by the guns. Now, four years later, I was holding Roy Carlson's book in my hands. Motke commented that its reading would give me a deeper insight into the people I *might* be dealing with in the future.

"Egypt?" I asked casually.

Motke grinned. "This I haven't said. First you get through the training, then we shall see when and where, *if* at all."

In all my subsequent readings, one thing most impressed me: Anonymity is the most important tool of an agent. Therefore I waited outside Gan Tamar for a man named Michael, the unit operations officer whom Motke had instructed me to meet.

At precisely the given hour, a bereted captain with three bars on his shoulders came marching briskly toward our rendezvous, spit and polish even to the pigskin attaché case he carried stiffly at his side. At the entrance to Gan Tamar he checked the time, then stepped onto the patio.

"You're looking for me," I said over his shoulder. He swiveled about to face me, a man in his mid-thirties, with huge ears fanning out from his head. A pleasant smile transformed his stern features, and he held out his hand.

I learned that Michael and I had similar backgrounds. Both Austrian born, teen-age emigres to Palestine. Recently divorced, he was just back from a two-year assignment in Europe, an old hand in Modiin and Mossad.[2] Later I was to learn that Michael was highly instrumental in bringing about German repayment to Israel and to Jewish victims of Nazi crimes.

"I hope we can be friends, Avri," Michael said, informing me that he was to be my host in Modiin during Motke's involvement with the battalion commanders course, the course I'd completed earlier. "I know you have a fairly complete understanding of what military intelligence is all about. That pleases us."

Michael shifted forward, hands cupped in front of his mouth, and in the old European fashion, he began to pick at his teeth. His eyes never left

2. MOSSAD. Central institute for intelligence and special missions. Comparable to the American CIA.

mine. "But there's one thing," he said, "the most important part of all intelligence: getting the information to those who can use it."

True, the most accurate intelligence in the world is worthless if it does not reach the proper sources in time. To mention it now seems too obvious, but not so when faced with the problem of getting it there.

"Because of this, Avri, that is where your training begins: transmitting and receiving information."

"Good. When?"

"Tomorrow." Michael laid change on the table and picked up his attaché case. "Let's go get your clothes."

"Where are we going?" I was up, ready to move.

"To your new residence."

In Michael's Willys jeepster, a type standard with the hush-hush people, we went directly to my lodging, then weaved in and out of obscure streets to Stricker Street in northern Tel Aviv, my home for the months to come.

On the second level Michael rapped on a door at the head of the stairs. A young, blonde, bespectacled, and not unattractive woman opened it. Martin Hauser stood behind her, his glossy dome brilliant in the light.

"I didn't expect you so soon, Shlomo," he said to Michael.

Michael's angry glare spoke volumes; Hauser had inadvertently blown Shlomo's cover name. When he said to me, "El-Ad, this is Mrs. Ruth Oren, your landlady," I blinked. Where were all these names coming from?

As we went into my one-room quarters, Mrs. Oren went out, closing the door behind her. Hauser gave me forty-five pounds' pocket money and a printed receipt with my new name, El-Ad Sarchi.[3] I signed the receipt, my head spinning, and Martin left me with Captain Shlomo Millet.

"Avri, you understand the necessity of the code name. From today on, all reports, letters, receipts, et cetera, coming from you will be signed "El-Ad Sarchi." Within the unit and in the files of Modiin, you will be known *only* as El-Ad Sarchi. Very few, even within the department, know your true identity; it's up to you to keep it that way.

"Tomorrow you'll commence training. I, myself, will keep a close eye on your progress. There are plans in store for you."

Wondering *what* plans, I set about getting used to my austere quarters. Its discomfort and newness (I was the first occupant) were proper symbols of the apprenticeship I had to serve.

As if clinging to the rope of a runaway horse, I began my training. In four frenetic months, I learned to build transmitters and receivers; the art of *slikim* (concealment of *anything* from cigarette papers to transmitters); Morse Code; and the labyrinths of cryptology. I had refreshers in judo, ex-

---

3. EL-AD SARCHI, *a nom de guerre,* a code name. El-Ad—"ever"; Sarchi—"illuminous."

plosives, photography, weapons—all the details necessary to achieve an objective and remain alive.

The only social event I attended occurred well into the third month. Rachel, my former Morse Code instructor, invited me to a party at her home. She was attractive, young, any man's cup of tea. Consciously or not, I hadn't thought of sex since the day I walked away from Shula. In fact, I had hardly thought of Shula. Tonight would be different.

By the time I arrived the party was in full swing. The phonograph blared loudly with popular South American tangos, yet the atmosphere was tense beneath the frivolity: fleeting faces, forced smiles. In our hearts each of us knew we were not a joyous people at this time in our lives, even as we sang our patriotic songs, danced our *Horah,* and shouted our freedom. As a motley collection of Jews from the distant countries of the world, the aloneness we felt and the mild state of fanaticism it forced on us weighed heavily on our shoulders, leaving us with with a sense of fatalism. Our laughter was not quite so carefree as we pretended.

Dancing with Rachel to the slow, moody music, her breasts swelling against my chest, I saw in her an intense desperation shared by all of us. Her restlessness, her grasping for completion, made her more vulnerable than she knew. At one point in our dancing, a revelation came to me. I suddenly recognized the demon that had been driving Shula. It seemed too simple, yet here it was, and I had found it while dancing with another woman. I saw it now in Rachel's face. *Desperation* had been Shula's source of restlessness, making her uneasy and rebellious. It was not the things she had wanted; instead her anxiety and discontent reflected her lack of security. Why hadn't I seen it before?

Training rarely varied; there were few surprises. During one of these days of endless routine, I was taken to Zrifin (Sarafand, its Arabic name) for psychological tests. The place hummed with activity, filled with eager aspirants for the officers academy, all younger than myself.

Six long hours of extensive individual testing followed, and there were more tests on the ensuing day, given in groups of eight. Our task was to solve and overcome field situations through our collective ingenuity. A psychologist rated my performance as excellent, as it should have been; I had commanded large groups of men in the past.

Once I had mastered the critical technique of secret written communications through the use of panchromatic paper, secret ink, and other chemical solutions, total emphasis was now placed on the art of sabotage. An old friend of mine from the Palmach, Captain Ellison, along with Lieutenant Natty of the Naval Underwater Demolition Squad, took over. I was no novice to the field of demolitions. A chemist came on the staff, a specialist in the manufacture of homemade bombs and devices made from chemical materials readily available in retail outlets. There was no limit to one's ability to improvise. A condom substituted as a remarkably effective improvised time fuse. Filled with a consistent strength of acid, the condom can be easily measured for its time-accuracy. The acid, eating slowly through the rubber, will eventually reach the surrounding chemical compound, bringing about a reaction: in this case, an ignition.

With the knowledge from my military background—the Haganah-Palmach underground movement, World War II, and Israel's War of Independence—I shortened my training period from the usual eight or nine months to a record four months. Remaining was a final examination, consisting of three field problems; I passed easily.

Motke made one of his rare appearances. "Avri, your performance was outstanding. I know you're pleased, and so am I. It proved my decision right."

Right about *what?* Had there been difficulties with my employment? Did I owe him some debt for speaking out in my favor?

"We're working to find the right cover identity for you," he continued, "but in the interim there'll be other subjects you'll have to become acquainted with."

Capt. Shlomo Millet, who had closely supervised my training, provided new books concerning the Egyptian army and its history. Now I knew for certain my future theater of operation. Shlomo sensed my impatience. My time was coming, he said; all I had to do was sit tight.

One day he handed me a typewritten page. "This is your new identity," he said. "Learn the details by heart. Your life may depend on it."

I glanced at the *curriculum vitae.*

PAUL FRANK

Born July 30, 1921, in Willmars, Oberfranken, Kreis Hammelburg, Germany

Father's name: Max Frank

Mother's name: Betty Frank (Maiden name: Levy)

Sister's name: Ruth Frank

Max and Betty Frank are deceased, killed during the war. Paul's sister, Ruth, married and emigrated to the United States.

Willmars is a small village of about 600 people; the Frank family were the only Jews residing there. In 1935, the family moved to Hammelburg. Max Frank opened a shop for household goods, clothing, and lingerie. The shop was Aryanized (confiscated by the Germans) two years later.

Paul emigrated to Palestine in 1937 and is presently a member of Maayan Zvi, a kibbutz near Sichron Jacob.

Education: Willmars Elementary School
            Gymnasium in Hammelburg

Documents: Vaccination certificate
No other known relatives alive.
No birthmarks or scars.

I was incredulous. "It's rather meager, isn't it?"

"That's all we have on him, Avri," Shlomo answered.

"Shlomo, I have to know more about Frank. We have to squeeze his memory like an orange."

Shlomo said it had already been decided that Paul Frank and I would meet soon. The name had a good German ring to it, but what disturbed me most was the fact of his Jewishness. Passing me off as an Aryan German from a German-Jewish background seemed dangerous. Hell! It seemed downright stupid.

Already I'd had reservations about the thoroughness of the training, and this transparent cover identity added to my tension. Yet who was I to question Modiin decisions? *The personnel in Modiin was thoroughly experienced and professional,* I rationalized—*highly professional.*

The day of my departure drew closer. After Motke introduced me to Josef and Jiddel Langfuss, brothers who were to help me establish my German identity in Zurich, Shlomo Millet drove me out to kibbutz Mayan Zvi to see my alter ego, Paul Frank. The closer we got the more anxious I became. I wanted an identity that would hold up under the most minute scrutiny, one capable of weathering the stiffest interrogation.

At Kibbutz Mayan Zvi, in a little one-room kitchenette-dwelling typical of collectivist living, we found Paul Frank. He looked like anybody in the world, except me. He was short, hairy, and overweight. Arched heavy black eyebrows obscured deep-set brown eyes. He had four years on me, and he looked older than that.

Instantly, it was plain that something had rankled him. Though not uncooperative, he volunteered nothing we didn't coax from him. Ignoring his obvious hesitations, we examined and cross-examined him regarding every detail of his past life.

When we parted, we found out what was bothering Frank. He wanted to be reassured that in lending his identity to what he called a worthy cause, he would not lose the benefits due him from German reparation.[4]

Shlomo attempted to reassure him. "Could I have something in writing," he asked, "something to safeguard my interests?"

The real Paul Frank did not enchant me, but I told myself that I was just uneasy—a natural feeling when one's life hangs in the balance.

---

4. GERMAN REPARATION. Compensation and restitution by the West German government for Nazi crimes committed against the Jewish people.

Chapter 3

Preparations for my send-off began in earnest. The plan was for "El-Ad Sarchi" to assume the role of Paul Frank, a former German soldier with a Nazi background. After obtaining a German passport in Zurich, I was to continue to Frankfurt am Main, Germany, to establish residence. Frankfurt's location in the American Occupation Zone was vital; for me so was its proximity to Paul Frank's birthplace, for it was believed that I could get a copy of his birth certificate there. In some way I had to come by a legitimate baptism certificate as well. Considering Frank's Jewish birth, arranging a Christian background looked formidable. No directives, only objectives.

"You have to find a way to get Frank's name on the church records, Avri," Shlomo emphasized. "Department 8[1] can always forge a baptism certificate, but we can't manipulate church records."

My orders called for a German identity card and a driver's license qualified up to heavy vehicles. The Frankfurt newspapers would supposedly present a wealth of possibilities for establishing myself, particularly ads requiring mechanical skills. Industry was begging for trained personnel. Getting a job with one of the larger German firms exporting goods and skilled labor to the Arab countries might be my springboard into Egypt.

1. Department 8. A branch of Israel's Military Security Services dealing with forgery, documents, photography, cryptography.

"We're throwing you into rough water, Avri," Shlomo said, choosing each word with great deliberation. "You've been taught to swim, but the direction of the current depends on you.

"First, establish your cover. Live, think, *be* a German. Avoid all contact with Jews, Israelis, and their friends—and the places they go. Above all, though, don't be overly security-minded. Nothing draws suspicion more than too much caution. Whatever the circumstances, act naturally, think logically. Cultivate yourself a habit; it may save your hide ten times over. Believe me, I know what I'm talking about."

Aside from the general transparency of my cover identity, a particular shortcoming disturbed me. I was Jewish—and circumcised. Only a small portion (28%) of the German male population had had the operation. I broached the problem to Motke and Shlomo, and after a moment Motke's faced brightened. "I have a suggestion. We will have a foreskin made of plastic. Something you can slide on or off."

Was this a joke? I looked at Shlomo and we both started laughing.

"What's so funny?" Motke demanded irritably. "It can be done. They do miracles with plastic these days."

"Are you serious?" I asked. "Can't you see it all in the Arab papers: Spy loses his shmuck! Israeli spy unmasked while *fucking!*"

Martin Hauser handled my final financial matters. "I explained to your wife, Shula," he said, "that, through me, she will receive a monthly allotment of 150 pounds. She also knows how to contact me in cases of emergency." The unit had accepted Shula as my wife.

"What did you tell her about me? Did she ask?"

"She only knows you're employed by the defense ministry. But I think she understands without knowing, Avri. She's quite a woman, but you know that. She's greatly concerned for you and sends her blessings."

"I'm glad she knows something," I said, feeling a warm glow sweep over me.

"To start, your monthly salary will be paid in dollars, $250 minus the allotment to Shula, will leave you with $165. It doesn't seem like much, but it should see you through while you're in Germany. Naturally you will be reimbursed for certain expenditures: rent, fares, things like that. Be sure to send receipts. I trust your word, but we've got a ginger-headed accountant that takes these matters very seriously."

The next day Shlomo and I dropped in on Jiddel Langfuss, just arrived from Asmara, Ethiopia. Jiddel looked something like his brother, Josef, only more intense. It might have been his gold tooth, but I liked him much better; he seemed warmer, more humane.

"When are you returning to Europe?" Shlomo asked him.

"I don't know, but certainly by Passover," he said.

My quick calculations put me in Zurich in less than two weeks.

"Paul, call my brother Josef. You have the number?"

"He'll have it," Shlomo asserted.

"I am closer to the German consul than my brother, but in my absence Josef can handle Paul's needs."

I preferred dealing with Jiddel, and on leaving told Shlomo so.

"It makes no difference. Both are crooks," Shlomo said. "If it were done my way, we wouldn't deal with either of them; but Motke made the decision."

We began the countdown for my departure.

Motke drove us out to meet with Col. Jehosaphat Harkabi, the acting head of Modiin in the absence of Col. Benjamin Gibli. I knew "Fatti" Harkabi from the Siege of Jerusalem and later in the regimental commanders course. His intellectual, analytical mind impressed me.

Fatti received us at his home. On the table between us was my personal army file. "Understand, we are expecting great things from you. I make no promises, but if you succeed you'll recapture your place in Zahal. Having your rank stripped away hasn't been easy for you, but if we thought you deserved it, you would never have been admitted to Modiin's ranks. Rest assured of that."

Fatti's words started a fire inside me. Was he saying that my rank would be returned? Or that the court-martial would be stricken from my army record? Or both? I waited until Fatti's mother left coffee and cake.

"You see, Fatti," I said, forking a wedge of cake, "my price for danger is merely one piece of good cake. However, if what I do buys back my rank, I assure you I will not refuse it."

"Just as it should be," Fatti replied, opening my file. "I'm summarizing here on the cover what I've said. If I'm off the job when you come back, my successor will pick up the obligation. You're witness to it, Motke."

Fatti handed me a typewritten page from the folder. "This is a contract between you, Zahal, and Modiin. It merely safeguards everyone's interests."

Certain stipulations stood out. At year's end the contract automatically renewed itself for three years unless Modiin chose to terminate the agreement without warning or explanation. If terminated they were obligated to pay me three months' salary. I had no rights of cancellation. Salary was the lowest on the Civil Service scale, but it was sufficient. I had no complaints. I was under the jurisdiction of the military Code of Law 1948. The payment provision to my son came last. Without comment, I signed.

Motke disclosed the date of my departure: March 29, two more days.

"Shlomo will accompany you to the airport," he said. "I'm on field maneuvers in the south, but we'll meet again sooner than you think. Meanwhile, *Shalom* . . . and don't let me down."

We gripped hands in farewell. Again a stab of animosity shot through me. Motke had said, "Don't let *me* down." Was he still trying to say that I owed him something?

The evening of the twenty-eighth Motke unexpectedly arrived at the apartment.

"Get your jacket," he said abruptly. "You're to see somebody."

We were racing eastward in his battered green Rover Salon before he spoke again. "Don't take this personally, but it's policy to investigate the motives of our people . . . why they accept certain assignments. Someone wants to talk to you about it." I was annoyed but held my silence.

At Ramla Prison, Motke pulled to the front of the old three-tiered former British police compound. We were expected. A trusty led us up to the second floor to a door marked "Dr. Rudi." Motke ushered me into an office where pipe smoke obscured the seated figure.

"This is Dr. Rudi," Motke said, "consultant for our people." Then he introduced me and left the office.

Dr. Rudi was white-haired, of medium height, and had benevolent features somewhat marred by unsteady, bloodshot eyes. He was a pipe smoker, like me. I took the chair he offered.

"How often during a month do you engage in sexual intercourse?"

Obviously he meant his first question to be shocking. It was.

"A gentleman enjoys and keeps quiet."

A slow smile spread over Rudi's face.

"If a gentleman is unable to talk about the present, perhaps he can talk about the past. How often did you masturbate before you lost your virginity?"

"I doubt if masturbation is the basic element of an agent."

"Would you please tell me why you're willing to take a mission you might not return from?"

I smiled. "There are many ways of committing suicide. Going to Egypt is merely one of them. Perhaps I might be of some use to Israel at the same time."

The doctor was quiet for a while. It was time to put things straight.

"Dr. Rudi, I'm being facetious. If you really want my motives, you're going to have to investigate my life a lot deeper than asking me how many times I masturbated. I'm going out for a lot of reasons . . . not the least of which is I've been a soldier for a long time, since I joined the Haganah at fourteen.

"Even in Vienna as a kid, I lived under tension. I was the child of a

Jewish Socialist. My father was three years in Woellersdorf Prison because he was a Socialist. He was in Buchenwald and Dachau because he was a Jew. I remember the nights he couldn't come home, all the things we didn't have because he was dedicated to his convictions. I remember his watching the windows for the police and the messages I passed from him to his friends in the movement. I remember my little, uninvolved, religious mother wringing her hands, fighting the tears.

"I watched Hitler's grand entrance into Vienna. From the Hofburg, the huge palace court, I saw his acceptance of Austria's loyalty. But I wasn't old enough to recognize the monster in Hitler. My father knew—he was one of the few who *did* know in those days. I still can hear the shouting in my ears. You know who were shouting? Austrians. And don't think there weren't friends among them.

"My father was not a very good Jewish father. We had little, my sister Ruth and I, except a stern example of a fighter. Warmth came from our mother. I may be much the same kind of husband and father myself.

"But another thing we have in common, my father and I. He didn't like or dislike a man simply because he was a Jew. I'm not going out on this mission simply because Israel is populated with Jews. It's just that anybody taking up Hitler's reins to liquidate Jews, or whatever, becomes, to me, the common foe."

I broke off a moment, realizing how tense I'd become.

"Dr. Rudi, whatever I am, I'm a good soldier, by training and instinct. It's the life I know best and want most. However you want to label it, that's the way it is."

"What makes you think you couldn't live life outside the military?" Dr. Rudi's little eyes were twinkling.

"The year after my court-martial was the most miserable year of my life. Everything crumbled around me." I paused. "I got divorced. But it wasn't the court-martial that destroyed my marriage; it was my marriage to the army that destroyed Shula and me."

"Why do you say that?"

"Even after the court-martial, I was still married to the army."

Dr. Rudi lighted his pipe, then nodded for me to go on.

"There's nothing more to say . . . except for one very important point. It's a thing we tend to mock, something we call Zionism. There's a lot of Zionism in me."

Rudi's eyes shone in understanding. "I see what you mean." He shifted forward. "A moment ago you spoke of being a soldier by instinct. What did you mean by that?"

The last thing I wanted was to dig deeper into the past.

"Just that I've lived my life with the knowledge that self-preservation is foremost. Hitler introduced that to me; the Arab has kept me aware of it."

Dr. Rudi stood. Extending his hand across the desk, he said, "Let me wish you luck for your future."

Outside, with Motke, I looked back at the impersonal fortress, a formidable sight from where I stood. Three stories high. I could only imagine how high its parapets would seem to one confined within.

I woke early on March 29, 1953, the day of my departure. I had just finished breakfast when Shlomo picked me up. Driving to Lod Airport he quizzed me on cover details, contacts, objectives, and a dozen other points. "Remember to report expenses. Alert us early if you have a shortage of cash so we can get more to you fast."

Inside the terminal Shlomo gave me my temporary passport, a *laissez-passer* stamped for Swiss entry. I checked in with Swiss Air and we were proceeding to passport control when Shlomo stopped me. Without a word he took my hand in his two and looked into my eyes. Then he went away.

I watched until he was gone. It was over—or was it? Somehow I had the feeling there was more. Probably my jitters overwarning me. I promised myself to watch that.

The police sergeant at passport control checked my credentials against his little black book. A bead of sweat trickled from my armpit as he looked closely at me, then beckoned another officer to his booth. "Mr. Frank, would you please come with us?" Where the hell was Shlomo? I was led through an unmarked door, where passport control turned me over to two unofficial-looking clowns who had to be security people. They stated that my embarkation papers might be a little out of order. Thirty questions later they searched the attaché case given to me by Department 8 but missed its secret compartment.

"You'll be responsible if I miss my flight," I said, feigning annoyance.

"You won't miss it."

They were finished. I was taken directly to the plane. Looking back, what I saw made me curse—but in German. *Verflucht noch einmal!* Shlomo and Hauser stood on the spectators' balcony, grinning. The last test. Refusing to acknowledge them, I stepped inside; my name was Paul Frank.

As I took a window seat, an envelope with $600 expense money was thrust at me by a one-armed man I'd observed in the customs area.

With a twinkle in his eye, he whispered, "This is for you. *Behazlacha!"* His path up the aisle was unhurried and straight. Another security man.

Chapter 4

Its engines biting into the hot, dry air, the Swiss Air Constellation slowly lifted off. Coming up below was Tel Aviv. Crossing the coastline, I watched the white strand of beach reach north to Haifa Bay, curving past Acre all the way to the Lebanon border. I was mildly shocked at the tininess of my country, at its vulnerability, but I was overjoyed to be going into action again.

I got through passport control; Avri Seidenwerg, settled soberly into his German identity, was now Paul Frank. I had awaited this day, my day of ordination, with a beating heart and a kind of proud humility. I envisioned myself *primus inter pares,* even though many had gone before me. According to the Bible, I was now a member of the second-oldest profession.

Zurich was just as Shlomo had described it. Leaving the terminal, I crossed the rain-swept street and rounded the block circling Schweizer Hof, a landmark hotel. I entered the lobby of the Simplon Hotel.

Jiddel Langfuss was not in. Depositing a note in his box, I signed the register, "Paul Frank," my first alias ever.

In my second-floor room, bone weary, I flopped down on the narrow bed and listened to the rain on the window. Langfuss, Shlomo, Motke, and the whole blasted entanglement disappeared from my mind. I slept soundly.

Wind and rain still raged when I went down for breakfast. This was my first return to Europe since seeing my father in Vienna, just after the war, in 1946. Enveloped by the soothing sounds of the weather, I thought of my childhood, lured by the strains of *Tales of the Vienna Woods* flowing from a radio.

At the Jemoly Department Store I bought a raincoat, neckties (the only ties I'd ever bought in my adult life), and shirts—just enough to get by. Most of my wardrobe I would buy in Germany. I then called Josef Lang-fuss.

"You'll have to wait for Jiddel to proceed," he said. "He'll arrive for Passover."

In my excitement I'd forgotten Passover. *Seder* began at sundown tonight. All these years and still we weren't free of the damned Egyptians. But for them I would be celebrating my heritage, joined with millions of Jews around the world—not here in the damp cold of Zurich. *Ten more plagues on the house of the Egyptians!*

At the German consulate the next afternoon, Jiddel was waiting im-patiently. Hurrying me inside, he was breathless with explanation. "Thank God you're not late. I wanted you to see the consul before he left. The new regulations are difficult even for the consul to circumvent. If you lived in Zurich, things would be easier; but you want a passport on the spot, and that's quite another story. I warned of such things in Israel."

"In Israel," I said, "you spoke quite the contrary."

"The consul wants to oblige me, Paul, but the first secretary—*Jemuch schamo* (May his name be wiped off the face of the earth!)—has voiced ob-jections. I've asked the consul to advise you; so be patient. Don't worry!"

My apprehension in dealing with German officialdom began to surface. The last encounter had been in Vienna, in 1938, when my mother had stood in line with me for hours while we applied for my emigration permit to Palestine. However, this time there would be no Nazi rifle butts herding me along.

Jiddel's nervousness, however, made me calm, until the sight of a most singular man, coming out of a door across the corridor, stood my hair on end. He was a typical Prussian bureaucrat: stiff, superior, narrow-visaged, an ardent Nazi-in-disguise. How had this one survived the denazification of the German foreign office? Langfuss was on his feet, greeting him effu-sively, introducing me.

The German first secretary!

"It is not a simple matter of minutes to straighten out Herr Frank's aims," he said. "He must go through proper channels." With this an-nouncement, he turned on his heel and left.

"This is the *goy* I warned you about, *Jemach schamo!* If not for him, your passport would be in hand."

The consul, however, proved to be cordial. He would help, but I lacked certain requirements.

"What kind of documents do you have proving your German nationality?" he asked.

I explained that I had lost my proof of birth. "Life, for me, was not very stable," I stressed, "first one home, then another. What few belongings I had disappeared. My father and mother died in Germany during the war."

Somewhere within the consul I'd struck a sympathetic note. "I understand," he said. "It's a shame."

"I do have vaccination and school certificates. But please don't hold poor marks against me," I added, smiling.

"Let's see what can be done." He picked up the phone and asked someone to come in.

To my astonishment, it was the Prussian. The consul showed him my documents, then asked, "By the way, Herr Frank, you have acquired nationality in Israel, perhaps?"

I answered in a vehement negative. "As you can see there, they granted me only the *laissez-passer* and not a regular passport. It even says I'm *staatenlos* (stateless)."

"I think Mr. Frank should have to fill out the necessary forms and apply for renaturalization," the first secretary said.

"I'm willing to personally sign for his renaturalization," the consul said, "so long as I have enough proof of his birth."

The first secretary beckoned me to follow him. Alone with him in his office, I decided, To hell with it! Pitching my voice sharply, I demanded, "Instead of helping me, why are you creating obstacles?"

Before he could reply, I began quietly to recite the pledge of the Wehrmacht: *"Ich Schwoere bei Gott diesen heiligen Eid das ich den Fuehrer des deutschen Reiches und Volkes, dem Oberstenbfehlshaber der Wehrmacht, unbedingen——"*

"Das genügt (enough)! Why haven't you said so already?" He leaned toward me. Indicating the absent Jiddel with a nod, he asked, "Why have you engaged *that* one to help you?"

"You don't know *why*?" I grinned. "Maybe I should have quoted the *other* oath, eh?" I meant the oath of the SS, certainly more impressive to the Prussian than was the Wehrmacht.

"There's no need. But tell me, why were you there in Israel?"

"The safest place is in the lion's throat."

Approval flashed in his eyes. He left the room with my two passport photos and the completed questionnaires. In ten minutes he was back with a German passport made out in the name of Paul Frank. I showed none of the astonishment I felt. He winked. I signed my name, paid the small filing fee, and it was all over—almost.

I didn't want any of my "Israeli" documents to remain on file in case my past should ever be checked.

"Is it possible for me to have my *laissez-passer?*" I asked.

He looked at me. "I understand." We went down the service stairs into the boiler room; he opened the file that he carried and tossed all the forms and questionnaires into the furnace. I watched, fascinated by the eerie glow on the Nazi bastard's face, thinking of my dead mother. I could easily have killed the man on the spot.

When the flame had eaten away the documents, he gave me a triumphant look. "How is that?" he asked.

My *Danke* sufficed; we were two good ex-Nazis.

Jiddel was astonished when I showed him the passport. "How did you do it?"

I grinned triumphantly. "I convinced the first secretary." The details were for headquarters only.

Anticipating crossing into Germany, I went to arrange the transfer of my visa to the new passport. An official at the Fremdenpolizei informed me there would be a delay because of the upcoming weekend. Concerned about a possible routine check on my passport and *laissez-passer,* I reluctantly left my credentials behind.

I returned to find my papers ready—except for one small item that stopped me in my tracks. There was a routine handwritten remark at the bottom of the visa: "Granted on the grounds of Visa Nr. 78391/25/B, Tel Aviv, March 16, 1953." The passport was worthless with "Tel Aviv" appearing on it.

I went back to the official who had helped me.

"You see, I represent international firms; my business sometimes takes me to the Middle East. If my passport shows a Tel Aviv origin, I can expect problems when applying for visas to Arabic countries."

"I'm sorry, Herr Frank, but that's our procedure."

I'd almost accepted his verdict, when a thought came to me.

"Suppose," I said, "we simply blot out 'Tel Aviv.' Could that be done?"

After a moment's deliberation, he blacked out the incriminating words with a pen and stamped over his initials. I hurried from the building. Frankfurt lay ahead.

The next morning I left Zurich by train. After four hours of Swiss scenery, the train began slowing.

"Passkontrolle und Zoll. Bitte Pässe vorzubereiten," a Swiss border official repeated, passing through the coach. He stamped my visa for exit.

The train lurched to a halt, and the German border guard got on. I caught myself tensing. I was loath to be shaken by thirteen-year-old fears from those last days in Vienna.

"Ihren Pass bitte?" They had entered the coach behind me. *"Ihren Pass bitte? Ihren Pass bitte? . . ."* they droned as they closed on me. But it was no drone to me; it was a siren.

"Ihren Pass bitte?" It was to me they spoke. I fought to keep from staring into their eyes as I handed over my passport. A surge of desire for revenge nearly overwhelmed me; I wanted to see in them the killers of my mother and my people. How was it that I had now become so fascinated by the object of my animosity?

"Your destination, Herr Frank?"

"Frankfurt."

"Haben Sie etwas zum verzollen?"

"Nichts," I said. "You can look in the suitcase for yourself."

"Danke. Ist nicht nötig."

They moved on. I breathed easier, directing myself to erase now the hatred for Germans in my soul. Right now, I was one of them, and German soil lay beneath me.

Frankfurt am Main. The city, half-leveled in the bombings, was now practically rebuilt, much of the remaining dichotomy visible from the train. Coming from Israel, with its rail span of 250 total miles, I marveled at the vast field of black-sooted railhead as the train pulled into the Frankfurt station. I was setting foot on German territory for the first time since 1945, when I had come as a soldier in the British army. In addition, there was a buoyancy, a desire to get on with my future. First, a birth certificate for Paul Frank.

I deposited my gear at the terminal and walked out to a street crowded with American and British uniforms, alive now to the fact that Frankfurt was the seat of the American-British occupation.

West Germany had usurped Switzerland's wartime role as the European center for espionage and political intrigue. Allied West Berlin, enclaved by East Germany, was the hotbed of the cold war. The Big Three, and God knows how many Communist networks, all were grabbing for a piece of what could be a very hot pie.

Knowing I was just another foreign operative crowding the midway did not allay my apprehension. This was *not* a case of safety in numbers. I was alone. But, I told myself, he travels fastest who travels alone.

From a rented room in a private home in Sachsenhausen, a district south of the River Main, I began acquainting myself with Frankfurt. Along with spending countless days at the public libraries refreshing my "memory," I checked out two neighborhood churches that might prove handy for my Christian indoctrination.

Time soon dictated a visit to Willmars, Paul Frank's birthplace. The past had to be tied to the present. I went by train to Bad-Kissingen, the famous spa, and then by bus to Mellrichstadt. After spending the night in a local inn, I set out in the early morning, walking the few miles to Willmars.

The village was scenically nestled amidst forested, rolling hills, on which cattle grazed in ankle-deep meadows. Sounds of their bells broke the valley's stillness. The few people on the village road greeted me with curious friendliness, and I dared to ask some of them if they remembered my parents. "Go to see the registrar," they said, without exception. "He is the last of the first. If anyone knows, he does."

Willmars's municipal house was a typical gray building. I climbed the stairs and found an elderly spinster, using an ancient typewriter; the two went perfectly with the musty dark of the heavy, wood-beamed room. She said that Der Herr Registrar would see me in a while.

He proved to be a white-haired gentleman of seventy or so, fully in control of his faculties. Giving him the passport and school certificate, I stated my purpose. The registrar scrutinized the documents twice before he looked up with a humorous glint in his eye.

"So you are *that* little Frank? I remember the day you were born. How are your father and mother?"

"They died in the war, Herr Registrar," I said, mildly alarmed.

"Sad. Very sad . . . but you have a sister, don't you? What happened to her?"

"She's married, the mother of two children."

"Where were you during the war?"

"I was conscripted in '42 and fought in Africa."

"That's strange. Your father was a Jew."

"But my mother wasn't, if you remember. By late '42, the front had deteriorated to the point that even *Mischlinge* (mongrels) were being conscripted." I grinned. Claiming that Paul Frank's mother hadn't a Jewish background was risky. However, if he accepted the lie now, later he might possibly recollect it as true.

"Ja," he said after some thought, "now that you mention it, I do seem to remember there was something about your mother. Wasn't the family of your father against the marriage?"

I nodded, my face properly serious.

"That's it. I am right. But your mother was a good woman."

My comment was a grateful smile.

"How many children were you? Two? How nice you're both alive."

Yes, *how nice*. Age had its blessings.

Lunch hour had come. The old man invited me to his house while his secretary searched the records before issuing the birth certificate.

At his home, he said, "My wife died fourteen years ago, may she rest in peace." Two hours later we were still chatting. The old man volunteered additional background on Frank's father, recalling that he had also served in the first war as an officer and that his brother (Frank's uncle) had once resided in Willmars. Herr Registrar might have been recollecting too much for his own good. This man had enough information about Paul Frank *et famille* to sink me in a security check. But this dark image faded when the secretary brought the birth certificate. My heart leaped; *no religious designation had been included.*

That afternoon, at the parish church, I struck gold. The parish sacristan informed me that all baptism, marriage, and death records of the 1920s (the decade of Paul Frank's birth) had been destroyed years ago in a fire. Now Frank's Christian baptism could not be disproved.

The next morning the old registrar accompanied me to the bus. "My home is yours whenever you can come, Paul. Don't forget me." His home had indeed become mine; I had slept the night there.

Backtracking by bus to Mellrichstadt, I picked up the train to Hammelburg to unearth another phase of Paul Frank's background. Hammelburg was a colorless railroad crossing of some 25,000 people. Like Willmars, it had been spared the batterings of war. At the *Rathaus* (town hall), I hoped to locate the address of the shop my father had owned. An attractive secretary checked the file index downstairs, then produced a file marked "M. Frank."

While she looked over the four pages of the file, I exercised an old skill: reading upside down. One page clearly showed that Frank's father was Jewish. Suddenly I felt desperation. The most routine check could ruin my cover story. I had to get my hands on these files. I looked at my watch: 12:15.

"Fräulein, I realize how abrupt this sounds, but would you have lunch with me? I haven't been here since before the war. The city is a stranger to me."

With a pert smile, she accepted. "By the way," she added, "my name is Krause, Fräulein Helga Krause."

"I'm Paul Frank."

"I'll have to tell my colleague upstairs I'm going. Please wait here, Herr Frank, it'll only take a minute."

She replaced the Frank file and went quickly up the stairs. I moved swiftly to the cabinet and stuffed the incriminating form into my pocket. I was looking out the window, when Fräulein Krause returned.

"Are we ready?"

"Very ready."

Lunch turned out beautifully. Helga obligingly talked about local events over the last years; to her, I was the late returning prisoner of war. She did my Hammelburg homework for me brilliantly.

On the train back to Frankfurt misgivings began to cloud my feeling of accomplishment. Fear can be a very positive force. Out of my growing doubt I decided to find another background. In the first place, I could not assume that there were no copies of the files relating to Frank.

There were other hazards. People. Countless Arabs had seen me in British uniform during the war. I'd even trained for the British parachute units in Egypt; Arabs had joined the Commonwealth army. Other Arabs may have known me as Avri Seidenwerg in Israel. There were a thousand such people who could recognize me from the past. Then there were the old registrar and his secretary.

A crude plan based on a story I'd once heard began to take shape in my mind. *In 1942, German agents, together with Arabs in sympathy with the swastika, had parachuted into the Jericho Valley in Palestine, aiming for Waadi Kelt. They evidently landed in a British trap. True or not, the eight men had never been heard from again.*

It was conjecture, but most likely the British had disposed of them after interrogation—a not uncommon fate for enemy agents during the war.

Why couldn't Paul Frank be one of those German agents?

The more I pondered the possibility, the more feasible it sounded. The trick was to reverse my story: I, as the German agent (whom I could safely dub Paul Frank), had escaped from the British. Unable to get out of Palestine, I relied on the cover given me by the *Abwehr* before the mission—that of an Austrian Jew named Adolf Seidenwerg—and volunteered into the British army at the time Jewish brigades were forming. I remained in Palestine after the war, living and working as a Jew. Now that West German denazification and the search for war criminals were on the wane, I felt it safe to return to the *Vaterland*.

At best the idea was sound; at worst it was no more farfetched than the Paul Frank guise under which I now hid. Every detail about the vanished German agents had to be known. *The conception was mine; its success hinged entirely on me.* Not since my coup in Zurich had I felt so good. With the new cover all things were possible.

Chapter 5

In May, Jiddel Langfuss came to Frankfurt to live, just in time to loan me money to get to Munich and my emergency contact. Despite my requests for funds in my reports to headquarters, none had arrived.

My emergency contact, Ben-Jacob, worked at Israel's Purchasing Mission at Theresienstrasse 43, in a beautiful residential area near the famous English Garden. The two-storied facade heralded the H.I.A.S. (relief fund) and IRO (International Relief Organization), but nothing indicated offices for Israel's Purchasing Mission, whose function it was to buy German products through reparations—conscience funds for Nazi atrocities. I presented myself to Ben-Jacob's secretary. "Regarding what matter do you want to see Mr. Ben-Jacob?" she asked.

"I've come to give him Michael's regards." (Shlomo's instructions.)

She beckoned me into a nearby office. Ben-Jacob, with typical bureacratic impatience, looked up at me.

"What can I do for you?" he asked.

What could he do for me? Hadn't the secretary repeated what I'd said to her?

I introduced myself. "I'm El-Ad Sarchi, Michael's friend. He sends his regards."

"Michael *who*?"

Was Ben-Jacob on the level?

"Hasn't Michael told you about me?" I asked.

Ben-Jacob drummed his fingers on the desk top. "I don't know this Michael, and I don't know you. Will you please be so kind as to enlighten me? I have no time for guessing games."

I was feeling like a dime-store spy. Furious, I barked at him, "Shlomo Millet is Michael *who*!"

Ben-Jacob's reaction was instant surprise. "Shlomo! Why didn't you say so before? I had completely forgotten he was this Michael. How is Shlomo?"

"Hasn't Shlomo advised you about me?"

"No. Good God, was he supposed to?"

Anger rode me while I told him why I'd come here. Ben-Jacob phoned for someone to come in. The man who entered was rosy-faced, in his mid-thirties, of medium height, and had wavy brown hair. A cigar drooped from the side of his mouth; he had a friendly face. Chanan Barel would have an active part in my operations until the end of 1957.

We were introduced.

"Chanan, do you have anything on El-Ad Sarchi here?" Ben-Jacob asked without pause.

"Nothing."

"El-Ad is an associate of Shlomo Millet. He needs expense money."

"We'll have to contact Shlomo."

Ben-Jacob advised me to call tomorrow, and he suggested a reasonably priced inn nearby. What was to be one night of inactivity became two. I made an appearance at Munich's infamous Buergerbraeu Keller, once a favorite haunt of a little-known political demagogue, Adolf Hitler. From here, he had staged his ill-fated attempt to overthrow the Bavarian government. Arrested, sentenced to an eight-month term, he dictated *Mein Kampf* to Rudolf Hess. Munich had supported Hitler's beginning; I wondered what the once bomb-ruined city felt about that now.

I treated myself to a typical German meal of Ochsenschwanzsuppe and Kalbshaxen, accompanied by a mug of dark beer. The evening wore on. Soon I was locked arm-in-arm with the rest of the drunks loudly singing the Biergarten songs. Paul Frank, I thought to myself, is becoming a damned good German!

By midmorning I read the letter Ben-Jacob handed me. The reason Ben-Jacob had not been alerted about me, Shlomo wrote, was that I'd arrived too early. My hangover increased my irritation at this oversight. Further, Chanan Barel would be my contact man; Ben-Jacob was being transferred. Shlomo's letter contained a thousand deutsche marks. I signed for the money, repaid what had been given to me the day before, and left the city.

Munich should have alerted me to the inefficiency of our foreign intelligence, but I was too inexperienced to draw definite conclusions about

Modiin's relationship with the Mossad. Modiin, I knew, had few facilities of its own abroad, but I was only now realizing how dependent it was. And I came to know something of the interservice competition on May 15, Israel's Independence Day.

For the first time in our short, five-year history, I was excluded from celebrating this proud and emotional occasion; I had orders forbidding my association with fellow countrymen. Yet the feast hall in the Jewish community of Frankfurt drew me like a magnet. From the dark, I viewed the entrance decorated by our blue-and-white flag and envied every person entering the hall.

"Well, it's really a surprise to see you here," a voice said beside me.

I started. Benjamin Magen, a lieutenant-colonel from the army, stood grinning at me. In mufti, he looked out of place. We both were, and we realized it. At a coffee shop safely away from the celebration, Benny professed to represent El-Al Airlines in Frankfurt. Strange, since El-Al didn't land here! Only later did he reveal his status in the Mossad.

No brighter than he, and thinking I could trust someone of the "second faculty," I discussed with him some minor problem needing another opinion. It was bad judgment of the worst kind; I'd breached security. In no time at all Benny had reported me to Modiin headquarters. It taught me a hard-learned lesson. Shlomo's wrath, in letter form, was soon followed by a mysterious late-month visit from Motke.

At 5:30 on a still, dark morning, a knock woke me. Frau Meier, my landlady, in nightgown and hair curlers, said anxiously that a man downstairs wanted urgently to see me.

I threw on my trousers and went down. The glass door framed the bulky silhouette of a man wearing a hat. Cautiously I opened the door.

"Guten Tag, Herr Frank," the man said, obscured by the night. Had the preceding moments not been so tense, I would have laughed. Motke stood smirking on the threshold, while Frau Meier eyed him suspiciously from the top of the stairs.

"It's all right," I said, "an old friend of mine from Bavaria."

She smiled nervously; she had lived the Gestapo years. "I *thought* he was Bavarian—his accent," she said.

Upstairs, Motke and I laughed at her remark. Apparently she mistook his Germanized Yiddish for a Bavarian dialect.

Motke had squeezed seeing me into his three-hour Frankfurt layover. I gave him an account of events, stressing the lack of coordination between headquarters and people in the field.

Motke grunted sardonically. "I'm not too pleased with some of the arrangements Shlomo made." He hesitated, then went on to what he had come to discuss. "I'm not going to say much about your slip-up with

Benny Magen. It's a security breach on *your* part. But never mind Magen, he's Mossad. Let them do what they please. Shlomo doesn't see it exactly my way, but the less you deal with Mossad people, the better it is for us."

Motke handed me two excellent postcard-size photos of me. In one I wore the German Wehrmacht and in the other the SS uniform. In the latter I had the Ritterkreuz dangling from my neck; in the former I wore the Iron Cross beneath the breast pocket. Department 8 had done a beautiful job.

"One more thing," he said. "Forget about Shlomo's friend, Chanan Barel." He dug a phone number from his pocket. "This is the number of Alisa in Munich; she'll be your letterbox. Once a month go there and submit your report to her. She'll have our mail to you. If you need anything, tell her. She'll attend to it.

"Avri, you've done a good job to date. But again, bear in mind that our enemies are not asleep. Keep away from Israelis in general, and Mossad people in particular. Avoid them like the plague. To us, they *are* the plague."

"But why? Don't we pull on the same rope?"

"Indeed we do, but in different directions."

I said nothing. Motke's position was adamant. The divisiveness—if I read him correctly—centered in a power-duel between Modiin director, Col. Benjamin Gibli, and the Mossad director, Isser Harel, a man apparently determined to bring Modiin under his personal supervision.

Mossad and Modiin, operating beyond Israel's borders, overlapped in function and objective, thus creating a crippling atmosphere of discord that neither could afford. Since the Mossad had nearly all the external facilities, Modiin had to rely on these. Both were competing for status, each jealous of the other.

I had time to tell Motke only a bit of my plan for a new cover identity. He gave me permission to change residences and instructions to enroll in a compulsory driving course to obtain a license. Two weeks later I had the license and my identity card.

In my quest for the urgently important baptism certificate, I chose the smaller of the two Catholic churches in the neighborhood. I attended mass and took solace at the Communion altar for several days before I felt the priest's questioning eyes on me. Over the next weeks he watched my humble portrayal of a man tortured by his conscience, a sinner seeking salvation.

One late afternoon, I entered the church and I went into the wooden confessional cubicle. A rustling of cloth in the adjoining cubicle told me that the priest had answered my ring. On my side of the wicker partition I waited for his first move.

"Yes, my son, have you something to confess?" he asked, his soft, nearly inaudible voice rippling my spine. "Put your trust in God, and you will have comfort."

"Yes, Father," I answered. As if under great pressure, I began hinting that I had done something terribly wrong during the war. I suddenly became overwrought. "I cannot finish, Father!" I pushed out of the confessional, rushing from the church.

At the next mass, the priest's eyes searched the congregation until he spotted me. I played the game as before. But at my third attempt to confess, I spilled out my role in the mass execution of Jews. "Father, I know I merely carried out orders, but they were human beings. I murdered, Father. I killed, in cold blood, people who never did wrong to me."

After offering panaceas for my soul, the voice on the other side of the wicker partition fell silent. I left, my sins established.

When I next saw the priest, it was in his study at the vicarage, and at my request. I explained my predicament—the destruction of my baptism certificate and my need for the document in order to gain entry visas to Arab countries since my job was dependent on it—and he understood fully. He asked for facts about Frank's parents and verifying documents. I knew that a single name on Paul Frank's birth certificate would prove disastrous: Frank's mother was a Levy. I decided to alter the name on the document to Leroy, a name with a French inclination, which would explain a background from Alsace-Lorraine. Luckily I'd noted the ancient typewriter used by the registrar's secretary in Willmars. Finding one to rent was not easy, but I finally was able to make the change. It was a good job, undetectable.

Dropping off my papers to the priest put our acquaintanceship on a more personal basis. He wanted to know all about me. Over coffee I obliged him.

Returning for the certificate of congregation, again I was invited for a chat. This time a heavy German wine having replaced the coffee, I was now certain the good priest was more concerned with my body than my soul. Certificate in hand, I got to the door as quickly as I could. He gently squeezed my arm and looked deep into my eyes.

"Son, you have gone through hell. Don't let your conscience torture you longer. Bear in mind from now on, those people whom you have sent to their death . . . were the killers of our Lord, Jesus Christ. So don't torture yourself."

For a moment I could not believe the monstrosity of his words. Anger raged behind my pious exterior as I nodded obediently. My knowledge of the efforts of other priests to save my people spared me from cursing the whole of Catholic priestdom. But I had my certification of baptism and had ferreted out another Nazi sympathizer, under reverent cloth.

My orders were to secure a job with a German firm trading in Egypt and, by hook or crook, maneuver a transfer to Egypt. I had been answering the local newspaper ads and, in several personal interviews, had elicited interest. But I had been unable to follow up with *Unterlagen* (proof) of my background.

Finally headquarters responded through Alisa, my contact in Munich, with a letter of former employment with Kaiser-Fraser, Willow Run, USA, stating that I had worked as service manager for its assembly plant in Haifa. (I actually had served in that capacity for a few months, my last civilian employment before entering Modiin.) Accompanying the letter was a diploma from the Technische Hochschule in Darmstadt, Germany, certifying my studies in mechanical engineering. The forged documents would do everything except get me to Egypt.

At length the futility of the pursuit struck me. Headquarters had again initiated a plan lacking logic. No firm was going to send a newcomer to Egypt when others, with proven experience and more seniority, were available. There had to be another way.

Headquarters granted me a brief visit with my father in Vienna, my first in seven years. I experienced a nagging problem. In 1949 father had remarried. He had met his new wife, Olga, in 1942 during their year of internment in England as suspicious aliens, a condition meted out to many politically oriented refugees. With the war's end, they returned to Vienna. Their marriage made me feel that my mother's place had been usurped.

Flying into Schwechat Airfield outside Vienna, I felt disoriented passing through customs as Paul Frank. The speed of the bus added to my growing anxiety. How would I react? Where would I stand in my father's life if I failed to accept his new wife, a woman he loved deeply. In the city the bus stopped at the BEA office.

From my window, Father and Olga were in full view. Unseen I stared at them while the bus emptied. Olga was exactly as she had appeared in the pictures father had sent to my sister in Israel. Though she was only fifty, from a distance the full gray in her hair belied her age; beneath the matronly image was a full-breasted, full-hipped woman who might even be called pretty. Her square face and prominent features reflected a strong character amazingly akin to my father's.

Father had changed. The powerful angular face with its high, strong cheekbones, the piercing eyes I saw behind spectacles for the first time, the thin, determined mouth, all belonged to a man a little more stooped and a bit more introverted. His sixty-three years were there. His years in political prison, his time in concentration camps, his internment in England, his part in the political reconstruction of Austria—all of this had marked him. Yet I saw the stoicism I remembered from childhood.

At that very instant, I accepted Olga without reservation. I stepped from the bus and embraced her tightly. Tears sprang to her eyes. I went to Father. We held each other close, his arms tightened in overwhelming gratitude for my response to Olga.

"I feared you weren't coming. Your name didn't appear on the passenger list; so we didn't go the airport. How did you get here?"

Intervening, Olga used my father's pet name. "Mundl, leave him alone," she said. "The important thing is he's here with us."

As time went on, I told Father that I was working for the Israeli government in a sensitive capacity. To an old revolutionary who'd dueled politically with the Austrian government prior to Hitler, that was enough. Later, using my childhood name, he cautioned, "Dolfi, know that this kind of work is similar to a big wheel. One day you are on the top, the next day you've been dragged to the bottom." I smiled condescendingly, unable to appreciate his wisdom.

Their small, comfortable flat was in the fifteenth district near the *Sporthalle* and the *Westbahnhof.* Father had now risen in rank close to the secretariat of the Austrian Socialist Party labor organization, a lofty reward for a man who'd spent his life fighting for the existence of the party. Olga was also a ranking personage within the party. An accountant, her work now was with the *Arbeiter Zeitung,* the Vienna newspaper. I answered all their eager questions about my sister Ruth, her husband, Zvi Swet, and their five children. But I could not tell them of my divorce, not this time. Ashamed to admit the failure, I had not yet abandoned hope of reconciliation with Shula.

Travel expenditures rose, and I decided it would be better to own an automobile. Headquarters would never make the outlay. So, with my own funds, through a friend of Chanan Barel's in Munich, I bought a 1952 green Plymouth convertible, monthly payments in dollars.

Upon returning to Frankfurt, I found that Jiddel, who had promised to clear the car through customs for me, had reneged again. I had to lay out the full custom duties. Before that, however, I had had an opportunity to use Jiddel's influence on one of our trips to Paris. I had forgotten the pictures attached to the inside of my passport, and when the French border guard saw snapshots of me in the Wehrmacht and SS uniforms, his charm disappeared. He ran his finger down a list of names in his black book. Suddenly he looked at me hard, dialed a number, and was joined by a man out of uniform. For two hours they grilled me. Thanks to Jiddel's intervention, the interrogators were finally swayed. It was apparent that a man—Paul Frank or someone similar—was wanted. The black book undoubtedly listed ex-Nazis wanted for questioning, or worse.

Now I decided to focus on my idea that Paul Frank was one of the Germans who'd parachuted into Jericho during the war. My search began for a Paul Frank whose service record would fit my invented past. Files of those formerly in the SS or the Wehrmacht generally were not open to the public. However, if I claimed to be searching for a missing relative who might be a Russian prisoner of war, the information would be made available to me.

Paul Franks were well represented in the archives but none suited my need. Digging anxiously into the files of those under the heading of *Auslanddeutsche* (Germans from foreign countries), I found a Paul Frank, born in 1921 *in Palestine!*

My eagerness renewed, I began reading all materials of the German *Abwehr* (military intelligence) and the SS; the library in Frankfurt was an excellent source for transcripts of the Nuremberg war trials.

One General Lahousen told of his having recruited German agents, *Auslanddeutsche,* for work in the Middle East. The editors of *Deutsche Soldaten Zeitung* (Journal of the League of German Soldiers) in Munich revealed that many of the Templars'[1] sons had served either in the SS or *Abwehr* because of their knowledge of Arabic, Hebrew, or English. I could now play out my story in a credible light. The story I uncovered was that of a real Paul Frank, born in Palestine, the son of members of the Templars sect, who was sent to Germany prior to the war. He was accepted as a full candidate in the SS and later taken into the *Abwehr,* where he proved himself in missions not disclosed. Having risen to the rank of major, he was parachuted into Jericho, Palestine, with several Arab allies, and there he was captured by the British.

I then added pure fiction. I, as Paul Frank, escaped from the British, assumed a Jewish identity, joined the British army in hopes of getting to the continent and, failing to do so, remained in Palestine until the heat was off former SS members. Only now had I returned to Germany.

It fitted my original concept in every detail. Except that now its credibility had to be verified. It happened that at this time Germany was forming its new army under the Federal Republic, and ads appeared regularly in the papers for former soldiers interested in joining. Amt Blank was the

---

1. KNIGHTS TEMPLARS. Originally called Knights of the Temple of Solomon from their house in Jerusalem, they were founded by nine knights during the Crusades to protect pilgrims. They grew in number and became the greatest of warriors in the Crusades, gaining wealth and power throughout Europe. Nearly demolished by envy and jealousy, they retain, through legend, special privileges from some in total power, such as Hitler. Jerusalem remains their ancestral home. Many later moved to Palestine, as did the parents of the Nazi major, Paul Frank.

ministry responsible, and, after applying, I appeared for an interview in Bonn.

My stomach in a knot, I explained my past activities.

"I have no documents to prove my claim, but I trust you have copies of my file and can substantiate my military past." I knew that few such files had survived the war.

In three weeks I was called back to the capital. A colonel disclosed that although sparse records remained of *Abwehr III*, my story had been corroborated verbally. I was to be accepted in the rank of captain if I were interested. With forms and a booklet describing the new German army, I left—with the exuberance of knowing that my story had passed the check. *I, as Paul Frank, was now credible in the eyes of German officialdom— free to add convenient details to my life as they were needed.*

A few weeks after I wrote to Amt Blank, explaining my decision *not* to join the new German army because of a job offer, Jiddel Langfuss introduced me to a *Fräulein,* an acquaintance of his who was interning at a Frankfurt hospital. Once the plain, angular, thirtyish spinster had told us about her relatives, she became sheer poetry to me. Her father was a board member of a large electronics concern; her uncle was General Bayerlein, once Field Marshal Rommel's chief of staff.

Whatever her liaison with Jiddel, it took only a few coffees for Jiddel's budding lady doctor to begin casting furtive glances at me. I took advantage of her infatuation and arranged for the three of us to visit her general/uncle in Ingolstadt. At the end of my only talk with the general— who claimed to have known of Paul Frank's parachute sortie into Jericho—I had a note of introduction to Gen. Wilhelm Fahrmbacher, the chief adviser to the new Egyptian army.

Summer came to Germany.

The last of my letters to the old registrar in Willmars returned. A note enclosed told of his recent death. The gentle old man's passing solved a nagging problem for me; he was the last of those who could identify me through my false birth certificate.

I had relocated in Dornbusch, a better neighborhood only eight minutes by car from downtown Frankfurt. My new landlady was widowed and employed by day, thus removing my need to be on constant guard. Having presentable quarters and a car, I could get on to a more convenient intimacy with Gundrun, a young woman I had met by chance, who proudly claimed that Hitler had been her godfather. Gundrun's father, among the first right-hand men to Hitler, had belonged to the *Blutordentraeger* (holder of the Blood Order medal). Each trip to the boudoir with Gundrun was especially stimulating because of these facts. My only lack of fulfillment was in not being able to tell her of my Jewishness.

Evading Frankfurt's summer heat wasn't easy. Often I rented a boat and toyed about on the Main River, sometimes with Gundrun, sometimes alone. On occasion I drifted over to the floating swimming pool anchored near the quay and soon came to be accepted as a regular.

On what turned out to be a red-letter day, I arrived early and sunned alone. On my stomach, head on my folded arms, I spent a long while eyeing a beauteous blonde's escaping white breast. Finally, shifting my view to the left, I stared directly into the armpit of a man I had seen there before. He was forty or so, short, deeply tanned, blue-eyed, and gray-haired, and he had a fascinating, dime-sized scar in his armpit. That was where members of the German elite of the war years and members of the SS had tattooed their blood-group identification. Now the incriminating tattoo was a scar. I accidentally brushed his arm. "Pardon," I said. His look was congenial, and he nodded.

"It's not easy to notice anyone else with such as her nearby." I indicated the blonde.

I'd struck a common chord; he peered closely at the girl. "I see what you mean. Very nice."

"I'm going up for a beer. Could I bring you one?"

He readily agreed. *"Ein Helles* [light one], if you will. I'll hold your place. It's too strategic to lose."

"Das ist richtig," I said, leaping to my feet. I bought two glasses of beer and returned to begin a friendship with Ludwig Pohl, a man I hoped might eventually lead me into neo-Nazi circles.

That evening, with a ballpoint pen, I etched the letter *A* into my armpit. Even after several applications it looked too fresh. I dabbed it with hydrogen peroxide. In a matter of hours the *A* was perfect; it had all the earmarks of a tattoo I had amateurishly tried to remove.

The next day I broke a date with Gundrun; Pohl was at his spot beside the floating pool. Eventually we went to the shower room together.

"I see you've done a better job of it than I have."

At his quizzical look, I nodded toward his armpit. Lifting my arm, I showed him my "tattoo." Without a word, he leaned to me and said, *sotto voce,* "Mine was removed by an expert."

"And mine," I said, "was homework."

"You'd better attend to it. One never knows."

"It looks like it's fading," I said.

"I don't know. It has to be better than that."

Pohl invited me to join him at the local league of the *Spätheimkehre,* (late-returning prisoners), which, in German style, held office in a beer cellar. Being introduced as his old friend seemed sufficient. On the occasion of *Kameradschafts Abend* (comradeship evening), I declined his invitation, lest I seem overeager, a pattern of behavior I would exercise often.

"Maybe next time," he suggested. "And you'll see, the company will be your cup of tea." The implications intrigued me. What *was* my cup of tea?

I was soon to find out. The next meeting was that of the ODESSA, locally fronted by the Waffen SS veterans' organization. Soon I was fraternizing with the aiders and abettors, the sympathizers. The meetings were fairly routine, always a speaker with a subject vindicating German atrocities, especially those of the Waffen SS, which, they claimed, was only the combat branch of the SS.

During my first evening, Pohl whispered to me, "That fellow over there with the split chin was a *Gruppenfuhrer,* and the one sitting beside him a *Standartenfuhrer,* the one with the green shirt." And so it went. Each man had held some rank in Hitler's elite. Pohl never spoke of his own rank, nor did he ask mine.

When the singing of old German soldiers' songs began, I always immersed myself, recalling the times we of the German Platoon sang for practice these same gusty tunes. When called upon for a solo, drunkenly encouraged by friends of Pohl, I broke into *Die Blauen Dragoner sie Reiten* (The Blue Dragoons Are Riding). Soon the room resounded with the song. When the "Bravo, Paul" died, I was one of them, an accepted fringe member with wartime accreditations. As a former German intelligence agent, I was to be trusted.

I was still stymied, however, by the lack of a job. Though only four months had elapsed since my arrival in Germany, when Jiddel told me of a friend of his in Paris who knew of a German industrialist interested in a business venture in the Middle East, I jumped at the chance.

In August, Jiddel and I drove to Paris and lodged at the *petite* Lafayette, a small hotel around the block from *le grande* Lafayette. Having accidentally bumped into Israelis periodically, I was not surprised when our first popped up in the lobby. Jiddel and I found ourselves listening to his adventures in Parisian night life. He was well into a story about his failing to take advantage of a certain Israeli woman at our hotel, who was having trouble locating her husband.

"She's running all over Paris trying to find him," he told us. "Showed me his picture." He broke off, adding what he considered a joke. "She claims her husband is a *spy* for our government."

He laughed. "What's her name?" I asked.

He told me.

Good God! She was the wife of a Modiin operative who had been assigned a mission before me. *And she was running all over Paris claiming he was a spy!*

Somebody had to shut her mouth. I went to the hotel receptionist: The lady was out until evening. I raced to the Israeli Embassy, which was contrary to directives, and came face to face with Etka Jiftach, the wife of Col. Shimon Jiftach, my former commanding officer in Zahal.

"What are you doing here?" we exclaimed in unison.

Etka answered quickly, "I'm part-time secretary to Colonel Sirkin, our military attaché. And you?"

"I have to see him right away, Etka. Is he in?"

"Not until the afternoon. Maybe someone else can help you." Etka spoke into the phone. In a moment the Mossad's Arieh-Mambush came in. I quickly related to him what I'd heard.

"She's been here already," he said, smiling wanly. "We know what she's up to."

Then why was she still on the loose? "You mean, you know she's showing his picture around the hotel?"

Arieh's face clouded. "No, we didn't know that. But something will be done about her stupidity, believe me." With a fast "thank you" he fled the room.

Later, in a chance encounter with the captain whose wife was looking for him, I learned that the authorities had sent her home.

"I heard about what you did," he said. "Thanks." He seemed humbled. I felt even more so. He was one hell of a chap.

Chapter 6

Promise was in the air. Paris led to my first tangible opportunity for a legitimate route into Egypt. Jiddel took me to a Mr. Eppelbaum, who had left Palestine for France years ago to establish an import-export company with dealings in Germany. Eppelbaum directed us to Herr Shroeder, a German manufacturer who wanted to market heavy machinery in the Middle East.

On Eppelbaum's lead Jiddel and I went to Bielefeld, Herr Shroeder's base in northern Germany, where Jiddel met with the industrialist to sell me as a man with good connections in the Middle East. Waiting in Shroeder's office, I met the man who would springboard me into Egypt.

His name was Faust. He was the owner of two plants specializing in the manufacture of electrical coils and coil-wrapping machines for industrial and maritime purposes. After listening to my thoughts on commercial ventures, he invited me to visit his plants. I tucked away the invitation until a letter from Shroeder brought an offer for me "to stop in Bielefeld at my next convenience."

I convinced him that Jiddel should handle negotiations with Israel while I, as a German with a past that was better left confidential, could negotiate the Arab market. After donning coveralls and monitoring his plant for several days, I was referred to Faust (the man I really wanted to get at) as a "young man to deal with."

Unknown to me, however, Jiddel had stalled my meeting with Faust in fear of being excluded from the deal. He had already presented my ideas to Faust as his own. They centered on the sale of surplus military matériel to Arab countries, a good possibility in view of the arms embargo. The tripartite agreement among the United States, England, and France had banned the sale of offensive equipment into the area. I had already located a source of this matériel through a major in charge of the U.S. procurement center in Frankfurt. Naturally the supply was limited, but I only wanted a route into Egypt. Also, I foresaw a pipeline for our people to filter into Egypt as business representatives handling matériel negotiations and technical training, while they kept an eye on military preparations.

After straightening out Jiddel—it was my show!—I drove to Offenbach am Main, Faust's plant ten miles from Frankfurt. His office epitomized the German *gediegen:* solid, dependable, and expensive, from the heavy furniture to the polished oak paneling. The art was original, worth a king's ransom, and the Persian rug was priceless. Faust himself, indeed, was the ideal picture of a German industrialist: heavy of stature, fleshy, with darting, intelligent eyes. He was a no-nonsense businessman; it had made him ridiculously rich.

Desperately wanting the association with Faust, I repeated my proposals, tying the sale of his products to military surplus. Faust proved the soundness of my scheme by mentioning inquiries from Lebanon and Egypt that demanded following up: One Egyptian firm had asked for an agency to market his electrical products. I minimized the Egyptian's skills in the commercial area, convincing Faust that initial probings should be handled by a German, like myself, who was familiar with engineering and military equipment.

After a short, nervous wait, Faust endorsed my proposal by suggesting that I *also* represent another plant of his south of Darmstadt. Stollberg, a plant manufacturing drills and tools, could be equipped for drilling gun barrels on short notice. Then, reluctant to associate his established plants with the sale of war matériel, Faust suggested the creation of a new firm, equally owned by himself, Jiddel, and me. Each of us would put up one-third of the capital, and to reduce initial expenditures, the firm would operate out of his plant in Offenbach.

It was incredible luck, though to me, luck is nothing more than preparedness meeting opportunity. However, I had no authority to approve such a large capital outlay. In a fast letter to headquarters, I outlined the developments. I was nagged by the possibility that headquarters would see too many trees and miss the forest. Lately my relationship with Motke had cooled as a result of impatience on his part, certain disagreements over my *modus operandi,* and several sniping reports from Mossad sources.

Instead of receiving a response, I got a letter from Motke accusing me of squandering money on cars, of being indiscreet (no details), and of failing to show tangible accomplishment. He even hinted at calling me back home. Long confused by the lack of coordination with headquarters, humiliated by the shoddy accusations, and sick of the petty intrigues and narrow prejudices of my Mossad counterparts, I sent Motke a two-word cable: "Coming home."

Chanan Barel contacted me from Munich immediately. A cable from Motke read: "Wait. Mordechai Almog arriving Europe. Instructions to follow."

While I awaited Lieutenant Colonel Almog, Modiin's logistics officer, I made angry attempts to convince headquarters of the soundness of the Faust proposal. Another cable came: "Almog will check the matter for decision. If positive, money no problem"—the first announcement I'd *ever* heard that money was no problem.

Over the last weeks a sticky political development had been taking place, one that endangered the Egyptian leg of my mission. The London-Bonn controversy was front page news. Anthony Eden had complained to Konrad Adenauer that mercenary German advisers were aiding the new Egyptian army just at a time when England was trying to retain its garrison on the Suez Canal Zone in the face of belligerent Egyptian nationalism. As reported Bonn had informed Whitehall that it had no authority to prevent German advisers from carrying out their private contracts as instructors to General Naguib's forces.

Chanan Barel told me that the British were fearful of German advisers assuming active commands if hostilities broke out. Apparently *un*reported in the news was Whitehall's ability to effect (somewhat) Bonn's cooperation. This was assumed, Barel said, when the German Embassy in Cairo informed the German advisers to use discretion in case of armed conflict. (Later I would learn that the German advisers were warned that if they led Egyptian troops against the British, their chances of being accepted into the new German army would be damaged.)

Meanwhile I drove to Vienna for a weekend with Father and Olga.

On Saturday afternoon I was sitting in a coffeehouse on the Kaerntner Strasse, the famous shopping street. Three men, roughly my age, were sipping espresso and chatting; I had known two of them fifteen years before. One was Hugo Krug, my sister Ruth's boyfriend from our childhood days in Vienna. Hugo had emigrated to Palestine in 1938, a year before me.

I sensed them staring at me. I paid the bill and was moving to the door when they confronted me.

"Haven't we met before? You look familiar."

"Years ago," I confirmed. "When we were kids together. I was a friend of your sister Lotte, Hugo. We played many times in St. Johann Park."

"Of course! You're Dolfi, little *Dolfi!* Ruth Seidenwerg's brother," Hugo exclaimed. He suggested I join them for a night on the town. I begged off but could hardly dodge an invitation for Sunday lunch at his home.

I hadn't liked Hugo Krug as a child, and I wasn't so certain about him now, but I went to his plain apartment where scarcity lay like a pall. Hugo's wife, Ruth, a lithe and curvaceous, reddish-haired beauty, looked totally out of place alongside the diminutive, dark-haired, Semitic-featured Hugo. I took to her immediately, despite her forced smiles of approval as Hugo sought to explain his recent return to Austria as an attempt to reclaim an old family shoe factory confiscated by the Nazis.

I did not buy his elaborate explanation. Hugo was now manufacturing shirts, but his wife's downcast smile belied his "thriving" business. Hugo was really attempting to justify his leaving Israel; those who had emigrated to Palestine and later returned to their country of origin were looked on in Israel as deserters. *Joreds* were regarded with contempt. Hugo, obviously, was home.

Explaining my presence in Vienna as having to do with industrial expansion, I said that I'd also seen our ambassador about some war-surplus matériel.

"If it's war surplus you're looking for," he said, "I might be of some help. I know someone who was an executive with Henschel during the war. A nice fellow, a *goy*. He knows about such things."

I said I'd be interested in seeing the *goy* on my next trip to Vienna.

On the drive back to Frankfurt, however, I wondered if Hugo was on the level. The Henschel concern had been one of the biggest armament factories of the Third Reich. Today it was a giant exporter of locomotives, buses, and tractors; it had recently been licensed to build American Sikorsky helicopters. If Henschel hadn't penetrated the Egyptian market, perhaps I could help them.

In that moment I decided to consolidate my whole concept. Instead of representing Faust and Shroeder exclusively, why not obtain as many agencies as possible, covering the whole range from light to heavy industry? *Exported equipment demanded maintenance, and maintenance demanded skilled workers. Israel had them. Through these agencies we could infiltrate Egypt.* Now, more than ever, everything depended on my meeting with Mordechai Almog!

I received instructions to meet Almog in Paris at a coffee shop near the Place de l'Opera. I phoned Jiddel in Frankfurt, asking him to be prepared to come to Paris on a moment's notice, with a partnership agreement with Faust. Almog might be more receptive to facts in black and white.

When Almog and I met, I went through my plan step by step. Almog seemed critical but knowledgeable, interjecting a question here and there.

"Avri, let me tell you about Motke's situation a while back," he volunteered. It appeared a total *non sequitur*.

"Please do," I said. This I wanted to hear.

"You have to understand his position," he began. "Then you might not think too hard of him. It took a while for Motke to realize that the reports reaching him about you were distorted. Until then he was not only disappointed but worried as well. He sent me out personally to investigate the sources. Here in Europe, I realized you'd actually achieved more than we logically could have expected. I wrote recommending he keep you on the job." He paused. "Motke did warn you about avoiding the Mossad people, however."

"That's true," I nodded.

In the end, Almog explained, Motke had stood up for me.

"All right," I said, "let's forget it happened."

Almog agreed to Jiddel's coming to Paris. He appeared with a raw draft of the Faust agreement that called for each of the three of us to put up twenty-five-thousand deutsche marks. The firm, Faust and Stollberg, would supply surplus war matériel exclusively to the Middle East. Of course Faust would not know that Modiin was represented.

Within twenty-four hours Almog had headquarters' approval and the promise of my share of the investment, which Jiddel would turn over to Faust.

I remained in Paris for further photography training at the apartment of Schmuel Toledano. Accidentally I learned that the Jordanian military attaché resided in Schmuel's building, and that across the street was the residence of the Syrian military attaché. Had I known these facts, I would have refused training in Schmuel's apartment. The possibility existed that my picture had been snapped by either of the Arab military attachés, merely as a precautionary measure. It was too late to complain, but the oversight would be in my next report. Let Motke wring the Mossad's tail!

A letter from Motke read like old times. Almog had taken home a favorable report. Motke stated that the importance of my Plymouth had been realized, and that headquarters would assume the payments as well as its upkeep. I hadn't realized how much being in Motke's good graces meant to me.

I knew exactly what to do with the extra money. I would fly Shula and my son to Vienna for a few days. The first break, I would join them; in this way, Father would meet the daughter-in-law and grandson he'd never seen. Fearing that headquarters would not approve, I wrote Shula directly.

I familiarized myself with Faust's operating processes at Offenbach. Meanwhile Faust had secured letters of appointment for me from two other important firms. Now I had sufficient credentials to apply for an entry visa to the land of the pharaohs.

The Egyptian Consulate was high alongside the south bank of the River Main, not far from my former lodging. Often I'd wondered what was going on inside that impressive structure. Now an Arab desked in the hall directed me to Fräulein Gaertner on the second floor. I explained to her the purpose of my visit.

"Are you German?" she asked in her efficient manner.

I said stiffly, "Of course I am."

"No offense meant, Herr——?"

"Frank. Paul Frank. I'll need a commercial visa extended for at least a month."

"It is our policy to inquire, Herr Frank. Are you Catholic?"

"I am. But not a very pious one." I grinned.

"You certainly don't look like a sinner," she said. The tension between us had flown. She didn't look too bad, once she smiled.

"If you would join me later for a cup of coffee, I would do all in my power to prove you wrong."

Fräulein Gaertner's full laughter and her acceptance of my invitation showed something else. "The formalities come first," she smiled. "Fill out these forms. I need two pictures and proof of religion."

Wanting to photograph the forms, I sought an excuse to take them from the building. I found it in the "date of departure" and "means of transportation," which, I explained, would have to be confirmed with Herr Faust of Faust and Stollbergwerke.

I left, promising to return the forms the next day. Before leaving for Munich, I called Fräulein Gaertner and explained that I wouldn't be back until the following week. I added, "Don't forget about our coffee."

"I haven't. Don't *you* forget it," she laughed. She was the first thing I heard about from Chanan Barel when I reached Munich.

"You're a godsend," he said.

"Why?"

"We know all about Fräulein Gaertner. Some time ago, I instructed Benny Magen to befriend her, however he could." He laughed. "He got nowhere with her."

"And you want me to do better?"

"Exactly."

My return to the Egyptian Consulate was with all necessary credentials, plus the letters of representation from the firms wanting to establish agencies in Egypt.

Having squared myself with Fräulein Gaertner, I was escorted to the consul's office. I took the chair but refused the Egyptian cigarettes.

"I'm a pipe smoker," I explained.

"So am I," the consul replied. "But today, I am not well; so I refrain from smoking at all."

Fräulein Gaertner's mimicry behind his back proved she liked me. I winked at her while the consul shuffled the documents.

"Everything seems in order, Herr Frank," he said. "I'll grant a three-month visa, but it has to be used within this year." He swiveled toward Fräulein Gaertner. "Take care of this matter."

Rising with the consul, I thanked him profusely.

"It is hoped your trip is rewarding both for you and for us. And try to enjoy our beautiful country."

"I shall do my utmost in both areas, sir."

Stamping the visa, the consul signed it with a flourish. I thanked him again and trailed Fräulein Gaertner from the office. Out of the consul's earshot, I said, "Can you meet me at Kranzler Coffee this afternoon?" She nodded. I touched her hand briefly, then walked out. Our coffee became coffees. Our relationship made Barel happy.

Applying for a *carne de passage* issued by the German automobile club, I turned up an unexpected piece of business—the ADAC's lack of information on Egyptian road conditions.

"Since you anticipate extensive travel in Egypt," the head of the ADAC office in Frankfurt said to me, "why not take notes? With your help, we can update our present maps."

I could hardly believe this opportunity. "It might be a good idea to give me your request in writing; the Egyptian automobile club should help, I would think." We shook on the agreement.

Headquarters seemed to have ignored one important matter: my circumcision.

At a previous gathering of the *Deutsche Reichspartei* with Ludwig Pohl, a conversation had brought me into the trust of Doctor G. After a heavy consumption of beer, he confided that he had served as a surgeon in the war. On his release as a prisoner of war, he had become active in associations that provided shelter for war criminals. He spoke of an illegal abortion patient dying. Dismissed from the medical associations, he had moved to the South.

"There are too many of Moses's children in the medical profession; otherwise, I would still be a doctor. They see in every one of us those responsible for Auschwitz, for mass sterilization of the inferiors," he complained.

"You are not alone. I, too, still suffer because of the Jews," I said.

"Tell me," he coaxed drunkenly. "You can trust me."

I asked if he had heard where I'd served during the war. "With Rommel in Africa . . . or somewhere like that."

"Something like that," I said. "I stepped out over Palestine once, on a special mission."

Doctor G's face lighted up. "So you were one of *those!*" he exclaimed.

"In order to go into Palestine, they asked me to undergo an operation so I could piss with the Jews."

Doctor G broke into a spasm of laughter. Grinning, I continued, "Now that the war is over, it bothers me so much that sometimes I begin to feel inferior."

His arm went round my shoulders. "Paul," he said, "do you know how many of us have been circumcised? If I had a deutsche mark for every one, I could set up a clinic right here."

"It's true," I said, "but to be chaffed for it by my girl friend—— You know what she does?"

"What?"

"When we're in bed, at the ready, she sometimes starts giggling. 'It makes me feel wicked to have a Jew in bed,' she says. How do you think I feel when she does that?" I was using the very words of Gundrun, my former anti-Semite bedmate.

"You should kick her in the ass," Doctor G said sullenly. "Who the hell is she? You are a good-looking boy! There are others, doesn't she know that?"

"The problem is deeper than that. I wanted to marry her, but because of the operation and her jokes, I don't see how it could last, do you?"

Doctor G stared into the depths of his beer mug. "You do have a problem. Maybe I can help. It might cost you a bit, and there's no guarantee."

"Anything," I said eagerly.

"Before I say more, I'll have to examine your defunct *Schmeisser*." He erupted in laughter. "That's good. A defunct *Schmeisser!*"

Now I called Doctor G. But I felt mounting trepidation. How did I know this fifty-year-old doctor wasn't a butcher?

"All right, Paul, drop your laundry. Let's inspect that *Schmeisser* of yours and see if it can be fixed up with a muzzle guard."

Breaking into a sweat, I trailed him into a tiny, disheveled room that served as both examination and operating room. Undressed and sitting on the edge of his stirrup-table, I endured his caustic remarks while he pulled and probed at my penis, which resisted the examination by trying to hide.

"Paul, you can count yourself one of the lucky ones. Whoever did the job left enough foreskin so that, with a few stitches, I might be able to extend it downward." He demonstrated. "You see, it's almost perfect."

I looked at it. I looked at him.

"There will be no complications, believe me." Could I believe it? That wasn't exactly a lollypop he was fingering. I was no longer acting; this was real fright.

"The fee is 150 deutsche marks. But for you, 100."

"Who quibbles at a time like this!"

Still chuckling at my remark, Doctor G applied the anesthetic to freeze the area. In a moment I felt only the sensation of icy coldness. The skill in his hands amazed me. Minor incisions, a few stitches, and it was done. Doctor G stepped back, critically appraising his handiwork. "Nice. Very nice indeed. Almost like new."

Gingerly I touched it. "When will it feel again?"

"Not for a while. No bath for ten days, Paul, and forget horizontal activity for at least a month."

A month! Shula would be meeting me in Vienna before then. "What if I don't forget it?" I asked.

"When you have an erection, you'll remember to forget."

I paid the fee and took off for the apartment. Only there did I dare take a closer look at my swollen and smarting penis. Good God! A fortnight after the surgery, I had my first urination without pain.

Headquarters instructed me that Jiddel, as a partner in the firm, was to receive mail from me through Faust and Stollberg and convey it immediately to Chanan Barel in Munich. Orders from Motke were simple. My mission was to tour Egypt as long as necessary to establish a permanent residence in Cairo; then I would return to Europe. En route to Egypt, when I reached Rome, I was to call a certain number and arrange to meet with a contact whose cover name was Abba.

I had already written Shula to book the first flight to Vienna. I had nothing more to do except sleep until morning, grab some clothes, and take off.

Snow came to Germany. Magic touched the ground.

In Vienna I got in touch with Hugo Krug and suggested I might meet the executive he knew at Henschel. Hans Schneider, of Henschel, Fichtel, and Sachs, suggested that he might supply me with such items as Mauser carbines left over from World War II Wehrmacht stocks, as well as almost every other sort of war surplus. But, as for my representing Henschel in Egypt, his response was guarded. Then suddenly he said, "I'll go to Germany and see to it personally. Leave it to me."

Within a week Hans Schneider had authorized me to negotiate on his behalf, as Henschel's representative for Austria. This document put the important Henschel name behind me in gaining a legal foothold in Egypt.

Shula cabled the date of her arrival: November 28.

As Father, Olga, and I, laden with flowers, drove to Schwechat Airport, the sun burst through for the first time in a week. When we learned that the flight would be two hours late, my father began teasing me about Jewish airlines and pilots, and soon we were in a heated argument.

"You are taking yourself too blasted seriously," Father accused. "Where is your Jewish sense of humor?"

But my father, in all his wisdom, had yet to realize that Israel was not a Jewish country, though most of her inhabitants were Jews. We young Israelis were akin to Jews in ancestry, but hardly in spirit. Our distinctive pride and fiery chauvinism made us a *new* people with self-confidence and an immense national conscience. Our Jewish humor was no longer self-derogatory. There was no force in our souls driving us to justify our being alive as an oppressed minority. In our land, we were not the minority.

I said it all to my father and saw it fall harshly on him. I looked at him, his lips pressed tight. I felt greatly relieved but ashamed; he was not one of those Jews against whom I raged.

"Son," he said, choosing his words carefully, "forgive me if I nipped at your pride. I understand. When I was a young man, I was blessed with the feelings you have. They made life worth living."

I'd never felt such closeness for my father. I took him in a hug and squeezed. Holding him at arm's length, I could only grin.

Then the El-Al DC-4 landed and Shula came down the stairs, the travail of the last hours in her face. I restrained my longing to hold her in my arms as we kissed; first I had to clear up one thing.

"Shula, we'll be staying with Father and Olga at their apartment. They wouldn't have it any other way."

Indignation flared in her face. "Staying with *them!* How could you put me in such a position?"

Restraining my writhing son, I said, "I couldn't help it. I couldn't bring myself to tell Father about us."

With a forced smile, I pushed myself toward the terminal. Father gave Shula the flowers and kissed her warmly, then turned to the only one of his grandchildren he'd ever seen.

Halfway to the city, Shula said, "Did you see Hauser? He came on the plane with me."

"Hauser!" I braked the car so hard Harel almost catapulted in the front seat. "Hauser was on your plane?"

"Yes, he boarded into Rome. He helped me with Harel."

"Did he know where you were going? That you were meeting me?"

"No. He said only to send you his best regards. You stand very high in his esteem, you know."

"Did you tell anyone you were meeting me?"

"I only told Shlomo I was accepting an invitation from my in-laws."

God! Sure as hell they knew Shula was meeting me, but why hadn't Hauser come forward to say hello? Maybe they didn't care since my work was done until I left for Egypt.

"Avri, is something wrong?"

"No, nothing is wrong. Maybe it is very right."

Shula, Olga, and Father fell in love with one another. Harel was delirious with joy. He had his father and a houseful of people who loved him. No one was happier than I, despite my private war with Shula. Together we drove everywhere; we even went for a two-day outing in the Alps. Father bragged about his grandson and showered him with gifts.

One day Shula asked me, "What do you think about Ben-Gurion's threat to resign?"

"I wouldn't worry about the old fox. He knows what he's doing."

During the past six months the situation in Israel had deteriorated sharply. Guerrilla activity on both the Jordanian and Egyptian frontiers had increased markedly, and the number of villagers killed rose daily, reaching crisis levels. A special army unit, 101, for retaliation purposes, strove to spread terror among the Arab villages to halt infiltration. This eye-for-an-eye philosophy had led directly to an incident that would be soundly condemned by not only the United Nations, but the world. Kfar Kibbiah, a border village across the Jordan River, had been hit by Israeli commandos on October 14, leaving sixty-six Jordanians dead and many wounded.

Ben-Gurion's handiwork, even though he was on leave of absence. Ben-Gurion's ruling party, clamoring alongside the rest of the Knesset, condemned the action and threatened to curtail his powers as prime minister. But the Ben-Gurion of my experience would not roll over defeated. His threats of resignation seemed just the sort of maneuver designed to bring his foes to heel.

Ben-Gurion accepted the authority of no man when it ran counter to his desires. He was proud and inclined to vindictiveness, embodying the strongest inclinations of Israel as a nation and a people. Once, in 1948, I was in charge of a convoy trekking slowly toward Jerusalem through Arab-controlled territory. My orders were to instruct Ben-Gurion, in his steel-plated Lincoln, that he had to follow precautions for his safety. Predictably, at one point he grew impatient, and he ordered his driver to pull out of line and go ahead. That was the last we saw of him until we reached Jerusalem. I was held at fault; why hadn't I deflated the tires on his car?

When I cornered Ben-Gurion's driver later, all he said was, "B-G kept mumbling, 'Nobody is going to tell me what to do. Drive on! I am responsible.' "

At the beginning Shula had disliked Vienna, not an uncommon reaction for Jews making their first journey to the Germanic countries; she saw an ex-Nazi in every face. At the end, however, she regretted having to leave. Morning dawned on mid-December, a cold, clear day, perfect for a motor trip. We had an open road to Rome, which afforded us the chance to discuss our problems. Shula told me she had no intentions of remarrying. Neither would she commit herself regarding our relationship, even after I disclosed the likelihood of my touring the Arabic countries as a German businessman.

At Bologna I learned that Ben-Gurion had made his threat a reality; he resigned the two offices he'd held jointly since the creation of the State of Israel: prime minister and minister of defense.

What had he done? Was it merely belligerent political blackmail, or was his decision final? There was only one Ben-Gurion. The Old Lion was looked upon as the modern Moses. He had led us to the Promised Land. He was the leader.

Drawing on the tremulous feeling in my gut, I could only imagine the reaction at home. Every stomach would be an empty pit. Many had clamored for his skin. Now they had it. What next?

A day later we pulled into Rome. I contacted Abba as instructed.

"Come to the embassy this evening." Abba saw my astonishment and added, "It will be very dark outside. At eight o'clock sharp, someone will bring you to the rear entrance."

At eight on the dot, I was led through the alley and up to the second floor, where Abba and another man waited. Abba handed me a thick envelope containing orders from Motke and private notes from Shlomo and Hauser.

My mission: Go into Egypt and establish residence as a German businessman. Provide an infiltration route for other Israeli operatives and set up a sleeper network under Motke's command! I would be lying low under my cover, rather than actively collecting intelligence information. Only before an outbreak of war would the sleeper network be activated to hit vital tactical and strategical military targets.

The order did not mean that I was to close my ears to information that fell into my lap. But first, I was to smell around, check out an infiltration route, then come out. Easy.

My one-dollar-per-day hazard pay for time spent in enemy territory was a tribute I neither expected nor wanted.

The letter suggested using secret ink for communication in this initial stage. Two dead letterbox addresses were inserted—one in Germany, another in Austria. Final instructions for the infiltration network would be given to me later.

I put a match to the order. Abba watched patiently. "I've got money for you."

The envelope contained $1,040. I signed the receipt. Abba asked for my passport for updating. I gave it to him.

"All set?" Abba asked.

"All set."

I was beginning to get that time-is running-out feeling.

The next day my passport showed that the words "Tel Aviv," stricken out in Zurich with black ink, were no longer legible to any light. A note from Shlomo read: *"Hals und Beinbruch* (Break your neck and leg)."

At two o'clock in the morning, I still lingered outside the airport with Shula and my son. My friend, Gen. Yitzhak Rabin, returning home after a year at England's Staff College, was inside the terminal. His presence would have attracted Arab intelligence people.

I was standing near the entrance when a green Mercedes convertible roared up, a Ford station wagon glued to its rear bumper. Behind the wheel of the Mercedes sat a voluminous mound of masculine assemblage decorated with a Bavarian hat, sunglasses, and a mustache. Pressed against him was an awe-inspiring, voluptuous blonde. The car stopped and the driver poked his head out.

"Tell me, please, where is Via Appia?" he asked in Italian.

I lowered my head for a better look. "Straight ahead."

"Mille grazie!" The Mercedes roared off.

Before the driver of the Ford could speed off, I stepped to the window. "Wasn't that King Farouk?" An irritable grunt and a yes came from Farouk's beleaguered bodyguards, as they raced off in pursuit of their charge. Of the millions of people in Rome, the exiled former king of Egypt had chosen me.

Almost five hours late, Shula's plane readied for departure. No words could say what I felt as I watched them leave, not knowing if I'd ever see them again.

Thirty minutes later I was on the road south. Reaching Naples, I drove across the mountainous peninsula of Italy and reached Bari on the Adriatic Sea by early evening. I dragged myself to the nicest hotel and slept until midmorning.

At the docks the S.S. *Enotria* lay at anchor. I turned over the Plymouth to the dock officer and I watched it hoisted on board by a giant derrick.

Going to Egypt. I looked forward to it with a fine anticipation.

Book 2

Chapter 7

1953 was running out.

Five days before Christmas I left for Alexandria. I awoke at dawn to feel the ship rising high on wind-torn waves and then dropping deep into the troughs with lurches that jarred the spine. Even through the closed porthole I could hear the wild screech of the wind. The *Enotria* had sailed into a violent Mediterranean storm.

The day before, on embarking, I found I had been berthed with two Arabs: Captain Tahar of the Sudanese Army, returning home after six months of advanced British military study, and an Egyptian doctor returning from a UNICEF conference in Switzerland.

The arrangement was opportune. I tested my German identity against their Arab mentality and found it airtight. Immediately they displayed the Arab's affinity for Germans by mentioning a fellow passenger: the new German ambassador to Egypt.

Outside a porthole, lashed by giant waves, I saw heavy black clouds consuming the sky. Captain Tahar groaned, his head cradled miserably in his arms. The doctor was out of it, one skinny leg over the edge of his bunk like an abandoned puppet's. At least he was silent.

Dozens of passengers headed for their rooms as I made my way topside. The wind was stabbing cold. The ship was rolling like a log adrift. I had barely made it to a deck chair when my stomach erupted with nausea. Frantically I dashed to the rail and let go. Lurching back to the chair, I nearly rammed a man strolling along the deck, apparently oblivious of the storm and the motion of the ship.

"Feeling better?" he asked, smiling down at me. "Even half the crew are no better than you." I saw a man of fifty, graying and scholarly. "My name is Kopf, Dr. Kopf. *Aus Freiburg, der Universitatstadt.* I am on a study tour of Egypt."

"Paul Frank," I told him, "a somewhat ill businessman."

He said, "A pleasure meeting you, Herr Frank, even in these trying circumstances."

"Danke." I was happier without him.

Two days later, when the Mediterranean shone smooth as a mirror, I learned that Dr. Kopf was head of a powerful committee of the West German Bundestag. In casual conversation Dr. Kopf confirmed the presence of the new German ambassador, Dr. Pawelke, and added that there was another envoy aboard accredited to Ethiopia, Dr. Bidder.

When he told me his touring base would be Cairo, I felt I was in luck. Few German officials abroad, I knew, had vehicles, and I invited him to drive with me to Cairo.

"Why, thank you very much, Herr Frank," he beamed, "but Dr. Pawelke has promised transportation in the embassy vehicles."

The last morning at sea brought Middle East weather, as the smudge on the horizon grew into a minaret atop a hillside mosque and then the sparkling city beyond the waterfront. It also brought the Egyptian health and customs officials out to us. One checked passports against a black book; the second, visitation and residence; the third affixed the triangle Egyptian stamp. Nothing to worry about—except the black book. A leaflet of regulations stated that all aliens must register with the Department of Interior within forty-eight hours and that this could be done at one's hotel or pension. Very clever that the movement of any alien could be plotted simply by his nightly residence.

Alexandria loomed near; the quay was just ahead. I managed to get snapshots of every naval vessel and military installation in view before the *Enotria* docked, and then the gangplank lowered into a swarm of screeching shouts and waving arms. Fighting my way to the landing, I saw two black Opel limousines flying small German banners, no doubt come to pick up Dr. Pawelke's entourage.

At customs I heard a shout: "Herr Frank!" A flushed Dr. Kopf trotted toward me. "Herr Frank, is your offer still open to Cairo? Dr. Pawelke finds no room in his cars for Dr. Bidder and myself." He cast an angry glance toward the limousines.

"Of course," I said.

"Wonderful! Wonderful!" he exclaimed. "I shall wait beyond customs with Dr. Bidder."

The ease with which I passed customs alerted me to the fact that I couldn't relax. Be smart, Paul Frank, I said, you've got perfect credentials and a perfect cover. There's nothing to worry about, except carelessness.

Outside Dr. Bidder and I were introduced, and minutes later we were cruising along the straight desert road toward Cairo.

Within an hour we'd caught up with Ambassador Pawelke's caravan, and I had made myself (and my car) available for Dr. Kopf's tours. As we closed slowly on the two limousines, both doctors strongly urged me to pass, knowing full well the narrow tarmac road hardly accommodated both big cars side by side. So I sent Pawelke's chauffeur onto the sandy shoulder and into clouds of dust. My passengers gave the ambassador polite but superior smiles as we sailed past.

Behind us Pawelke's car suddenly surged forward, horn blaring, lights blinking frantically. I pulled over, and the three of us alighted to face an apoplectic Dr. Pawelke. He did an odd thing. Instead of attacking us for blinding him, he chose a tack that took away his advantage.

"How dare you fly that flag on your car!" he fumed. "Only the German ambassador or his representative has that privilege."

Calmly I said, "I haven't had the questionable pleasure of being introduced to you, sir."

Dr. Kopf introduced us. "Dr. Pawelke, Herr Frank was so kind as to offer us transportation after you found yourself unable."

I stepped forward with a short Teutonic bow and extended my hand. The ambassador took it, unable to refuse without offending Kopf.

"Allow me to apologize, Excellency," I said, "but the pennant is the official banner of the German auto club. In an unofficial capacity I am representing them here. I have no intention of insulting you with its similarity. If it displeases you, I will remove it."

Kopf and Bidder stood tall beside me. Obviously Dr. Pawelke had no choice; he was dead wrong.

"Well, it is rather deceptive in its outward features." Herr Ambassador pulled himself up in the best German tradition. "Herr Frank, I have made a mistake. I extend my apologies." Pawelke turned smartly to my companions. "Dr. Kopf and Dr. Bidder, I feel it a privilege to invite you gentlemen to the embassy immediately on arrival in Cairo. Herr Frank, again you have my apologies, as well as an invitation with Herr Doctors. Please accept."

"I'm honored, sir."

On the road again, I was astonished at my luck. Less than three hours in Egypt and already invited to the embassy. Who would believe it!

Two hours later we were at the pyramids of El Giza. Eastward the Nile Valley, a narrow ribbon of green, wound viperlike from the south toward the Mediterranean, holding the powerful Nile River, the literal artery of

Egypt. On its other side, the desert rose up again, stretching to the Red Sea. To our right lay the Western Desert—400 miles of sand, all the way to Libya's border.

Meanwhile Kopf had been giving a running commentary on Egyptian geography and history.

"You know, Cairo is not a pharaonic city but an Islamic one."

"With the influx of our countrymen, it shall soon be a Teutonic-Islamic city," I injected gaily.

Dr. Bidder laughed. "Herr Frank is right. We shall succeed where Field Marshall Rommel failed!"

Kopf wanted it clear about Germany's foreign interests. "Today," he said, "our industrial recovery depends on our commercial drive back into the Middle East. No wonder so many of our countrymen are coming."

"*Ja,* and half the Afrika Korps is assembled here. But I doubt they are interested in furthering Germany's commercial needs."

I wanted a reaction, and Kopf countered me strongly. "Former German soldiers contracted to the Egyptian government have nothing to do with Bonn!" I dropped the subject.

We were on a seven-kilometer road leading straight to the heart of Cairo. Before crossing the Nile, we wound our way through Dokki, a suburb of foreign embassies, stopping in front of a three-leveled villa adorned with the German Eagle. An Egyptian servant in smartly starched whites and fez picked us up at the policed gate and led us in through a garden. Ambassador Pawelke greeted us like long-lost friends. We were presented to Herr Kindler, the first secretary, and Herr De Hass, the commercial attaché.

The ambassador rigidly announced: "Tomorrow is Christmas Eve, gentlemen. Drs. Kopf and Bidder, we of the embassy invite you to join our party tomorrow night. You will come, too, of course, Herr Frank."

I hadn't been invited, I'd been ordered. But my God! I'd forgotten Christmas.

"Of course he will come," asserted Dr. Kopf. "We are residing at the same hotel and can come together."

What Kopf said was comforting. Actually, Bidder had recommended the Hotel Windsor to Kopf, and I'd said that I hoped accommodations were available for me there, too.

Accommodations were plentiful. In my room, oblivious of the heat, I fell asleep to the rumbling rhythm of the big overhead fan, smiling at my luck.

In the morning Dr. Kopf was engrossed with travel guides over breakfast. I greeted him and ordered coffee.

"Herr Frank, I'm having some difficulty deciding where to go first. Have you a suggestion?"

I told him I was free until after Christmas. "Whatever you decide is fine."

"Good," Dr. Kopf beamed, "we have the entire day at our disposal. Let's get acquainted with the city."

Cairo was a spectrum of startling contrasts, for Egypt had shared her heritage too long and intimately with many conquering armies over the centuries. Many Moslem Arabs, native to other countries neighboring the Mediterranean, appeared to be more Christian than the host of Europeans within their midst.

I noted the absence of British army uniforms. After seventy-two years the Commonwealth soldier was on his way home, except for garrisons in the canal zone. Both of us noticed the obvious reversal: During the war, Germans had been cursed to the face of the Britisher; today people cursed the Britisher openly. A shift in policy, a shift in slogan.

Back at the hotel, our passports were returned with red marks beside the entry stamps. Routine. As the booklet had indicated, foreigners' movements could be well tracked.

I soon discovered that somebody had tampered with the hair-rigging on my suitcase. Although I had nothing tangible to hide—it still was a good lesson. Everybody was an informer, or could be. Driving to the embassy, I mentioned it to Dr. Kopf. He smiled wisely. "I also had a visitor. It appears we should get used to this kind of service."

First Secretary Kindler greeted us and led us into a large gathering of local dignitaries of the German colony; they stood around a Christmas tree so small it could only be symbolic. The room was full of polite conversation and tinkling ice. Ambassador Pawelke greeted us with a perfunctory handshake and an offer of Scotch whisky. Soon De Hass, the commercial attaché, joined our circle, as did Dr. Bidder. In due course we were introduced around the room by De Hass, who billed me as "a representative of some of Germany's largest concerns." However inflated, it sounded more authentic from the mouth of the commercial attaché, considering my relative youth.

One man intrigued me: Dr. Wilhelm Voss. Both Chanan Barel and Shlomo had mentioned him. A former SS general and director of both the Skoda arms factory in Czechoslovakia and the Hermann Goering Steel Mills, Voss was the man entrusted by General Naguib and Nasser to reorganize the Egyptian economy. (It was Voss who would recruit German experts to plan for armament factory construction in Egypt and the Sudan as a joint enterprise of the Nasser regime and Alfred Krupp. Because of his previous association with Skoda, he would stress the merits of obtaining Communist arms—and the 1955 Czech-Egyptian arms deal would result.) The strain between Ambassador Pawelke and Voss was obvious; Voss was the uncrowned ambassador in Cairo.

"Herr Frank, I understand you are planning to reside in Cairo," Pawelke said as we shook hands good night. "If I or any of my staff can be of help, please let us know. If I'm not available, then speak personally to De Hass or Kindler."

My God! The man was practically giving me a carte blanche invitation. "Thank you very much, Herr Ambassador," I said. "If I may, I'd like to ask your advice from time to time, sir."

Pawelke beamed proudly. "Of course, Herr Frank, of course."

There is no greater compliment than to seek the advice of someone older.

Kopf and I dropped Bidder at his hotel. The good feeling in my gut stilled any wariness in my mind. I couldn't wait to submit my report to headquarters. I glanced at Dr. Kopf beside me, a powerful politico. I found myself rather liking the man.

"It's going to be a very nice stay here," I said.

Kopf looked at me, then at the city night. " Let us hope so," he said.

Christmas demanded little of me except for the embassy party. Out in the totally Moslem city, the holiday was hardly felt. Kopf and I took rooms in a pension on Suliman Pasha Street. It was time for me to make a move.

I called on the Pharaonic Engineering Company, Ltd.—a firm that represented the British Marconi Radio Industry (the telephone monopoly in Egypt), the Italian Mareli, plus other products in the radio-electronic field—in Midan Towfidiah. Farrag, the owner, greeted me in the effusive Arab fashion and told me that Faust had alerted him to my coming.

Farrag was optimistic about marketing German products. "My brother is a lieutenant colonel in the army signal corps, and he has access to the tenders handed out by the war ministry." Farrag caught me off guard, he wanted an agency for distribution of Faust and Stollberg wares to the Egyptian government. That would have made me expendable. I suggested that arrangements might be made for his sole distributorship after a trial period of six to twelve months. By that time, I hoped, Farrag would have outlasted his usefulness to me. Fortunately he bought the challenge, offered me an office in his shop, and arranged a luncheon with his brother, the lieutenant colonel. Outside he made no effort to hide his awe of my green Plymouth convertible, sparkling in the sun. Covetously he touched the smooth glaze paint, then drew back. Egyptians, I came to realize, are ashamed of their lack of technical skills, which Germans symbolize. An Egyptian can learn to drive and repair a Western automobile, but he knows in his heart that he cannot manufacture it. Even with a rich cultural heritage, had the centuries of serfdom, I wondered, become irrevocable? If so, this was tragic. Even for an enemy.

"I have no such car as this," Farrag confessed enviously. To Farrag, any man bringing a car to Egypt for only a few months must command quite a position with his company, an impression I hoped to leave with any who might question my age.

Passing the general post office, I asked if there was mail for Paul Frank, and the clerk introduced himself. G'abber, a man worth knowing because of the dangers of postal censorship, seemed impressed with Germans and, like many other Egyptians, he was fluent in English. He handed me a small parcel postmarked Vienna. In the car I inspected it carefully, positive that the censor had gone through the harmless material on Henschel and Krauss Maffai's products.

Outside the pension a bald Arab in dark glasses and suit, standing across the street, caught my eye. He looked up briefly, then resumed his post behind a newspaper.

From my upstairs window, I studied the man, then checked my suitcase. Somebody had been at it again, an expert. Who would be searching my things? The man outside was gone. Next door, Kopf's shower stopped, and with my ear against the wall I heard voices. It was nearing the hour for Kopf and me to resume our city tour. I dressed quickly and knocked on his door.

"Come in, Herr Frank, I want you to meet Machmoud."

I shook hands with the guardian angel from the street! Kopf explained that Machmoud had been recommended by a friend of his. "I dropped Machmoud a note the moment we landed so that he could show us around."

"I am at your service," Machmoud confirmed in halting German.

I smiled politely, troubled by Kopf's explanation. How had Kopf informed him of the address when neither of us had known, until yesterday, where we would be? Maybe Kopf wasn't altogether aboveboard. Good for him. If he was busy with other things, he wouldn't be watching a simple businessman like me.

Machmoud was another story. Speaking some German would render him invaluable to the Egyptian Mukabarat, the general security service. Keep him close. He declined my offer to join us at the movie.

"But soon I will join you. Dr. Kopf is anxious to see the Sakara Pyramids and Memphis this week."

Kopf and I went searching for an Arab film (most of the movies were American films, dubbed). The movie house we chose was astir with rustling paper, the crunching of chickpeas, and the shouting of the audience to the screen characters. Everybody was a participant. The innocent love story closed as the hero chased the chiffon-clad heroine across the desert, both starry-eyed and singing, "*Ya ayni* (My eye), let us sing together till the end of our life." Another Egyptian fantasy had been fulfilled.

A week later Kopf, Bidder, and myself, guided by Machmoud, set out for Memphis, the capital of the pharaohs. After studying the mammoth statue of Rameses II, we tracked a sandy path through a lonely grove of palm trees to the pyramids of Sakara, the world's oldest stone edifice.

Gazing up at this huge structure, I felt atremble. It was here that my people, the B'nai Isra'il of the Koran, did back-breaking work, and it was from here that Moses led my ancestors on the forty-year trek to freedom. Now I, a descendant, stood here, a free man involved in safeguarding the future of my people from the same former enslaver. Strange.

In a letter in my file a Heliopolis firm inquired about an electrical coil, produced by Faust's Offenbach plant. Calling on Moens, the general manager, I learned that the firm operated the streetcar system between Cairo and Heliopolis as well as owning the electrical power plant in Heliopolis. Moens, taking my engineering credentials at face value, soon had me involved in a technical discussion that was considerably over my head. To make it worse, he addressed me as "Herr Engineer."

I became enthusiastic about binding myself to the firm Moens managed. An Israeli agent or two might be planted here, and in the event of war, the whole transportation and power systems could be brought to a standstill through cold sabotage. I told Moens that a company specialist would answer his questions. Moens liked the idea, and he invited me to dinner at the Semiramis Hotel, where he had his office. His firm owned the hotel.

During the endless sight-seeing, I became friendly with Machmoud; on one occasion I invited him for a drive along the Nile. As I explained my business activity to him, he said proudly, "I know all the German military experts here. Gen. Wilhelm Fahrmbacher is a good friend of mine"— Fahrmbacher! I had a note of introduction to him from General Bayer-lein—"and so is Admiral Baron von Bechtoldsheim. Would you like to meet them?"

"Indeed I would," I said, "but later, after business." I grinned at him. "You know how we Germans are."

"Do you know Engineer Römisch?" he asked. "He works with the rocket industry. He, too, is an electronic engineer."

Now I was an *electronics* engineer! "I don't believe I know this Römisch."

"I have met him at the gliders' club. If you care to meet him, it can be arranged. He goes often to the airfield."

Concealing my eagerness, I gave Machmoud brochures of the German concerns I represented, hoping to tie him to the offer I'd made earlier: Any deal he brought together would earn him a finder's fee.

All I could learn about Machmoud himself was that he claimed to be a small clerk in a government office. No doubt we were observing each other from behind fraudulent masks, but I sensed no suspicions on his part.

After Kopf and Bidder left Egypt, I had him all to myself. Promptly I set up a meeting with him at the gliders' club.

The Egyptian Air and Gliding Club operated on the military airfield, part of a huge compound containing the newly created Egyptian parachute unit. All I had to do to have access to this restricted area was join the club. Gliding around would open up Cairo's military installations to my camera.

Machmoud, I thought as I breezed up to the military police roadblock, *you are a sweetheart!*

"Andak!"

I halted; within minutes I was cleared to proceed. Machmoud had left a note with the duty sergeant.

"Wait a minute, *bleze,*" the sergeant requested, waving to a man inside the guardhouse.

The man, roughly my age, came toward the car. His proud bearing did not fit the scruffy suit and shirt he wore; but it did fit the brown eyes and hair and the jagged scar running from his cheekbone to the cleft of his lower lip. The scar, too crude to be the result of Prussian dueling, marred what was otherwise a good face. It shone white against his deep tan. What I saw in him as he stuck his head in the window, requesting a ride to the Air Club, was a man down on his luck.

As he directed me, I asked him his business.

"Nothing," he said, not the least intimidated by his lot. "I just got stuck in this miserable hole. Right now I'm trying to organize fare back to Germany."

The rest of his story was as whimsical as his attitude. With a friend, Robert "Bob" Jansen had driven a prewar plywood German car through Europe, the Balkans, Turkey, Syria; and en route by boat, from Lebanon to Egypt, the car had burned in the ship's hold. His friend had gone back to Germany to collect the insurance. Bob chose to hang here and look for a job.

"Maybe you can help me find one," he tossed out.

"What do you do?"

"I'm a mechanic, and a damned good one. I can fix this car if anything goes wrong."

We were driving on a broad plain that stretched four kilometers to the Mokattam Hills, a chain reaching from Cairo southward almost to Helwan, and I could see the hill labyrinthed with caves that served as ammunition depots. Several well-placed, powerful charges might be sufficient to blow those hills sky high—and take a piece of Cairo with it. Farther on it came to me that not only was this spacious area the landing strip for the glider club, but it served as a drop zone for the parachute units. On the northeast, it also touched the air force base and Al Mazar, Cairo's international airport complex. I knew I had to become a member. Outside the club Machmoud reminded me of my promise to repair the towing apparatus that hoisted gliders into the air.

Thank God for Bob Jansen, the mechanic. I presented him to Machmoud as an old friend of mine from Germany.

Inside, the club's president, a man holding military rank, was eager to have us join. When he asked about my previous experience, I told him (whetting Machmoud's curiosity) that I had been a paratrooper. While he gave Bob Jansen and me applications, Machmoud told him I was an engineer, intimating that I would solve the riddle of the malfunctioning winch.

"What luck!" the officer said, grinning broadly. "Allah has sent you to us, Herr Frank. Nowadays we are towing the gliders with automobiles, but sometimes the glider fails to unhook from the towing line and it plunges right on top of the car. It is no soft landing!"

By late afternoon, thanks to Bob's skills, my standing as an engineer was upheld. Jansen had a look of gravity, defiance, determination: the look of a finely skilled technician face to face with his machine. He fondled it and took its measure. That night, over mugs of beer, I thanked him for giving me a hand.

"I thought you handled the situation quite well," he said, with an amused look.

"What do you mean by that?"

"You looked as if you'd never seen such a thing before."

"Oh, that," I said, smiling. "You're right. I don't remember seeing anything quite that old before."

Bob Jansen would bear watching. He was intelligent, observant, and possibly valuable. But I knew how valuable only when he told me more about his stay in Egypt.

"I'm living at a German hospice maintained by the Evangelic church. It only costs a few piasters a day. The place is clean, the food bearable, and if I sleep with one of the sisters the blessings are free of charge." I laughed with him. "Up to last week, I had a roommate, Count Willi Kubie. But Willi, what with his degrees in chemistry and nuclear physics, decided to leave when he landed work with the rocket industry."

"Are you still friendly with this Kubie?" I asked, hoping.

"Sure, you'll meet him."

Bob Jansen's precarious economic state made him vulnerable. I proposed that if he helped me with my work, when I set up an office he would go on the payroll. He accepted. Not only did he help with my correspondence, but his very presence bolstered my cover.

As time would prove, I could not remain silent about my past. Leaving the pension one day, I deliberately placed my passport on the table; inside were the two pictures of me in German uniform. When I came back, the passport had been disturbed. Proof of Bob's curiosity would come to me later when Machmoud revealed that Bob had told him about my having been a highly decorated major in the German army. When Machmoud confronted me with the facts, I gave him an impatient look. "Do me a favor, my friend. Forget about my past. I don't think it healthy to discuss it."

The act had exactly the desired effect: Machmoud couldn't keep his mouth shut. The evasion of my past led directly to meeting my first German military expert, Colonel de Bouche, a ballistics and artillery instructor. The colonel told me straightaway that Machmoud had spoken of my past. Colonel de Bouche provided valuable details on the rearmament of the Egyptian army. And from his references to his colleagues, I was able to pinpoint their functions as advisers to the Egyptian military and paramilitary organizations.

Within a few weeks, my new acquaintances included an interesting cross section of the German colony. Strangely, it worried me. I could not ignore the free information given me at every turn. Yet my job was to smell around, get a feel of the place, and establish myself.

I had to get headquarters' reaction. "He who rides a tiger cannot dismount at will." I wrote a detailed report in secret ink between the lines of a long letter to Faust and Stollberg.

Meanwhile two firms in Alexandria had queried the company, seeking individual agencies. To follow up the correspondence, Machmoud and Bob along for the ride, I sped across the lower delta area of the Nile, north to the port city.

Two weeks before, I had postponed accepting Machmoud's offer to introduce me to a former German navy captain, Baron Theodor von Bechtoldsheim. But after I finished my business conferences, I let Machmoud talk me into meeting the chief adviser to the new Egyptian navy. He directed us along Corniche Drive to a three-story villa on Sultan Hussain Boulevard. The house was encircled by an iron fence and there was a uniformed policeman.

Machmoud was known to the guard. We took the stairs to the second level. Machmoud introduced Bob and me to Ruth von Bechtoldsheim, a tall, attractive woman in her mid-forties. Though we had arrived unexpectedly, she was perfectly poised as we waited for her husband to return and listened to Machmoud tell about the goings-on at the Helio-Lido, the German experts club in Heliopolis. (Who in hell was this Machmoud? Why was he so well informed?)

I had envisioned Theodor von Bechtoldsheim as a giant of a man. When he entered, I saw him to be shorter than his wife and slim of build, with a sensitive but weather-beaten face. He was typically German: hospitable but guarded. Surprisingly he was especially reserved with Machmoud; there was almost an undercurrent of distrust.

Von Bechtoldsheim and I quickly developed a mutual feeling of regard. Since Machmoud spoke very little German, I revealed my skepticism of him to the baron, which drew the baron out. But I told Machmoud I'd related to the baron how helpful he'd been.

Machmoud was flattered. "I like Germans," he said. "I hope to go to Germany and study or work there. The baron has even offered his help in that direction."

Bechtoldsheim nodded in reassurance. "Possibly Herr Frank can be of more assistance, with his interests in heavy industry."

What I had in mind for Machmoud was considerably more devious. With his knowledge and potential value, headquarters might have considerable interest in him—he might work for Israelis *whom he thought were German.*

Driving back to Cairo, I held an open invitation to visit the von Bechtoldsheims whenever possible. The long, silent ride over the desert made me sleepy. I kept sliding the radio dial across the band, trying to find music other than the screeching Egyptian sounds. At last, something by Tchaikovsky. Abruptly the music ended. An announcer came on—speaking Hebrew! We had been listening to the Voice of Israel.

"Verdamt noch einmal!" I muttered loudly and spun the dial. "One station I like and it's played by the Jews!"

Bob leaped on the dial, turning it back. Machmoud watched us. Bob insisted on the classical music. I refused.

"Listen!" he said angrily. "If you expect me to listen to that screeching Egyptian shit instead of the Jews' station just because they're Jews, then turn the damned thing off!"

Wonderful! Bob's outburst allowed me to play my role of *Juden*-hater to the hilt for Machmoud. While I protested, underneath was a thought: Why didn't intelligence utilize *Kol Israel* the way the BBC had been used during the war? Coded messages could be sent over the airwaves, with none of the shortcomings of secret wireless transmission.

"How much for your thoughts?" Bob said. His observance of detail was astute; spies cannot be mediocre actors, I thought.

Another concern nagged at me: My achievements to date had come almost too easily. There was the danger of my becoming careless. And if I got careless, I was dead.

The next time Machmoud mentioned Gen. Wilhelm Fahrmbacher, the chief adviser to the new Egyptian ground forces, I begged off.

"There's no hurry, Machmoud. Nobody is going anywhere." I hoped to convince him that meeting German experts was not my most important aim. "Maybe next week."

As a patron of the Helio-Lido Club, I would befriend many of the officers, both German and Egyptian. No top secrets ever came to my ears, but I gathered lots of information about political events. Once Bob heard that the Egyptian army was hiring German maintenance crews for their growing panzer units, and he asked me to speak to Colonel de Bouche on his behalf. I did.

De Bouche directed me to Maj. Gen. Oskar Munzel, a veteran panzer commander on the Russian front, who was training Egyptian tank units.

One afternoon, at Machmoud's call, I rushed to the Helio-Lido; Munzel was there. Under a canopy beside the swimming pool, Machmoud presented me to the old general.

As I sat, the general fired a question at me.

"What is your business with this fellow Machmoud?"

"I merely became acquainted with him through Dr. Kopf, whom I believe you know."

The general leaned to me. "I would take careful steps with him if I were you. I think he has a job other than the one he tells about." Munzel twisted in his chair and glanced scornfully at Machmoud. *"Dieser Affenpinscher!"*

"I have nothing to hide from him, Herr General."

"They never report the truth!" he hissed vehemently. "They're all a bunch of liars."

I told him what Bob had heard about the hiring of maintenance crews. "My friend Jansen would be a good man to have," I said.

"Ach!" he muttered irritably. "The worst problem we have with the Arabs is maintenance. They don't seem to learn. To give you an example: This past July 23, on their Independence Day, forty panzers were allocated from the arsenal. Would you care to know how many passed the tribune, Herr Frank?" General Munzel stretched out his booted feet and interlocked fingers across his watermelon belly. "Twelve! Can you believe twelve out of forty?" He shot forward, taut with the incredibility of his own story. "And one lost a track and almost ran down the saluting stand."

Laughing uproariously, I said, "Thank God things have changed."

"You *think* they've changed! A thousand times I've tried to beat into their dense heads that pretty paint and big identification numbers do not a fighting panzer force make!" The general chuckled at his own humor.

"I tell you, Herr Frank, for my part, your friend would be on the job tomorrow. But there are those who think they know more than an old panzer warrior like myself." He studied his iced lemonade for a moment. "It is my opinion, Herr Frank, the Egyptians will never have an army."

Weeks later, General Munzel, in an explosive, open confrontation with Nasser and General Ibrahim, banged his fist on the desk and stalked out of Egypt.

Dr. Albert Degener, chairman of the new German-Egyptian Chamber of Commerce, received me with a brief lecture about Germany's position in the Middle East. The whole Middle East, he said, was in search of an objective power. Egypt—profoundly hostile to Britain, France, and, to a lesser extent, Italy; leery of Russia and suspicious of America's procrastination under Eisenhower and Dulles—had few alternatives. Germany most fitted Egypt's requirements. With the present state of Arab nationalism, the fact that Germany manifested no imperialistic designs enhanced her position. To Dr. Degener the German businessman's future in Egypt looked fruitful.

Within the week Colonel Farrag, brother of the owner of the Pharaonic Engineering Company, alerted me to the secret plans for the construction of an oil pipeline from the city of Suez to Cairo. The pipeline would have three underground pumping stations. The job required more than a hundred miles of construction and months of work using skilled labor and specialists, many of whom would have to be imported from Europe. The source of Cairo's oil supply would be a strategic target in the event of hostilities. I urged the Farrag brothers to get me the confidential details so that my German firms might bid on the project. The colonel promised to do his best.

On my next trip to Alexandria, I dropped in on the von Bechtoldsheims. They made me feel at home, but one thing about Herr Baron bothered me. Though the barriers of German formality were crumbling, he persisted with the formal address, an annoyance in my dealings with all Germans.

In the baron's study after dinner, I commented that while aboard the *Enotria,* I had noticed three warships performing smart battle maneuvers. "I thought they might be Italian or Egyptian until I saw the blue-and-white flag of the Israelis."

"Oh, yes, the Israelis. They are bloody efficient!" The baron's comment drew a disquieting glance from his wife, who had entered with coffee and her highly reputed strawberry cake. "You would never encounter the Egyptian navy so far out to sea. They are afraid to steam beyond sight of land." Could all I was hearing about Egyptian military ineptitude be believed?

The baron asked me about Bob Jansen. Soon the conversation included Bob's friend, Willi Kubie.

"Ah," the baron exclaimed, "if this Kubie is involved in the rocket project, then you should have the chance to meet my friend, Dr. Rolf Engel. He might prove valuable for your business interests."

From Rolf Engel, the head of CERVA, Egypt's rocket industry, the baron went on to tell me how the rocket project had begun in Egypt. After the coup in July in 1952, the military junta had taken over the rocket factory that had been built during Farouk's rule as the beginning of an ambitious rocket weaponry plan by ex–Premier Nahas Pasha in 1951. A team of German experts was brought in as a part of the private German firm owned by a Herr Fuellner. After a year, a test flight was carried out. Dissatisfied, the Egyptian government proposed that the firm formally enter the government.

Herr Fuellner refused and was forced to leave Egypt with those who sided with him. The balance of the rocket team was brought into CERVA, headed by the baron's friend, Dr. Rolf Engel.

According to the baron, the unofficial ambassador to Egypt, Wilhelm Voss, was in close contact with Konrad Adenauer's defense ministry, contrary to public disclaimers that Bonn had nothing to do with Germans under contract. General Naguib had appointed Voss head of central planning, and as such, chief adviser to the Egyptian war ministry. Voss had brought the baron to Egypt.

The ramifications were enthralling. The baron's brother, who had been the last German military attaché to Britain before World War II, was now lecturing on military history at the Pentagon in Washington.

The Americans certainly were cognizant of the two Baron Bechtoldsheims, which made it extremely likely that information flowed handily among the United States, Germany, and Egypt. Interesting.

I was learning all the time that more lurks in the silent brain war than meets the eye or ear. The enemy hid everywhere.

Chapter 8

Dr. Count Willi von Kubie, Bob Jansen's friend who worked with CERVA, was in his late twenties, aesthetic, bespectacled, with a winning, naive smile. He had come to Egypt on a tour of the Middle East, having completed advanced degrees in chemistry and nuclear physics. Kubie, a romanticist by his own admission, instead took a job with a construction firm that was building a bridge in the vicinity of Luxor; but, unaccustomed to physical labor and overwhelmingly unsanitary conditions, he became violently ill.

On his feet again and penniless, he accepted a job as a photographer with the Egyptian rocket industry. Though photography had been his lifelong hobby, the position was shamefully beneath his abilities, and so was his salary. (Had he been contracted to CERVA outside Egypt, his pay would have been based on the European rate.)

I explained to Kubie about the German firms I represented and, as I had with Machmoud and others, offered him a percentage for his help. He jumped at this, suggesting that I meet Engineer Kurt Hainisch, production engineer for CERVA, a man Machmoud had mentioned. Apparently CERVA badly needed special materials for rocket production, and Kubie quickly set up a meeting with Hainisch at the Semiramis Hotel, site of half the deals, shady or otherwise, made in Egypt.

I disliked Hainisch instinctively for his marked resemblance to Hitler's propagandist, Joseph Goebbels: small, thin-lipped, gray-faced, with a hard, overbearing behavior. I invited him and Kubie to dine.

"Sorry, I have no time, Herr Frank. Let us have a drink and proceed to the point." Which turned out to be two points. "Herr Frank, Kubie has told me about your hand in surplus military matériel. Does it include small arms? Rifles, for instance?"

"Small arms are no problem," I said.

Hainisch nodded curtly and moved to a second point.

"Whether or not you know it, rocket production cannot go far without a particular type of steel sheet. Its supply from Germany demands the permission of the Allied controlling powers."

"I know," I lied.

"Can you supply it?"

"Herr Engineer, provided the quantity is not so great as to attract attention, I see no insurmountable problems."

"I understand," he replied. "I will provide you with specifications."

"At your convenience."

"Back to the matter of surplus," he said. "I have an acquaintance who might be interested in speaking with you; I'm sure you're heard of him: Haj Amin al Husseini, the former mufti of Jerusalem. Do you have a list of supplies which can be shown to him?"

I nodded. What Jew didn't know that rabid Arab anti-Semite? If the Jew and Israel had an archenemy on the face of the earth, it was the grand mufti of Jerusalem, the Moslem spiritual leader.

"Within a few days," I said, "but the list will not include weapons. And I am willing to meet with the grand mufti at his convenience."

"Do you know him, by chance?" Hainisch asked.

"Not personally. During the war I dealt with several of his men." Hainisch did not know of my German background in detail; my implication was lost on him. But I was well aware of Husseini's personal attachment to Hitler and his stay in Germany during the war.

Kubie entered the talk for the first time. "I have mentioned to you that Herr Frank parachuted into Palestine during the war."

Hainisch said, "Oh, yes, I remember. Good." He stood. "Herr Frank, the moment I have the specifications for you, we can proceed from there." He nodded curtly and left the room.

"He's a bastard," Kubie was saying. "Nobody at the plant likes him. Even his boss, Dr. Rolf Engel, handles him with caution. But as long as you do business, who cares?"

I agreed.

The avalanche of my acquaintanceships—Dr. Kopf, Ambassador Pawelke and staff, Machmoud, Moens, Bob Jansen, Theodor von Bechtoldsheim, Willi Kubie, Hainisch, and others of import—was almost nothing compared to what awaited me on my second visit to Farrag and his brother, the lieutenant colonel, at their office in the center of Cairo.

Trying to hide their pleasure, they revealed their surprise: the complete secret plans for the construction of the Suez-to-Cairo oil pipeline, *and* the underground pumping stations! The map pinpointed the underground power plants, the power lines, and the existing facilities at each city. However, the fly in the ointment was the deadline set for acceptance of bids on the secret tender.

If headquarters were to become involved, they would need to work out a thousand details, requiring time. Time the Egyptian government wasn't allowing.

I made my decision. I would rush to Europe with the plans and see to their immediate implementation.

A problem loomed: Leaving the country voided my visa. A permit of residence required an exit visa for each trip outside the country. What if I had to get out within hours? So I applied for another simple entry visa.

But an entry visa required additional letters of recommendation. I went directly to the German embassy and presented myself to Ambassador Pawelke, emphasizing the importance of a German firm building the proposed pipeline. He called in Commercial Attaché de Hass. I showed them the blueprints.

De Hass dictated a letter addressed to the office of the Egyptian ministry of interior, stating that I represented important German companies, and that they, as official representatives of the West German government, would appreciate my having a multiple-entry visa.

The minister of the interior issued me the multiple-entry visa without delay; further, I was allowed to retain the letter of recommendation given me by the German embassy. By late afternoon I had booked passage on the SS *Enotria,* sailing from Alexandria.

Earlier, through the cooperation of Moens, general manager of the Belgian-owned streetcar and power companies in Heliopolis, I had managed to get Bob Jansen a job in the maintenance department of the Semiramis Hotel. I had learned from Willi Kubie that he had been given the job of photographing the blueprints of all radar installations to be erected for the air force. German Professor Goerke, one of the world's foremost experts on radar, had planned for their completion in two to three years. Despite my eagerness to get my hands on these blueprints, the time to move was not yet.

At the Helio-Lido Club one day, I found Machmoud seated beside the pool with an elderly couple. Machmoud jumped up, beckoning me over.

"Herr Frank, may I present my friend General Fahrmbacher and his wife?"

General Fahrmbacher! *Wilhelm Fahrmbacher, ex-general in Hitler's army, artillery expert, chief adviser to the new Egyptian army.* My mind was racing in high gear; I saluted Herr General with the short Prussian bow and kissed Frau Fahrmbacher's hand.

"Machmoud has spoken highly of you," the general said. "Please join us, Herr Frank."

Fahrmbacher, close to sixty, hardly epitomized the movie image of German generals. His fading blue eyes, thinning white hair, and rosy cheeks made him look more like a kindly shopkeeper.

"Herr General," I said, "I was given a letter of introduction to you by General Bayerlein. But when I arrived here, you were out of town."

"Yes, my wife and I. We were on our wedding trip."

"Hochzeitreise!" I cried. "Congratulations!"

General Fahrmbacher seemed amused. "Hasn't Machmoud told you? I married my wife two months ago."

"Wilhelm!" Frau Fahrmbacher interjected. "It is longer than that. Have you forgotten already?"

"Are you married, Herr Frank?" she asked, obviously wanting to change the subject.

"No, I'm not."

"Have you family in Germany?"

"My family died during the war. An American bombing attack."

"We all live with our tragedies, don't we?" she said sympathetically. "Won't you come visit with us, Herr Frank? We've only just moved, but you are welcome."

I thanked them and promised to visit their new flat on my return from Germany.

The day before my departure I met again with Kurt Hainisch. He supplied me with a list of materials and specifications needed by CERVA.

"I expect no miracles," he said, handing me a separate piece of paper. "Write to me here if there are questions. My private address. The less certain people at the plant know about this matter, the better."

"I understand," I said. What I really understood was the likelihood that Hainisch was lining his own pockets. (Soon I would learn of the discord between him and his boss, Dr. Rolf Engel, the head of CERVA, which would eventually turn into an open power struggle.)

"Herr Frank, are you, by chance, in any way connected with INTER-ARMCO?"

My smile Hainisch could interpret as yes. But letting him assume my involvement with one of the largest private European dealers in surplus-arms (run by an American, a former CIA employee) couldn't hurt, even though Israel had been among INTERARMCO's customers.

Back at my place I explained to Bob that I was leaving my car with Bechtoldsheim in the hope of doing business with the Egyptian navy.

Before leaving Cairo the next morning, to further entrench myself with the German embassy staff I picked up a letter from First Secretary Kindler to his daughter. Kindler's explanation for wanting the letter mailed in Germany was that it contained money. However, Kindler, a diplomat, was under no restriction. Like so many others, he was avoiding censorship.

In Alexandria I checked in at Hotel Cecil, which had become my quarters there. Ruth von Bechtoldsheim, over a toast, suggested we all drop the formal *Sie*. "We like you, Paul, and we hope you feel comfortable with us." Our friendship was sealed.

Theo revealed more of himself and the people surrounding him, including the Egyptian Admiral of the Navy, Suliman Azzazat. Then they mentioned their daughter, Charlotte. She had fallen in love with an Egyptian Jew, and to break up the affair, they had sent her back to Germany.

"We think Charlotte is going to correspond with the boy," Theo said. "What we are asking you to do is speak to our daughter."

"I'll do what I can," I said.

Ruth looked at me, her eyes misted. "Thank you, Paul. Thank you so much."

"I've prepared a letter to her, Paul," Theo said. "I'll give it to you in the morning. Please see that Charlotte gets it."

It was late when he dropped me off at the hotel.

The morning broke hot and bright. Theo drove me to the harbor, and we were invited to the brigadier's office, where Theo was treated with great deference. As we prepared to leave, the brigadier informed us that Herr Frank would not have to go through the normal control channels.

He turned to me. "Herr Frank, the baron's friends are mine. Whenever I may be of service to you, please don't hesitate to call."

I thanked him. Before long I would have reason to take up his offer with great urgency.

After an eight-hour delay due to another fierce storm, the *Enotria* docked in Brindisi, Italy's disembarkation port of the Adriatic. Mid-February was as cold as Egypt is hot as we crossed the mountainous Italian peninsula.

Rome was a stopover. I got in touch with Benjamin Rottem, my new contact, because I wanted headquarters to know I was in Europe. Also I was short of money.

Benjamin, one of the few *Sabras* (Palestinian-born Jews) I had encountered operating outside Israel, was Mossad. I had hardly dealt with anyone in Europe who wasn't. It was now clear that Modiin, without personnel or facilities in Europe, could not function independently of the Mossad, which had both. I wondered again if simple interservice rivalry was Motke's reason for cautioning me not to trust Mossad people, or was it his own personal prejudice?

Leaving Benjamin at the terminal, I bought a train ticket to Munich, went downstairs with my luggage, rented a private booth, bathed, and wrote a note to headquarters advising them of my itinerary. Still with time to kill, I dropped in at a stationery store and bought a blue leather diary. (From this day on, I would record everything in the diary: business details openly, secret activity in code. Little did I know the importance this diary would play in future political events.) At a nearby coffee shop I filled in my activities to date. Later I gave Benjamin my sealed report to headquarters, and he returned the letters various Germans had asked me to post in Germany. All had been photographed. I signed a receipt for the money he had for me.

Hours later, letters in hand, I was on the Munich-bound express racing toward an urgent meeting with Chanan Barel. Unfortunately Barel was gone; I felt that the oil pipeline blueprints were of such importance that I decided not to wait. So I dealt with an old acquaintance of mine, Lt. Col. Chananya Levanon, new to his Mossad post. I handed over all the material on the proposed pipeline from Suez to Cairo.

"That's quite a fish you've gotten hold of, my friend," he said. "But we would have had our hands on it soon enough."

I ignored his remark. The important thing was that Israel had them. I showed him the letter of recommendation from the German ambassador in Cairo.

"How did you manage this?" he pressed.

"Nothing to it, my friend."

More professional jealousy! I simply couldn't figure it.

In my quarters at the Carlton Hotel, I buried myself in writing a detailed account of the past week. (From my beginning reports on the Zurich affair, I had begun a catalog of field reports already known in Modiin headquarters as "El-Ad Sarchi's volumes.") I also wrote a short letter to Shula.

Chananya returned the pipeline materials and my passport, both photographed for headquarters. No mail had been sent to me, but Chanan Barel was returning in the evening.

At dusk I dropped by his office and picked up a letter from Motke and Shlomo that dealt with my previous reports. Shlomo agreed that communication in the field wasn't functioning as it should but again promised to take care of it. (A steady flow of communication had been promised me before going down to Egypt. The flow had proved to be a dribble.)

A note from Shula mentioned our days together in Vienna. All was well. She still had her secretarial job with Solel Boneh. Harel was doing fine in school.

At nightfall I was on the fast train to Frankfurt to hand over to Faust the plans for the pipeline. But Faust was out of town when I reached his plant at Offenbach am Main. The company's secretary, authorized to handle company affairs, dealt with me. Through Faust the tender for construction of the oil pipeline would be submitted to the major European companies expert in this field, with Faust and Stollberg as middlemen. Within two hours I had briefed the secretary on this and the inquiries from Egyptian firms seeking independent distributorships. I felt I was again astride that tiger.

My new Cologne contact, Poldi, seemed to be a keen observer of security precautions. His instructions for my first rendezvous with him were, to say the least, circuitous. When I finally sat in his car, I was certain that no one was trailing me.

Poldi, who had emigrated from Germany to Palestine in his youth, knew all about the German traffic to Egypt. Many Germans were profitably employed in the Nasser-led junta's military and paramilitary organizations. Most of those he named were wanted for war crimes; many had assumed Arab aliases. Others, such as Fahrmbacher and von Bechtoldsheim, were contracted.

In a sealed letter, Motke instructed me that I was free to pursue any information, so long as it didn't interfere with establishing myself as a businessman. Headquarters had decided not to equip me with a wireless transmitter, preferring the secret-ink method for now. Also my suggestion to use the Voice of Israel to convey messages was under consideration. The usually laconic Motke's note revealed him as deeper than the cold intelligence officer he was portraying.

"I hope that one day we will be able to forget all our struggles and take our boys to a quiet fishing place. There, while we watch the calm waters and our youngsters beside us, we can say that we have reached this peaceful time because we have contributed our share." And a postscript: "By the way, do you like fishing?"

It was a dream Motke had described. Where was a quiet place right now? Certainly it wasn't inside me. Yet Motke, Shlomo, Hauser, and the rest of them at home wouldn't let me down. We were as one.

(It was only later that I found out about Poldi's overt function with Israel's Purchasing Mission in Cologne. As a mission security officer, his cover was blown. Using an overt operative (Poldi) to contact a covert operative (me) did not fit any idea of the rules of safety in conspiratorial activity.)

En route to Vienna, I stopped in Munich to see Charlotte von Bechtoldsheim. She was all Theo and Ruth had claimed: lovely, charming, intelligent, and twenty. Reserved on the telephone, she opened up the following evening at the Schwabinger wine tavern. Respectfully, Charlotte accused her parents of being old-fashioned, blind to the changes in

Germany since the war. Secretly I admired her for having the courage to involve herself with a young Egyptian Jew; openly I played the advocate.

I promised to deliver a letter to her young man in Egypt and not to divulge its existence to her parents—knowing, all the while, that the promise would have to be broken.

Hans Schneider awaited me in Vienna. There was no problem in procuring rocket time fuses for CERVA. I would take along a surplus-arms list, and samples of the time fuses would be mailed to me at Bechtoldsheim's address. By late evening, over a table in Grinzing, the famous wine district of the city, our formality had dissolved.

My relationship with Hugo Krug had also solidified. Though Hugo knew nothing of my true mission in Egypt—he could only assume Israeli intelligence involvement—he could be trusted. He had a need to pay Israel for what she had done for him.

With Jiddel, whose enthusiasm appeared to have waned for some reason, I rented a car and drove to Paris and a conference on the oil pipeline bid with Faust, his brother, and the company's chief engineer. There would be a delay in securing offers; so I advised him to forward the bid to me in Rome.

Having felt at odds with Jiddel during the entire trip, I reminded him of the payments that were to be made to Faust and Stollberg. Faust had informed me that Jiddel had promised the balance of the money within a reasonable period, and since Faust seemed content with that, I let the matter drop.

Going through Munich to pick up Charlotte von Bechtoldsheim's letter, I arrived in Italy exhausted. My trip had been like an ignited string of Chinese firecrackers: Brindisi. Rome. Munich. Frankfurt. Cologne. Munich. Vienna. Frankfurt. Paris. Frankfurt. Munich. Rome again. It seemed as if the past ten days had been spent getting on and off trains, in and out of cars.

No mail awaited me. Since I couldn't return to Egypt without something to show for the trip, I canceled the reservation and planned to book a flight to Alexandria when the materials arrived. It meant Rome for a few more days.

Italian newspapers announce on the 25th of February that Nasser, as deputy prime minister, has deposed President–Prime Minister Naguib. Nasser is proclaimed the new prime minister of the Republic by the ruling Revolutionary Command Council, the Nasser-led military junta.

As expected Naguib had been unable to withstand the radical fervor of the younger officers in the Revolutionary Command Council. He had preferred to balance the economy before demanding the withdrawal of the

British from the canal zone. Nasser, using as his excuse a clash among the now-legitimate party, the National Liberation Organization, and the Naguib-oriented Moslem Brotherhood, moved to disband the brotherhood and clap the leaders into jail.

Unknown to me until my return to Egypt: Naguib was held under house arrest. Demonstrators, protesting junta rule, decided to support Nasser as prime minister, provided that there was a return to constitutional government. The lines were drawn; the cavalry was behind Naguib; other forces supported Nasser.

Nasser feared civil war. A compromise was reached. *On the twenty-seventh, only two days after Naguib's resignation, he was returned to office,* proclaiming that a constitutent assembly would be elected.

By the third day the Rome postal clerk, wearied by my many appearances, greeted me with a letter and small parcel from Vienna. I studied the catalogues, technical pamphlets, and arms price lists sent by Hans Schneider. The origin of the German rifle K-98 was given as Spain on the list when in fact it had been manufactured in Czechoslovakia and was being marketed as ex-Wehrmacht stock. The parcel contained a sample of the time-clock fuse. In the small, round, aluminum casing was the mechanism for exploding rocket warheads.

Nothing on the pipeline bid. Calling the Offenbach am Main plant, I was told that the bid would be mailed directly to me in Cairo. I was eager to go.

Chapter 9

Olympic Airlines' DC-3 coughed and shook across the Adriatic Sea to Greece. A night's sleep in Athens, six more hours of flying, and we landed in Alexandria. Ruth met me, explaining that a last-minute meeting at the admiralty had detained Theo. He finally arrived, tense and apologetic. To get my car, he drove me back to the admiralty at Ras el Tin, thinking over his problems aloud.

"There are going to be problems over adviser contracts with the government, I can see it. Admiral Azzazat reassured me that nothing has changed, but *something* is brewing."

Something was right. The power struggle between Nasser and Naguib was jeopardizing the contract of more than one German adviser who had openly sided with Naguib. Another factor: the Americans. Secretary of State Dulles was wooing Nasser with his policy of friendly impartiality and his promise of aid. And the Americans were openly negative about the ex-Nazis advising the Egyptian military.

"Stop by the admiralty whenever you can, Paul; I want to introduce you to some people in procurement." He flashed a knowing grin as we parted. "You know the old army saying: 'Well lubricated is well traveled.' "

Lubrication, *baksheesh,* bribery. Theo was playing the game, too. Now, I decided, was the time to offer him a finder's percentage.

My tie to the Bechtoldsheims was cemented when, on the condition that this would be our secret, I gave them their daughter's letter to her Jewish-Egyptian boyfriend. It must have been her farewell to him, because as they finished reading it, they glanced warmly at each other. I was now a trusted member of the family. It was strange to find myself genuinely concerned with former Kapitan zur See Baron Theodor von Bechtoldsheim, a mercenary training a navy vowed to eradicate Israel. At a party thrown the next night for the Alexandrian German community, Theo presented me to his colleagues. One was Spachmann, of the naval advisory team, an expert in submarines and torpedoes. (The British were fearful that his expertise in underwater demolition might be applied to their shipping along the canal.)

Next, Professor Goerke. My adrenalin raced. He might have been the world's foremost expert in radar and electronic guidance systems, the one whose radar blueprints Willi Kubie had photographed.

From among the gathering, volunteers were sought for whitewashing the German plot at El Alamein cemetery. I enlisted.

Back in Cairo, I thought of Theo's words: "Well lubricated is well traveled" as I stopped at the German embassy to deliver to Kindler some pumpernickel bread and, to the bald de Hass, hair tonic. They were speechless. In my absence, they had checked on me. With astonishment, both demanded to know why my military record had been kept quiet. My answer was a modest smile.

A similar reaction came from General Fahrmbacher at army general headquarters compound near Heliopolis. His office—maps, filing cabinets, documents, an air of seriousness—was fitting for the head adviser of the new Egyptian ground forces. He, too, was blunt about my not informing him of my military past.

Suddenly everybody was investigating me. Although my record would certainly help establish me, I was conscious of the danger.

At the Fahrmbachers some nights later, I related developments in the *Vaterland*. They responded with a childish enthusiasm, even to my suggestion that we tour the countryside in my car.

"It's too bad so many historic sites are in restricted areas," I said.

The general brushed aside the problem with a gruff *"Ach!* I can fix it."

We were to have many sight-seeing outings.

Having released my room before going to Europe, I bunked with Bob in a charred two-room house near the burned-out Shepperd Hotel, at the center of European Cairo. I offered him space with me, rent-free, if his Egyptian girl friend would help us relocate.

Flat #7, Bank de Lyon Building, on Sharia Adli Pasha, was in the heart of the city—perfect. Aside from the landlord's insistence that we retain the house servant—and the danger of having an alien about the place—it was ideal.

Willi Kubie and Machmoud became daily visitors. Willi showed me some rocket pictures he'd taken. He said that the first operational

Egyptian rocket, with a range limited to several miles, was being developed. Increased range might threaten Israel's security! The Egyptian rocket industry now became my number-one priority. My report was en route to headquarters before the weekend at El Alamein cemetery came around.

Twenty-five men, women, and children from the Alexandria community showed up that Saturday morning. I walked among the rows of crosses marking fallen German and Italian soldiers. The desert light was gold; this was also a burial place for British, Australians, South Africans, and soldiers of all nations who had died here in November 1942, when Rommel's advance across North Africa ended as he faced the Allies.

It took me back to another year, 1944. Italy. I was a member of the Jewish 462 Co-1, RASC, quartered in a village north of Arrezo. Strolling among the vineyards one day, I had happened on the abandoned grave of a German soldier, a helmet askew on the upright. No inscription identified him, only an age: eighteen. If the inscriber had tried to point out the insanity of war, he had succeeded. With paint and tools, I returned, planted flowers, and painted the cross white. On the marker I wrote: Unknown German soldier, *only* 18 years of age. I left the village with the local priest's word that the young soldier would not be forgotten again.

Now, here at El Alamein, I knelt beside the grave of an Italian soldier whose weathered cross rendered his name illegible. One of the Germans said, "Only the graves of our boys." I stayed there as long as it suited me. Then I replied, "We fought here together, remember? He was a brother-in-arms."

The man winced under the scrutiny of the others. "I didn't mean it that way," he said.

The story made the rounds. Theo had already heard it when I stopped by to pick up the time fuses for CERVA's Kurt Hainisch—and discovered that the package had been opened by the censors.

Theo's outlook was one of acceptance. "All our mail is censored."

Here was a matter beyond control. There was only one thing I could *not* do: Be careless.

General Fahrmbacher and I frequently visited historic sites—though the Fokker-Wolf aircraft plant at Helwan was hardly historic. With the Arab defeat in 1948, the Egyptians approached Klemens Fokker, the top German designer. I was viewing the result: the first successfully flown, light training plane, and the frightening beginning of more lethal planes. (Years would pass before Israel realized the futility of Egypt's grandiose dreams for constructing combat aircraft.)

On our outings, Fahrmbacher told me of his plan for creating an

Egyptian strike force of fifteen divisions, based on the old Reichswehr structure of 1933.

"Egypt needs another seven to eight years before they can sustain the logistics of large fighting groups. Until then, I think that small groups, not more than company strength, should be built to expertly man their few modern weapons."

His logic seemed sound. Prior to Hitler's building of a massive army, such efforts had been limited under the Versailles Treaty. The elite cadre forces they developed became the basis for a huge fighting machine. Fahrmbacher mentioned the deployment of troops for the defense of the Sinai Desert, citing an upcoming inspection of proposed fortifications from northern Sinai all the way south to Saint Katherina Monastery. Since nearby Mount Sinai was where Moses supposedly received the Ten Commandments, I said: "I would like to visit there. It has been my dream to see where the Ten Commandments were handed down."

"I didn't know you were religious," Fahrmbacher said, amused.

"No, Herr General. It is only of historical interest."

"If I arrange passage for you on the inspection tour, can you afford a couple of days away from your business?"

"Herr General, I wouldn't miss it for any reason."

The political struggle was again peaking, a replay of the February crisis when Nasser forced Naguib's two-day resignation. In the streets demonstrations resumed. I was caught up in a miniriot along Suliman Pasha street and only the jab of a mounted policeman's thin bamboo prod made me realize that to him I was no innocent bystander but a hated foreigner. Later Theo gave me a transparent identification tag to hang around my neck. It bore the inscription *Ana Almani* (I am a German), and the stamp of the Egyptian ministry of interior.

"It's lighter than your Knight's Cross, isn't it?" he said jokingly.

More of my fabricated past had spread to Theo. He also held the Knight's Cross, which made us brothers of the order. However, Theo had proof: a pocket-sized certificate. I didn't even know if the real Maj. Paul Frank appeared in the list of some seven thousand soldiers of the coveted Knight's Cross. A dangerous oversight.

One day I inquired about his troubles at the admiralty.

"My contract will not be renewed," he said.

"Why?"

"I don't know why," he said. "They avoid me. I've requested to speak with Admiral Azzazat, but he never finds the time. Did I tell you that my office has been searched?"

Theo's disclosure bothered me. If he wasn't trusted, then probably his associates were under observation. But until this could be verified, and especially until we journeyed to Libya on a trip we had planned, I had to stick. The Western Desert could be a route for either infiltration or escape.

Willi Kubie, bemoaning his underpaid position, refused a loan. "It won't help, Paul. I have to find another way to make money." I let it pass until after my lunch date, which Kubie had arranged with Hainisch at the Heliopolis Palace.

Hainisch, showing us into the dining room, suddenly greeted two Arabs at an isolated table. I tensed, recognizing a man I knew only from pictures: Mohammed Said Haj Amin el Husseini, the mufti of Jerusalem! Husseini was the most vicious Jew hater alive who was not running for his life—and the man who had turned Arab unrest into murderous rioting against Palestinian Jewry as far back as the 1920s. During the war he had lived in Germany as Hitler's unofficial link with the Middle East, recruiting Moslem volunteers for the German war effort. Although his political influence was at an end, he was still a wily serpent. What other reason would Hainisch have had for making known his need for surplus weapons?

Beckoned to the mufti's table, I was totally aware that it was on a secret parachute mission into Palestine with several of Husseini's Moslem volunteers that Abwehr Major Paul Frank had disappeared. I wondered if Husseini remembered that he had sent so many unwary zealots to their graves in the name of his fanaticism.

My introduction as Paul Frank, former Abwehr major, brought Husseini's companion, Abdul Latif, to his feet, winking at me so that only I could see. Terror gripped me. Had he known the real Paul Frank? Anxious moments elapsed before I remembered the rumor that the Frank mission was betrayed by one of Husseini's men, a British collaborator. Was Latif alerting me that he knew the story, knew I was a fake?

"Is this your first visit to Cairo, Herr Frank?" Husseini asked in his soft, perfect English. His beard, once fiery red, was now white; he seemed older than his sixty-odd years.

"No, Your Eminence," I said.

"Business or pleasure? Or both?"

"Both, Your Eminence."

"That is wise, very wise."

The waiter interrupted to take the order. Hainisch politely refused for us, claiming business.

"But you are not going to refuse coffee," Husseini insisted.

"I could never resist a good cup of *khawa,*" I replied, holding on to Husseini, not knowing if the opportunity would ever present itself again.

Latif caught my eye with a look of curiosity as the mufti exclaimed, "Oh, you speak Arabic?"

"Only a few words, Your Eminence, which I learned years ago at the Oriental Institute in Frankfurt."

"Herr Frank has had some interesting experiences during the war," Hainisch inserted, but I cut him short.

"Nothing of importance, Your Eminence. Like all the others, I only did my part in the past. And the past is gone."

The mufti nodded in understanding; the lost past undoubtedly meant more to him than it did to me. Abdul Latif broke in.

"Herr Frank, I understood Herr Hainisch to say you were in the Abwehr."

"Why do you ask?"

Latif smiled the legendary Arabic smile of patience. *Infuriating.* "I have seen you before. I, too, was in Germany during the war, activated by Intelligence."

Latif left me no choice. "Herr Latif, in the Abwehr we were taught a basic principle: Keep to yourself and survive." I paused, looking at him. "As you can see, I have survived."

Silence descended on the table.

A slow smile of understanding rose from Latif's bushy mustache to his dark eyes. "You are right, Herr Frank. Absolutely right." Again his wink. I felt no safer during the remaining ten minutes of the conversation, for now Husseini seemed to be testing me.

"Have you ever been in the Klopstockstrasse, Herr Frank?"

"If Your Eminence is referring to the Jewish Institute, no, I haven't been inside. However, I walked past the building on many occasions." The confiscated Jewish Institute had been the object of extensive negotiations between Husseini and the German foreign office. Husseini finally won and occupied the building. There had been no Jews alive in Germany to protest. "If I am not mistaken, wasn't Your Eminence moved from there to Zaue on the lakes of Schwieloch because of the air attacks, and from there to Oybin?"

"How did you know that, Herr Frank? Were you there?"

"Don't forget, Your Eminence, I was in the Abwehr." Husseini could interpret my answer any way he liked.

I felt better when Hainisch suggested we leave. The mufti nodded gracefully. "It was a pleasure making your acquaintance, Herr Frank. I am certain we shall meet again."

Latif gripped my hand. *"Auf Wiedersehen,* Herr Paul Frank."

"Auf Wiedersehen."

Hainisch lingered at Husseini's table. When he joined me, his face smug, he declared, "Herr Latif recognized you immediately. He was supposed to have performed as your wireless operator on your mission into Palestine in 1943, but he parachuted in earlier."

"That is too bad," I said, overjoyed by the news. Either I bore a remarkable resemblance to the deceased Paul Frank or Abdul Latif was a bigger liar than I. Still, a pang of fear lingered in me.

Without referring to the mufti, Hainisch suggested we could do business on small arms if the price was a little more favorable.

"Of course I have to consult with my people in Europe, which will take time," I said.

Yes, Herr Hainisch, a lot of time. Talking was one thing; delivering arms to my enemies was quite another.

Chapter 10

Theo and I stopped off one day at a bazaar run by the Evangelical church in Cairo, where I bought at auction a coveted all-channel Blaupunkt radio, and then Theo called Dr. Rolf Engel, head of the rocket industry and Hainisch's immediate superior. Engel invited Theo for lunch. Since I would be driving, I was included.

Rolf Engel's villa, on a quiet street in Heliopolis, was stoutly guarded. His career went back to Wernher von Braun's staff on the V-1 and V-2 programs. With the armistice, he had developed the French Veronica missile. His place at the top of the world's rocket experts hadn't lessened his charm.

Theo spoke of his contract-renewal problems. "They hint I am guilty of certain indiscretions," he said, "but they tell me nothing specific. On the other hand, Admiral Azzazat claims that only a lack of funds, or policy changes, would force him to cancel my services."

"Suppose I speak to Voss about this," Engel volunteered. "He is the power without portfolio. But I don't have to tell you about the Egyptian style; one hand rarely knows what the other is doing." Engel laughed. "I myself could sing a song on that. The government wants to take over and make us technical employees. Of course, I'll do everything possible to maintain CERVA's independence. You see, we all have our burdens dealing with the junta, Herr Baron."

For the first time it was made clear to me that the rocket industry,

CERVA, was actually a union of military and private enterprise, with a civilian, Count de Lavison, chairing the board of directors. As Engel explained difficulties in the rocket's technical process, I made a few remarks, drawing on what Hainisch had told me. Engel was curious.

"What is your field, Herr Frank?"

I explained my connection with Faust and Stollberg and other German firms. "I'm a mechanical engineer."

Engel stared absently at Theo for a moment, then at me. "I could use a man like you on my team, Herr Frank. Maintenance in Egypt, as I'm sure you know, is a problem. Soon we will have to buy the heavy machine tools needed for mass production. There are also certain mechanical matters that might fall into your field."

I had to extricate myself. "That's very complimentary of you, Herr Engel. For the time being, I am quite happy with my work. However, if I can be of help, please don't hesitate."

Engel was open about his distrust of his staff, and I read Kurt Hainisch between the lines. To gain Engel's confidence, I told him of my association with Hainisch. His response proved me right.

"Yes, I have been aware of it all along. You are quite right to be candid, Herr Frank. May I suggest that from now on you negotiate with me. I have the last word." He smiled politely. "On everything."

I knew I would have to avoid involving myself in the animosity between the two men.

The Faust and Stollberg bid on the proposed pipeline arrived; I turned the secret blueprints, specifications, completion timetable, and estimate of cost over to Farrag, who submitted them to the government. (Decision was reached several months after I had fled Egypt, and the contract was awarded to an international consortium through political pressure.[1])

Bob and I set out for Port Said via Zagazig to Ismailia. My mission was to survey British installations and troop deployments in the canal zone and to plot a road description for the German automobile club. Though British concentrations were hardly secret, key redeployment might be significant. There were strong rumors of an agreement on evacuating the zone, a maneuver my country could ill afford. British presence restrained Egyptian militancy by way of the Sinai Desert.

The timing was opportune. For three years the zone had been a hotbed of Arab guerrilla activity against the British garrisons, dangerous even for civilian traffic. But in the last two months, with Nasser and Naguib holding everyone's attention, hostilities had ceased. Into the hands of the guer-

---

1. In July 1956, Nasser attended the opening of the first oil pumping station on the Suez-to-Cairo pipeline.

rillas would go whatever arms I might furnish for His Eminence, Mohammed Said Haj Amin el Husseini, the mufti of Jerusalem.

Neither Ismailia nor Port Said had changed since 1943, when I had been there as an eighteen-year-old volunteer in the British army.

We returned to the delta road and made our way to Alexandria and the Bechtoldsheims. Theo, terribly disturbed, said he would be unable to make the Western Desert drive to Libya. A warning from Admiral Azzazat not to leave Egypt had thoroughly unnerved him; they were treating him like a spy, he said.

However, he decided that Ruth and Franz, their fifteen-year-old son, would go. I was relieved. As yet headquarters had little information on Egyptian desert outposts or security measures there.

In preparation for the four-to-five-day journey, I asked General Fahrmbacher for a permit to cross into Libya. When the Egyptian automobile club informed me that road maps were unavailable for the restricted area, we used Franz's school atlas.

The day before departure I drove out to Al Mazar Airfield at Engel's request. To my surprise Hainisch met me at the gate. Fine. Earlier, to allay his suspicions, I had told him of the luncheon with Engel. Like a fellow conspirator, he had thanked me for telling him.

"Engel informed me you were coming," he said. "He suggested that I be present."

A clever man, Herr Engel. He greeted me like an old friend and, as if he did not know that Hainisch and I were acquainted, introduced the two of us. In this three-way round robin, everyone was deceitful.

"Herr Hainisch and I have already met," I replied.

"Oh, yes. You told me. It completely escaped my mind."

For the next hour, we talked about Engel's most severe impasse: lack of proper propellant. Then, showing me around the plant, he spoke confidentially. "I did not bring up the subject of machine tools in front of Hainisch because our thoughts differ drastically. Soon we'll figure out something to both our advantages."

Whatever that might be, the important thing was getting Engel's confidence.

It was in the comfortable, warm winds near the end of March that Ruth, Franz, and I left for the drive to Libya. Ruth diligently jotted down details of the route for the German automobile club, but there was little to note other than the narrow asphalt road slicing through the yawning yellow void of desert. Its isolation sets the brain to imagining the beginning of the world.

For Ruth and Franz, the tiny hamlets that fell behind us were only dusty, monotonous names. For me they were history, embodying the motto of the desert raiders: "Who dares, wins." It was in El Daba that members of the Jewish German Platoon infiltrated captured segments of the Afrika Korps, to elicit vital information for Montgomery's advance against Rommel.

Mersa Matruh was our stop for the night. It consisted of the military governor's quarters, the railroad station, a church and mosque, and a few shops. Even the water, drawn from artesian wells, was rancid with grit. We settled in Hotel Rosetta on the beach.

The governor, a lieutenant colonel, was impressed with the Bechtoldsheim name. Cool drinks and dinner were prepared for us. Fatigued, Ruth begged off.

The colonel invited me to play one game of chess. However good or bad he was, I could not afford to beat him in front of his subordinates. It went nip and tuck for twenty minutes until I was defeated, and glad of it. "I congratulate your game, colonel." Enthusiastic jabber from his aides. I retired for the night.

Morning brought a roadblock every fifty kilometers; two soldiers were stationed at each post. The little traffic was military. Looking north, only yellow rocks, saltbush, and gray earth met the eye.

We came to the bordertown of Sollum, a village locked in the arc of a shallow bay, with a sheer six-hundred-foot escarpment behind it. We pulled up to Custom and Passport Control. Beside the lazy eyes of several camels and their Bedouin drivers, the nondescript official in a dusty black suit seemed totally out of place.

"The military governor phoned ahead," he said, bowing grandly. We spent a half-hour over coffee, then drove past the crenellated battlements of Fort Capuzze and onto Libyan soil.

A hundred miles of desert road took us past Tobruk toward Derna, through rough terrain once packed with reinforcements for Rommel's push into Egypt. Mersa Matruh brought another game of chess with the military governor; it was a draw. He said, "Your next trip, don't bother getting a permit in Cairo. I will issue whatever is needed."

Back in Alexandria we found that Theo's contract was not being renewed. I stayed until his audience with President Naguib.

Cairo's Abadin Palace, 500 rooms in restrained Buckingham Palace motif, faced a great square where on each July 23, the anniversary of the 1952 overthrow of Farouk, the heads of government address thousands. Theo introduced me as his confidant, and we were taken to Naguib's office. I mentally pinched myself.

President and Prime Minister Mohammed Naguib, in his early fifties, avuncular and deeply tanned, with close-cropped, graying hair and mustache, was the picture of health, and he had a Peterson briar clamped between his teeth. His high-windowed office was graciously decorated, masculine, and comfortable. As we were served coffee, Theo broached the matter of Naguib's reinstallment as prime minister. Naguib smiled wistfully, toying with his pipe, unaware that he had only a short while more at the post.

"These young officers," he said, "they believe the Americans are better than the British, and the Russians are better than both. They will learn their lesson; they will learn."

This was the first mention I had heard of Russians (it would be well into the following year before the statement would have any meaning, at which time Nasser would negotiate an arms deal with the Czechs, promoted by the USSR). Naguib preferred to retain the German military advisers; Nasser did not. Naguib spoke briefly of this before breaking into praise of Theo's work. "The Republic owes you a great debt of gratitude, Herr Baron," he said in impeccable German. He gave no reasons for Theo's dismissal; it was obviously Nasser's doing.

A photographer took their picture together, then Naguib graciously gave me an autographed picture of himself. The next time I would see him, he would be gardening in his yard, reduced to titular president.

Obermayer, Theo's aide, was leaving for Germany to become an officer in the new West German navy; Theo expected him to wind up as an admiral. I joined the quayside farewell party and sealed our relationship by giving him the coveted Blaupunkt radio I had bought at the church bazaar. Speechless, Obermayer invited me to visit with him at Regensburg an der Donau anytime.

Leaving the port, Theo, Ruth, and I encountered Admiral Soliman Azzazat and Commodore Rageb Fahmi of the Egyptian navy. Theo introduced me as a man potentially valuable to the navy's procurement branch. The admiral suggested that we arrange a meeting.

Over dinner at Fahrmbacher's a few days later, Herr Roser, a guest and a former SS major general sought by the Russians for war crimes, asked not so offhandedly when I had last been to Alexandria, explaining that a high official of the junta's new police had been forced off the road and his car overturned by an automobile answering the description of my Plymouth convertible. I denied it, but Bob and I had been involved. The limousine had crowded us on the narrow desert road, and our reaction sent it into the deep sand. We kept going to avoid identification. Fortunately no one had been hurt.

Herr Roser was full of surprises; he claimed to have known Paul Frank's father!

"Yes, I remember your father *quite* well, Herr Frank," he said. "I met him in Palestine before the war, just before he moved your family back to Germany."[2] He paused; all I could feel was panic. "And, I might add, you favor him quite remarkably."

"I am very proud of that," I mumbled.

"You have every reason to be," Roser nodded. "He was a true German."

Willi Kubie's financial situation was desperate. He hoped that through me some German firm might buy the rocket techniques developed by the CERVA team. I promised to speak to Engel regarding his salary, and I cautioned him about divulging CERVA secrets. I was leery of traps.

"Besides," I said, "how can you get out copies of the blueprints? When I toured the plant with Engel, they were as large as wall maps."

Willi laughed. "Paul, I'm a photographer, remember? Those blueprints can be reproduced to the size of your thumbnail. Nobody would ever know."

Despite my eagerness, I delayed. The material was dynamite. Once I would have taken a risk to acquire it, but now that I was sure I had it, Willi could wait.

The newspapers reported England caught in a squeeze play: The United States was pressuring her to evacuate the canal zone, and even letting out word that if the Egyptians attacked the garrisons the United States would not interfere. (Dulles appeasing Nasser again.)

Countering American pressure, Israel protested the evacuation because of the lack of guaranteed passage of Israeli ships through the canal.

While the British vacillated, Henry A. Byroade, the United States expert on Middle East affairs, stated in an inflammatory speech that Israel should cease its eye-for-an-eye belligerency. Two days later, on April 13, he announced that American aid to Israel would be cut, and aid to the Arabs increased. A blow to the heart of Israel.

On April 17 Nasser became all powerful, ascending to the office of the prime minister while still chairing the Revolutionary Command Council. The RCC consolidated the army's grip on the government, reducing civilian control to a whisper.

Wild speculation ran through the German community concerning the future of all Germans in Egypt. Discussing it with Bob, I decided I had to jump on Nasser's bandwagon. I wrote a letter, stating our admiration for his aims and our desire to help, and we decided to deliver it personally to army GHQ in Heliopolis.

2. Paul Frank's family had made its home in Palestine since the 1900s, as had many Germans of the Templar sect.

After some confusion at the GHQ gate, we were directed to the officers' club in Cairo, then to Mohammed Ali Palace, knowing that a telephone call would precede us. It was the seat of the junta on Roda Island on the bank of the Nile. Darkness was falling on Cairo as we reached the checkpoint. One sentry raised the barrier; the other went into a shoulder arms salute. Again the German automobile club banner had been misinterpreted, but a red-bereted NCO demanded identity. I thrust the letter toward him.

"A personal message for Colonel Nasser."

"Nasser." The magic word. At the palace entrance a duty officer took over; the captain knew our names.

Bob handed him the envelope. "This is intended only for Colonel Nasser."

His face eased into a slight smile that held a private challenge. "Would you like to deliver it personally?"

"We'd be delighted," I answered.

Still smiling, the captain spoke at length on the phone.

"Only one of you may go in."

Bob's look carried doubt. In my gut was the same feeling, only more so. *He* didn't know who I was.

"I'll go." I followed the captain.

Behind me, Bob called out, "Don't leave without at least a million-dollar order!"

I laughed. It helped.

Beyond a beautifully manicured and lighted courtyard, we took a flight of steps to the second floor and went through a guarded door.

On a sign from the sentry, we went in.

An officer at a desk nodded. The captain knocked on a door to his right, and I was ushered in. For an instant the faces of the uniformed and muftied men comprising most of the ruling Revolutionary Command Council were a blur. They were all staring curiously at me, wondering who was I to breach their inner sanctum.

One man stepped forward: Lt. Col. Gamal Abdul Nasser, now prime minister.

Behind him were Salah Salem, minister of national guidance and Sudanese affairs; Abdul Latif Boghdady, wing commander and minister of war; Ali Sabry, officer in air intelligence and principal negotiator; Zacharia Mohieddin, minister of interior and, therefore, as head of security services, a man who would soon have dealings with me; and others who would stay at the pinnacle of Egypt's military government under Nasser.

Nasser's forbidding countenance, dominated by the hawk nose and jutting chin under fiercely dark eyes, disappeared when he smiled. He shook my hand and asked me my name and my business.

I congratulated him on his victory over Naguib and told him about my business taking care to mention only those German advisers whom I suspected were in his favor—names that brought smiles of satisfaction to the room. Nasser shook my hand a second time, then moved with me to the door, wishing luck and Allah's blessings on me.

"And thank you for the letter," he added. For a moment our eyes locked; he had the ability to freeze your attention. "I will read it now."

"Thank you, Colonel Nasser, for your time."

All the way back to the flat, one fantasy was in my mind: *How easy it would have been to liquidate them all.*

I relayed to headquarters my penetration of Nasser's lair. Nasser was as yet an unknown quantity, possibly only a single step away from a firing squad. He had little of the self-assurance with which he would one day capture the imagination of Egypt's populace and influence the world.

Gerhard Mertens—once a member of Germany's Green Devils parachute brigade and now architect of the Egyptian parachute unit—had me to dinner. I had met him a month earlier on a three-day trip to the head of the Gulf of Suez with Theo and his sons. We had bivouacked with his group, and our backgrounds as parachutists brought us together, relating war stories. Later in the evening came the cruel jokes at the expense of Jews, which I, both ashamed and angered, participated in. Only Theo and his sons refrained.

Now Mertens, at Villa Marghita, was holding court for a mixed German and Egyptian group. Outstanding in his long black kaftan and white headgear was the mufti of Jerusalem. Mertens introduced me to Lt. Col. Zacharia Mohieddin, minister of the interior and head of security services.

"We have met before," Mohieddin told him, referring to the delivery of my letter to Nasser.

Mertens drifted away; Mohieddin cut our social chitchat short. "Herr Frank, have you ever considered working for us in our government? With your military background, you could be of great service to us."

This was dangerous ground. "You flatter me, Colonel Mohieddin. But it is difficult to see how I could be of service to Egypt more than I am now as a businessman. Too, certain obligations are not easily laid aside."

Mohieddin eyed me thoughtfully. "I see," he said. "But should you ever decide to change your mind, please let me know, personally."

"You have my word, Herr Minister."

My cover background was a complete success, and Mohieddin's offer meant one thing; he was recruiting me for security. My begging off was merely to gain time to alert headquarters, and my note was on the way when the eagerly awaited Sinai trip with General Fahrmbacher came about.

The general and his party had set out two days earlier on the long tour of the proposed desert defenses. I joined them at control station #3, on the canal. My reason for delaying was to convince the general that Saint Katherina Monastery and Mount Sinai were my only interests.

Fahrmbacher was fuming from the heat, and the car's comfort appealed to him. He rode in front with me, while an Egyptian colonel and captain took the back seat. After a night at Port Taufiq we reached Ras Sudr, where manganese mines, and most of Egypt's oil production were concentrated.

All the way south was a beautiful, dangerous, desolation, the sun the boiling eye of God. I avoided consulting the map; the Egyptian officers viewed me with less then total trust. At one bivouac, my two bottles of Scotch lessened their suspicion, and I was given a chance to glance at the maps a fuming Fahrmbacher had spread across his lap, red-penciled lines encircling defense locations. He was upset, ripping down notes in German and muttering unflattering remarks about the strategic comprehension of Egyptians.

On another night a heated debate broke out on tactical matters. Fahrmbacher insisted that not holding certain positions in the Sinai was pure folly. His arguments were openly contested. Later, as I prepared the back seat of the car for sleeping, Fahrmbacher came with a flashlight and the map. "Look here," he said, "if the Jews take the Messerkamm, Gafgafa has no chance at all. Taking at the same time the Mitla Pass, nothing stands between them and the heart of Egypt. Dropping paratroops at the Barrage Dam north of Cairo will put the city in their hands within twenty-four hours. Am I right?" he asked, handing me the flashlight. The map was the rough defense plan for Egyptian deployment. I turned a serious face to the general. "A glance is sufficient to see where the rabbit will run." Then, indicating the Egyptians with a nod: "Don't they understand it?"

"You have seen for yourself what is understood," he said, his mouth a determined line. "Anyway, they are not deciding it."

He went grumbling to his tent. I climbed into the sleeping bag borrowed from Willi. Fahrmbacher contended that whoever held the Messerkamm, a strategic knife-ridge to the rear of Bir Gafgafa in the northwest sector of the Sinai, controlled the axis from Abu Ageila to Ismailia on the Suez Canal. Holding Mitla Pass controlled the central area of the Sinai, blocking Israel's advance toward the city of Suez at the head of the Gulf. Only the coastal route from El Arish toward Port Said remained as a penetration point. There was nothing in the south Sinai except Sharm el Sheikh.

The twin-track road reached an end. We left my car at a frontier post and climbed along the bed of Wadi Farran toward the ancient, gray granite walls of Saint Katherina Monastery. Raised in a basket elevator to the top of the wall, we were greeted by the six monks and the abbot, who showed us invaluable scriptures and icons as well as the catacombs, then asked for our names in the guest book. I signed *Paul Frank* with a flourish below Fahrmbacher's. (Two years later, at the capture of the monastery by Israeli forces, a friend, who knew something of my story leafed through the guest book and saw the names.)

Fahrmbacher, alone with me all the way back to Cairo, gave way to his thoughts. In spite of his advice, the Egyptian general headquarters was planning a more exposed and less defensible defense line near the Israeli border.

"If the Jews are clever," he said, "they will roll up the Egyptian front from the rear, take Mitla, Gafgafa, and Massa and stand on the threshold of Cairo."

That evening I sent a letter back to Unit 131 headquarters. The future shone a little brighter that night for Israel.

Day by day I gained insight into the activities of my fellow Germans. The recently established Staff Security Cadre seemed to be structured like Hitler's SS: shock troops and secret police. The Economic Department was a true replica of the SS Witschaftsamt, with a special Jewish section that had worked at full speed to register all Jewish property.

As a child in Austria I had grown up during the beginnings of a nightmare; now history was repeating it.

Chapter 11

The second week in May I received an ominous invisible-ink message from headquarters on Faust and Stollberg stationery: Proceed to Paris at the end of May and bring your car. The order pounded with urgency. My job was to prepare for departure without arousing the suspicions of either the authorities or my German acquaintances.

I decided to bring negotiations with Dr. Rolf Engel to a head. Engel, Hainisch, and Professor Goerke, the radar expert, had discussed the experimental rocket with me and had demonstrated the propellant's burning. The fact was that the Egyptians had a tactical rocket; a guided missile would come next.

Meanwhile my negotiations with CERVA, via Engel, had deadlocked. The problem was Count de Lavison, chairman of the board. Earlier, Engel and I had worked out an order for machine tools amounting to $240,000. Under the table, Engel would pocket a percentage. However, de Lavison had vetoed it, preferring to use his own connections. Engel, furious, came directly to the point.

"We have to do something about this Jew," he said.

"Jew?" I asked in genuine astonishment.

"Of course, Lavison is a Jew! He bought his title from the Vatican. The Jew Levinson is now the Catholic Count de Lavison."

"Herr Engel, permit my saying that it seems to lack logic for him to block his own interests; he is the biggest private shareholder in the firm."

Engel rarely equivocated. He didn't now.

"What it really amounts to, Herr Frank," he said testily, "is sabotage. I am certain he works for the Jews. But everyone is too impressed with the Jew's money and influence."

"Is there no way to get proof?"

"Maybe through your connections in Europe you might find out who he meets on his frequent trips there. Three weeks ago he went abroad for two days." He peered at me. "On his return, more obstacles for me."

"It's possible I might. It's worth a try."

"Paul," (the first time Engel had addressed me informally), "if we can prove he has questionable connections, he is out. It could be the beginning of big business for you."

Given the sensitivity of Egypt's rocket industry, how could de Lavison's Jewish background be overlooked? The count, for a very important reason, would be my first piece of business in Rome.

In Israel I had been told that our scientists had invented a device that, through microwaves, could detonate explosives 300 miles away. If I could furnish the tools Engel wanted, then it would be easy to load the machinery with explosives. At any time the entire rocket factory could be blown sky-high! It was too great an opportunity to miss because of this Count de La-vison.

Bob Jansen was leaving with me to marry his long-time girl friend in Germany, and for a totally selfish reason, I had offered to pay his boat fare to Italy: The sale of CERVA's rocket secrets had come up again with Willi Kubie. I had refused to take out the microfilm, not knowing if Willi was bait in a trap. However, Bob was so happy to be leaving Egypt that he offered to smuggle out the Sphinx.

The word of my trip abroad spread among my friends, and soon I had special chores on my hands. Fahrmbacher gave me a letter for his daughter, who lived in the Bavarian Alps south of Munich. Theo arranged a meeting with Admiral Suliman Azzazat's adjutant, who took me to Commodore Rageb Fahmi. Angered over the junta's demand that she abandon the canal, England had embargoed equipment and spare parts. I was asked to secure projectile explosives for naval guns and spare parts for radar installations.

Meanwhile Engel and Hainisch were using me as a table-tennis ball. The first assumed my loyalty; the other demanded it. Besides giving me a letter for Herr von Karaman, an adviser on aerodynamics to NATO in Paris, Engel entrusted me with an equally confidential mission to Brussels. It was the first I'd heard of the planned production of the Matador missile in Egypt. Secret negotiations were under way with a Belgium firm; Engel wanted to convey to the owner the feasibility of CERVA's participation.

The day before departure Hainisch came with a letter for his wife outside Paris. "No one is to know about this letter, Herr Frank. You understand, of course."

I nodded, understanding much. Hainisch's conflict with Engel was now an open battle. Steaming it open, I found that it clarified much but also added a greater mystery. The letter read: "I told Engel that I would use the microfilm against him" and asked her to hide the films.

I explained to Engel my dilemma over telling him about the letter.

"Do you know the contents of the letter?"

"I would not open a man's mail, Herr Engel."

"May I see it?" To my show of hesitation, Engel remarked, "Only with a man of honor do you repay honor."

"But Hainisch must never know," I insisted.

"Of course not."

Engel's face paled as he read the letter. If I'd had doubts of his trust, they were washed away.

"Paul, I can never truly reflect my indebtedness to you."

Bob and I set out for Alexandria. I stopped by Theo's and picked up another letter for Charlotte. Theo wanted to accompany me to the ship but I declined; the friendship of former Kapitan zur See Baron Theodor von Bechtoldsheim was becoming a liability in Egypt.

Willi Kubie awaited us at the port. While I busied myself with the shipping of the car, Kubie passed the rocket blueprints, now thumbnail-size microfilm, to Bob. At sea, Bob, grinning like the cat that had eaten the mouse, told me he'd gone down into the ship's hold and put the matchbox containing eighty-five square negatives into the trunk of my car.

It was a slow, impatient passage to Brindisi. I could hardly wait to pass on my bag of tricks to headquarters.

Disembarking at the Adriatic port, I took the matchbox of microfilm through customs, clutching it in hand while lighting my pipe. We drove to Rome and put up at Hotel Ferrovia, my usual quarters.

Benjamin Rottem and I had business to transact.

"Does the name Count de Lavison mean anything to you, Benjamin?" I asked.

"The name is familiar. Why?"

I told him about my conversation with Engel. "I have to know whether he really is working for us. A plan depends on it."

"To my knowledge, he isn't connected with us," Benjamin said. The only connection he knew about was the son of another large shareholder in CERVA; through him Mossad had gotten the layout of the rocket plant at the cost of several thousand dollars.

Benjamin was to verify de Lavison's status with the Mossad. "Should he not be connected," I said, "within a week after I return to Egypt, start sending letters to de Lavison written in simple secret ink so that any fool could detect it. Write that you have acted in accordance with his advice—anything that will cast doubt on his allegiance."

"Why don't I sign the letters with 'Bass,' my blown cover name? The Egyptians know it. You can inform Engel that de Lavison met someone named Bass," Benjamin grinned.

"Is the name Bass well known to them?" I felt uneasy. Perhaps my contact was a red flag.

"Believe it," Benjamin said.

"Then why are you my contact? Has it occurred to anyone that this might endanger my life?"

"Forget it, Avri. All the safety precautions are taken with you."

"Maybe you can forget it, but it's my neck in the noose."

Benjamin wanted to know what was in the matchbox. When I told him, he was stunned.

"I don't understand! We've been chasing those blueprints for months and all we got was the layout of the factory! How did you do it?"

I left him in the dark.

Driving into Zurich, I couldn't believe it was only fourteen months ago that I had come to the city as a raw Modiin operative in search of a German identity. In Munich Bob left for Dusseldorf by train, after making me swear to visit his parents' home the following week.

I told Charlotte von Bechtoldsheim about her father's problems in Egypt and, on learning of my trip to Paris, she said she wanted to come along—to play games I wasn't about to play with Theo's daughter.

I drove to Cologne to pick up a letter from Shlomo that had been channeled through Poldi. My Paris contact was to be informed of the date of my meeting with Hainisch's wife; Modiin wanted to lay its hands on the material Hainisch held against Engel. Leverage. The tone of Shlomo's letter showed headquarters' concern over Egypt's rocketry progress. Shlomo added: "Blueprints are being evaluated. At first sight, they are outstanding material. Convey detailed report on how they were acquired."

I did just that, adding my memory road maps of the two desert areas and my photographic negatives.

This done, I sent the notes from the trip to Libya to the German auto club and received a grateful reply.

In Dusseldorf Bob Jansen's parents received me graciously, as their son's best friend. Bob and Edith, his girl friend, wanted to go to Paris, and, having acquired chaperones, I phoned Charlotte. We picked her up en route. My change of mind was also due to her desire to visit a friend of her father's, Colonel Mohab, the Egyptian military attaché to the Netherlands, a man I'd met at Theo's. I hoped to renew our acquaintanceship.

Arriving in Paris, I put Charlotte in a room by herself (only the next morning did I discover the extent of her wounded feelings), set up a meeting with Frau Hainisch, and phoned my contact. My instructions were to keep her with me as long as possible to allow search of her house. To avoid implicating me, any materials would be photographed on the spot.

Frau Hainisch proved to be charmingly outspoken. Before reading the letter over coffee in a Paris café, her comments about Engel were anything but ladylike; and when she read it, she left immediately, rejecting my offer to drive her. The moment she was out of sight, I was on the phone. More material had been found than anticipated. Five minutes after our people had cleared the house, Frau Hainisch appeared. . . . *Close!*

I delivered Engel's letter to Herr von Karaman, who reminded me remarkably of Ben-Gurion. From him I learned that Rolf Engel was a founder of the *Verein Für Raumschiffahrt* (Association for Experimental Space Flight); a member of the Research Council of the Third Reich; and, after the war, an adviser to the National Aeronautical Research in Paris, where he became closely associated with von Karaman. These two scientists, in collaboration, meant that something big was in the offing.

No word yet as to whom I was to meet in Europe.

On our arrival in Brussels, Charlotte called Colonel Mohab, Egyptian military attaché to the Low Countries and director of Egyptian Intelligence in Europe. He had already been directed to follow Admiral Azzazat's suggestion that my samples of explosive materials could be routed through Egyptian military attachés in Europe.

My main piece of business in the Low Countries was to deliver Engel's message to Dr. Somerville, owner of the firm producing rockets for NATO.

An elderly gentleman, he awaited me in his laboratory in Rotterdam and took only a moment to digest Engel's note. "That's dandy," he said. "Tell Engel that I am willing to go into the venture."

Apparently Dr. Somerville believed me to be Engel's confidant and I could not ask him to elaborate. After a fast tour of the plant, he said, "Come and see me again when you are in Brussels." I fully intended to accept.

Returning to Germany, I dropped off Bob and Edith in Dusseldorf and drove a sullen Charlotte to Munich.

I'd reached a conclusion regarding my chronically inflamed penis: Paul Frank was well enough established that no harm would be done should my circumcision be revealed. One addition to my cover story would take care of it: Before dropping into Palestine, he had understandably undergone circumcision to fit his assumed identity as a Jew.

Doctor G was all smiles when I called on him in Frankfurt. Another hundred deutsche marks changed hands and I was a changed man, with only temporary inflammation for my troubles. Incontestable: Sex has its place in a spy's life, or else the "silent" war is also hell.

I received a message from Poldi in Cologne to proceed to Paris and get in touch with my contact. This was what I had come for!

One day in the second week in June, as I waited at the Chez Maitena coffeehouse on Boulevard St. Germain, Motke's tall, bearish frame came into view! Our encounter was casual by design; startling by its unexpectedness. We took a small table under the café's sidewalk canopy.

"You've come a long way, Avri," Motke began. "No one is prouder than me."

"Let's hope it's justified," I said. "It's been easy so far."

"Luck didn't do it alone, my boy. You got results; you proved yourself beyond all expectations."

When the blonde waitress came, Motke looked at his watch. "Order for yourself. I have to meet someone for a half hour. I'll be back." With that, he hurried off.

While admiring the strolling women famous for beautifying Paris, I puzzled over Motke. His presence in Europe was always connected with some big operation. When he reappeared, a jerkiness in his normally lumbering gait caught my attention. Trouble—something—snapped at his heels. He dropped into his chair, more tense than I had ever seen him. His direct stare did nothing to allay my apprehension.

"Avri——" Motke looked at everyone within earshot, then back to me. "Avri, I haven't seen the rocket blueprints—they were en route to Israel when I left—but they're quite valuable." His expression eased. "How did you get them?"

I couldn't restrain a smile. We both knew about the efforts our Mossad competitor had expended pursuing these very plans. I briefed him on my acquisition from Willi Kubie.

"You've made no friends in the Mossad!" Motke said lightly. "Neither have I, huh?" We laughed, pleased. Then he asked soberly, "What's going on in Egypt?"

My three-week-old puzzle, the message ordering my return to Europe with the car, was nearing a solution. I wished to hell he would get to that little item.

"It's very simple," I concluded, "the whole country is in chaos. Nasser has the government under control but nothing else."

Motke nodded. "What about the German advisers? Won't Nasser look hard at them since they supported Naguib all along?"

"That's hard to say." It depended on how much Nasser valued their services. And Modiin's files on German advisers (I had contributed my share) disclosed that they did everything from stamping documents in

Cairo to creating concentration camps, SS style, deep in the Western Desert.

"It's fairly clear that most of the contracts will be renewed. Until something better is offered to Nasser."

"Jerusalem is afraid of just that," Motke said. "Afraid of their staying and afraid of what will replace them." He leaned closer. "Let's make a supposition, Avri. Suppose Nasser cancels most of the contracts, which he will be forced to do if the United States has its way. How will that affect the German businessmen? Like yourself, for instance?"

I replied readily. Nasser wasn't likely to bother *any* businessman. Egypt needed badly to keep its commercial avenues open to the world. Its main export crop, cotton, had dwindled to nothing; foreign credit was leery of the new regime. Egyptian private money, even more uncertain of the government, withheld investing in a shattered economy. Besides, foreign governments weren't griping about Nasser's foreign trade efforts. An independent Egypt was an Egypt free of world subsidy. The budding war machine was the feared ogre.

"About the only unifier the Egyptians have is their push to rid themselves of the British. Quite frankly, from what I gather from rumor, it won't be long before Nasser reaches some kind of agreement with Whitehall. When that happens, I think England will hand over the canal to Nasser."

"That's what we have to stop," Motke said grimly. "But that's in my briefing to you. I'll get to it later."

His eyes were strangely alight; barely contained excitement lay somewhere behind the broad face of the Polish-born Jew.

"Listen very carefully. Israel is in very grave trouble." Jerusalem is afraid the situation is deteriorating by the hour. Avri, do you realize what will happen if the British pull out? They'll abandon to Nasser the mightiest military bases in the Middle East: thirty-seven military installations, including two fully equipped airfields, docks, dumps, hospitals, radar stations and some of the world's largest ordnance depots. It took the British thirty-eight years to build and equip them." He paused. "With those forward bases, Nasser's air force will stare right into our eyes. And his troops can move around the Sinai at will. Worst of all, they'll leave Nasser a hero to his people. He'll have complete control of the canal. When, not if, he nationalizes the canal, Israel's shipping will be shut off forever." Motke sat back, his eyes dark and challenging. "And you know how quick an Arab can get a whim."

I knew, as did every Israeli.

Now, with Egyptian troops holding Sharm El Sheikh and the two tiny offshore islands, Nasser could strangle Eilat.

Hoping to lift our spirits, I suggested that Nasser was too short of armament to launch a new war. But a nagging recall was how the British had willed a treasure of arms to the Arabs when they evacuated Palestine in 1948. With a new and larger inheritance, show of force was possible.

"Israel has a second point of concern: the United States," Motke said, unappeased. "Secretary of State Dulles's courtship of Egypt scares the pants off Jerusalem. However, it's no secret that Dulles doesn't trust Nasser. If something should happen to make Dulles more distrustful, Israel might be the beneficiary."

Motke was hinting at the purpose of our meeting. Whatever it was, it had something to do with me.

"America," he said, "wants Egypt aligned with the West against the Russians."

It was true. The United States had attempted an alliance with Farouk's government and had failed (which might account for the rumor that the American Central Intelligence Agency had been instrumental in Farouk's overthrow). Yet Dulles had also failed to sway Nasser. It was easy to understand: How could Nasser get excited about Russians thousands of miles away, when the hated English were camped not more than a hundred miles from Cairo?

So Dulles had concentrated on the northern tier Moslem countries— Turkey, Iran, Iraq, Pakistan—who were more vulnerable to the Russian threat, and Nasser had been working against him.

"But," Motke said, "Dulles hasn't given up on him." He grinned.

The United States wanted to fill the vacuum that would be created by Britain's departure. "What America really wants," I said, "are bases to completely ring Russia."

"Right. The cold war isn't without its victims, you know. And its pawns."

America, I knew, would have to pay a heavy price to make a pawn of the paranoid Nasser. Egypt had been under foreign domination too long. We agreed: Nasser wanted aid and nonalignment.

"The Americans know the game, Avri. They just don't know how much it's going to cost." Motke's eyes swept sidelong, then returned. "Anyway, Israel is not prepared to share in the expense."

I doubted there was much we could do about it, and I said as much. Motke came up with his somber, lazy, all-knowing smirk.

"That depends on whether we can stop Britain's evacuation. If we succeed, we more or less keep the status quo: border skirmishes with the terrorists and an armistice about as fragile as we've had since forty-nine. But if the Tommies do go, with the additional arms and a little pep rally for the hysterical masses, you can bet your ass Israel had better brace for another round."

I had to ask a disturbing question.

"If America fills the Middle East vacuum, where will it leave us?"

"Isolated."

"Isolated? America will abandon us?"

"It's not so difficult to imagine, Avri. We're a welfare state with little America needs, except our democracy. Egypt is a welfare state with everything America needs." Motke's face became doleful. "Nasser won't tolerate their arming us at the same time."

Cold anger swept over me. The United States had closed its ears. To trust Nasser was to commit the most colossal stupidity. Rumors of high-level talks had run rampant throughout the German colony. The Aswan High Dam, to be constructed on the Upper Nile, was part of those discussions. Also the United States was pressing for the ouster of the German advisers. The situation was almost too paradoxical not to be humorous. When Palestine was under the British Mandate, we did our utmost to get rid of them. Now it appeared that we had to keep them in the area for our own protection.

Overwhelmed by the danger confronting our country, I said, "I only hope we're not fresh out of a David for the Goliath."

Motke smiled thinly. "We have a way . . . and you are involved." Involvement, hell! As Motke went on it sounded as if I were in the lead! "With a great deal of chaos and confusion, making it look as if things are completely out of hand in Egypt, we can give the British Parliament all the excuse it needs to retract its decision to withdraw the troops. They know that to pull out is risking the loss of the canal to Nasser, if not now, eventually." Again he leaned forward. *"We can furnish them with the excuse to retract. To stay."*

I told him to go on. He did, making his points one by one, distinctly.

"We've only to convince the United States of Nasser's instability; show them how unpredictable he is, how helpless. Show them that any agreement he makes is only good so long as he controls the government.

"We have to destroy his credibility. Everything he says in negotiation must be made out to be a farce. And it has to be shown to the world.

"If we poison the atmosphere around him, then what little trust the West has placed in him will end abruptly. Then we have accomplished what must be done for Israel."

"You've told me everything except how all this is to be done."

"By sabotage actions. And you will command our people."

Slowly, deliberately, I propped my chin on my closed fists. Our eyes locked. I had no instant thoughts—only feelings. Most of all, I felt relief. Tension, built up over the past few minutes, slid from my shoulders.

"It's about time somebody did something," I heard myself saying, stunned by the boldness of what Motke had revealed, but surging with pride. *Sabotage!*

Eagerly I waited for more.

"Right now, Nasser wants peace and quiet." Motke spoke intently. "If we sabotage selected Anglo-American and Egyptian facilities, everybody—and Nasser will be the first—is sure to lay the blame on either the Moslem Brotherhood or the Communists. Or both!" Motke clenched his fist. "Nasser will turn on the radicals with all the vengeance of a *Jihad*. He'll mass arrest them, forcing them to retaliate. And you know as well as I, the Moslem Brotherhood only retaliates violently."

"And when the fire subsides, we fan it a bit," I added. "Besides, who would suspect us?"

I looked beyond him, at the picture he had painted. It was certainly possible. The fragile moratorium Nasser had extracted from the Moslem Brotherhood was mutually explosive. A spark could set either of them off. And everybody hated the Communists.

"Dulles doesn't need much help to completely disillusion him," Motke went on. "Nasser is playing too much the prima donna, making things too difficult. He's deliberately sabotaging Dulles's progress in the other Moslem countries.

"If Dulles gets his bellyful of Nasser, he'll stop pressing the British to get out of the canal. Might be Dulles will use their presence as leverage to get what he wants from Nasser."

My mind was busy keeping up with Motke. Would the actions he projected really destroy Nasser in the eyes of the Americans? However, for me to question the wisdom of the decision was to question Israel's top planners. I accepted Motke's confidence as my own.

"Avri, you have hesitations." His easy smile disappeared. "There's no alternative except to sit back and let the world decide our future. The Jewish people did that once, and you know the results."

Motke's allusion to Hitler's gigantic atrocity aroused personal memories. Still, his pragmatism frightened me. An eye for an eye and the end justifies the means were Middle East rules of conduct I had to question. But the question was for myself, not for Israel.

I looked long at my friend. "Why me, Motke? Why was I selected to head the operation?"

This I could question. My success in Egypt having been more swift and effective than any of my superiors had anticipated, it seemed unwise to throw away Paul Frank.

Motke didn't hedge. "You were not the first considered, Avri. We have a man in Egypt, operating as a lone wolf like yourself, but he is not as flexible as he would have to be. Avraham Dar is a blabbermouth; he blew his cover a long time ago. Another man was to come up from South Africa, but he chickened out.

"You were next. At first, we felt your value was too great to risk."

Again he paused. *"But right now, nothing is more important to Israel than this."*

I had an odd new kind of feeling, and Motke had not yet finished.

"Avri, if there is no alternative, there is more to plan." Motke hesitated, studying my reaction. I gave none. He went on. "It might be necessary to deal with those Germans who are vital to Nasser's war program. Then there are important Egyptians. . . ."

"Yes?" His words had drifted to a stop.

"We are to draw up a list, Avri, you and I. A list for elimination. It may come to that. Tomorrow we'll make the selection, go into details."

I don't know what my face showed, but I felt fear, pride, anticipation, elation. All these filled my head and overflowed my lips in one word: "elimination!"

Sudden awareness of my reckless anticipation frightened me.

"It's good that you've breached Nasser's security. We see that it can be done." Motke took a deep breath. "Avri, there is no time to waste. The sabotage actions must be carried out immediately."

One question remained for me. "Motke, who decided about this operation? Was it Gibli?"[1]

"Higher."

"The chief of staff?"

"Higher than Dayan."

"Then it has to be the minister of defense."

"Lavon is an activist, but not he. Higher."

"It cannot be the prime minister. Who, Motke?"

"I told you: the highest authority."

Then it hit me. Of course! There was no higher authority!

I suddenly realized what he was implying, recalling Gibli and Dayan's weekly pilgrimage down to Kibbutz Sde Boker in the Negev Desert where the Old Man had exiled himself from a government he had built and rejected. There lay the answer.

"Is it him, Motke? Is it Ben-Gurion?"

But Motke would not commit himself verbally; he was afraid to mention God by his proper name.

The answer lay, however, in his face.

The significance of his statement gripped me completely. His phrase, "the highest authority," spoken in emphatic tones, would return to me again and again over the years, in times of crisis. At this moment, however, I was caught up in a scheme that I was unable, as yet, to fully comprehend.

---

1. Col. Benjamin Gibli, director of military intelligence.

After we parted, I walked along the Seine, digesting the impact of Motke's revelation and pondering hard my selection to head the operation—when businessman Paul Frank had every chance of entrenching himself for years to come in Egypt. It was a golden opportunity for an Israeli agent. Was it wise to risk it?

As it turned out, I would have a lifetime to debate that point.

Book 3

Chapter 12

The double-barreled charge of emotion with which I sailed back to Egypt wiped out any similarity to my two previous passages. The orders with which I now sailed were of such magnitude that to be caught in their execution meant my certain death. There would be no mercy in Egyptian hearts for me. Aboard the slow ship, I stewed in my anxiety, consumed by my orders—orders of first national priority, according to Motke.

Sabotage actions are to be taken immediately. Concurrently, elimination of those men listed must be prepared for so that assassination can be carried out on notice.

Those on the list were living, breathing men, some of whom I knew and liked. Nasser, Naguib, Fahrmbacher, Bechtoldsheim, Admiral Azzazat, Zacharia Mohieddin, General Ibrahim, head of the army. *Cripple by sabotage, maim by death.* Motke's words—my orders.

Motke had sketched out the conspiracy network in Egypt as he knew it. Set up in 1951 by Maj. Avraham Dar (my recruiter) prior to Motke's heading Modiin Unit 131, it was made up largely of youthful volunteers from the ranks of local Jewish organizations. Since the beginning, except for the few who had been secretly trained in Israel, they had been held in limbo.

The bleak picture that Motke had painted of the network only added to my eagerness to take command; organization was chaotic in both the Alexandria and Cairo cells; morale was low; communication with headquarters had been abandoned; leadership was nonexistent; so was experience in either conspiracy or sabotage. Their loyalty to Israel was their best asset, Motke emphasized. Despite the shortcomings, I felt I could shape the group into a viable sabotage team. And that task would probably enable me to keep my assassination role in perspective.

I did not seriously question the puniness of the network Motke described; I didn't feel it my place to do so. Israel was too vulnerable to embark on a double cross of her American and British benefactors without having tied all the loose ends together. Her chosen course of action, frighteningly Machiavellian, was fraught with enormous repercussions. In intelligence operations dishonor lies not in the commission of the act so much as it does in its discovery.

Whatever the ramifications of my country's scheme, my task was clear: Take command of the Alexandria cell and render it operational for immediate sabotage action. (The Cairo cell would be activated later.) And at all times I must be prepared to deliver death—on order. My objectives were to spread sedition and unrest—and poison the political atmosphere against Egypt in the international arena. Sabotaging Anglo-American establishments would disrupt America's courtship of Nasser by making it appear as if Egypt's populace was actively subverting his promises. These violent acts would throw Egypt backward into internecine warfare; force Nasser to crack down on the extremists opposing his rule; and give England's Parliament cause to retract her intent to abandon the Suez Canal to a man unable to control his countrymen. Keeping the British 80,000-man garrison along the canal would give Israel more time, more protection from any impulsive Egyptian move.

But the greatest guarantee of all would be through assassination of key military advisers and government figures. Each target—man or structure—would be identified by a code name, the humans designated as vegetables (Farhmbacher: carrot). All of the codes were transmittable either by secret ink, wireless, or one of the two Voice of Israel programs, "Program for the Housewife" and "Program of your Choice," an hour-long music show.

Knowing that at any moment I could receive the dreaded directive from one of these sources hounded me, to say the least. To capsize the aims of my German and Arab "friends" was one thing; to extinguish a human life was quite another.

And the enormity of the plan ate at me. We hadn't come very far if we, as the chosen people, had to resort to assassination. To do this was to align ourselves with Arab mentality. I lived a silent plea that those at home who had conceived and ordered the plan knew what they were doing.

I went to Vienna to see my father. Completing arrangements with Hans

Schneider while there, I left for Rome where Benjamin Rottem informed me that, according to his Mossad superiors, CERVA's chairman, Count de Lavison, was not connected with our agencies. Motke had already approved of my scheme to incriminate the man. Stoutly, Benjamin assured me the incriminating letters would reach Egypt immediately after my arrival. He gave me a thousand dollars, mostly singles. "Count it," he said.

I counted until one of the bills, flaunting the oval stamp of the Israel National Bank, chilled my blood.

"You've just handed me my death warrant," I said with venom, shoving the bill in his hand glad this was not Egyptian customs. Both of us went through the stack of bills twice. Neither of us wanted a slip-up.

This time I was going back to Egypt as a plunderer, a destroyer of life, a made-to-order killer.

Admiral Azzazat, responding to my cable of arrival on June 29, sent word to forgo inspection of the car and my personal belongings. Customs could impound the shell fuses for the navy, the specifications for electronic radar parts, the price lists for the navy's procurement department, or even the weapons list for Hainisch, I didn't care. It was the transmission schedule, the *Moby Dick* code book, frequency crystals (some concealed in my attaché case), and other network items that concerned me. I breathed easier as the entry stamp was pressed into my passport, the customs inspection avoided.

I found that even though Theo had been reinstated as a *persona grata,* he and his family were leaving Egypt within the week. I brought them up to date on Charlotte and broke away, promising to return shortly.

I drove circuitously through Alexandria's European section before stopping at a service station near my destination. Leaving Theo's boys (brought along for cover) with the car, which I ordered washed and lubricated, I sought out Philip "Henri" Nathanson's house. I carried a tripod used for photographing paper work, a piece of equipment whose possession would be difficult to justify. A stout, middle-aged, awkward woman answered my knock.

"Is Philip home?" I asked in English, the language I would use hereafter with the ring members to hide my true identity, hoping they would think I was from one of the northern European countries.

She appraised me casually. "Are you Robert?" Her knowledge of my code name for this operation momentarily stunned me. "I'm Philip's mother. Please come in. He's upstairs."

I followed, wondering if Motke knew that the spying business was a family affair with the Nathansons.

Philip Nathanson was a slim, good-looking youth of nineteen or twenty.

I handed him the tripod, which he studied approvingly. "It's good that you've come," he said. "We've been expecting you."

"How do you know *who* I am?" I asked, putting bite into my words.

He smiled pleasantly. "You're Robert. We've been alerted of your coming."

"So it seems."

Nathanson, trained in Israel, had a perfect front for his well-equipped attic studio. Photography was ostensibly his hobby. He had a small quantity of explosives in two VIM containers; more was buried in the backyard. Even though he proudly announced they'd been practicing explosive sabotage in the desert, I didn't inquire into the amount remaining, since Motke had assured me there were sufficient explosives on hand to initiate action.

"How soon can you arrange a meeting with 'Pierre'?"

"By tomorrow noon."

"Good. In front of the bookstore on Rue de Banque. Twelve noon on the dot."

To impress Nathanson with the absolute necessity of using conspiracy procedures at all times, I insisted on using his code name.[1] I had seen enough already; the cell was dangerously lax. (Nathanson had used Pierre's real name and seemed to know all about him.)

During my absence Rolf Engel had asked Theo about my return. Since outer-city phone calls could not be placed from private telephones, Theo went with me to the Marconi radio office. I reached Engel in Cairo, telling him guardedly that my mission for him had been "successful in every respect."

The next morning, leaving Hotel Cecil, I strolled up Rue de Banque. At exactly noon Nathanson walked up with Victor "Pierre" Levy. Their punctuality gave me hope as I crossed the street. Levy, unlike Nathanson, could have been northern Italian. Whereas Nathanson had a shock of reddish hair, Levy's was dark and trimmed short, and he sported a Clark Gable mustache. Both were likable, direct, and eager. I wanted to deal with Levy alone, trusting Motke's suggestion that he was the best choice to act as head of the group. At my hint Levy suggested Nathanson leave us. We chose to sit in an indoor restaurant.

"You have regards from your girl friend."

Levy's face lighted up. "You have *seen* her?"

"I am only a messenger," I smiled, having delivered Motke's communication.

Levy inquired about Avraham Dar's well-being. I was speechless. Unwittingly he had confirmed Motke's words: Dar was a loudmouthed

---

1. Author's Note: For the sake of clarity code names will be omitted generally.

braggart who had blown his cover by talking. Yesterday Nathanson had also brought up Dar. "Tell me about John Darling," he had said. "You know John Darling—Avraham Dar, a commander in the Palmach." I merely nodded. "Dar is fine. He sends regards."

Levy made no attempt to hide his excitement as I briefed him. "You can apprise the others of what I've told you. You will command the group, Pierre," I said, "answering only to me." The elimination task I kept to myself.

Levy's assessment of the situation was even grimmer than I'd expected. Nearly everything was wrong. Besides there being no conspiratorial apparatus and barely enough explosive materials on hand, it looked as if I had exactly three-and-a-half people in Alexandria to sabotage the entire Middle East policies of America and Britain: Levy and Nathanson were ready to act; Reuben "Roger" Dassa needed only convincing, according to Levy; Shmuel "Jacques" Azar (after hearing Levy's opinion) I considered a large question mark. Later it would become an exclamation point—of his own. These four made my three and a half.

Eli "Alex" Cohen,[2] trained in Israel as our principal wireless operator, was, I gathered, too busy with his work to get involved.

Meir Meyouchas, according to Motke, had hedged on setting up a workshop for preparing bombs and the like with the 500 Egyptian pounds[3] given him by headquarters. He also refused to return the money. I was ordered to get it from him.

If the group I held was the Israeli David, then my country was in desperate trouble. I was a man ordered to move a mountain with a firecracker.

But we were committed, and Israel was too threatened for us to delay. The decision had been reached by the highest authority. *Impossible* was not in Zahal's vocabulary.

I saw deeply into Levy's silence. "Do you have doubts? This won't be a picnic, like blowing up harmless holes in the desert. Practice is over. If you back out, nobody will hold it against you. We will part as friends, and you will never hear from us again. The decision is yours to make. Don't be ashamed."

I knew beforehand Levy's decision, but I wanted it clear that this was no spy novel. Pursuit meant battling security forces with a sympathetic population at their backs. Losing the cat-and-mouse game could mean imprisonment or death.

Without a word Levy pressed my hand. It was enough. I gave him the new frequency crystals for an immediate transmission to BASE.

---

2. The principal figure of Zwi Aldouby's *The Shattered Silence*.
3. Approximately $1,500 in June 1954.

"Until Eli Cohen cooperates, you will act as wireless operator," I said. "Can you do it?"

"I was trained in Israel. I can do it."

"Good. Begin according to schedule. BASE is listening for us."

"What's the message?"

"Contact established. Phase two to be executed without delay."

From the hotel that night, I conveyed to headquarters (covertly in a business letter) a picture of what I'd found here. Besides demanding an immediate supply of explosives, I again requested false passports for the group. We might have to run for it sooner than anyone expected.

July 1 rolled up on the calendar, hot and clear. To touch base with my Cairo acquaintances, I rode the Desert Line bus to the capital and brushed my presence across the scene. Then I returned for a late afternoon meeting with Levy. But first I visited Willi Kubie.

It seemed a pity that Willi's noble heritage hadn't included more vigorous physical equipment. I tracked him down through CERVA and his landlady to the hospital, where he was recovering from an emergency appendectomy; he was in little shape to discuss the rocket microfilms. Egypt had not been Willi's lucky charm.

When I told him that an Austrian pyrotechnic firm had offered only three thousand Austrian schillings, he replied, "I don't care. I need it," his voice thin.

I arranged to get him half of the three thousand immediately, promising the remainder as soon as the Austrian could come up with it. His face lighted with gratitude.

"It's all right, Willi," I said. "I know you'd do the same for me." I left him. It did not occur to me that a change might be taking place in me. Looking back now, it apparently didn't matter whom I lied to.

Levy was having technical difficulties with the wireless. He wanted me to go to the apartment at Rue Hospital 18, ostensibly a studio for Azar's painting classes, not only to check the transmitter but also to talk to Dassar and Azar. He had failed to convince them to participate directly in the action. They weren't yet sold on the fact that a man had been sent to command them.

I hesitated, extremely reluctant to expose myself to all of them. A violation of conspiratorial procedure. I had hoped to command exclusively through Levy; however, time was pressing me, and the wireless was of paramount importance.

Apartment 107, Rue Hospital 18, Alexandria, had been cleverly chosen. The busy thoroughfare allowed an unobtrusive entrance and exit. Seven stories high and the tallest structure around, it was ideal for wireless transmission. The antenna would rise well above nearby buildings.

Levy introduced me to bespectacled Shmuel Azar—medium height, late twenties—and to Reuben Dassa, just over five feet, barely in his twenties.

"I'm Robert," I said, making a cursory sweep of the room, which contained two chairs, a bench, a chest of drawers, a desk, and a few paintings that were on the floor, leaning against the bare walls. Exposed for all to see was the complete transmission apparatus: radio, transmitter, Morse key, earphones, tubes, crystals, and a smattering of spare parts.

I was furious, but I casually picked up the transmitter, looking at Shmuel Azar, whom Levy had said was an electronics engineering instructor at a technical school. He looked perfectly blank.

"Safety precautions should not be neglected," I said, my manner easy, taking in the lowered window shade. I raised it halfway. "It's a beautiful day outside. Few people would lower the shade after the afternoon siesta. And what artist blocks out the beautiful sunshine?" I looked at Azar, then at the canvases. "One has to remain true to his cover story."

Dassa's fiery black eyes, matching his hair, exposed a sudden willingness to be a part of the team. "We have a *slik* to hide the gear," he said, moving quickly to the equipment.

I stopped him. "Leave it. I have a few things to say." I wanted them all at ease. "I understand your misgivings, but things have changed. Modiin realizes that mistakes have been made. That's why I'm here. You know what we have to do. All that is expected of you is your best effort. If the action is against your conscience, now is the time to speak up."

After a long silence, each quietly showed his willingness to involve himself: Dassa's eyes were shining with excitement; Azar, Egyptian-featured, stood nervous and wary; Levy had taken the role of commander.

"I'm glad you're here, Robert," Azar said. Whatever his cause for hesitation, he was trying to measure up.

"Thanks. Let's get to work."

We soon determined by the signal that the transmitter's output was weak. The problem was either in the transmitter or the aerial.

"Have you checked out the other SAMIR transmitter?" I asked Levy.

"The other is in Paul's possession." His look was one of astonishment at my ignorance of the fact. All I knew was that Motke had mentioned two SAMIRs and a Zenith portable radio for powering them.

"Where's the Zenith?" I asked.

"Paul has that, too," Levy said. "But I can get it from him."

"How can you? He's in Europe."

"Robert, you are mistaken. Paul returned before you got here."

There is no word to describe my consternation and anger. Dr. Moussa "Paul" Marzouk had been the subject of a conversation between Motke and me. Paul had demanded that he be allowed to head the network in

Egypt and, when Motke refused, had threatened to take steps in retaliation. All I could think of now was Motke's promise to me that Marzouk would not be allowed in Egypt after his threats.

I hid my frustration. "Then get it first thing!" I said. But right now we would have to use the transmitter and radio we had on hand.

On schedule Levy sent out our call signal and, pausing, transmitted our ciphered message. He was good, completing the transmission quickly. The briefer the time on the air, the less opportunity detection equipment would have of zeroing in on our transmitter.

Switching over to the prearranged wavelength and frequency, we waited for BASE's answer. Levy tuned the old wood-cabinet radio, slowly moving the indicator back and forth across the band. Suddenly faint, high-pitched dots and dashes came through the radio speaker. Then it stopped dead. Levy had caught only the end of it, but that was enough. Communication was established. We could go ahead with the operation.

Chapter 13

On July 2 at 11:00 A.M., without Levy or Nathanson's knowledge, I observed their approach to Alexandria's general post office. Street activity was routine as they disappeared inside, each with a parcel in hand, each calm and purposeful. A few minutes later they reappeared without the parcels, and they walked out of sight. Nice and easy. The target I'd selected was a guaranteed success, a good beginning for them.

I was having coffee after lunch at Theo's when the sound of fire trucks racing downtown along Sultan Hussaine Boulevard catapulted Clemence, the six year old, to the window.

"Four fire trucks!" he exclaimed.

Four trucks from this part of town meant that more would answer the alarm from other stations. Shortly I excused myself to go into town. Clemence, always ready for a ride, went with me.

The thoroughfare leading to the post office had been cordoned off. It teemed with firefighting apparatus, firemen, police, and spectators. Parking, I took Clemence by the hand and mingled with the spectators surrounding the post office entrance.

Words of excitement darted about us. "Bombs! Post office! How many? Man bleeding! Postal workers! Move back! Ambulance! Communists! *Yuchra Bayetcoum!* (Their homes be eradicated!)" Black smoke lingering in the still air revealed the work that the potassium and sulfuric acid incendiary bombs had done.

Later in the evening a jubilant Levy gave me his account. After reconnoitering the post office, he and Nathanson had sandwiched the incendiaries between two rectangular cardboard plates, which slid easily through the mail-chute slot.

"Everything went off without a hitch!" he exclaimed, overwhelmed with his success. I had to bring him down.

"The target was a pushover, Pierre; the police were asleep. Next time will be more dangerous." He sobered immediately.

Days later part of the post office still was closed. Nothing had appeared in the newspapers or on radio. Strict censorship was withholding all inciting news from the populace, the radicals, and the world.

Levy had the responsibility of apprising headquarters of the action by letter as well as by wireless. He didn't know it, but I would also inform headquarters by mail. I urged him to pressure Meir Meyouchas to return the 500 Egyptian pounds or face whatever action was necessary to collect it. Azar was still a reluctant participant, even after his agreement. "He's willing to help in every way except carrying out the action," Levy said. "I think it's only a matter of convincing him, Robert. He's afraid, that's all."

"You know him, I don't," I said, accepting Levy's evaluation. I would have to talk further with Azar.

Dinner honoring the Bechtoldsheims' departure, after two years in Egypt, was at the home of Melki Keludian and his wife. Melki's daughter, Nina, and her husband, Hannes Zenker, a German, were there. The Keludians were wealthy, influential Armenians of long residency in Egypt who had befriended the Bechtoldsheims. The evening was sadly festive; we all were losing good friends. I did have mixed emotions, however, since Theo was on my elimination list.

Engel had company at his home in Cairo, but he excused himself to hear what had transpired with Professor von Karaman in Paris and Herr Somerville in Rotterdam. Pleased, he then asked me about Count de Lavison.

"I can't say just yet, Herr Engel. I'm waiting for word from friends to substantiate your suspicions. It may take a week or more." The incriminating letters from Benjamin Rottem were not yet en route.

Engel was disappointed. "The moment you have something, please let me know at once."

I drove to army general headquarters to pick up Fahrmbacher, very much aware that the general was *carrot* on the elimination list. I waited at the gate. Shortly the general came toward me with two armed soldiers aheel, their fingers literally on the trigger. My heart leaped in my throat. Fahrmbacher *never* went escorted!

I fired up the engine, shifted into gear, and had my foot on the clutch when he lowered his head into the window. One wrong word and I was taking his head with me.

"It's good to see you again, Paul," he said, climbing in. He saw me staring at the soldiers. "For my protection." His laugh was strained. "The Egyptians claim they received information that the Jews want to kill me."

A bolt of cold fear shot up my spine. "Kill you!" I stammered. "Why would they want to kill you?"

"Because I am training the Egyptians, I imagine." He slapped my shoulder. "But with you, old fox, I am safe." I managed a grin. "I'm leaving my watchdogs behind." He motioned his escort back into the compound.

"Are you sure, Herr General, the Egyptians aren't exaggerating?"

Fahrmbacher sighed; he seemed to be under great strain. "Not this time, I'm afraid. They have definite information."

And at this moment he rides with his executioner! How had the Egyptians gotten the information? So far as I knew, Motke and I were the only ones outside Israel who knew about the elimination list. There had to be a leak. But who?

Levy was prompt; he had sent someone to Cairo for the second SAMIR transmitter and Zenith portable radio in Marzouk's possession. I asked, "Were there any problems getting the gear from him?"

"None," Levy said. "But the transmitter doesn't operate any better than the one we had; both are too weak. We only get three-by-three of the maximum five-by-five output."

There was no alternative but to return to the dummy studio. The difficulties with the transmitter proved simple. The radio off which the wireless operated was connected to the master aerial atop the building; this diminished our transmission energy. In exploring the situation, we discovered that we risked detection; the high-pitched dots and dashes pushing along the master aerial overlapped regular radio broadcasting. Any sharp-eared radio listener in the building could quickly discern them as Morse code. We would have to erect our own aerial.

Alternating transmitting sites, to offset any chance of police detection, meant that Levy would have to transmit from his home until the antenna was erected, in order to maintain the schedule established with BASE. I had insisted that we stick strictly to the schedule, two or three times weekly, alternating the hour and location, with no night transmissions after the day's air traffic had ceased. Levy had hollowed out a niche in a thick dictionary for transporting the tiny wireless.

Even if we'd had the antenna, the old radio lacked the band spread to pick up the frequencies on which BASE transmitted. Theo's Hallicrafters, which he'd tried to sell me, would be the ideal receiver. And I had it in my possession the day I stood with Theo and Ruth on the fantail of the SS *Enotria,* awaiting Admiral Azzazat's arrival for the sailing lunch honoring Theo's service to the Egyptian navy.

As the admiral's staff car braked at the gangplank, and he strutted toward us with his entourage in tow, I calculated the possibilities of killing him. I saw the difficulties; this man was never alone.

Lunch was correctly social. On leaving the admiral suggested that if I ran into problems with the procurement staff, I was to let him know.

Saying goodbye to Theo, Ruth, and the boys was awkward, as most sailing farewells are. I settled for a kiss from Ruth and a firm, silent handshake from Theo. It would do for now; their home in Germany would be mine as well.

With Theo's Hallicrafter and Ruth's painting easel (for Azar's studio) tucked in the car trunk, I went to a meeting with the president of the Misr Bank, a quite paradoxical affair. In Vienna Hans Schneider had introduced me to Dr. P. Schwilly, the executive director of a Swiss consortium, who asked me to negotiate with the Misr Bank on the collateral the bank was putting up for a loan. The paradox was the international Jewish money behind the investment group. Thinking of millions of dollars of Jewish funds being pumped into the industrialization of Israel's bitterest enemy unnerved me.

I visited the Keludians and mentioned giving up my flat in Cairo.

"Don't rush into taking another," Melki Keludian injected. "My partner's flat in Cairo is available for at least a fortnight."

It sounded ideal. If something went wrong, another location might shield me should the authorities get on my tail. I thanked him.

I was getting to know Shmuel Azar better. Waiting outside an electrical supply store while he bought aerial wire and a battery for the Zenith portable, I began to understand his reluctance. Azar was an intellectual, an introvert *in extremis;* his conflict was one of loyalty. As a Jew he offered himself to his people and Israel; as an Egyptian, he was bound morally to the land. I had sensed his pride of country when he told me that, as a student at the French-Egyptian gymnasium, he had been chosen to represent his school in the National Student Committee for Egypt's independence. Law of the blood split by the law of the land. What a conflict!

He had some interesting observations on the potential effect of our sabotage. Historically, he explained, each time the British and Egyptian governments reached the verge of an agreement over British withdrawal, pandemonium would break loose in the streets. Britain would sever negotiations on the claim that the Egyptian government did not represent the people, for it was unable to maintain order. Further, who would guarantee that the signatory government would be around next year to honor the agreement? Who would guarantee the safety of aliens or British subjects? Now I understood headquarters' reasoning. *Israel was only using Britain's thought process.*

Later in the day Levy gave me Meyouchas's retort to our demand for the 500 Egyptian pounds; if we bothered him again, we would have reason to fear him. Suddenly it was not the 500 pounds at issue, it was the danger to everyone.

"Arrange a meeting with Meyouchas for me." Levy's eyes demanded some explanation of my intentions. "I'll give him one last chance." But the swiftness of events made that decision impossible.

I gave the Hallicrafters and easel to Levy for delivery to the studio—telling him there was no chance of erecting a new aerial without gaining entrance to the premises above the studio, which would be a matter of suicide.

"BASE will simply have to strain its ears until we can find another solution."

On my return to Cairo from Alexandria, Nina and Hannes Zenker rode with me back to their flat. I moved out of my flat, dumped my belongings into the trunk of the Plymouth, and went to Fahrmbacher's house. Since the Voice of Israel's broadcast hour came during our lunch, I had to get to my car radio.

"My wallet is missing," I said. "It must have fallen out in the car seat. Please excuse me!"

"By all means," Frau Fahrmbacher agreed. "Go! Thieves around here are like magpies."

I rushed to the car, going through the motions of searching for the wallet, catching the Hebrew voice: *" . . . and here is the answer for Mrs. Sarchi. To improve the coffee party, add English cake or some cake of that sort. And everybody will praise you for it."* Then shortly the repeat: *"And as I have advised you, Mrs. Sarchi, don't forget to add the English cake, and your party will be a success."*

Loud and clear, home base! I read you five by five. *An English target or target of that sort. English or American.* My choice.

I shut off the radio, warmed by the word *add* spoken twice in the message. *Add* meant that BASE had received Levy's transmission of our firebombing of the post office and that we should strike *again.*

I encoded this information in my diary: "message received, 9 July."

I rode back to Alexandria with Melki, his wife, and the Zenkers. We went to the Keludians' seaside bungalow at Agami, a resort area ten miles west of the port city. Alone on the beach at noon, I listened again to "Program for the Housewife." I was taut with anxiety, wondering when the order would come to kill someone, who he would be, and if I would live beyond that act. My toes bit into the sand as the female announcer came to the message for Mrs. Sarchi. A repeat of yesterday's. I rolled onto my back, letting the tension drain from my body. Thank God! No word on *carrot* or *radish* or any of them.

The last days had been hectic, filled more with worry than activity. In the afternoon, stretched out on the sundeck with Hannes and Nina, I forgot the fixed realities—where death followed the slightest mistake. Later, in my diary, I entered the second radio message received, dated July 10.

I told Levy that on July 14 we would strike the U.S. Information Service libraries in both Alexandria and Cairo. Carrying out simultaneous strikes would point to a widespread terror organization (such as the Moslem Brotherhood or the Communists).

"Now what about Jacques (Azar)?" I asked. "Has he made up his mind yet?"

"No, but we can count on Roger (Dassa)," Levy said.

"Good. But press Jacques. We need him." Since my pep talk at the studio, I was certain of Dassa. I now had three people. I needed Azar. "Whoever handles the action in Alexandria will include the Ramla District streetcar terminal," I added.

"I don't think we can, Robert. We don't have enough acid."

I looked at Levy in disbelief. Not enough acid to make *three* incendiaries? Inwardly I cursed Motke for misinforming me and, worse, for not sending us a new supply. I had heard *nothing* from headquarters regarding either the explosives or the escape passports for my people.

Israel, according to Motke's urgent briefing, was in jeopardy dire enough to embark on a plan aimed at sabotaging the West's Middle East policies, yet I was given no tools to work with. My chagrin bit deep.

"Forget the streetcar terminal," I said, trying to hide my bitterness. "We'll hit the two U.S. Information libraries. We'll give the Americans a dose of it!"

A few days later I met Levy and Nathanson. As planned Levy had brought Nathanson to Cairo to reconnoiter the library together in case either of them had to initiate the action in Alexandria with Dassa. Azar was still a big, fat question mark.

I gave them a fast briefing on how we would case the library in the American embassy compound. Parting, we agreed to enter an hour before closing. When the time came, I watched as they entered the heavy wrought-iron gate on Scheich Brachat Street. They passed the Egyptian police guard and were already in the library when I reached the second guard, posted in the lobby. Levy, I noticed, had deposited his briefcase with the guard as requested by a sign on the desk.

Two women librarians hardly glanced up as I walked among the shelves. From the corner of my eye, I saw Levy and Nathanson watching me. I took out a book, marking the spot to plant an incendiary, then shoved the book back in. Levy came around after I'd moved on, confirming the place. At the door of the film library off the main room, I caught Levy's attention. He nodded: Plant the other incendiary close to the film library. Film is a volatile fuel for any fire.

I'd already figured out that the best way to slip the incendiaries past the lobby guard was in one of the most common sights in Egypt: a spectacle case. Everybody wears sunglasses in summer, and everybody carries a case.

But our shortage of incendiary ingredients, especially sulfuric acid, was a recurring problem. What HQ had told me at the outset of my mission, I had learned, was not the case. Explosive ingredients could not be purchased openly at local pharmacies or chemical houses. I had already tried. Each purchase meant having to identify oneself. The authorities routinely checked such purchase ledgers. Thwarted, we had to locate another source. The question was where.

Since the Bechtoldsheims' departure, the Keludians had taken over my social welfare. At the Semiramis Hotel one night, Melki had introduced me to various local personalities for whom the Semiramis had become something of a replacement for the royal court that Nasser's junta had struck down. One was the former Princess Farida, Farouk's sister; another, a former minister of commerce. So it went. Everybody was an ex-something, and all of them potentially valuable to me.

On the evening of the thirteenth, after I'd reconnoitered the library in preparation for tomorrow's action, Melki insisted on squiring me about town. We wound up at Cairo's most famous nightclub, the Auberge Pyramid. A man of considerable influence, Melki was accosted frequently by acquaintances, who bombarded us with drinks.

At midnight an alarm sounded in my head: *Somebody was watching me.* I could feel eyes on my back. Melki was a blur as he tried to convince me to invest in his import-export business. Excusing myself to go to the rest room, I scanned the room.

"Good evening, Mr. Frank. Nice seeing you."

It was the head of Egyptian internal security, Zacharia Mohieddin. "Would you care to join us?" The two men with him were unknown to me.

"Thank you, but I'm the guest of Herr Melki Keludian."

"Of course." Mohieddin cast an appraising glance at Keludian who looked at that moment like a former habitué of Farouk's royal court. "How is business? Good, I hope."

"Slow at the moment, Herr Minister, but I'm optimistic."

"No doubt you will succeed," Mohieddin replied with a sly grin. (From your mouth to Allah's ear, I mused.) "But you can always work for us. I have been told you are a good man to have around."

"Again I'm honored, Herr Minister. However, I haven't changed my mind. In any case, thank you again for your offer."

I continued on to the rest room. His offer was intriguing and the stakes high. In fact, so high that I had already queried headquarters. Again, no word.

The last show had just started when I returned to the table, the audience rapturously watching the writhing belly dancer. The puritanical nationalism of the junta had veiled her traditionally bared midriff. I glanced at Mohieddin's table; it was empty. Herr Minister had to set an example.

Tension was getting the better of me by the early afternoon of the fourteenth. As usual the bus from Alexandria was late. When I saw Levy and Nathanson step down together, I breathed easier; even more so when they left the parcel of chemicals with me.

Arranging to meet them again at 5:00 P.M. I sent them off to a movie, went back to the car, parked in front of the Egyptian automobile club, deposited the parcel of explosive chemicals under the seat, and applied myself to deciding where to assemble the devices. Renting a hotel room was out of the question, as was taking Levy and Nathanson to my temporary flat. Doing it in the car, which they might be able to identify later, was against every warning in my nerve ends. But so was not hitting the targets.

At five of five, I cruised past the American embassy and USIS Library. Everything was normal: the usual in-and-out traffic, the guard at the gate, routine police patrols near the compound. Parking on Suliman Pasha, I went to meet the waiting Levy and Nathanson and led them back to the car.

"Hop in! Quick!" The way I had wedged the car in, they had no chance of seeing the license plates. At a spot near the Nile, watching the graceful *feluccas* sailing up and down its placid length, I kept a lookout while they prepared the incendiaries, placing a plastic bag of potassium chlorate in each spectacle case, then placing a condom filled with sulfuric acid on top of the potassium. It would take two or three hours for the acid to eat through the rubber and reach the potassium, causing a high-intensity ignition; by then the library would be abandoned for the night.

I dropped Levy and Nathanson off at Liberation Square, each with a spectacle case in his shirt pocket. They were brave but now brutally aware that this was no longer child's play. I looked past their anxious smiles into the dark sunglasses hiding their furtive eyes.

"Good luck," I said, wishing I were planting the incendiaries. To make sure they left the library safely, I drove around several blocks and nearly missed their exit. At the far end of the street Nathanson patted Levy on the back.

Mission accomplished. I thought of Dassa and Azar taking simultaneous action at the Alexandria USIS Library. But it was no time for accolades.

That evening distance screened those of us at Gerhard Merten's house in Heliopolis from the sound of bells clanging through the city in answer to the fire alarm. I was jolted from my preoccupation, however, when Mertens informed me that my car had been observed at the British Naval Attaché in Alexandria during my first return to Europe, when Theo Bechtoldsheim had my car. Mertens told me outright that Theo was known to have close contact with the British. This explained much about why his contract was canceled.

Leaving Mertens late, I detoured to get a glimpse of the library. The street leading past the embassy compound was cordoned off. Security forces were evident in plain clothes, late as it was. Two armored cars stood alongside the fire brigade. The police were anticipating violence.

Though I had no idea of the outcome of the Alexandria action, I left for the Semiramis and another drink, humming old German army songs. Hitting American property would give Dulles and his cronies something to think about. Nasser, too.

Engel was ecstatic that I had discovered that Count de Lavison's liaison in Italy was a man named Bass, a man allied with the Jews. The letters had to be en route by now.

"There's no time to lose!" He sprang to the door. "Now I can report this to army general headquarters. Let's go, Paul."

"I have a very important appointment in the city," I said, trying to extract myself from this web of my own making.

"I have to be in town, as well," he countered. "I'll ride with you and report on the way in. It won't take long."

Reluctantly I said, "Fine. As we say at home, 'We're caught together, we hang together.' "

Engel grinned, understanding the comradeship of accomplices. On the way I mentioned offhandedly that if I were investigating the case I would take careful note of de Lavison's correspondence, especially that coming and going to Italy.

"Excellent," Engel said. "Thank you."

We were escorted into a building separate from that housing Fahrmbacher's office, where a colonel absorbed Engel's brief appraisal noncommittally. "Are you certain, Mr. Engel?" he said at length. "This is a very serious accusation."

"I've told you what I know, colonel. Herr Frank will bear me out. Suspicion is *never* certain. My job is to report it, yours is to substantiate it."

The colonel moved past Engel's chair, then hesitated. "Your problem may be somewhat out of my area. Excuse me." When he returned, he said he was sending us to military intelligence headquarters and Col. Osman Nouri.

A nondescript building on the road to Heliopolis turned out to be the headquarters. Inside it was a fortress. Col. Osman Nouri, a career officer Fahrmbacher had once presented to me as his liaison to the Egyptian general staff, was now deputy head of military intelligence. He was flanked by a captain and another colonel. Engel, unaware of my prior encounter with Nouri, made the introductions.

"Herr Frank and I have already had the pleasure," Nouri said, offering his hand. "How is business these days, Herr Frank?"

Amused at Engel's mildly surprised reaction, I said, "It couldn't be better, colonel. And you?"

"Our usual problems," he smiled, sitting on the edge of his desk. "What can I do for you gentlemen?"

Engel related his suspicions about de Lavison and what I'd learned in Europe. "I elicited Frank's aid because of his wartime experiences," he added.

Nouri's smile was complimentary. "Yes, we are aware of Herr Frank's exploits."

When Engel spoke the name Bass, Nouri whispered something to the captain who left and returned as Engel was finishing. The captain said to Nouri, "His name is known to us." Nouri nodded. "We will investigate the matter, Herr Engel."

"Thank you, colonel."

He took from Engel the particulars on CERVA and de Lavison. "Herr Frank, if you by any chance have a minute sometime, please call me." He handed me his card.

"I will, colonel. Thanks for your time."

Outside, Engel made no effort to hide his surprise at Nouri's familiarity with my record. "Colonel Nouri is a very powerful man, you know," he said. "He is right under the wing of Interior Minister Mohieddin."

"Mohieddin once offered me a job with his security forces. Nouri is following up, I imagine."

Engel bestowed one of his rare smiles on me. "Just remember, Paul, I have first option on your services."

Engel's next destination was the American embassy, which was back to back with the USIS Library. I stole a glance at Engel. Was he luring me? First to military intelligence headquarters, now to the scene of our crime committed only eighteen hours ago. If he was setting me up, he was doing it beautifully.

"Why not?" I said. "I'm already late for my appointment."

"You might find it interesting."

Leading the way to the office of the military attaché, Engel entered without knocking. The office, like the corridor, was jammed with trunks, filing cabinets, and heavy crates. Several men and a couple of secretaries were sorting out a huge stack of files heaped on the floor. New steel cabinets were obviously replacing the wooden ones. An American, small and with a crew cut, greeted Engel.

"What's this, Colonel Evans?" Engel said.

"Forgive our housekeeping, Mr. Engel, but as you can see, we've had quite a disruption here."

Another American, also in mufti, came around. Colonel Evans presented Colonel Ebert, who was replacing him as military air attaché.

Engel, introducing me as "the man entrusted with the messages to Somerville [regarding the Matador missile project] and to von Karaman, the professor in Paris," revealed to me that he was dealing with the Americans. I wondered if the Egyptians were aware of it.

Engel asked Colonel Ebert if he was moving the office now that he was taking over. Both Evans and Ebert laughed heartily.

"Oh, no," Ebert said. "We had a fire last night. The Communists are up to their old tricks." He indicated the back wall, which had been cleared of filing cabinets. "We're wall to wall with the library and film room. Somebody planted a bomb. No damage in here, but we decided to store our documents in steel cabinets from now on."

Colonel Evans surveyed the disarray. "Whoever did the job here and in Alexandria did good work!"

"In Alexandria, too?" Engel said. "I've heard nothing of it."

"Naturally. It's being kept from the public."

"Ah, politics," Engel mused.

Engel further confirmed his collusion with the Americans when he set a time to talk further the next day. Colonel Ebert, at our departure, invited me to have coffee with him anytime. (I would see Ebert again half a year later in Munich.)

Alexandria might have been under martial law, so thick were the police and armed soldiers on every corner and in front of public buildings. I toured the area of the USIS Library on Rue Fuad. Most important to me was the fact that Azar had acted with Dassa. I now had *four* men with which to undermine the Middle East politics of America and Britain!

Chapter 14

The next strike I planned for the evening of July 22, the onset of forty-odd hours of continuous celebration commemorating the overthrow of the monarchy. Beginning with the fireworks, Egypt's populace would be in the streets throughout the night and the following day.

In a cast-iron mailbox, in the center of a great square where the huge rally was planned for Alexandria, I intended to plant dynamite. Fragmenting the mailbox into countless deadly missiles, the makeshift grenade would fell or maim scores of people.

I apprised Levy of my plan.

"But we have no explosives!" he cried.

"I'll try to come up with some." I knew where they'd come from: the bunker storing CERVA's explosives at the testing ground. "What's the situation with acid. Have you found a source?"

"We're dry as the desert, but Jacques is trying."

"Keep him at it."

Alone in Cairo, I was worried. BASE was silent. If they were responding by wireless, we were unable to pick up their frequency. Of equal concern was the absence of any mail at all. Had I been detected by censorship? Dozens of questions forced me to drop in unannounced on Col. Osman Nouri at military intelligence headquarters.

The duty officer said that the colonel would see me shortly. As I waited, anxiety grew into fear. I might be setting up my own arrest; I was an Israeli saboteur. Suddenly every movement around me was threatening, every gesture a signal. The feeling was almost unbearable. Finally a sergeant came and led me to Nouri's office.

"Good to see you, Herr Frank. I assume," he said, "you've come to discuss placing your expertise at our service."

What a relief to be able to smile. "Sorry, not this time, colonel. I came to enlist your help."

"My help! What could I possibly do for you?"

"I think censorship is holding my mail for some unexplained reason." I displayed my concern. "There are samples coming for Admiral Azzazat, and Dr. Rolf Engel as well."

"Have you approached the admiral?"

"I didn't want to bother him. I'm sure he has more important things to do. . . ."

"And not I?" Colonel Nouri grinned.

I laughed. "Not that at all. I merely feel more at home with intelligence than the navy. I did go to General Fahrmbacher. He directed me to you."

"I'm glad you came. Give me a minute to see what can be done."

Nouri left the room. I stayed in my seat, wary of Nouri's professional suspiciousness. He'd already baited me by deftly placing a ruler across some pages on his desk, daring it to be touched. Professional habit? Clever.

On a bookshelf to my left were lines of books, most of them dealing with Israel. My eyes wandered along the titles. Suddenly two of them stopped me cold: albums of the Palmach and Haganah!

In the Palmach album was a group picture of the Palmach's "German Platoon"—*and the face in the first row, third from the end, was mine, clearly recognizable!*

Nouri returned before I'd completely recovered, his eyes scanning his desk. "I've checked," he said. "Provided your mail was received in Egypt, you will get it right away. It has been sent, no question of that." When I expressed my gratitude, he again brought up my employment with Egyptian security.

While declining his offer again, I fed my curiosity. "In what capacity do you see me serving?"

"Your experience is invaluable, Herr Frank. We also know of your understanding of Arabic and Hebrew. In an advisory capacity, I would imagine."

A hell of an opening, I thought, but still up to headquarters.

In my mail the next day were parcels of samples and brochures from Hans Schneider, several letters from Faust and Stollberg—and nothing from headquarters except a postcard from Shlomo, giving me none of the answers I so badly needed.

We had to have sulfuric acid. Without it, no incendiaries. The celebration was just around the corner.

Late that night I drove out to CERVA's testing ground, nerves tuned only to my objective. Parking outside the compound, I made my way to the dimly lighted barbed wire enclosure. The jeep patrol was elsewhere at the moment. Its absence made me even more edgy.

Time. Do it. I bellied under the lowest wire and in a crouched dash quickly reached the wall beside the door of the bunker housing CERVA's explosives. I flattened against it, my heart slamming in my ears. With a wedge I snapped the padlock, the sound cracking the quiet night like a rifle. I was inside. I closed the door behind me.

My eyes were filled with pitch black; my ears rang with my pounding blood and the sound of my breathing. Coming without a flashlight was a mistake, but I had been here before with Engel; the bunker was only room-size. Reassured I moved forward with my hands out before me. I had to get explosives and get out. Urgency drove me in the blackness. I reached down and, groping blindly, discovered a wooden crate, its top loose. I lifted it, my hand exploring gingerly and closing on a familiar object. A British Mils hand grenade; I had thrown enough to know one, even in darkness. I stuck it in my pocket.

I moved to my left, blind as a bat without sonar. I groped for another crate and moved my fingers over oiled cloth. TNT wrappings! Several bricks of TNT lined half the box. Quickly I took one and turned back toward the vertical stripe of near-light that marked the door. The weight of the TNT package in my hand brought a mental picture of the exploding cast-iron mailbox in Alexandria, and the felled humans.

I eased the door open, scanned the compound, and stepped out, resnapping the padlock.

Halfway to the fence in my running crouch, I was blinded by a pair of headlights. I dived, scurrying back to the bunker steps. The grenade in my pocket, the TNT in my hand, and the jeep coming toward me—I could think only of escape.

The lights of the jeep danced. On it came, then swerved sending its three riders on through the night. I watched the red glow of the taillight move away. Jumping to my feet, I raced for my car.

As I drove away from the danger, my logic returned. The TNT brick demanded a detonating primer that I didn't have. But by the time I'd reached town, I'd thought of a method for detonating the TNT without a primer: the hand grenade.

I would wrap the TNT brick for mailing. After dropping it in the mailbox, I would drop the hand grenade, the pin half-pulled, and dangle a cord attached to the pin outside the mail chute. Here I counted on human curiosity. There had to be dozens who would tug on the cord. All it took was one.

When I arrived in Alexandria, Levy had good news. Azar had lifted a tiny bottle of sulfuric acid from the laboratory of the technical school where he taught part time. It was enough to construct incendiaries for two movie houses in Alexandria and the two in Cairo, plus the luggage storeroom at the main railway terminal. Planting the TNT brick in the mailbox on the twenty-third was my job.

One fact gnawed at me. *Had Azar not taken the acid, and I the TNT brick, we would have missed the perfect strike. Where was headquarters? They had assessed the importance of this.* I couldn't figure it.

The Zenkers and Keludians invited me to one of the better restaurants for dinner. Afterward Melki asked when I might be returning to Germany again; his wife had to go to Bad Kissingen, a thermal spa for medical treatment, but she was afraid to fly alone.

"As you know, Herr Keludian, in business one never knows. One day no, the next day yes. But soon, I think."

"Good," he said. "Please let us know."

"All I need is forty-eight hours' notice, Paul," Frau Keludian said in her gentle fashion. (Within three weeks, I would fly with her out of Egypt to safety.)

On July 22 I passed Cairo's Radio and Rivoli movie houses and checked their evening schedules. Later, after Dassa, Azar, and I had reconnoitered the cinemas, I advised them to exercise extreme caution in carrying out the sabotage and then to return to Alexandria separately. Since it was the anniversary of the revolution, every policeman and militiaman in Egypt would be on duty; every radical in the country was a potential threat beginning tonight.

At dusk Egypt flashed into festivity. Cairo was hot and dry. Loudspeakers blared shrilly, car engines raced, horns honked incessantly, laughter screeched everywhere. It all reached us in Hannes and Nina Zenker's high-rise flat in midcity. While they complained of the noise, my thoughts were with Dassa and Azar down below, braving the streets and the omnipresent police, depositing the incendiary suitcase at the train station and with Levy and Nathanson, wading through the Alexandria melange, slitting theater seats in balcony and mezzanine, inserting the spectacle cases.

Nina wanted to ride to the Nile shores and watch the fireworks. My watch read nine o'clock. One or all of the theaters should be on fire by now.

The streets were jammed. I steered along Suliman Pasha, following the flow of traffic toward the Radio Theatre. But the street was blocked by the fire brigade and police vehicles. Blue smoke was pouring from the Radio's entrance.

"Arson," Zenker said.

I glanced at him, surprised. Hannes had always been detached from political events. "What makes you think arson?"

"What else could it be? Haven't you heard? The Communists and the Moslem Brotherhood are on the warpath again. Everybody is talking about it. It's everywhere, even in the small towns."

"I haven't seen anything in the papers about it."

"Of course! They only write what the junta wants the people to hear. They're very careful to hide it from foreign consumption."

At the Nile, unable to find a parking space, we drove to the Mena House near the El Giza pyramids and from its veranda watched fireworks against Cairo's cloudless, blue night sky.

Going back to their flat, I drove past the Rivoli. No fire damage, but the presence of policemen at the entrance told me that the action had been carried out.

At midnight we settled down, anticipating our dawn drive to Alexandria. From the balcony where I bunked, I could hear the clang of fire-engine bells racing in the direction of the railway terminal. *Dassa and Azar had hit their third and last target.* I slept not at all.

Alexandria was asleep at seven-thirty in the morning, grabbing a few hours' rest before resuming the celebration. The sidewalks and streets were littered from the night-long party. Dropping the Zenkers at the Keludians', I passed the Metro Theatre, Levy and Nathanson's target, expecting to see evidence of fire and confusion.

Everything was normal, not a policeman in sight. It was disturbing. Could the conscientious Levy have abandoned the strike?

At 9:50 I was posted for our ten o'clock rendezvous. Fifteen minutes later, still no Levy. Enough time remained for me to make the alternate rendezvous; he didn't show there either.

I raced to the studio on Rue Hospital. From the street I checked the window shade. Pulled to the middle of the window, it indicated all clear. Controlling my dread, I gave the building a half-hour watch, then climbed the stairs. The quiet told me that nobody was inside. Back down in the lobby, I slid a note into the mailbox: "Meet me at 3:00." Levy would know where. Invisible bloodhounds were baying in voices only I could hear.

At the Keludians, while they conversed on trivia my head spun in growing anxiety. I soon left.

Three-thirty. No Levy. Nor had he picked up the note.

A danger bell began to sound in my mind. The city had once again come to life; now was not the time to plant the TNT brick in the mailbox.

Up the street a familiar figure popped into sight. Azar. I stepped out, motioning to him.

"When did you return from Cairo?" I asked.

"Last night, after we planted the incendiary at the railway station."

Good man! "Have you seen Pierre?"

"He was to meet me this morning, but he didn't make it. I was going to the studio to give him my report."

Careful not to infect Azar with my alarm, I said, "Yes. And we need their report. How soon could you contact Henri (Nathanson)?"

"An hour—maybe more."

"I'll stay here. Get back as quickly as you can."

"You don't think something happened, do you?"

"Probably not, but we can't take any chances. And don't contact Henri yourself; have a friend do it."

Minutes dragged like hours.

Every fiber in Azar's body seemed afire when he came back.

"Nathanson has been arrested, Robert! A friend at the Jewish community center told me the incendiary exploded in his pocket. When he came running out of the Rio, the police got him. He's in the hospital now, badly burned."

Hot fear swept me. The police had Nathanson. The first bowling pin! All I could see were the others, falling with him.

"Pierre has to be warned. Where does he live?"

"I don't know."

"Find out! And be back here by nine. Do you have a key to the studio?"

"It's at home."

"Go get it. Go, man! There's no time to waste."

Azar disappeared into a growing crowd.

When darkness fell, I hurried to the back of the building and checked the drainage pipe that ran up the wall, thinking it might hold my weight; but I dismissed the idea. If anyone saw me, the police would be all over me. I went back to the street, watching, waiting, my mind racing. Nathanson captured, Levy gone. I had to empty that studio!

Azar returned, wobbly with fright.

"Levy was arrested entering his house!" he exclaimed.

My mind filled with the beginnings of catastrophe. Two down! "Did they find anything on him?"

"He had his briefcase, I think."

"Pray to God the transmitters are in the studio! Did you bring the key?"

A frantic smile touched Azar's face. "I had it on me all the time."

I had no thought of rebuke, only of getting upstairs. The police would know about the studio soon enough. But Azar's hesitation was clear. He was terrified.

"Don't be afraid. I've had the house under observation all day." Azar wasn't convinced. I tried another tactic, drawing on my hints to Levy and the others all along; that their cell was only one of a larger network strategically located throughout Egypt. "See that man across the street?" I pointed out an innocent bystander. "He's one of ours. The building is covered by our people. They're standing by." Finally, in angry desperation, I told him to come along or forget it.

"I'll go with you, Robert."

We made it into the empty studio. I took a second to gather my wits. First things first. I lowered the shade, blocking out the city. Azar produced a candle, adding a ghostly aura to our fear. Above the window was secreted one of the SAMIR transmitters; the other we couldn't find. Levy must have taken it home in the hollowed-out dictionary. Probably the police had it.

"Is there someone reliable who can approach Levy's parents to see about the SAMIR?"

"I'll see a friend and have him tell Levy's sister what to do," Azar said.

In a few minutes the studio was clean. Meticulously I scoured every cranny. In a hollowed-out *slik* atop the closet door, I found money, old letters from headquarters that should have been destroyed, and an old transmitting schedule. I burned everything flammable and flushed the ashes down the toilet. Azar gathered up what I couldn't take. We left.

Ordering Azar to dump everything he carried into the sea, I parted from him. I immediately drove to the Cornish and dumped all except the SAMIR, Morse key, and crystals. Headquarters had to be alerted in case they had a contingency plan for just such an emergency. But I didn't know if BASE would be listening in except at scheduled transmission time. With Levy captured, even wireless contact was risky. The authorities might have taken our wavelength and frequencies from him.

I flagged down the first taxi and went directly to the Marconi telegraph office. I handed the clerk a telegram that read: "Pierre and company went bankrupt. I'll remain here to save whatever can be salvaged of our investment. Please advise. Signed, Reli (This was a pet nickname for my son, which Motke and Shlomo knew)." The telegram was directed to an emergency address in Vienna.

At Hotel Cecil I asked for my room key, anticipating plainclothesmen stepping out for the arrest. Since early morning—when Levy had failed to show—in every person, movement, or dark corner, I saw an ogre crouched to spring on me. The desk clerk handed over a message from Melki Keludian. They were awaiting me at their home.

In my room I transferred the transmitting equipment from the bag to the guts of the Zenith portable. I might have breathed easier had not I thought of the car. Levy and Nathanson could identify it even without the license number. How many green 1952 Plymouth convertibles were there in the whole damned country? I took a taxi to the Keludian home, telling them that my car was going into the garage the next morning. Melki offered me his second car, a Chevrolet, for a few days.

"By the way, if my present deal goes through, I'll be traveling to Germany on short notice. Soon." I chuckled. "Keep it under your hat. I don't want my competition to smell out potential negotiations."

The anniversary celebration was fading when the Zenkers dropped me off at the hotel. In my room I looked out on the now quiet city, my mind filled with thoughts of Levy and Nathanson and with the threat of what *had* to follow.

Courtesy of Reuters News Agency, the morning news was on the lobby teleprinter. Not a word on the arrest of Levy and Nathanson, nothing about the fire bombings. The silence rang clear; the hunt was on, but under wraps.

I moved to a room in a German pension across town where I had stayed before. In the event of my arrest, the German authorities would be notified by the loyal proprietors.

I felt I could buy some time by having the Plymouth painted. The local Chrysler dealer, Herr Keil, had discussed the possibility of a trade with me. We agreed on price and time, and I placed the Plymouth in his hands.

The Zenkers picked me up and we drove to Agami. I brought along the Zenith portable with the transmitting apparatus inside. In my overnight bag was the TNT brick and the hand grenade; I had missed my chance at carnage.

Nevertheless the sabotage had to continue. Striking again would, I hoped, take some of the pressure off Nathanson and Levy. Nathanson had been caught in the act, but Levy had a slim chance. I knew in my gut that neither of them could resist Egyptian interrogation methods for long.

Returning to Alexandria, with the TNT brick and hand grenade safely buried in the sand near the Keludian condominium, I picked up Melki's Chevrolet just before meeting Azar, who was verging on hysteria.

"Have you warned Dassa?" I asked.

"I don't know if he's back from Cairo."

"Find him. Set up a meeting as soon as possible."

Azar was wild-eyed. "Yes. I will!"

"Did you dump the gear in the sea? Do you need money?"

"I dumped everything like you said. No, I still have the money you gave me."

"OK, get going!"

Fear had ripped Azar apart. I hoped that Dassa, wherever he was, still retained his senses and could help me initiate another strike right away, on widely separated targets.

If he wouldn't act, by God, I would.

A business-as-usual facade was almost impossible to assume for the grand opening of the San Stefano Hotel and its nightclub. But Paul Frank was still in business! Even dancing with former Queen Narriman, King Farouk's ex-wife, did little to dispel my tension. Nor did her invitation to visit with her later in the week help. I promised to call, knowing, with regret, that the opportunity would never arise.

After sleeping the night at the Keludian home, I drove into town. The inner city was an armed camp. A state of emergency apparently had been declared overnight. At the hotel I learned why.

Several Moslem Brotherhood members had been arrested on suspicion of sabotage. Clashes had broken out between sympathizers of Naguib and Nasser. The Moslem Brotherhood had attempted to free their comrades from the local police station. In a fierce exchange of gunfire, a policeman had been killed and several wounded. A chain reaction, as predicted by Motke, had set in.

Dassa had been arrested getting off the train from Cairo. Azar was the lone survivor. And he wouldn't be free long.

"I'm smuggling you out of the country," I told him.

"How will you do it?"

"Leave the arrangements to me. Whatever you do, don't stay at home. Stay anywhere, but not home. Tomorrow we go!"

The paint shop had done nothing more than strip the Plymouth of its bumpers and chrome. The shop foreman, with typical Arab verbosity, passed the buck. "In three days it will be ready. *Inshallah.*" *God willing.* I couldn't help smiling bitterly. My case precisely.

The shop kept the car overnight to reinstall the bumpers and chrome, then I picked it up early the following morning, promising to bring it back within two days. Thirty minutes later I was ready for the long drive through the Western Desert to Libya, my planned escape route with Azar.

In Saad Zaghlul Square, he joined me on a bench.

"Aren't you taking anything?" I asked, surprised to see his hands empty.

"I can't come with you, Robert." He saw my bewilderment. "There's no real need for me to leave the country. If they knew about me, I would be under arrest already."

"Are you crazy? It's only a matter of their finding you."

Azar dropped his head. "I can't leave my mother. I am the only one she has in the world."

"She'll get along," I said, refusing to abandon him. "Sooner or later, one or all of them are going to give up. Egyptian interrogators don't wear kid gloves, not with Jews! No harm will come to your mother. They'll question her and that'll be the end of it."

"I cannot leave, Robert."

Suddenly I realized that, past his earlier terror, Azar was now reasonably calm. His decision was firm. Suspecting the seed behind it might be resignation to his fate, I pressed him to lay low for a while, somewhere out in the country. To reassure him, I lied, saying I'd mobilized all our people in Egypt and that they were standing by to kidnap Nathanson from the hospital. With kidnap in mind, I had actually managed to pass Nathanson's room at the hospital. It proved only one thing to me: There would be no kidnapping, not without a reinforced rifle company.

Azar's decision had up-ended my plans. The car was serviced for the dash to Libya, and I had geared myself psychologically. Azar's behavior nagged at me. What had happened to reverse him? He could not tell me, and conjecture had a bitter taste.

My returning the car to the Chrysler paint shop foreman the same day threw him into consternation. Keil welcomed me with more sales talk. This time he found me eager to sell the car. Keil was sure he had a buyer in tow.

Seeking release from my feeling of utter helplessness, I recalled the oil storage tanks on the road from Alexandria. In Melki's Chevrolet I drove out to Agami in the late afternoon on the pretext of picking up my Zenith portable, which I'd purposely forgotten the day I buried the hand grenade and TNT brick in the sand. I stopped on the way and purchased ingredients for a long-burning Molotov cocktail.

After digging up the hand grenade, I prepared the Molotov, then headed back toward the city. The oil storage tanks, I saw on approaching them, had a series of crisscrossing oil pipes connecting the main tanks. Leaving the engine idling, I fired the dry wick and shoved the Molotov among the pipes. I flew back to the car and sped around the bend, thankful that I hadn't been spotted.

Alexandria's suburbs came alive with fire trucks. My rearview mirror showed the sky darkening with billowing bluish-black oil smoke. The sight suddenly made me realize that I no longer counted absolutely on headquarters. It was not a matter of anger, it was simply a fact. When I needed them, they were not there. Why? But it was now clear to me that, by stealing the TNT and the sulfuric acid, we had been following their original directives without their help. I was adrift, veering this way and that as the winds of my circumstances dictated.

I stopped by the Hellenic Shipping Company and booked passage on the next ship to Italy, August 7, knowing that I would never make the sailing. If security were suspicious of me, discovering my departure date might deter their moving on me. But with the car stowed, I'd hidden myself from them very carefully. I still had time.

Back in Cairo, Engel dealt with all our business before I steered the topic around to Count de Lavison, trying to find out if the incriminating letters had been discovered by censorship. To my dismay Engel related that Colonel Nouri had found nothing in de Lavison's correspondence from Italy.

Engel's disappointment couldn't match mine. Benjamin "Bass" Rottem should have had the letters rolling three weeks ago. What was the delay?

"Could it be," I suggested, "that censorship is keeping quiet about it? After all, de Lavison is not a nobody."

"I'm on the same train of thought," Engel said, "especially in light of the arrest of the Jews. Some sort of widespread network, I've heard."

I'd already encountered dozens of rumors concerning the "widespread Jewish network," most of them way off base. Much was known but buried under secrecy.

Willi Kubie was finally up and around after nearly five weeks of confinement. In the month of my return, I had visited him periodically, keeping his hopes alive with lies about possible sales of the microfilmed rocket blueprints to European markets. He was eager to discuss the matter.

"I've received word from my friend in Europe. We may have a buyer for your material," I said. Willi became excited, already feeling the money in his pocket. "I told my friend that you wanted a guaranteed payment even if it didn't turn out to be what the buyer wanted."

"But, Paul, I never made that condition."

"I'm aware of that," I said, "but with the risk you took, the buyer should pay for a look. Let me handle it."

Willi was crestfallen. "Whatever you think, Paul." He wanted the money right now.

"Can you get more of it in case he's interested?" I asked.

"It's no problem. Let me know and I will have it ready in a few hours."

Willi had revealed all I wanted to hear. On leaving Egypt I intended taking every bit of military information I could carry.

Another diversionary tactic had taken shape in my mind. In Melki's Chevrolet, I decided to go to Alexandria via Ismailia instead of the direct desert route. It was dusk when I passed the Suez shore town. Ahead was

Camp Moaskar, the large British army installation Bob Jansen and I had mistakenly entered weeks ago on the tail end of a British escort vehicle.

I stopped and smeared the license plate with mud. Under way again, the hand grenade in my left hand and the pin pulled, I came abreast of the sentry post around the bend. Heaving the grenade, I floored the accelerator. The explosion erupted behind. Tracer bullets probed the ground alongside me until an oncoming British lorry forced them to hold their fire, all I needed to sail out of range. No British soldier was about to leave the Suez Zone, for fear of the Arab.

Safe, I cleaned the license plate and continued to Alexandria. Picayune, yes. But something.

Headquarters' silence was maddening. Surely our disappearance from the airwaves had made them take notice. It was as if we'd been abandoned. I couldn't really believe that, except in moments of exhaustion.

On the twenty-seventh England and Egypt agreed on evacuation.[1] After seven decades on Egypt's soil, the British were withdrawing from the Suez Canal—a measly meow was the only response from the English lion, as Nasser planted a heavy foot on its tail.

Egypt was ecstatic. It had achieved what it had hated, plotted, and died for: eradicating the final vestige of ancient colonialism. They were a free people at last.

Israel had failed. *We* had failed. We could sabotage every installation in Egypt now to no avail. On the horizon I heard a resounding *"Ya'ish Gamal* (Long live Gamal)!"* Nasser was a hero to his people. Nobody could bring him down. Not Israel. Not America's Dulles. Nobody.

Disdaining the risks, I dropped by the Hotel Cecil in Alexandria to check for messages. It was all I could do to stay calm when I saw Col. Osman Nouri conversing with a group of civilians. He came to me, smiling. I braced myself for the crucial encounter.

"Good to see you. I trust you're still thinking about our discussion?"

"All the time," I said, sounding as if I meant it. "What brings you to Alexandria?"

"The usual. Business."

I was certain his business concerned Levy, Nathanson, and Dassa. "Quite a show of military we have today," I said.

"Yes, Colonel Nasser is here with General Naguib. It always demands my presence in some capacity or another." Indicating the news teleprinter, he said, "Excuse me, I must catch the latest."

No messages awaited me; I drifted over to Nouri's side and watched the long sheet rolling from the machine. The only news item relating to our ac-

---

1. Documents were signed October 19, three months later.

tion read: "Egyptian Security Service has cracked a Jewish-Communist spy ring and arrested its members. As far as it has been established, the ring is responsible for recent outrages of arson and bombing. Investigations are continuing and further arrests are anticipated."

The scene was deadly ironic. Colonel Nouri, a key man in security, was standing by my side as we read of my men's arrests. I noted in the communique the hyphenation of Jews and Communists. We had established that if any of us were captured, we would claim to be Communist-inspired, disavowing any association with Israel. Levy, Nathanson, and Dassa must have stood up to it. A good diversion.

"Congratulations, Colonel Nouri, you've had quite a success," I said.

"Oh, yes. But success is not complete until we have their leader. It is only a matter of days; then it will be all over for them." His benign, confident smile got to me.

"Good hunting, colonel," I smiled cheerfully. "You have my blessings for a difficult task."

"Not so difficult." Almost as if bragging, he added, "My opposite number is giving me a hand. The end is near."

I could not believe my ears: *My opposite number is giving me a hand.* His *Israeli* opposite number? It could not be! I dismissed Nouri's claim as more Arab braggadocio. But it was so unlike him.

When Nouri had rejoined his colleagues, I went straight to the bar and had a long Scotch; I could not shake the ominous import of his words. Had he meant his opposite number in a country other than Israel? He had not merely been boasting. Colonel Nouri was above the usual Arab folly.

When I dropped in at the Chrysler agency, I learned that Keil hadn't yet completed the papers for selling the Plymouth.

I felt a powerful sense of danger. I lay low till the day I was to meet with Azar in a last attempt to change his mind about escaping.

I was there twenty-five minutes early. The thoroughfare streamed with traffic. From the doorway of a juice vendor's shop, I observed nothing unusual until two Arabs in plainclothes stopped opposite the shoe shop where Azar was to post himself. Shortly one of them appeared to acknowledge two other Arabs loitering diagonally across the street, apparently window shopping.

Goddamn! This was a trap! Quickly I stepped out into a knot of strollers while I tried to figure out how the police had known. At a distance I stopped: Azar had to be warned. If we were separated now, neither of us would know how to contact the other.

Ten minutes remained of the hour. I headed for the next street, parallel to our meeting place. At the corner I drew back. In the middle of the block two station wagons pulled up to the curb. Five men alighted. Even at this distance I recognized Azar as one of them. Hurriedly they dispersed. Only Azar remained, glancing about; then he, too, was gone—*to meet me.*

I leaned against the stone wall, incredulous. *Azar was the treacherous bait in a trap—a trap set for me.* The cowardly bastard was giving me to the Egyptians! *He was handing them my life.*

Sure that my identity had not been discovered, I tried to think. How long would it take them to identify the ringleader?

From the Marconi telegraph office, I called Willi in Cairo and told him I was going to Europe. He understood that he was to prepare the secret microfilm.

Melki Keludian was pleased to hear of my plans. But even pulling strings, the next available flight out was three days from now, because of Egypt's tourist season.

Seventy-two more hours on Egyptian soil! Yet I had no choice. Azar had prevented a run through the Western Desert to Libya; he would have told the police of my plan to smuggle him out. Aship I would be a virtual prisoner until we reached international waters. The air seemed the only logical escape. I would be free until the plane took off—free to run and hide, if necessary. Making my getaway behind Frau Keludian's skirts held the greatest chance of success.

On returning to Cairo, I learned that Keil had encountered unforeseen obstacles in disposing of the Plymouth. New regulations required any automobile seller to appear in person at the traffic department and custom service. I told Keil of my proposed trip to Europe, ostensibly by boat. "Isn't there some way the problem can be dealt with through outside channels?"

"You have connections, Herr Frank; enlist their help. If the customs problem is solved, I can handle the change of ownership. That will only take a few minutes."

Summoning my courage, I raced to the customs and harbor police headquarters in Alexandria to see the commanding officer, the brigadier I had met with Theo. Very jittery, I was escorted into his office. *If anyone would be on the lookout for me, it would be this man.*

The brigadier inquired about Theo and his family, then listened to my problems. Instantly he handed the documents to an aide who, while the brigadier and I chatted idly, expedited the matter. Twenty minutes later, after paying the necessary customs duty and effusively thanking the brigadier, I rushed back to Keil.

Within the hour I had half the sales price in hand, $470, half of what I'd paid for the Plymouth. The other half, due when the Plymouth changed hands (too late for me), I could kiss goodbye. The price of a life—$470!

I drove back to Cairo in Melki's car and dropped in on Fahrmbacher,

Engel, Machmoud, and others, leaving them with the impression that I would travel by boat as usual, and that I was taking my car to trade on a new Mercedes in Germany.

Machmoud wanted to see me off at the port. He was adamant. Since I had been in Egypt, his ready availability to my needs had made me certain he was attached to the German Table within the security service. To allay his suspicions (if he had any), I asked him to keep my typewriter until I returned.

Willi joined me at the Tahrir Square bus station with microfilm negatives of the Egyptian rocket's guidance system and, unexpectedly, detailed copies of the secret radar scheme designed by Professor Goerke. Willi explained that he had simply tossed it in, thinking it might be of value. I took it. We parted with a handshake—and another loan to him. *Shalom, Willi!*

Frau Keludian was packed and ready. Melki had booked a TWA flight at 6:30 A.M. at Cairo International Airport, for the next day. August 6. We drove to Cairo, picked up our tickets, and checked into the Heliopolis Hotel.

During the night my nerves almost gave way. Every sound, every step seemed to signal my end. If worse came to worst, I had a makeshift plan of escape. Jumping out of the hotel window (I was careful to rent a room only a flight up), I could escape in Melki's car, race to Port Tawfiq fifty miles away, and, on foot, skirt along the edge of the Red Sea. From my previous visit with Fahrmbacher, I knew the area to be patrolled by camel riders of the Frontier Patrol. By overpowering one of them, I could possibly make my way to Eliat. With a great deal of luck it might work. Anything was better than to end here.

Morning came. Downstairs, Hannes and Nina Zenker joined us for breakfast. Mine was four cups of coffee, all my knotted stomach would accept. Frau Keludian talked me into buying some local jewelry for Lore, the German girl I supposedly was in love with, a fictitious widow of a best friend.

Melki drove us to the airport. Sitting in the back amidst luggage we couldn't cram into the trunk, I managed to slip the tiny transmitter in among Frau Keludian's personal things in her handbasket, and the matchbox containing the microfilm into her coat pocket. Of all people, she would be least likely to be searched.

Tension had my guts on fire. Within a half hour, it would be all over. We were having coffee when our TWA flight was announced. *Now.*

We approached customs. I hung behind the Keludians, wanting a clear field to run if, God forbid, I had to. Slowly, erratically, one passenger after the other was passed through the line. In my hands was Frau Keludian's basket, over my arm her coat. She passed.

"Frau Keludian," I said, stepping to the desk, "please hold your things for a second." Passing Frau Keludian her basket and coat with a wink at the officials, I said, "Once a gentleman, always a gentleman."

They grinned. "Your bag, please," one of them said. I handed over a clean attaché case for inspection. It was returned.

"Please proceed to passport control."

Frau Keludian was already through.

The passport official, a captain wearing the insignia of the dreaded security police, took my passport and leafed slowly through the pages, scrutinizing each entry. He flipped back to the first. My name and picture stared out at him. Bristling with efficiency, he shuffled through a card index at his elbow—the dreaded black list.

Fear leaped into my throat. Ready to bolt, I spoke casually to Frau Keludian.

When the captain's meticulous tour through the card index was completed, he stamped my passport and handed it over, looking for the next.

The walk across the tarmac to the plane seemed endless. Boarded and settled, my head still ballooning, it seemed an eternity until we raced down the runway. Then we were airborne, but flying over Egyptian territory, still subject to recall by the security services. (I had already decided that if that should happen, I would try to stand off the plane crew and fake a hijack if necessary. I had nothing to lose up here. I had everything to lose down there.)

The pilot's voice came over the intercom: "Ladies and gentlemen, we are now flying over the famous pyramids of Giza. To allow you an aerial view, we will circle so all can get a look. For those seated on the right side, please be patient. We will make a right-hand circle for you. Thank you."

As the plane dipped toward my side, I saw the Mediterranean far ahead and the pyramids below. Then the wings leveled off. In a few minutes the yellow beach fell away under the wings.

I had made it.

Chapter 15

I spent a quick week in Europe, where I surprised a few people (reports trickling from Egypt had led them to suspect my arrest), and then I was ordered home for debriefing. Odd, how much easier for headquarters to find me in Europe than in Egypt. Thoughts of Levy and the others plagued me. Since my escape, I'd tried to view their predicament as all a part of the spy game, but to say that prospects of their fate deeply disturbed me is a feeble understatement.

Even so, excitement gripped me now. *I was going home!* I had not set foot on Israeli soil in a year and a half.

The flight itself seemed interminable, but I was full of myself and Israel as *Havanu Shalom Aleichem* sounded in my ears on deplaning at Lod Airport. The first person I recognized was the one-armed security man, the last man I'd seen on leaving. Then Motke strode up. Without words, we bear hugged. A fast zigzag through the crowded terminal to his chauffeured Henry J, and we were on our way to his house.

I was bursting with questions. Shula? The boy? Shlomo? I feasted on the sights as Motke drove us to an unpretentious little house with a yard that reflected the labors of a man who took pride in ownership. I thought of Motke's note of a few months back, inviting me and my son to fish with him and his son in some quiet, peaceful spot.

Nina, Motke's wife, embraced me excitedly. Food (a Jewish mother!), then a tour of the premises, an exhibition of Motke and Nina's new son, finally a bed.

I came awake abruptly to a tug at my shoulder, seven hours later.

"Mensch, es ist spaet!"

"Avri, you're home!"

Motke's loud laugh stopped me. In my sleepy stupor, I was still not home. I shook my head, shaking out Paul Frank.

Later, over coffee and cake, I related to Motke the whole story, from my departure for Zurich to my arrival earlier this morning. Motke listened in heavy silence, with only grunts of acknowledgment; his eyes were somber. My accusations leveled against Modiin's incompetence and the crippling competitiveness between Modiin and Mossad deeply disturbed him. But nothing I said about my run-ins with the Mossad were new.

"I want you to write a full account of all you've told me," he said. "Take all the time you need; I must have it in writing."

Capt. Shlomo Millet and Martin Hauser stopped by, but at Motke's request little detail of the mission was discussed. For two consecutive, almost incommunicado days at Motke's home, I wrote my lengthy report, no detail deleted, no one spared, not even myself. The report was a near-criminal indictment against headquarters—its shortcomings, its dilettantism, its negligence—and professionally damaging to Motke.

That was regrettable, but I owed it to those left behind in Egypt to tell it the way it happened. On the top page, in bold capital letters, I wrote "PARASHAT PIERRE" (The Pierre Affair).

Motke expressed his position simply. "There're two sides to every coin, Avri; you only know one. I understand your feelings, though I think you were harsh in your judgment."

My response was even simpler. No comment.

Motke had kept me practically in isolation. Shula had no idea I was in the country, not even when Motke stopped the car outside her flat late at night. One should never surprise his ex-wife, I thought nervously, as Motke knocked on the door.

Shula stood silhouetted in the threshold. She had never looked more beautiful. We were in each other's arms, her lips searching every bit of my face. There were no words.

And Harel. Now five years old, he had grown unbelievably. I spent two joyous hours with him clinging around my neck before he dropped back to sleep.

Shula and I talked late. I was pleased to my gut that she had been accepted so completely into the intelligence community.

"I couldn't believe you were dead," she said. "Motke says when it comes to the worst, you're at your best. You don't know how they esteem you, Avri."

Pride showed in her every expression. Once she'd had no pride at all in my being in the army; now she seemed to feel its importance. It was almost morning when we fell asleep, Shula's short blonde hair fragrant against my cheek. Almost immediately, Harel joined us, wedging himself between us. I embraced them, enjoying, forgetting.

Five wonderful days later, a Modiin major came with a topographical map of the Sinai Desert, getting every detail of my trip down the east bank of the Gulf of Suez with Fahrmbacher. He wanted more detail than I had given in my rough maps to headquarters.

Headquarters had yet to assess the full extent of the catastrophe in Egypt. All the information filtering out alluded to wholesale arrest of Jews for questioning in connection with the cell, indicating the Egyptian authorities believed it to be a widespread and well-organized network. Motke had word that all the other Alexandria and Cairo people (unknown to me) had been arrested with the exception of Victorine Marcel Ninio, a young woman Levy had once suggested as my courier. Despite the danger, Motke thought she could be rescued.

"What are your chances of going in and bringing Ninio out?"

"It all depends on my cover."

Paul Frank had yet to be connected to the sabotage.

"Are you willing to take the risk?"

"Have we ever left anyone behind, Motke?" Even though I had never seen her. Victorine Ninio was one of us.

The final decisions on Ninio's rescue were left to me. I decided not to tell Shula; she would learn of the mission soon enough.

Motke, I learned, had personally supervised my activities as case officer, having, for some unexplained reason, taken over from Shlomo after our strike on the American USIS libraries on July 14. Shlomo, when I next saw him, was surprised to hear that except for the one postcard he'd written me, nothing more of his correspondence had reached me the entire month of July.

"Do you know what we call your field reports?" Shlomo asked.

I couldn't imagine. "What?"

"El-Ad Sarchi's volumes. At first we were skeptical because you moved so fast, but cross-checking verified everything you reported. So we gave it your special name." He shook his head. "You were born for this kind of work."

The following week was tough, commuting daily between Tel Aviv and Haifa; I spent the days in a refresher course at Modiin's training ground and nights in a crash course in forgery. Modiin hadn't Victorine Ninio's exact description, and the French passport with which I hoped to bring her out of Egypt had to be filled out when I saw her. In addition I would forge all her travel documents on the spot. A very tricky affair.

Final preparations were in force. Shula knew that I would return to Europe, but not to Egypt. She more than suspected something, however, when I suggested we remarry. She consented, asking no more questions. Two years of our divorce had been a long time. Too long for both of us.

To Motke I placed three conditions on my going back into Egypt: 1) the unit was to lend me 4,000 pounds to lease a flat for my family; 2) arrangements must be made for the wedding; and 3) I was to be provided with poison.

Final decision on the loan was the responsibility of the director of Modiin, Col. Benjamin Gibli; the wedding arrangements were being made; but Motke hedged on the final condition.

I hadn't the slightest fear of being thought melodramatic in requesting the poison; I simply knew Egyptian interrogators would eventually find my breaking point. Though I talked about a fifty-fifty chance of success in rescuing Ninio, I believed the odds greater than that. The Egyptians could be waiting for me. Motke wanted a reason for my unusual request.

"You want a reason?" I said. "I hate pain! I'm ticklish! I can't stand being shouted at!"

Motke understood that my contrived, comic outburst was serious. "OK," he said finally, "but we won't call it poison. We'll call it *chomar monea* (an antidote to life)."

One late afternoon, Motke drove me to army general headquarters in Ramat Gan, to the office of the director of military intelligence. Col. Benjamin Gibli I knew mostly by reputation, having met him only once, during our War of Independence. In the fighting for Jerusalem, Gibli had held a key position in SHAI.[1] During that period he gained a reputation as a man capable of arousing strong and diverse passions in those around him—both loyalty and intense dislike. Gibli held the dubious distinction of presiding over the only field court-martial ever held in Israel that resulted in an execution.

The man was Meir Tobiansky, a technical graduate and emigre from Russia, who had reached the rank of major in the British army in World War II. During our War of Independence, he was in charge of the main Haganah depot in Jerusalem. SHAI, certain that a spy ring was handing over information to the Jordanian forces, investigated, and the slim evidence led to Tobiansky.

Lt. Col. Isser Bari, head of intelligence, was convinced of Tobiansky's guilt. When advised that Tobiansky could hardly be brought to court on the evidence collected (largely circumstantial), Bari suggested a field court-martial, headed by Benjamin Gibli, then head of intelligence in Jerusalem. The field tribunal convened and, in a couple of hours, using in-

---

1. Pre-State underground intelligence.

formation furnished mostly by Gibli, found Tobiansky guilty. Bari had demanded the death penalty, and the sentence was carried out.[2]

Dalia Carmel, Gibli's secretary, a tall, slender, young woman sergeant, directed Motke and me into Gibli's office.

"*Shalom*, Avri," Gibli greeted me, coming around his desk to shake my hand. "You've changed since the war. For the better."

I laughed with him, a little taken aback by Gibli's almost movie-star appearance; he was not unlike Gregory Peck. He was in his mid- to late-thirties, sharply dressed, slender, and tall. Still a full colonel, he was the only department head in Zahal who hadn't the rank of general.

Gibli set me at ease, but I could sense his ability to ruthlessly denigrate a man with a word. Motke was silent, aware of whose show it was. Gibli said, "The Modiin family is proud to have you with us; those in Zahal who have reason to know of you, feel the same. You have done an excellent job."

I thanked him, quickly grasping the opportunity to broach a subject I'd been thinking about since Egypt. I wanted all those under my command officially listed into the ranks of Zahal. "They deserve it," I said. "It's the least the nation can do to show its gratitude. If they ever reach Israel's shores, they'll have something waiting for them."

Gibli was thoughtful for a moment. "Rest assured we'll do all we can. There are obstacles to overcome." He came to the point. "I've read your report," he said, "and your remarks are being taken with extreme seriousness. I think all those involved should sit together and learn how to avoid such mistakes in the future."

I objected to the word *mistake*. "Blunders is more the term," I said. Neither Motke nor Gibli liked my assessment.

Gibli addressed Motke. "Have you asked Colonel Washben at Department 8 why the security passports for our people in Egypt were never delivered when Avri requested them?"

"I sent a memo, but he didn't respond," Motke said.

That would have been even before I had gone back to Egypt to command the group, over two months ago. "If it takes that long to answer a memo," I said, "no wonder the passports were never delivered."

Gibli threw a long glance at Motke, then scribbled something on a pad. "I'll deal with it," he said.

At our leaving, Gibli assured me that my conditions for going back into Egypt on the rescue mission would be met, and I was given a raise in basic pay to help pay off the 4,000-pound loan. I had the impression, as I left Gibli's office, that he was going to deal with a lot of things.

---

2. Meir Tobiansky was posthumously exonerated, and Ben-Gurion restored him to the rank of captain in Zahal. Tobiansky's remains were transferred to a military cemetery under full military honors. Lt. Col. Isser Bari was brought to trial for his part in the execution.

I was riding high the morning Shula and I set out for the Rabbinical Court in Ramat Gan. Shlomo and Hauser were already there in the registrar's office, attending to the preliminary marriage formalities. With but a minor snag (my ID card did not show my divorce), which Shlomo quickly took care of with the aid of Department 8's forgers, we got the marriage permit with a hearty *Mazel Tov* from the rabbinical clerk.

At mid-afternoon we were at the chief rabbi's office in Jaffa. The required ten men were gathered as witnesses, along with Motke, others of headquarters staff, and some of my instructors. All except Motke, Shlomo, and Hauser were mystified as to why I was marrying my own wife. Few, I realized, knew of the divorce.

Shula and I returned to our tiny flat in Haifa. There was no time for a second honeymoon, but I cared only that it should last the night. It had been a long time since my court-martial over a refrigerator that was hardly worth a minute of a man's life; yet it had taken three years of mine.

As fast as I had come to Israel, I was ready to go again, my mission definite: Bring back Victorine Marcel Ninio out of Egypt.

I left Israel with all my important (and angry) questions unanswered. *Why had Dr. Moussa Marzouk been allowed to return to Egypt when Motke said he wouldn't? Why hadn't I been told? Why hadn't Modiin been better informed of the state of its so-called network? Why weren't there sufficient explosives on hand and why hadn't we been sent more? Why hadn't the security passports been delivered as I'd requested, so that some of those in custody might have escaped? Why had Shlomo been relieved as my case officer? Why hadn't I received the letters Shlomo claimed he'd written? Why hadn't the letters been sent to Count de Lavison when it had been cleared, and why hadn't I been informed of the change of plan?*

Whys! I had a thousand questions and no answers, only hedges. Left unanswered was the major question of all: *Why the hell had headquarters left us in an extremely critical international sabotage operation with absolutely no control?*

At Paris's Orly Airport, my contact took my British credentials and returned my German ones. I was Paul Frank again. I felt no discomfort in returning to the familiar role. I scribbled postcards to my friends in Germany, Austria, and Egypt. A fast train trip to see Poldi in Cologne added little to my understanding of what was happening in Egypt. I had to check further to find out Paul Frank's status in Egypt.

Theo Bechtoldsheim, when I called him at his home in Rendsburg, knew nothing of my involvement in Egypt. Theo would have warned me.

In Frankfurt I found a letter from Fahrmbacher in response to one I'd sent prior to my going to Israel; a short note from Willi Kubie; and one from Machmoud reminding me to locate a sponsor for his coming to Germany to work or study. Faust had received the usual business letters from Egypt; nothing in them implicated me.

However, Faust was indignant about Jiddel Langfuss's failure to pay into the company my share provided to him by Modiin, a payment now eight months in arrears. I was furious with Langfuss for having risked my good relationship with the German manufacturer. At the moment, though, I had no time to settle accounts.

In Munich I had to see to the engine repair of the 1953 Mercury I was buying. The delay was becoming critical. I had already arranged my departure by ship from Napoli to Libya, the first leg of my mission to rescue Ninio. My plan for her escape (and maybe mine) was for us to drive through the Western Desert into Libya. Though a travel permit was mandatory, I was certain that I could count on my former chess partner—the Egyptian colonel who commanded the area from Mersa Matruh—to give me the permit on the spot. I had no alternative, despite the risk. With the roundup going on in Egypt, a flea couldn't pass through Egyptian air and port customs.

Rushing to Cologne to inform headquarters of the delay, I bumped into Theo Bechtoldsheim at the train station. Theo revealed that he was trying to keep his financial head above water; so I suggested that we join in dealing with the Egyptian admiralty. (The Egyptians were still sending him inquiries regarding the acquisition of war supplies. Later we would submit offers, *in person,* to the Egyptian consul in Frankfurt. Fräulein Gaertner was still working there.) Leaving Theo with monies on account, I returned to Munich.

I drove straight through to Rome, punishing the Mercury, but I missed the ship's sailing by six hours. Instead of going directly to Benjamin Rottem, who was to give me the equipment for forging Victorine Ninio's passport, I killed a day, rebooking my passage to Benghazi, Libya. When I finally met with Benjamin, he handed me a message from headquarters.

"Return to Germany. Cancel plans."

Having keyed myself emotionally to whatever risks the mission held for me, I was hit hard by the news. But as I learned from Benjamin, if I hadn't been late, I would have been aboard ship because the message arrived *after* I was supposed to sail!

All I could think of as I headed back was *What the hell has happened?* Had Ninio been arrested? In Cologne, Poldi told me that someone was waiting in Paris. Get there fast!

Early in October, I reached an out-of-the-way coffeehouse and Col. Benjamin Gibli. What was important enough to bring the director of Modiin himself?

"What happened?" I asked. "Why was the mission canceled?"

"The name Paul Frank appeared in a British newspaper," he said coolly.

My heart stopped. The Egyptians knew about me!

"The British paper is the only source that brought up your name," Gibli replied to my next question; he handed me an article from the *New York Times*. "Here's something else."

EGYPT CAPTURES 'SPIES'

Charges Ring Was Directed by
Israeli Intelligence Officer

CAIRO. Egyptian security forces have seized members of an alleged spy network said to be under Israeli direction.

Col. Zacharia Mohieddin, interior minister and chief of military intelligence, said today at a press conference that the gang had been engaged in gathering military, economic and political information throughout the Arab world.

It sought to create internal disturbances in Egypt and in this task had the cooperation of certain societies and organizations hostile to the present Egyptian regime.

Investigation has shown that members of the ring were trained by Israeli intelligence departments in the use of firearms, wireless transmitters and codes, the minister declared. Some also received training from Communists in France.

I quietly put the paper down and looked at him.

"I'm here," Gibli said, "to see our people get the best legal aid we can mobilize. You'll be glad to know, Avri, that we've enlisted them as officers in Zahal. They'll automatically receive the benefits when they're released."

"*If* they're released."

"They will be, they will be. You know that everything possible is being done for them."

This I knew.

Since Paul Frank's name had cropped up, Gibli suggested I return to Germany and continue to function as if I were in no way connected with the name in the British newspaper; I would establish my own firm in Germany, an "umbrella holding company," or "roof" organization for various agencies that I would acquire to service the Arabic countries. He further ordered me to keep in touch with my friends in Egypt, to keep abreast of developments.

During the next days in Paris, I learned of a Radio Cairo broadcast by Zacharia Mohieddin, whereby he *outlined the entire network set-up, the motives behind the actions, the actions, and something of the arrests.* There was apparently little that Egyptian intelligence didn't know. Later in the month, Egyptian news media disclosed the government's indictments against twelve men and one woman. Two were to be tried in absentia: Avraham Dar, alias John Darling, the network's recruiter, and myself, as Paul Frank.

Two charges had been brought against the accused: transmitting military, economic, and political secrets to Israel via clandestine radio transmission; and sabotage of all the targets we had struck on July 2, 14, and 22.

Significantly the indictments followed the *Bat Galim* episode. On September 28 Israel had sent the cargo ship *Bat Galim* into the Suez Canal to demonstrate to the world Egyptian restrictions in the waterway; it hoped to show that the Egyptians would exclude Israeli ships and cargo, in violation of the 1951 UN Security Council resolution requiring free passage. The *Bat Galim* was captured and impounded, and its crew imprisoned, as expected by Israel's planners (headed by Col. Benjamin Gibli, so it was said).

The *Bat Galim* incident was a sister action to our sabotage action in Egypt, planned to forestall Britain's evacuation of her troops. Our sabotage action was meant to halt the agreement to withdraw, and when we failed, the *Bat Galim* was sent into the waterway to halt the final signing of the agreement. Withal it was signed on October 19.

To the extremist Moslem Brotherhood, which felt that the British should simply be kicked out of the canal zone, the lenient terms of Nasser's evacuation agreement seemed more an alliance with the British than an Egyptian victory. Their fury led to an assassination attempt on Nasser by one of their members on October 26, which in turn gave Nasser the excuse he needed to squash the Brethren once and for all. (After a November trial, six Brethren, including the would-be assassin, were hanged.)

We feared that this new furor would have a decidedly detrimental effect on the trial of our people. And their trial date drew closer.

Chapter 16

I drove to Rendsburg with Charlotte Bechtoldsheim, for a weekend with her parents. Theo returned with us to Bremen for a meeting with an arms dealer. I sat in on the meeting, learning that the world of private arms merchants is a small but select one. Although secrecy is a byword, the man had heard rumors that Theo and I were acting as go-betweens for the Egyptians.

Theo suggested that we drop in on Gerhard Mertens, who was in Germany on a parachute-buying mission for the Egyptian government. I had definite qualms about the encounter in Hanover when Mertens indicated on the phone that he was accompanied by two Egyptian air force officers and Colonel Moheb, Egyptian air force attaché to the Low Countries. I'd met the latter with Charlotte almost six months before.

At our meeting neither Mertens nor the Egyptians even hinted at my connections with the sabotage. However, I remained at the ready until Cologne, where our two-car caravan split. For I knew that they knew.

In Paris Theo and I submitted a detailed request to dealers for arms. Theo's motive was financial; mine, to seek business connections for the firm I was establishing in Munich. The insight I gained in the negotiations proved invaluable. I learned that arms merchants lurked everywhere, selling to anyone, without conscience.

Since the English newspaper article had exposed Paul Frank's connection with the sabotage, I knew for certain that any further dealings with the Egyptians meant they were willing to forgive and forget if they could cultivate my loyalty. And I was almost as certain that they did not know I was an Israeli operative, even though it had been charged by some of the arrested and subsequently released as fact by Egyptian propaganda. The Egyptians had to believe that I was a German mercenary selling his services to the highest bidder. It had to be! There was no other explanation for their behavior toward me.

In establishing the firm Engineer Paul Frank Import-Export in Munich, I enlisted the aid of a friend. Baron A. von Vietinghoff had held an important position in the Third Reich during the war, and, being a man of jurisprudence assigned to a high post in the Protectorate of Czechoslovakia, he knew everybody worth knowing in German heavy industry. Also Hugo Krug had come to Munich to live and work with my firm.

A month earlier, while visiting my parents in Vienna, I learned that Hugo had been arrested for nonpayment of debts. I covered the relatively small sum for him and offered him a job with the firm. From all reports, Hugo was a shrewd businessman, and I needed him badly. On my departure, it was understood that he would join me. I had already explained the firm's objectives, omitting Modiin's involvement until Hugo received security clearance. We had to do something about his Jewish appearance; so we passed him off as an Armenian by the name of Krugian.

Out of the blue the two Egyptian air force officers who had accompanied Mertens on the parachute-purchasing mission invited me to an evening in a *Bratskeller*.

"We're interested in enlisting your services," one of them said outright. "You know the right people, you have the right connections, and your experience has merit. You are a good man to have around." These were almost the identical words Minister of Interior Zacharia Mohieddin had spoken to me. Were they quoting him? Was Mohieddin still interested in my working for him? There could be only one explanation: *The Egyptians believed that I was a German mercenary hired by the Jews. My suspicions were true!*

I couldn't commit myself without headquarters' go-ahead. Motke's reply to my query was both categorical and carte blanche: "First establish your firm in Munich, then pursue the matter."

Though my German cover miraculously had held up, I couldn't shake the Damoclean sensation of sitting under a double-edged sword. Double agents were in a game of winner-take-all, and if the enemy thought I was one, I *was* one.

Meanwhile I was shuttling back and forth making myself known to the best German firms. All were interested in Middle East markets but were unwilling to give away sole representation to a new and unproven company.

Baron von Vietinghoff, who had accompanied me during most of the initial negotiations, suggested that since Israel was a growing market in which European manufacturers had great interest, perhaps by solidifying deals with the manufacturers themselves, rather than their wholesalers, I could demonstrate a track record to the wholesale companies I sought agencies from. The idea was sound.

Thanks to Germany's reparations payments, Israel had seventy million dollars to spend in Germany each year, most of it through Israel's purchasing mission in Cologne. However, the reparations agreement specified that purchases would be directly from the manufacturer without the services of a middleman.

Poldi arranged a meeting for me with Avigdor Dagan, deputy head of the purchasing mission. Dagan was willing to assist me, provided he received explicit instructions from Israel's minister of finance. But Dagan didn't think that possible because many influential people had tried to exert personal pressure on the finance minister to gain their ends. In explaining the reparations agreement, he provided me with the loophole I needed.

"Have you encountered German manufacturers who refuse to deal with Israel for fear of jeopardizing the Arab market?" I asked.

"Indeed we have!" Dagan said emphatically. "And some of them, unfortunately, are producers of products we can get *only* in Germany. But what are you driving at?"

"If my firm could supply you with these products you can't buy from the manufacturer, would you give me the purchase order?"

"I think so, yes . . . provided we get it at cost and without delays in delivery of other goods."

On the heels of this tentative success, I was called to Paris to meet with Colonel Gibli a second time to discuss what moves I had made in establishing Engineer Paul Frank Import-Export.

"Take your time," he advised when I'd briefed him. "Nobody is expecting immediate results. In this field it doesn't happen overnight." He handed me typed pages. "Have a look at this."

It was a report by George Watson, an English lawyer representing Max Benet, a lone-wolf Modiin operative captured in the roundup in Egypt.

I totally forgot Gibli as I read the pages. Watson's report pointed out the difficulties in providing the accused with counsel. It had taken a strong French protest to gain counsel for Dr. Moussa Marzouk, a French national from Tunisia. Maitre Ahmed Rushdi, a former Egyptian minister of justice and chairman of the Egyptian Bar Association, was assigned the defense. Most of what Watson had to say dealt with the trial, as an observer for the World Jewish Congress.

I learned that Victorine Marcel Ninio had attempted suicide by jumping from a window to evade her interrogators, suffering a broken leg and other minor injuries. Another Jew, unknown to me, had hanged himself for fear of arrest after Ninio's incarceration.

When I finished, I could only gaze somberly into the middle distance. What could I say; I knew that the worst was yet to come.

The trial of the thirteen opened on December 11. All but one pleaded guilty. Dr. Moussa Marzouk pled: "I am guilty, but not the way the first charge puts it." His plea was entered as "not guilty." The accused were fighting to avoid the death penalty. As expected, they all were throwing the entire blame on Paul Frank. "Paul Frank threatened to denounce us to the authorities for having visited Israel if we would not participate. . . ." became a prelude to each one's testimony.

Victor Levy: "I have confessed everything I have done, but I want the court to know I took the whole affair as fun. I am Egyptian before being a Jew, and at no time did I think that I was causing harm to Egypt, my country. I will never live or die as an enemy of Egypt."

Shmuel Azar: "I never meant to betray Egypt. I dumped an incendiary device in the sea rather than hurt innocent people and my country." (Not quite, but he might just as well have. Instead of slitting the theater seats and inserting the devices into the stuffing, he had dropped the spectacle-case incendiaries on the floor, where they did little damage.)

Philip Nathanson: "I am no Zionist. Israel doesn't interest me."

Dr. Moussa Marzouk: "John Darling (Avraham Dar) deceived us. I refused to cooperate with him as soon as I found out he had other motives in his mind."

Victorine Marcel Ninio's stand was most impressive. When the prosecutor asked her to repeat the statements she had made during interrogation, she was silent for a moment, then her voice fell loudly on the hushed courtroom: "I don't remember what I said. They mistreated me during the interrogation." This defiance of the tribunal took courage.

The *New York Times* brought the first news concerning Max Benet's suicide. On December 21 he slashed his wrists to avoid testifying in court. Benet had been kept under tight surveillance following an attempt to swallow potassium cyanide, smuggled into his cell. This time he made it.

The question of justice was not even present in the Zionist spy trial. The presiding judge in the tribunal had no more control over the outcome than I did. It was a show trial, a game of cat-and-mouse, a *pas de deux*. The verdict would be political, coming from Nasser and his policymakers.

While the tribunal was hearing evidence and weighing it, Zacharia Mohieddin said in an interview to NBC: "There is a leftist Zionist network operating for Israel intelligence. Its aims are to . . . maintain contact with the government of Israel in a war with Egypt . . . to perform acts of sabotage so as to disrupt Egypt-American relations. Most members of the network have admitted that they were working for Israel. In addition to this, there are established facts that Israel intelligence had organized this network to work for it."

The Egyptian authorities knew everything there was to know, as I said—except about me. They did not know that Paul Frank was an Israeli intelligence operative, only a supposed German mercenary.

December was nearing its end as the world watched the trial. I wanted to make several contacts in Belgium, Holland, Germany, and Austria before the holidays.

In Paris I picked up Lt. Col. Uzi Narkiss and his wife, Ester, having promised to drive them through Europe. My old friend Uzi was on leave, studying at France's war academy. In Vienna they met my father and Olga. Stopping off in Frankfurt before our return to Paris, I went with Baron von Vietinghoff to a chemical firm that had refused, out of fear, to do business with Israel's purchasing mission.

"As long as you buy our products for *your* firm, Herr Frank," the plant's export manager said, "what you do with them afterward is your affair." It was a big breakthrough, both for my firm and Israel's purchasing mission. The Engineer Paul Frank Import-Export firm received its first order for the mission.

December 31, 1954, I celebrated Sylvester night with my German friends in Munich. An incident before midnight proved to me how much I had become one with my cover.

Helmut Wïthrich, a German film producer who'd helped me find an office for the firm, a violent anti-Nazi and good friend, soon dropped his German reserve and approached Shamona Branitsky, whom Helmut knew to be an Israeli. He said belligerently, "How come you're so friendly with Paul Frank? Don't you know he's a dirty Nazi? He was in the 'Pig Corps' (the Schweine-Staffel, or SS)."

"Come now, Helmut," Shamona said appeasingly, "Paul was no Nazi. He is a good friend."

"He was a Nazi! Once a Nazi, always a Nazi!" He turned on me. "Paul! Are you a Nazi?"

Amused, but outwardly indignant, I said, "Lay off!"

"Paul was no Nazi," Shamona said to Helmut.

"Ha! You don't believe me! Paul, take off your shirt. Let's see if you are the proud bearer of the *Blutgruppen-Zeichen* (blood group tattoo under the armpit of SS members)." Helmut wouldn't be shooed off. "Come now," he demanded, "don't be shy. Half the girls here have seen you with less on; so pull off your shirt."

"Paul," Shamona said, pretending to take the matter more seriously now, "maybe we'd better go into another room."

"All right, you bastards," I said, "have it your way. But there's nothing wrong with being a good German."

Half-pushed, half-wobbling, I made it into the next room, trailed by Helmut, Shamona, and Capt. Alexander Barnett, an American orthopedist in the medical corps.

"Alex," Helmut ordered, "you are not only a doctor and an officer, but also a gentleman. Exposing this Nazi swine in our midst is your honor. Please carry out the examination." Helmut's seriousness, his inebriation, his weaving, glassy-eyed authoritarianism brought smiles all around.

"Are you ready?" Alex asked, disliking his role.

I stripped off my tuxedo jacket and bared myself to the waist. Alex made a perfunctory examination of both my armpits and stepped back. "Nothing there to substantiate your claim, Helmut."

Helmut rushed forward and examined my underarms impatiently. "This bastard has gone through plastic surgery!" he shouted. "I knew it! They all did it!" He was nearly in tears.

I put my arm around his shoulder. "Helmut, you are right. I was a Nazi—but a bad one. If I'd been a good one, you would have gone through the chimneys instead of spending the war in Paris making films for the Third Reich."

We all broke up, even Helmut.

Early in the gray morning, Shamona and I made it to his flat. I'd only closed my burning eyes when the phone began ringing without pause. Poldi, without explanation, ordered me to go to the *Schweizer Hof* in Zurich. Immediately!

"What's this all about?"

"I haven't the foggiest. Happy New Year and good luck."

At 8:00 P.M., January 1, 1955, I stood at the *Schweizer Hof 's* reception desk. Room 207 was ready for me. I had hardly removed my coat when the phone sounded. I picked it up, listening to the long-distance hum.

"Yes?"

An unfamiliar voice, speaking in English, said, "Mr. Frank?"

"Yes, this is Frank."

The voice switched to Hebrew. "Take the first plane to Paris. Contact the usual number. You're expected tomorrow. Advise no one of your movements. I repeat, *no one!*"

"I understand. *Shalom.*"

I pulled on my coat, grabbed my suitcase, and caught the next flight bound for Orly Airport.

By 2:00 A.M. I had a room in Hotel Touring in Paris, not far from

Avenue Lafayette. After catching a couple of hours sleep and breakfasting, I called my contact.

"At two, at the Arc de Triomphe, someone will wait for you," Israel Chashal said.

"Who is it?"

Israel chuckled. "I don't know. It's all mysterious, like the real thing!"

The weather was typically winter Paris—gray, windy, and raining—when I arrived. Lt. Col. Mordechai Almog, Modiin's administrative and logistics officer, stood wrapped in raincoat and hat in the drizzle.

"*Shalom,* El-Ad. Follow me."

Trailing him down Avenue Wagram, I turned onto a little side street and went into a cheap hotel not far from where Jehosaphat "Fatti" Harkabi, on leave from the deputy directorship of Modiin under Colonel Gibli, lived while studying at the Sorbonne. I mentioned that I'd recently seen Fatti.

"Fatti doesn't know I'm here," he replied. "Nobody knows." When we were settled in his room, he continued, "I've come to see you on a matter of the greatest importance, a matter which is for your knowledge only. And I have not come here at all. Understand?"

Behind drawn curtains and lighted by a small lamp, the room was both alien and friend. "I understand."

Almog brought out an envelope sealed with clear tape. "I have a letter for your eyes only. Even I don't know its contents."

"Who's it from?"

"I'm only the messenger."

Carefully I read twice the one-page message written by Motke's hand and signed by him. It was an appeal for my understanding, an outcry for my help. The silence was heavy in the room as I read. He recapitulated the tragedy in Egypt and spoke of dangers from certain people in Israel's defense department who were dying to divest themselves of any responsibility in the tragedy.

> . . . These people are trying to destroy what is dearest to our hearts: Zahal. There is a power struggle going on, and the other faculty (Mossad) has a strong hand in it. If Zahal is dear to you, as I know it is, I want you to forget everything concerning the actions carried out before the twenty-second of July. The orders you received from me in June, when we met in Paris, were merely orders of communication and planning. *Nothing else!* The order to start sabotage actions was transmitted to you *only* on the seventeenth of July. If you have any notes, memos, letters from home, anything indicating otherwise, destroy or alter them.

On your arrival home, announce to anyone who asks that you have arrived in accordance with the order conveyed to you, but due to your activity, you were unable to come immediately as demanded.

Remember: The airport here will be watched. I was ordered not to see you before you meet with Defense Minister Lavon or the prime minister.

I approach you knowing your concern for Zahal. I know you will make the right decision. Destroying this letter will be a sign that you will act in accordance with my instructions.

Motke

I looked long at Almog, who peered at me from his vantage point beside the dim lamp. Already I knew that I was going to do as Motke asked, though I hardly understood the reasons behind it. I had no idea why I was to deny to all that we had carried out actions on July 2 and 14; it didn't make sense; there were so many who knew otherwise. I knew only two things: I trusted Motke implicitly because no man loved the army more than he; and my love for it forced me to battle anyone seeking to bring down the only institution in Israel I believed to be free of corruption.

The attack on Zahal by persons trying to extricate themselves of responsibility smelled of political expediency, and, deep in my soul, I scorned party machinations. I was a soldier. The army *was* Israel. I had been willing to kill for it. I would do what Motke asked.

Under the watchful eyes of Almog, I shredded the letter and flushed it down the toilet. Almog's expression was one of subtle relief, the only reaction he'd allowed himself since handing over the envelope.

"I knew this would be your decision," he declared, pressing my hand between his. "We all knew we could count on you."

Suddenly it occurred to me that Almog had forgotten he was only a messenger: Uninvolved messengers don't have opinions. Almog then inferred that the letter had been brought out of Israel in the diplomatic mail pouch, since he had been under the scrutiny of the Shin-Beth.

"By the way," he said, "you have regards from Gideon Raphael."

I had never met Gideon Raphael, but I knew of his position with the foreign service. He was Colonel Gibli's friend and, I suspected, the conveyor of the letter to Europe. "Give Gideon my best," I said, honestly flattered by being taken into Motke's confidence and the confidence of all those standing with him.

"Go home at your first opportunity." Almog looked at me through slitted eyes. "And Avri, forget you have seen or heard of me. Not even my ghost. *Shalom*, and good luck!"

Armed with an Israeli identity, I boarded a plane for Zurich the following day; from there I flew to Rome to catch an El-Al flight for home.

As fate would have it, Almog was inside the terminal in Rome. Beckoning me into a urinal, he told me to remain a night in Rome; we could not be seen arriving home on the same plane—and the airport was being watched, "as Motke said in the letter."

So he did know its contents. But we were in action now, and the matter no longer held interest for me.

I rode into the city and put up at Hotel Modern across from the terminal. With the rest of the day to kill, purely by chance I strolled past the stationery store where I had bought my blue, leather-bound daily diary almost a year before.

Suddenly a plan flashed into my mind: Motke had told me to alter or destroy any record of the actions prior to receiving the fictitious order on the seventeenth of July. I entered the shop and inquired if they still had any 1954 diaries. To my joy the shopkeeper had one almost identical to mine. I went back to the room and, with several pens, duplicated the new diary as befitted the false action report. I rubbed and smudged the pages to add wear and age.

Whether I was simply following my conception of Motke's orders or what, I don't know. But it was a good job, totally undetectable. I looked at the two diaries: the original, the *real* me—I had lived it; the duplicate, *Motke's* me—a distortion by omission and alteration . . . a lie.

Each gave me a sense of achievement, though of different kinds. My satisfaction lay in the belief that both would be of benefit to Zahal.

Chapter 17

Though I arrived unannounced at Lod Airport, the one-armed guardian was waiting to rush me outside to a figure hidden by night shadows. Motke. "I couldn't meet you inside. Come, we're going to Benjamin's house."

Driving rapidly but circuitously toward Col. Benjamin Gibli's home, Motke was grim, expressing himself harshly about Defense Minister Lavon. I asked him why all the secrecy.

"Avri, give me credit. Don't ask questions. I once took you under my wing when you needed it. Trust me."

I trusted him. I shut up.

His near declaration that Lavon was trying to evade his responsibilities in having given the order to commence the sabotage action in Egypt seemed quite an inconsistency, though I didn't voice it. At our June meeting in Paris, when I asked him who'd given the orders, Motke had said, "the highest authority," a cut and dried statement to *any* Israeli. The highest authority meant David Ben-Gurion, even though Ben-Gurion was retired to the desert, free of all government responsibility. Also, Motke had specifically discounted Lavon as having given the sabotage order. He had said, verbatim, "Lavon is an activist, but not he. Higher."

However—since Ben-Gurion, on his retirement, had hand-picked Lavon to succeed him as minister of defense—it had *appeared* to mean that Ben-Gurion had sanctioned the sabotage action and left Lavon to order it. My superiors had initiated it and I, in command, carried it out. Now, if I read

Motke right, Lavon was trying to save his political hide by blaming others, namely, my superiors in Modiin. Political expediency.

Suddenly I understood what Motke had meant in his secret letter. He had written: "In the wake of the tragedy in Egypt, certain people are trying to rescind their responsibility and are willing to cheat and lie to destroy what is close to our hearts: Zahal!" This had pointed straight to Lavon, a civilian. Believing Motke, I was prepared to fight Lavon all the way. It was him or Zahal, and Zahal was us. Motke said that a court of inquiry was already studying the matter, and that I would be called to testify.

It came as a great surprise to see Avraham Dar waiting with Colonel Gibli, who, like Motke, was tense and nervous. Gibli wasted no time on formalities.

"Defense Minister Lavon thought we were trying to hide you from him. He demanded that we bring you home for interrogation, but we held him off. Should you be asked, say that it was hard for us to contact you and that you returned as soon as you could without jeopardizing your work."

"Does this apply to everybody?"

"Everybody outside this room. Lavon is an embittered man, Avri. He'll do anything to get what he wants. You'll be seeing him tomorrow, after you see the chief of staff."

"What does he want with me?"

"He wants to know if you and your people carried out any actions in Egypt prior to the twenty-second of July. If he can get you to admit that you struck targets *before* that date, then he will claim that as proof to free himself of the responsibility of having given the order to act. He will say he gave no such orders."

Gibli paused to let me digest the seriousness of what he was saying, which coincided with Motke's letter. I was silent.

"He'll try to break you down," Gibli continued. "He has to get you to admit that targets were hit *prior* to the action on the twenty-second, and then he will deny giving orders for those strikes. He'll put pressure on you by saying that nobody will believe you because of your past court-martial. He might even claim that you initiated the sabotage on your own. If that gets him nowhere, he'll try to win you over by promising you a bright future. He'll promise you anything. So be on guard. Pinhas Lavon is a master at twisting words. Beware of signing anything. Without realizing it, you may write your own verdict."

Startled, I interpreted Gibli's "write your own verdict" to mean Lavon's winning, and that his winning could mean, at the very least, loss of everything I had regained. I looked at each of them. Avraham Dar, who had sat quietly, was very much a part of the conspiracy—and this, I suddenly realized, was definitely a conspiracy.

"Avri, the letter from Motke, the one Almog gave you in Paris. Did you grasp its meaning?"

"For the most part. Otherwise I wouldn't be here." Gibli accepted my statement. It appeared that he did not intend to go deeper into the conflict between Lavon and us. But one thing was certain, and it gave me courage: The conspiracy against the minister of defense was not limited to a few. I needed nothing more to convince me that I would faithfully abet the fight against Lavon. My conclusion was neither simple nor based on logic; it was entangled in a series of understandings.

First there was the Zahal, not a national army in the usual sense of the word, as one thought of the British army. Zahal, for us, embodied all the values stemming from the critical years when, as Palestinian Jews, we were forced to fend for ourselves against the Arabs and their British benefactors. Our army, the direct offspring of our underground organizations, a civilian military in which every man and woman offered up his or her life, had been the crucial factor in the miraculous creation of Israel. It was the one institution beyond corruption by political machinations. It was establishment. It was the only body in Israel, besides the courts, that the man in the street believed in unquestioningly.

For me the question of loyalty was a powerfully motivating factor. I trusted those who gave me reason to trust. I had had a powerful example in my father, who, when I was a child, had voluntarily accepted the socialistic responsibility of his co-workers in Austria in the early 1930s and had gone to prison while his friends remained free to carry on their work. I had learned from him loyalty to a cause—loyalty carried to a fault, as it turned out.

I trusted Motke and Gibli simply because they were my superiors and beyond suspicion. Authority in Zahal was first and foremost based on trust.

Also I had a personal debt that could not be ignored. Modiin, and Motke in particular, had accepted me into its ranks and given me back my life when there seemed no hope. Because of this I had reclaimed my family, my pride, everything.

Lastly there was Pinhas Lavon, a man of whom I knew little more than what I could glean from negative rumors. He was prominent. We knew *of* him, but we did not *know* him. He was not a soldier, never had been, and his ability to head Israel's defense had always been heatedly questioned.

Suddenly, Gibli threw at me, "When did you receive the order to commence operation?"

For a fleeting second, I was perplexed; then I realized he was testing my reflexes in anticipation of Lavon's questions. "You should know," I said, adhering to the conspiracy's version of the facts. "I wrote in my reports that I received the orders to prepare the ring on July 17, and the go-ahead order on the nineteenth. We struck on the twenty-second." This ruled out our July 2 actions against the general post office in Alexandria and our actions against the United States Information Service libraries in the port city and Cairo on the fourteenth.

A smile of satisfaction spread over his face. Motke brought out a stack of my reports sent from the field: one was missing, my condemning Affair Pierre report.

I asked Gibli about it.

"Forget that such a report ever existed," he said emphatically, almost angrily. "You have never written it." Exactly what Motke had said in his letter: " . . . forget about the existence of the Pierre report."

Over the next hours, with Gibli and Motke instructing me, I altered my previous field reports even further than I had in Rome, to coincide with the new version of the sabotage.

The revised version of the action was as follows: I received by wireless a forewarning order on July 17; two days later the order to strike came. The *one and only* action initiated by the ring was carried out on the twenty-second, against the four theaters in Alexandria and Cairo, plus the train station baggage compartment in the capital city. All other orders or actions previous to the seventeenth of July heretofore ceased to exist. And so did any actions against the British and Americans.

I would not understand Gibli's insistence on the new version of events until later. Right now I only saw Lavon clawing at Zahal's throat to save his political hide.

We finished at nearly four in the morning, all of us jumpy and irritable. Motke carefully pieced the reports together, taking great care to smudge the papers to give them a look of wear. If I hadn't participated, I would have sworn the reports were the originals.

While we straightened up Gibli's parlor, an automatic reflex caused me to slip into my attaché case a piece of paper, in Gibli's handwriting, indicating various changes in my field reports. In a fit of pique he had scribbled the notations I was to make in one of the reports. Thinking about it, I wondered whether or not I trusted the entanglement of our actions. Was it my sense of justice? Was it because I feared the pragmatism that filled this room? Or was it self-preservation? Because of these unanswered questions, I also failed to apprise them of my real or my revised diary. All I knew was that I wanted some proof that this night had existed.

"I want to caution you about seeing the chief of staff in the morning," Gibli said. "Don't be alarmed. Dayan will ask you only *one* question: Did you and your people carry out any actions prior to the twenty-second of July?" He checked to see if I had it, then went on. "His adjutant will fetch you from the hotel early. After you've seen Dayan, Motke will meet you."

"And," Motke added, "you have not seen us tonight—or at all!"

Gibli said with a grin, "You can ask Dayan why you haven't been allowed to see us yet."

Full of conspiracy, content that we had acted to halt the civilian menace, I was driven by Dar to Jacobson pension in Tel Aviv. At 5:00 A.M., I was asleep, only to be aroused at 7:00 A.M. by the chief of staff's adjutant.

Within minutes we were bound for army general headquarters outside Tel Aviv. I was nervous, having to face Dayan so soon after the coaching, afraid he might not limit himself to the single question as Gibli predicted. Most of all I was curious to know how Gibli knew that Dayan would ask only one question. And why only one?

We entered the rear entrance of general headquarters compound. I was ushered into a small waiting room adjacent to Dayan's office, my last encounter with Dayan was strong in my mind.

It was in October 1948, and the siege of Jerusalem was on. The Jordanian legion controlled the road to the city, blocking our path except for an improvised, limestone-base "Burma Road" cutting across the countryside. Heavy traffic stirred up fogs of white dust in the dry climate, demanding every traveler's cooperation on the twin lanes. I was then in charge of the rear headquarters of the Harel Brigade, traveling with Shula toward Jerusalem in an army jeep, when Moshe Dayan, soon to be military commander of Jerusalem, came hurtling headlong in his car, the swirling dust blinding everyone he met. Determined not to choke on his dust, I switched into his lane. We were nose to nose when the game of chicken halted. Dayan and I piled out of our vehicles, dust swirling around us.

"Move out of my way!" he said, more authority than he possessed thrown into his order.

I shook my head. "I don't have to swallow your dust; drive slower."

"I order you to move!" he barked furiously.

"I am not moving."

Dayan was indecisive. He shook his head in frustration. "You stubborn fool!" he fumed. I watched him get back in his car, glaring at me while pulling out and around, this time at a moderate speed.

Now here the maverick was, six years later, chief of staff of the Israeli army. It was predictable that Ben-Gurion, a mustang himself, would appoint him to the job. He had seen himself in Dayan.

"*Shalom*, Moshe," I said, not altogether certain how to address him.

"*Shalom*, Avri." Dayan gave me one of his legendary slight, crooked smiles, his face half-hidden behind the black patch covering his left eye. "It's good to see you. It's been a long time."

"It has been a long time," I said, grinning.

I took the chair he offered.

"Let me come straight to the point," he said. "I have one question to ask you." He paused. "Did you or your men carry out any actions prior to the seventeenth of July?"

Electrified by the near-exactness of Gibli's prediction, I tried to read Dayan's mind. Gibli had said the twenty-second, not the seventeenth, but it came to the same thing. Dayan's one good eye pinned me, yet revealed nothing. The black patch seemed to hide his face from all commitment. Was this part of the rehearsal, an extension of last night's coaching?

"No," I said finally. "We acted only on the twenty-second."

"That's all I wanted to hear," he said. His edginess disappeared with my statement. "You'll be seeing the minister of defense later today, and at a later stage you'll appear before a board of inquiry. Your superiors will advise you when and where."

"How can I be advised by them?" I asked, thinking it a good time to place Gibli's suggested query. "I'm not allowed to see them."

"You can see Gibli now, I have nothing against it." Dayan came from behind his desk and placed a hand high up on my shoulder. "Avri, you're doing a great job; it's good we have such men as you. All the best."

Though feeling myself aligned with Gibli, Motke, Dar, Almog, and others—even Dayan—in an effort to crush Lavon, who was anathema (so I believed) to the well-oiled machine Zahal had become, I walked out of general headquarters confused as to Dayan's position in the conspiracy.

Granted, Gen. Moshe Dayan was a man of few questions, but it was clear that he was decidedly not after the facts. I had spent exactly twelve minutes with him. He could reach no conclusions with one question and one answer, especially a single answer from the man who had led the action and knew *all* the details emanating from Egypt.

I suspected from Motke and Gibli's attitude that the chief of staff was part and parcel to the conspiracy. I was certain that his one-question interrogation was intended to ascertain my loyalty to the conspiracy (without me there was no conspiracy), and his refusal to mention anything else remotely related to it indicated his determination to hide his involvement. The fact that he had been away in the United States in July, while the sabotage action was being carried out, did not in itself prove his uninvolvement.

I was deeply thoughtful about this. Waiting for Motke and Gibli to meet me at a nearby coffeehouse, I happened on an old issue of the *Jerusalem Post,* printed near the end of December. It carried Prime Minister Sharet's speech to the Parliament regarding the Egyptian affair:

> The trial which is held in Egypt against 13 Jews has inflamed feelings and caused profound indignation in Israel and the entire

Jewish world. It must arouse the concern and anxiety to all those *who seek justice and peace everywhere. . . .*[1]

The Parliament Foreign Affairs and Defense Committee has studied the grave matter and will continue to do so. . . .

In my previous address to the Parliament in November, I said that Egypt's uncontrolled action gives *no evidence that her rulers have acquired a sense of international responsibility or moderation.* How far Egypt is from that spirit may be judged by the plot that is being hatched in Alexandria, a show-trial of the group of Jews *who have fallen victim to false libels of espionage and from whom confessions to imaginary crimes appear to be extorted by threats and torture.*

This somber assumption has meanwhile been proved correct and stands revealed as a cruel and shocking fact in light of the statement made by the defendant Victorine Ninio in the Cairo Military Court, that she was tortured during preliminary interrogation, and that it was by the means of torture that she had been *forced to make false confessions of crimes that were never committed.*

The Government of Israel protests most strongly against practices that seek to revive in the Middle East of today the methods of Medieval Inquisitions. *The Government of Israel rejects emphatically the fantastic libels that appear in the charges made by the Egyptian prosecution which accused Israel authorities of outrages and internal plots against the security of Egypt and its international relations. . . .*

We look upon the Jews who have been falsely accused by the Egyptian authorities of such serious crimes as victims of their open enmity against Israel and the Jewish people. If their (the network) crime is Zionism and devotion to Israel, then this is the crime of which great numbers of Jews all over the world are guilty. We do not believe that the Egyptian junta should see any advantage in deliberately bringing it upon themselves that they have spilled Jewish blood. *We call upon all those who seek to further peace and stability and supportable relations between the nations to prevent this dangerous perversion of justice.*

I was perplexed by the prime minister's stance. For a head of state who knew the truth of the accusations, he'd taken a curiously extreme position of martyrdom for the accused, especially when the possibility existed that he might have to retract.[2] This was not Moshe Sharet's style, not unless he

---

1. Author's italics throughout.

2. The Israeli government has never publicly admitted responsibility for the sabotage actions in Egypt.

was lying purely for foreign consumption. It would be very hard for him to admit to America (Dulles) and England what his military had done against them.

On the other hand, if Prime Minister Sharet did not as yet know the facts, his position was potentially dangerous; the action had been initiated and executed without his knowledge, or that of his cabinet.

For myself I decided that the prime minister had no knowledge of the action prior to or during its execution, and I was doubtful if he knew the truth even now, six months after we had carried it out.[3]

Motke joined me at the prearranged time to hear of my twelve minutes with Dayan. I withheld my thoughts about Dayan's involvement and sent Motke away smiling. Then Gibli came to hear. From him, I had to know more.

"Where was Dayan all the time we were carrying out the action? Why didn't he know about it?" Behind my questions was the knowledge that Dayan knew almost every move Modiin made.

Gibli, to my everlasting amazement, was jestful when he said, "Dayan is a fox, Avri. He knew when to go to the United States."

Leaving Gibli satisfied, I met Shlomo Millet. Without being specific, he warned me to be careful about involving myself in "certain things that are going on."

"Something is very wrong," he said finally. "Just be sure to cover your back. Everybody else is."

What in hell did Shlomo's oblique remarks mean? With lingering apprehensions, I went with Shlomo to Defense Minister Lavon's official flat near the Habima Theatre in Tel Aviv.

Pinhas Lavon, nee Lubianiker, had come from Poland in the 1920s, to be nurtured in the socialistic atmosphere of the *kibbutzim* (collective farms). Shaped by its ideals and goals, he rose through the ranks of the Histadrut, the powerful labor federation. Intellectually head and shoulders above his colleagues, he attracted Ben-Gurion; in 1950 Ben-Gurion appointed him minister of agriculture, then to a short tenure as minister without portfolio. It was believed that Lavon was being tutored to become prime minister. When Ben-Gurion tapped him as acting minister of defense in the summer of 1953 (upon Ben-Gurion's leave of absence from the government to study Zahal's needs as Israel's arm of defense), this feeling became a certitude. In December Ben-Gurion angrily retired, leaving Lavon permanently in the post.

However, it was said that Ben-Gurion very quickly considered Lavon a wrong choice. Rumor had it that Lavon was solely responsible for the

---

3. Subsequent developments bore out my conclusions.

dissension that disrupted the traditionally smooth chain of command among Zahal, the military, and the civilian ministry of defense. (The whys and the wherefores of the rumors about Lavon's impossibility were not to filter down to me until much later. At the onset of the conspiracy, I knew only that Lavon was a very unpopular man with the various department heads, especially Chief of Staff Dayan and Shimon Peres, director-general of the defense ministry; both men were Ben-Gurion's protégés, both were subordinate to Lavon as minister of defense. The main criticism of Lavon was that he had neglected to consult with Prime Minister Sharet on matters of policy.

Lavon's installation at the top of the defense pyramid, it seemed to me, made him part of the whole but not integral to it. Lavon had been placed to oversee a defense organization evolved by Ben-Gurion and manned exclusively by his people. (Having held both the prime and defense ministerships simultaneously since the founding of the State, Ben-Gurion *was* the ministry of defense.)

In view of what I knew at this time, Lavon seemed out of place. As a threat to Zahal's well-being, and as a man politically ambitious enough to harm Zahal in pursuit of his own ambitions, he was dangerous. I was against him.

His door opened to my ring. Ephraim Evron, the minister's aide and secretary, invited me in. I disliked him ("Call me 'Eppie,' everyone does") automatically; in behavior he was a typical bureaucratic yes-man.

Minister of Defense Pinhas Lavon came into the room, nodded, then sat at his desk.

"So you are the man from Egypt, eh? Where have you been hiding? Your people couldn't get hold of you."

His heavy bluntness seemed to border on arrogance, raising my hackles. No *Shalom*, no social amenities, nothing but a frontal assault. I rebelled against his rudeness. I did not take into account the fact that I had been conditioned to expect it.

Lavon looked just like his pictures, except that, being rail-thin, he appeared to be more stooped than I had imagined him. His prematurely gray hair and his hangdog countenance belied the sharpness of his tongue. Lavon's brilliance had brought him a long way in his fifty-odd years, but he was going no further.

I replied, "I don't sit behind a desk in my work. The moment word reached me, I returned home." It was difficult to hide my antagonism.

"I know that. Tell me, did you have enough explosives to carry out all the actions?"

Eppie Evron was efficiently scribbling the minutes of our conversation. I paused, determined not to fall into any of Lavon's verbal traps.

Avri El-Ad as a soldier in the British army in 1943 and with Shula shortly after their marriage in 1948.

Vienna, 1956: Avri, Shula, and their son, Harel. Below: In the Austrian Alps with his father, Siegmund Seidenwerg, and his father's second wife, Olga.

Col. Benjamin Gibli, Israeli director of military intelligence, in 1954.

The president of Egypt, Gamal Abdel Nasser (left) with his successor, Anwar el-Sadat.

Avri's identification as Paul Frank, his cover in Egypt.

Mohammed Said Haj Amin al Husseini, the Grand Mufti of Jerusalem.

Bob Jansen driving Avri's car on the way to Port Said.

The U.S. Information Center library fire set during the Israeli sabotage action in Cairo on July 14, 1954.

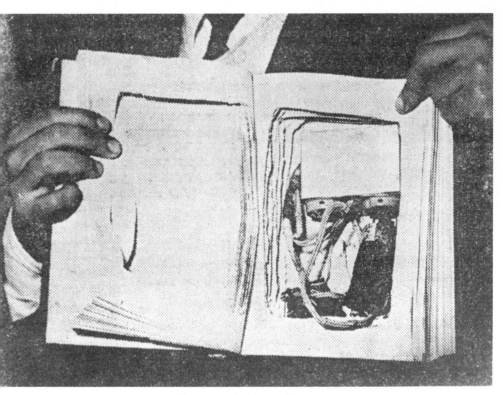

The concealed transmitter.

The second sabotage operation struck the luggage room of the Grand Union railway station in Cairo on July 22, 1954.

Operatives Victor ("Pierre") Levy (left) and Philip ("Henri") Nathanson in an Egyptian prison.

Shmuel ("Jacques") Azar being led into the courtroom.

Maj. Avraham Dar of Israeli military intelligence.

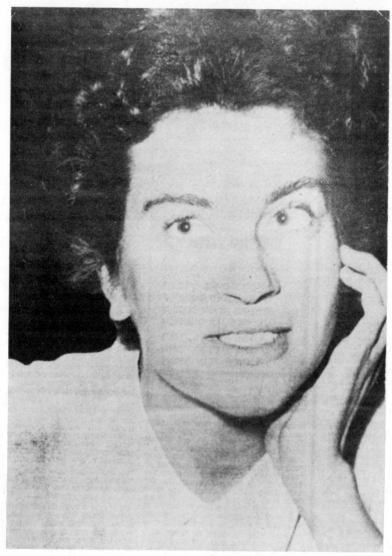

Victorine Marcel Ninio on trial.

Newspaper accounts of the "Zionist Spy" trial in Egypt and of the later Lavon Affair.

Israel's Defense Minister, Pinhas Lavon (left), listening to the army's chief of staff, Moshe Dayan, in 1954. Behind them: Shimon Peres, director-general of the defense ministry.

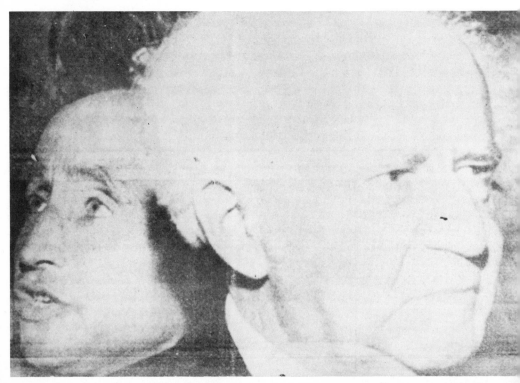

Prime Minister David Ben-Gurion and his confidant, Isser Harel, director of Israel's intelligence and security services.

Jacob Dori, Israel's first chief of staff in 1949, later a member of the Olshan-Dori commission. Right: Premier Moshe Sharet in 1955.

Avri El-Ad and Hugo Krug, photographed by secret camera during business negotiations with Mercedes-Benz.

Meeting place with the Egyptian intelligence officer in Vienna in 1957: the Europa Coffee House.

Levi Eshkol, then Israel's minister of finance and later prime minister. Right: Dr. Benjamin Halevi, presiding panelist in Avri's trial.

Avri in Ramla Prison in 1960, welcoming outside guests to a performance of the drama circle.

Ramla Prison. The second window, third floor, indicates the cell Adolph Eichmann would occupy in 1961.

Yigal Allon, Israel's minister for labor in 1964, later its foreign minister.

Avri El-Ad, six months after his release from prison in 1967.

"Not as much as we needed, and I so informed headquarters. The men had practiced demolitions in the desert, but this is not——"

"I don't want to know about the background," Lavon broke in. "I want to know if you had enough to carry out the actions."

"Oh, yes . . . for the first actions, certainly."

"Are you keeping up?" Lavon asked, looking at Eppie. "Yes, continue," Lavon said to me.

"Continue about what? I have answered your question."

"So you had enough for the post office in Alexandria and the libraries. . . ."

"What post office? What libraries?"

Lavon was startled. Evron stopped taking notes.

"You said you had enough explosives for the first couple of actions, didn't you? Well, were the first actions against the post office and the American Information libraries?" Lavon's voice hardened to open hostility.

I acted contrite. "That's not what I said, honorable minister. I said we had enough explosives for the first actions, which were the movie theaters and the railway terminal."

"So who else planted bombs?"

"Maybe the Moslem Brethren, or the Communists." I shrugged. "A lot of these things happened. Bombs were on Egypt's daily agenda."

"Maybe your people acted without your knowledge," Lavon shot back. "What did you know about them? They were all local people."

Though repelled, I remained calm. "I don't like that insinuation. They are *our* people. They never acted without my knowledge. They were good people, and they did everything in their power to fulfill their tasks."

Lavon shifted the direction of his attack. "What about yourself? You haven't the cleanest vest, if I remember correctly. Perhaps you carried out the actions on your own?"

His allusion to my past court-martial angered me. "That's not the case."

"What would you say if I told you that your superiors informed me that you acted on your own, without orders, for reasons known only to you? What do you say to that? Do you think they are lying?"

These seemed to be exactly the tactics Gibli had predicted.

"I don't think they told you any such thing. If they did, they're lying. Why don't you have them confront me if you believe them?"

"That's what they claim, but, nevertheless, I had my doubts when I learned more about your background. With your abilities, I think you could go far if you don't mistakenly get involved with the wrong people. Do you understand?"

I nodded, recognizing yet another tack.

"Tell me. Could it be that other people, unknown to you, carried out the actions? You couldn't have known everything that was going on in Egypt."

"That's true. However, you overlook one point. Uncoordinated actions would have endangered everybody. If that had been the case, it's possible that we might have chosen the same target, or one nearby, simultaneously. Somebody would have walked into a trap. No, the assumption that other people, ours, as you suggest, operated without coordination, is farfetched. I can't believe it."

"Then could it be possible that you misunderstood the orders given you by Lt. Col. Motke Ben Zur? He did give you the orders, didn't he?"

"What orders? When?"

"When you met him in Europe. The orders to attack, to start operations."

"Again there's a misunderstanding. When I met Motke, he gave me command of the network. Nothing more was discussed than setting up communications and the *possibility* of activating the network . . . no specific orders were given."

"No objects or targets were mentioned?"

"Certainly! Motke wanted to know the risks involved in attacking public facilities like railroad stations, government offices, theaters, and the like. Knowing the situation in Egypt, I gave him my assessment."

Lavon looked at me long and hard. "You still maintain that neither you nor your men threw bombs in the post office?"

"I've already told you. By the way, when was this action against the post office?"

Lavon searched through some papers before him. Reading from one of the pages, he said, "On the second of July. You don't know about it?"

I paused, faking some mental calculations. "That's impossible. Arriving on June twenty-ninth as I did, there wasn't enough time for me to contact the ring and organize action on the second."

"When *did* you receive the order to activate the network?"

"To the best of my recollection, on the seventeenth of July."

"How can you be certain it was the seventeenth? Do you have a copy of the cable?"

I chuckled. "Honorable minister, on enemy soil one does not keep copies of sabotage orders. But I do remember that it took four to five days to prepare for the action on the twenty-second, the eve of celebrations for Egypt's independence. Yes, I am almost certain it was around the seventeenth."

Lavon drummed his fingers on his desk a long time before he asked, "After your arrival here, did anybody ask you about this specific date?"

"Chief of Staff Dayan asked me this morning if we initiated action prior to the seventeenth. Nobody else."

For five hours, interrupted twice by beverages being served by Lucia "Lucy" Lavon, a petite, lovely woman nearly twenty years her husband's junior, the grilling continued. Lavon was brilliant, cunning, cynical, benign, benevolent, and threatening, as he probed for a truth he was beginning to realize he was never going to get. At the end I was drained, but he was a nervous wreck. His face had paled at first, but now his hands were taut and trembling, his voice reduced to a whisper.

I almost began to feel sorry for him. (I did not yet know the central issue and purpose of the conspiracy against Lavon: Gibli was claiming that Lavon conveyed the action order to him on July 16; Lavon denied it, vowing he'd never given the order, at any time.)

At Gibli's house, I gave him a full account.

"I knew what I was saying," Gibli said, grinning triumphantly despite the aura of fear permeating the room. "Did he give you anything to sign?"

"No, but Eppie Evron took notes."

"Ah, that *Voos-Voos*![4] Yes, Evron is worthy of his master. Tomorrow, beware putting your name to anything."

"How can I refuse? Lavon is the defense minister."

"Find an excuse. *Any* excuse."

Motke drove me home to Haifa, but now I didn't even know where home was. Shula, in my four-month absence, had leased a new flat. I couldn't wait to get there, away from the intrigues.

On the way, Motke gave me more instructions. "You'll have to write another Pierre report in accordance with the directives Benjamin and I laid out to you, one adhering to the readjusted dates and orders."

"Do you need it tomorrow?"

"I need it *yesterday*!" Motke grinned. "But I assume you'll be busy with more interesting things tonight."

We rode in silence for a while. Something within Motke was bursting to come out. When it came, it was bitter.

"You might be getting a new commanding officer. I may be leaving the unit."

I was stunned. "Why? Is it because of what happened in Egypt?" Motke remained silent. "If it is, I'll leave with you."

"It has nothing to do with you," he said, almost resignedly. "You've done an excellent job; you will remain."

I accepted his explanation for leaving Modiin, that he was to participate

---

4. Slang for a nosy Jew who always asks, "What, what?"

in the general staff course, preparing him for a raise in rank. (Later I would learn that quite the opposite was true. Already he was a victim of the scheme against Lavon.)

We reached a shopping center on Mount Carmel overlooking Haifa and stopped in front of a two-story duplex.

"The light at the top of the stairs is yours."

I took the stairs slowly, feeling pride as I read on the doorbell, Avri and Shula Seidenwerg. I was finally home again, safe from machinations for a few hours.

The following morning, with heightened anxiety, I read some news clippings Motke had given me. The defense of the thirteen had rested its case. Hassan El Gedawy, one of the Egyptian defense counsels, had appealed to the court for mercy.

"These boys," he pled, "should be spanked and sent home. They fell an easy prey to adventurers and to temptation, and even blackmail. The court should sentence the alleged ringleaders, John Darling and Paul Frank, who have not been found, and Max Benet, who has committed suicide in his cell, but not these kids." He further claimed that when Paul Frank came to Egypt in June, he asked them to repay him for the good time they had had in France and Israel by setting fire to the Alexandrian central post office. "Frank's plan was calculated to lead progressively to more serious crimes by his subordinates, who were trapped by his threats."

According to other clippings, the accused admitted in court to operating secret wireless transmission to Israel, claiming pressure from Paul Frank, who threatened to denounce them to the authorities for having visited Israel.

Other accounts reported that the court had moved to Alexandria to make an on-the-spot examination of the post office and the American Information Library.

Featured was a picture of the Hallicrafters radio, intact, the one I'd ordered Azar to throw in the sea, the one he told me he'd dumped. Why had he lied? Simple fear of facing me with his defection? He hadn't gone to the police until he felt he was lost. Otherwise all would have been lost from the start.

I realized that Lavon had access to every article written about the trial; and, having read the accused's testimony, revealing the events as they'd actually occurred, *Lavon knew that I was lying.* With Gibli and Motke telling the same version, he knew that they were lying as well. Who else had lied to him? All faces were against him.

Suddenly I saw the formidable wall against which Lavon was butting. He knew the facts but couldn't get anybody to admit them. He was fighting a conspiracy far tighter than I imagined possible. Somebody had to break if he were to win.

I vowed that it would not be me. The responsibility for damaging Zahal would not rest on my head. (Too late I would realize the lie in that.) Before meeting with Lavon again, I handed Motke a completely revised version of the Pierre report, stressing our new story line.

This time Lavon's interrogation was better prepared, but it led him nowhere. At the end he handed me a typed summarization of our previous meeting. I read the pages. He had taken some of what I'd said and matched it to his truth, yet it was essentially my statement. Seeing my lies on paper made me uneasy.

I was terribly confused now as to why Lavon would want me to sign my statement, which was merely a version of the events as Gibli and Motke had concocted them, except for Evron and Lavon's intentional alteration of a meaning here and there.

At Gibli's I rehashed the meeting with Lavon, hoping Gibli would clear up my confusion. But he volunteered nothing. It was as if I were being trusted *only* to a point.

"Did you sign the statement?" Gibli asked.

"Not immediately," I said, leading him. "I wanted to read it first and——"

Gibli sprang from his chair, his face ashen. "What do you mean, *not immediately!* I told you not to sign!" He was taut as a coiled spring, his hand clutching a glass of Scotch. Something happened I'd seen countless times in movies, but never in life—the glass splintered in his grip.

Realizing I had gone too far, I told him to calm down. "I haven't signed anything, Benjamin."

Motke arrived. The three of us then decided that when Eppie Evron offered the statement for my signature, I would demand that it be submitted first to my superiors, a stalling tactic.

But Eppie never brought the statement. Three days later I was instructed to appear before the investigating board of inquiry.

The Olshan-Dori Board of Inquiry, an ad hoc panel of two, was investigating the debacle in Egypt. It had been called by Prime Minister Sharet at the insistence of Lavon, after he had failed to break through the wall of lies condemning him for being the highest authority ordering the action in Egypt. Central to the inquiry were two questions:

> First, what was the extent of the ring's sabotage activity in Egypt? Had the ring struck on July 2, 14, and 22, as confessed by those on trial in Cairo, or were the accused coerced into confessing to crimes committed by other parties?
>
> Secondly, did Defense Minister Lavon give the order to Modiin Director Gibli on July 16 to carry out sabotage action (as claimed by Gibli and seconded in a ruling by the general staff headed by

Dayan), or had the defense minister *never* issued the action order to Gibli at any time (as *he* claimed).

Unraveling the controversy left only two possible conclusions for the panel. If Gibli got the action order from Lavon on July 16 and the ring's first action took place on July 22, then the panel could logically conclude that those on trial had been tortured into confessing falsely to the actions against the Alexandria post office on the second, and the USIS libraries on the fourteenth, crimes not of their doing. Thus Israel would be rescued from the consequences of having initiated military sabotage against America's political posture in the Middle East.

If, on the other hand, Lavon was found never to have given Gibli the order to commence any action in Egypt, then the only logical conclusion was that the ring had in fact been ordered by someone else to initiate action against United States property on the fourteenth.

Reaching the latter conclusion meant that Gibli, a ranking colonel and director of military intelligence, was lying, as were those of us supporting his contention that the only action the ring initiated in Egypt was on the twenty-second. Condemning Gibli was to admit that a clique of military officers had undertaken military action to alter international diplomacy without the knowledge and consent of both their military and civilian superiors; and that, to save themselves, the clique had instigated a conspiracy to place the final responsibility on the man they most disliked and the man most vulnerable, Defense Minister Pinhas Lavon.

The outcome would be simple. If Lavon *had* given Gibli action orders on July 16, then he alone would be culpable, and therefore, still alone, he would be subject to censure. At worst he would be dismissed from his post in disgrace.

The alternate result was the damning one. If Gibli were lying, then Israel had to contend with international repercussions, admitting that the confessions of the accused in Egypt were true. Also the admission would indicate that Israel had an internal problem of near-mutiny in the one institution in the country in which the man in the street had complete confidence: the army. To admit that Gibli and his fellow conspirators were guilty was to bare to Israel's populace the ruinous confession that the army was ridden with Fascist tendencies.

Besides that the State simply could not afford to dismiss those who might be involved in the conspiracy; rotten as they might be, they were simply too powerful and important to the State at this time. Some means would have to be found to control them.

The toss-up was heavily weighted against Lavon. It was him or the State.

Did the country really want to know the true facts of the imbroglio, I wondered, as I arrived to give my damning testimony in the framing of Lavon. Along with my concern for Israel, I should have been exercising a little enlightened self-interest.

Jacob Dori had been Zahal's first chief of staff at the creation of the State, and Jitzak Olshan served as president of the Supreme Court. Both were men of concern and integrity, men whose very inclusion in this investigation indicated its gravity.

Strangely the Olshan-Dori panel was not a military inquiry, even though the circumstances to be studied were purely of a military nature and of the utmost secrecy. The panel had been appointed in December by Prime Minister Sharet on Lavon's insistence, five months after the debacle in Egypt, when it was formally concluded by the general staff (headed by Dayan) that Lavon had given the order to commence action—a conclusion that Lavon was repudiating vehemently. Hence his demand for a full inquiry.

The board convened on January 2; I made my appearance on the eighth. The board sat in session at an inconspicuous private flat in Tel Aviv, apparently not wanting to chance its discovery by unauthorized persons. I sat before Jacob Dori, a short, frail, bald man wearing huge, black horn-rimmed glasses. Jitzak Olshan, a hard man who looked like anything but a judge, had his well-known scarf around his neck. Both men looked wrung out and confused. Olshan stated the purpose of the session.

"We expect the truth. Also be warned that everything concerning your testimony is to remain secret. Only by the permission of the prime minister himself are you allowed to divulge the details of your appearance here."

The questions were as I expected. When I had seen Motke, what was said in Paris in June? What were the specific communications orders, the gist of the planning? All were directly related to when, where, and how. My answers were totally in context with the revised version as discussed and plotted by Motke and Gibli.

"Who do you think was responsible for the actions prior to July 17?" This was the day preparation orders were supposedly transmitted to me in Egypt.

Denying that we had struck the post office or the USIS libraries, I said, "Various possibilities. The Moslem Brethren, the Green Shirts, the Communists, any of the nationalists."

"When did you receive the order to alert your people?"

"On the seventeenth."

"When did you first act?"

"The twenty-second, the eve of Egypt's Independence Day."

"When did you arrive in Egypt?"

"On the twenty-eighth or twenty-ninth of June. Let me check my diary." From my briefcase, I extracted my revised diary, carefully obscuring the presence of the original. Dori asked, in astonishment, if keeping a diary wasn't against elementary safety precautions. I smiled. "Not to keep one would be illogical for a German businessman who records everything of his various meetings, conversations, et cetera. The question is, who can interpret what is written?"

Motke was at Gibli's when I arrived. Gibli asked me how it went.

"OK. My diary convinced them," I said, deciding finally to divulge the existence of my two diaries.

"What diary?" both of them nearly shouted.

"The one I took my reports from."

They were stunned.

"You showed them your *diary*!" Gibli said.

Motke caught on. "Wait a second, Benjamin. I think Avri has something up his sleeve."

Gibli calmed down. "Yes, tell us the story of the diary."

I gave my account of the two diaries, then showed them the revised one.

"Where is the original?" Gibli asked.

I hesitated about ever giving it up, for it was a convincing link to the truth, except that which could come from Levy, Dassa, Nathanson, and Azar; but the mood of the trial in Egypt didn't give me much hope that they would be telling their versions for a long time, if ever. Finally I handed it over.

Both Motke and Gibli scrutinized it entry by entry. Gibli said, "It's cleverly arranged. I think it would be wise for Motke to take the original for safekeeping."

I was given back the revised diary, certain that I had relinquished the original forever. (When I gave my original diary to Gibli and Motke, I did so fully believing our trusts to be equal—equal in our commitments to each other, equal in our united efforts, and equal in the integrity and justice of our collective efforts on behalf of Zahal and Israel. Otherwise I would not have relinquished the diary, for it was *me*, my very life in what honor I possessed. My immediate instinct told me to keep it, but my trust in these men was absolute; it overcame my sense of fear of separation from the true record.)

Gibli and I remained alone after Motke had left, discussing again what had happened in Egypt. During the conversation I mentioned my encounter with Col. Osman Nouri in the lobby of the Hotel Cecil, where, after we'd viewed Reuters' newscast together, the colonel had said that his opposite number was giving him a hand in smashing the network. Gibli, seated on the sofa, buried his face in his hands without comment, remaining that way for several minutes. His reaction was directly tied to what I'd said, but I couldn't fathom it. I only knew that it deeply troubled him and alarmed me.

On the tenth of January, I was instructed to be at the Jordan Hotel in midafternoon because someone wanted to talk to me in Room 5. The message hadn't come through regular channels. Secrecy abroad was one thing, secrecy at home quite another; my imagination was going full speed when I knocked at the door.

Jacob Dori stood facing me! Studying my surprise, he got right to the point, though it was plain he was searching for the right words.

"Avri, I know you are a good man, and I also know you've done a splendid job. Nobody has ever doubted that the security of Israel is closest to your heart. You have proved it. Therefore I've decided to have this talk with you. Mind you, only a few know we are here.

"All my life I have been an activist myself, but in a democratic manner. In a democratic country (God forbid that Israel isn't democratic) it cannot be that a group of army officers can make policy for the entire state, not even when they are guided by feelings that they are doing it for the best of all concerned, feelings that the security of the state is in jeopardy. The security of the state is not the monopoly of one man, or even a group of officers. It is a matter that concerns all of us." Dori paused, pain written on his face. "So, please, I am appealing to you, if you have said something before the committee that did not reflect the true situation, or you have withheld or forgotten details which you are willing to tell me, please do so."

I was in turmoil. Dori had touched my conscience, which had grown more painful by the day in anticipation of the board of inquiry's findings. Lavon, I was reasonably certain, would be saddled with the responsibility of the debacle in Egypt by virtue of the order he supposedly gave to initiate the action. In the roar of things, I felt that his political career had to end; there seemed no other way for him. And, for the first time, because of the consequences for him, it struck me forcibly that Lavon might be telling the truth.

And Dori was telling me something I had only suspected: Officers had conceived their own foreign policy and had carried it out, contradicting a basic tenet of Israel's law, whereby any action involving an Israeli soldier on enemy territory must have the approval of the defense committee of the prime minister's cabinet, thus making it a democratically responsible action.

Cabinet approval of military actions is significant. Israel lacks a written constitution specifying the responsibility of the minister of defense, the chief of staff, or the prime minister. According to some legal interpretations (disputed by other men of jurisprudence), the commander-in-chief of Zahal is the minister of defense, not the prime minister or the president, as might be customary in the constitutional democracy. Cabinet approval presents a check and balance against the caprice of an insurgent minister of defense, although other social remedies do exist.

Israel's army is a civilian force, and while its officer corps is a professional one, there exists a tradition of having a responsible chief of staff who would demand confirmation from the cabinet before undertaking any major action on orders of the minister of defense. Under Ben-Gurion, it had been guaranteed: He had served simultaneously as both prime minister and defense minister.

It seemed, as I heard Dori, that the process of checks and balances had broken down under the drive of ambition and discord among the three men holding the major offices: Prime Minister Sharet, Lavon, and Dayan. They had split the spheres of power into personal arenas of control.

My mind raced, urged more by feeling than understanding. I was on the precipice of spilling out the entire imbroglio when Dori stopped me cold.

"Take your time, Avri; don't tell me now. I'm going downstairs to the lobby. When I come back, give me your answer."

He left, and in the space of his absence, the opportune instant passed. I knew I would never tell him the truth, and I never did—not until my trial three-and-a-half years later, at which time the conspiracy found a new victim—me.

How history might have changed for Israel, had I spoken then! Had I been able to foresee what was to take place, I might have eliminated the destruction of innocent men and seen to the punishment of the guilty simply by telling the truth. In a blind attempt to protect Zahal's innocence, I was dooming it and Israel to a perpetual lie.

At the time I had nothing in the world to lose. Later I had everything to lose. Life allows no replays.

Chapter 18

The Olshan-Dori Commission of Inquiry presented its findings[1] to Prime Minister Sharet on January 12, 1955: "In the final analysis, we regret that we have been unable to answer the questions put to us by the Prime Minister. We can only say that we were not convinced beyond any reasonable doubt that Col. Benjamin Gibli did not receive orders from (Lavon). We are equally uncertain that the Minister of Defense did in fact give the orders attributed to him by Gibli."

In lesser words, a draw! The conspiracy had failed to indict Lavon beyond doubt; at the same time, it protected Gibli and Dayan. The raging issue between Lavon and Gibli, unknown outside the government and the military, remained unsettled. Testimony from those of us wedded to the conspiracy—and from Lavon's enemies who were innocent of the frame-up—guaranteed the lack of a decision. It is to the credit of both Olshan and Dori, given the lies and distortions presented to them, that they did not rule outright against Lavon. (Jacob Dori's plea to me in the hotel room prior to rendering their findings clearly indicated that he and Olshan had not been fooled; at the end, they were plainly unable to ferret out the crime they suspected was being perpetrated.)

The investigation's critical shortcoming was the limited list of witnesses, a consequence of Olshan and Dori's faith that intrigues of such proportions were impossible in Israel's military establishment. They believed that

---

1. The Olshan-Dori protocol is still considered secret. However, parts of it have been released to selected personages for study.

the art of internecine intrigue belonged to the Arabs. In their worst nightmares, they could not imagine that some of Zahal's highest ranking officers, indeed, the highest, would purge a civil superior with criminal tactics. Because of their gullibility, only department heads and key military officers, twelve in number, were summoned as witnesses. None of their subordinates—men whose testimony could have ripped the conspiracy to shreds—testified.

It was a diverse cast of characters:

Defense Minister Pinhas Lavon (1) had only his aide, Ephraim Evron (2) to support his denial of ever having issued a sabotage order to Gibli. Theirs was a brave but futile effort.

Modiin Director Col. Benjamin Gibli (3) spearheaded the conspiracy, sticking unswervingly to his claim that Lavon had given him the alert order on the fifteenth of July and the action order on the sixteenth, both orders verbal and unwitnessed. His word against Lavon's.

Head of Modiin Unit 131, Lt. Col. Mordechai "Motke" Ben Zur (4), Maj. Avraham Dar (5), and myself (6), along with Gibli, so far as I knew, were the core of the conspiracy. Though the three of us could not verify Gibli's claims (none of us had been present at either of his two unwitnessed *tête-à-têtes* with Lavon), our perjurious testimony contradicted Lavon simply by supporting Gibli's assertions that no sabotage actions had been carried out prior to the action on July 22, at Nathanson's capture. This meant, circumstantially, that Lavon could have given the sabotage orders on July 15 and 16, and that they could have been transmitted to me in Egypt on July 17 and 19, per our testimony.

Chief of Staff Gen. Moshe Dayan (7), Gibli's silent partner, testified as neither accuser nor defender of either the defense minister (his superior) or the Modiin director (his subordinate). Lavon was too fearful to openly accuse Dayan of collusion with Gibli, both because of the latter's popularity and because of his own non grata status in the defense establishment. Thus, free of such charges, Dayan perjured himself and also presented "objective" testimony detrimental to Lavon's professional abilities as head of defense; he did this by volunteering examples of Lavon's behavior in the past, in which the defense minister had sought to disassociate himself from military actions for which he had given prior approval. Dayan was contriving to present these instances as yet other examples of Lavon's custom of trying to clear himself of responsibility for an action *after* it had been carried out with his approval.

However, it was not noted that the prior actions to which Dayan referred had been disclaimed by Lavon *because they exceeded in scope and force the plans he had actually approved.* It was Dayan's duplicity, in presenting one plan of action for Lavon's approval and initiating quite another in fact, that caused their early split. This was a little-known contention because Lavon was loath to complain—and thus admit that he did not have control of his defense department. More than once he had covered for Dayan and Gibli by taking responsibility for military actions that he had approved in more limited versions. The mishap in Egypt was an instance, however, when he was not assuming responsibility for anybody—contrary to Dayan and Gibli's belief that he would cover for them. It was Lavon's refusal that forced the issue, leaving them no choice but to frame him with the responsibility.

Maj. Shlomo Millet (8), though not active in the conspiracy, had sufficient facts of the events to blow Gibli's case against Lavon wide open. Yet he remained silent, knowing that Lavon was being framed. He opted for preserving Zahal's image, as did the Department 8 head, Lt. Col. Hayim Washben (9).

Director-general of the defense ministry, Shimon Peres (10), Lavon's subordinate and another Ben-Gurion protégé, actively supported Lavon's ouster, though the extent of his knowledge of the conspiracy was unknown to me. Peres had great animosity toward Lavon, much of it based simply on the fact that "Lavon did not do things as Ben-Gurion had." Lavon had cut off Peres's free hand, which had been allowed him by Ben-Gurion; Lavon held him accountable for all his decisions. But Peres also had more personal reasons for wanting Lavon destroyed. At his appointment as defense minister, Lavon discovered that a brother of Peres, a partner in an electronics firm, had a lucrative, privileged contract with the defense ministry. Lavon put a stop to the nepotistic contract. And Peres, in testifying before the panel, did all he could to put a stop to Lavon.

Dayan's deputy chief of staff, Gen. Josef Avidar (11), testified no further than what he knew: that he had seen Lavon and Gibli talking privately on one of the days Gibli claimed he received a verbal order from the defense minister.

Isser Harel (12), director of the Mossad and chief executive of all security services (he chaired the committee of secret service directors), was outside the fraternal crises. However, Isser owed his lofty position to Ben-Gurion, and Ben-Gurion wanted Lavon out; in addition, Isser had always been Gibli's staunchest competitor; so he wanted to see *both* of them ousted.

Olshan and Dori's January 13 decision was already history. There was no turning back; the impossible had occurred: Israel's military hierarchy had carried out a criminal purge. Even had there been a wholesale confessional, a people's faith had been shamefully compromised. Once done, some betrayals are never retractable.

The fact remains that someone might have spoken out—and many could have—and there would have been no conspiracy, no frame-up. Had someone only brought forth the fact that Motke gave me command of the network and the order to initiate sabotage action at our June meeting in Paris, a full six weeks prior to the July 15 and 16 dates in contention between Gibli and Lavon, then Gibli's claim that Lavon gave him the orders on those dates would have been precluded.

But Gibli, certain of himself, knew his customers. He knew that none of us in the conspiracy, nor any of those who hated Lavon, would upset the plot. Though not active in the conspiracy, we were, in my mind, guilty for acquiescing. My only excuse was that I was a latecomer to the party; the others were not. They knew what was going on but didn't want to know the details. Each had motives that colored his testimony against Lavon, and all sought, in part, to protect Israel from the truth that a dangerous precedent had been set. Thus it was better that Lavon stepped down, even if framed, than to demoralize the public with the indictment of his purgers. In doing this, they were protecting themselves. There were no warriors on this battlefield, only snipers.

The conspiracy against Lavon began in July 1954, and, step by step, continued right into January 1955, when it became a matter of record in the Olshan and Dori decision. Six months of demoniacal machinations.

Unknown to me the conspiracy was already in motion as I fled Egypt on August 6. Upon my arrival home somewhere near the middle of that August, when I submitted my condemning Pierre Report on the debacle, I was completely ignorant that any such machinery was in force. On my second return in January—to answer to Lavon's interrogations, join the conspiratorial collaboration with my superiors, and take part in the Olshan-Dori inquiry—I still did not know the truth. That Lavon was the victim of a conspiracy, I knew; that he was not trying to disassociate himself from a blunderous decision but instead trying to ward off a blatant framing by his subordinates, I did not know.

I was a part of the forces in motion, but the true reasons had been hidden from me. Motke and Gibli's pretext to gain my cooperation was well chosen: By stating conclusively that Lavon was attempting to save his political future by blaming Zahal (through my superiors), they persuaded me to join them blindly. I trusted Motke and Gibli, and they took advantage of my faith in them. They had to.

I do not believe I would have joined them for *any* reason other than the one they presented to me. I cannot be certain; history is easy to second-guess. But had I not joined them, there would have been no conspiracy. Unable to depend on my blind obedience to them, they were forced to lie to me. They had no choice, and I bought the lie.

As time went by, gradually associating me more and more with the conspiracy, in both practice and spirit, I began to see the real motives behind the conspiracy. I became more or less accepted by the conspirators; I became a conspirator myself. At this juncture, it was too late to go back. And when I attempted to go back, when I *had* to go back to stop a runaway lie, I found that I had a tiger by the tail—and "he who rides a tiger cannot dismount at will." I tried to get off, to bring justice to Lavon *and* Israel, but nobody was prepared to listen. Nobody wanted to listen. Don't rock the boat; Israel cannot survive the scandal. Let the dead dog lie. It did—in Lavon's lap.

Some powers-to-be in Israel at the time of *my own* framing in 1959, when I attempted to clear away the ugly cancer from my country's conscience, were so determined not to let out the truth of the past that they were committed to burying the truth, in silence, with me: ten years in Ramla Prison.

Here, from all the available evidence, is how the conspiracy must have happened:

On July 24, following Philip Nathanson's July 22 arrest outside the Rio Theatre in Alexandria, Gibli had my cryptic cable stating that the ring " . . . went bankrupt." Within a few days, he would learn of the wholesale roundup of the cells in Egypt. Gibli had not anticipated this swift collapse. Hardly more than three weeks had elapsed since my return to Egypt to set the Alexandrian ring into motion. Now he faced a possible catastrophe. He was no longer dealing solely with a military intelligence operation, but with a situation wherein loomed international repercussions for Israel—and the threat of his own ruin.

The sabotage operation had been exclusively his action, initiated without the knowledge or approval of the prime minister (Sharet) or any of the government charged with responsibility for external military actions. Nor had there been joint planning with the Mossad, a consequence of the crippling competitiveness between our two foreign intelligence arms. More importantly for Gibli, *he had not secured a written action order from Defense Minister Lavon, a prerequisite for any military action extending beyond the state's borders.*

Gibli stood alone in the present dilemma. His only military superior who had given general approval to the sabotage scheme was the chief of staff; but Dayan had been in the United States since July 7. Immediately Gibli began plotting to protect his military future, the ultimate goal of which was his appointment as chief of staff.

However, several considerations complicated his plotting. (1) All those arrested in Egypt would undoubtedly confess under the inevitable torture. (2) Exposure of the sabotage actions was imminent. Egypt's propaganda machine would take full advantage of Israel's blunder. (3) Exposure would result in international sanctions through the medium of the United Nations, and especially from the United States, in light of Israel's past difficulties with Secretary of State Dulles. (4) Despite Israel's strict censorship, which could muzzle local news media, the foreign press was untouchable.

Gibli anticipated inquiries by the prime minister through Isser Harel, Mossad chief. In deference to his long but silent feud with Isser, Gibli braced for the worst. He feared that Harel, armed with vital bits of information on the sabotage (furnished by Mossad operatives abroad), would be eager to discredit him. Gibli had headed Modiin almost from its creation, and it was his determination that had held at bay Isser's ambitions to make Modiin secondary to the Mossad.

General Moshe Dayan further complicated Gibli's bleak situation. Gibli had no illusions that the chief of staff would stick by him now that the sabotage plan had failed in such monumental fashion; Dayan was not a man to champion failures. A pragmatic man himself, Gibli well understood the options open to Dayan. (1) Dayan had left for the United States on July 7, a full week prior to the action against the USIS libraries on July 14; therefore, he could disclaim any knowledge of the strike on America's institutions. (2) If forced, he could admit to having given general approval to the plan, but final authority rested with Defense Minister Lavon, both his and Gibli's superior. (3) He could deny any knowledge whatsoever of the sabotage because there had been no witnesses to any of his discussions on the subject with Gibli. Dayan's word against Gibli's forced a confrontation that Gibli wanted to avoid at all costs.

However, one card in the otherwise uncertain deck favored Gibli. He could count on the extreme antagonism between Dayan and Lavon, a discord that went back to their simultaneous rise to the top defense posts. Dayan, as popular as Lavon was unpopular, was the backbone of Ben-Gurion's defense establishment. Lavon, the civilian outsider, was at once alienated from the department, which remained as Ben-Gurion had left it; in addition, he was almost vindictive toward and certainly intolerant of those who isolated him at the top of the defense pyramid. His ire focused on Dayan, and direct communication between the two men had broken down. (In a counterploy for independence from what he claimed was Lavon's intolerable interference, Dayan had once offered his resignation, knowing that Lavon would be forced to refuse it.)

Taking advantage of Lavon's hostility toward his subordinates and his rupture with Prime Minister Sharet, Gibli theorized that if he could maneuver without involving Dayan, he could count on the chief of staff's support in pointing the finger of responsibility at Lavon. *But Gibli had to have received an order from Lavon to commence the sabotage action.*

His blueprint for the frame-up was based on his word against Lavon's, a not-too-threatening possibility considering Lavon's unpopularity. Gibli recalled a general staff meeting on July 15, after which he had spoken privately with Lavon. General Avidar, temporary chief of staff during Dayan's absence, could attest to their *tête-à-tête* but not to the subject discussed. Since the staff meeting had dealt with problems of British withdrawal from the Suez Zone, it seemed logical in Gibli's mind that others would accept the fact that Lavon might, at that time, have given him the order. Thus two goals would have been accomplished, both necessary for Dayan's cooperation: (1) Lavon's having ordered the first sabotage action on July 15 would make absolutely impossible all prior actions, including the strike against the American libraries. (2) Claiming that day and occasion, and the urgency of the moment, would legitimize Gibli's having received a verbal order in lieu of a written directive, which would have been delayed through normal channels. In addition Lavon's giving the action order at that time would remove Dayan from all responsibility, since he had left the country a week earlier. (The possibility of Gibli's having received a verbal order directly from Lavon, without it having gone through routine channeling in Dayan's office, was easily credible since communication between Lavon and Dayan had broken down. Lavon, with Dayan's approval, often approached Gibli directly.)

Gibli had another powerful card to play if Dayan failed to go along with him, but it was a doomsday trump. *Gibli could simply tell the truth!* Playing this card would admit to the world Israel's guilt in striking her allies' institutions in Egypt in an attempt to alter their political directions. Admitting that the planning of the sabotage scheme had begun in the spring of 1954 between Dayan and him, and throwing in the obvious compliance and aforeknowledge of David Ben-Gurion, was to threaten the very existence of the established government. Speaking out would expose everyone to investigation of responsibility. Though Gibli stood to lose the directorship of Modiin, and thus all chance for a generalship and position as chief of staff, Dayan faced dismissal as chief of staff, the last post on his way to minister of defense, the job he wanted on leaving the army. For the two, it was swim together or sink together.

However, upon receiving my foreboding cable on July 24, and lacking certain assurance of Dayan's cooperation, Gibli hesitated. While Motke concentrated all his telltale evidence in a safe place (the operational file, my field reports, my later Pierre Report, etc.), Gibli sent a letter (probably by hand) to Dayan in the United States, apprising him of the network's collapse. In his reply Dayan advised Gibli to secure something in writing attesting to the fact that Lavon had given the action order.

While improvising his defense, Gibli came up with another fact to make his story more credible. He remembered having visited Lavon's flat on July 16, the day after the crucial staff meeting, to discuss a topic current at that juncture. Gibli's revision was to claim that Lavon had given him only the order to activate the ring on July 15 and, on discussing the matter further on the sixteenth, the verbal order to commence action. Gibli was safe on both dates: Both conversations had been witnessed but not overheard.

But there was something else to be considered. Lavon, on learning through the international press the details of the confessions of those arrested, would demand to know the truth of their statements. However, it was a simple matter for Gibli to take the position that the confessions were false statements extracted under torture. The Egyptian government, he could claim, had done so to disrupt the strong ties between Israel and the United States. (Gibli's reasoning became a prophecy: Egypt and Israel's propaganda on the debacle was conducted exactly along those lines.)

On about July 28, at the first public exposure of the saboteurs' arrest, Gibli set his scheme in motion. He informed Lavon, who, anticipating inquiries to his office, calmed Gibli by taking the responsibility of answering to the prime minister on a situation he knew very little about—other than what Gibli told him. As Gibli had expected, when Prime Minister Sharet learned of the arrests from the press, he instructed Isser Harel—who, as Mossad chief, answered only to the prime minister—to investigate. Isser contacted Gibli, who, probably in panic, lied. He told Isser that no order for action had been given, only orders for preparation and planning.

Gibli remained noncommittal as long as my status in Egypt was still a mystery. If I were captured and the Egyptians had proof of my role as an Israeli intelligence operative—proof that could be easily furnished to them—then my hanging was a certainty. If I confessed, Gibli could say I talked under torture; if I said nothing, he could claim that I had initiated the sabotage action on my own. Either way freed Gibli of responsibility, making unnecessary a conspiracy to frame Lavon.

At the beginning of August, prompted by Isser Harel's failure to get anything from Gibli, Prime Minister Sharet asked Lavon for the details of the mishap in Egypt. Lavon, not knowing the full picture because of Gibli's obfuscations, replied that he was conducting an inquiry. Isser Harel, eager to undermine Gibli, then voiced his suspicion of Lavon: "Lavon has kept quiet . . . and his claim that he is investigating the matter without interrogating the chief of staff, Gibli, and others does not point in this direction. If he is really doing it this way, his sole purpose is to clean himself . . . and not to investigate to the core of the matter."

My unexpected escape from Egypt on August 6 limited Gibli's options. Since only a handful of people knew of my participation, he ordered me home. My condemning Pierre Report was damaging to Motke, and it incriminated Gibli.

Then the plan to rescue Victorine Marcel Ninio was presented to me. It would be much later before I would realize that Gibli concocted the rescue mission to get rid of me. Had I gone in, it would have been a simple matter of alerting Egyptian intelligence to my presence and identity. As it was, I arrived in Rome too late to make my sailing and received the message warning me not to go.

The only avenue that remained open to Gibli was the frame-up against Lavon, and he could not do that without convincing me that Lavon was trying to destroy the army for his own political future.

When Dayan returned on August 19, Gibli outlined his scheme. However, Dayan needed assurances that it was foolproof. Checking, he found that his deputy, General Avidar, could attest to Gibli's *tête-à-tête* with Lavon on July 15.

Dayan's next step was to sound out Lavon through Ephraim Evron, which had long been normal procedure. Eppie's response was that he had heard a conversation between Lavon and Gibli in which orders were given for planning, but none to commence action. Dayan countered with a near-accusation that he attributed to Gibli: More than an order for planning had been given. He knew that Eppie would take the insinuation back to Lavon, thus moving the situation off dead-center. He needed for Lavon to commit himself.

Still uncertain, Dayan visited Ben-Gurion at Kibbutz Sde Boker. Though officially reporting on his fund-raising tour of the United States, Dayan revealed the imbroglio between Lavon and Gibli and they discussed means by which the state could bail itself out of the dilemma.[2]

It is illogical to presume that Ben-Gurion had not been privy, or party, to the planning of the sabotage. Periodic treks to confer with him by his protégés, Dayan and Shimon Peres, Lavon's subordinate as director-general of the defense ministry, and also by Gibli, were well known. Undoubtedly Ben-Gurion was hungering to right the wrongs done by Sharet and Lavon, both his appointees upon his retirement, and he wanted a part of the action. Action was his life's blood. He had already called Lavon a mistake, and his faith in Moshe Sharet had dwindled markedly. Ben-Gurion realized that Lavon's ouster would reinstate him as head of Israel's military.

Whatever the full substance of their talk, Dayan immediately advised Gibli to submit to him a written report. Dayan justified his request by saying "(Lavon) might try to rescind the responsibility as he did in the case of one of the retaliation raids."

---

2. Their discussion is according to an insertion in Ben-Gurion's private diary.

Gibli correctly read Dayan's motives: With his scheme on paper, Dayan could always claim that he had been falsely informed of Lavon's ordering the action. Gibli delayed the report while he went to Europe to organize legal defenses for our people soon to go on trial.

But Gibli had a more cold-blooded reason for delaying the report. I was already in Europe preparing the rescue mission, and my death would have cured all his ills. To further comfort him, my Paul Frank cover name surfaced, making my capture a certainty.

At the same time Dayan was determined to get Gibli's report on paper, still trusting his word that everything was under control in Modiin; thus Dayan ordered Gibli's deputy to submit a summary of the Egyptian affair. Col. Juval Naaeman, ignorant of the goings-on, relayed the message to Motke, who, confident that Dayan was acting in league with Gibli and himself, submitted a full and accurate report through channels.

Dayan was stunned: *Motke had given the facts, not Gibli's scheme, and he had omitted Lavon's giving the action order.*

To convince me of the need for urgency in our June meeting in Paris, Motke had thrown the "highest authority" at me as having ordered the action. His direct implication—that this was Ben-Gurion—was understandable. But, having had no direct access to superiors above Gibli, he had omitted it in the report to Dayan. Motke had trusted Gibli's word, as I had trusted his. The *cordon sanitaire* was complete: Ben-Gurion was protected by Dayan; Dayan by Gibli; Gibli by Motke; Motke by me; and me by Levy, Nathanson, and Dassa, who were safely imprisoned in Egypt.

Since other eyes had seen Motke's report, the conspiracy was blown as far as Dayan was concerned. He had no choice but to disassociate himself from Gibli but not necessarily from the conspiracy. The conspiracy still served a twofold purpose: It protected Israel from responsibility in the actions against American and British property, and it presaged dethroning Lavon.

Upon his return from Europe on September 19, Gibli was dumbfounded by Motke's report. As Motke related it to him, Dayan's reply was that he understood Lavon had ordered the action and that therefore his role should have been included in the report. (It is obvious that Dayan was hiding his participation from Motke as he had hidden it from me. Motke might *know*, but the topic was never to be broached with Dayan.)

Gibli understood only too well the ramifications of Motke's blunder. Dayan now held a powerful club over his head. He could only apprise Dayan that he would disassociate himself from Motke's report. He would submit his version, which consisted of conspiratorial facts that framed Lavon and left Dayan clear. In doing this Gibli's actions established for Dayan that old law of command, *primus inter pares*—first among equals.

Gibli submitted such a report, but only after he had persuaded Motke to disavow his own report, by appealing to his loyalty to the army and to Israel. Conjecturing dismissal from the army, or worse, Motke depended upon Gibli to protect him.

Motke did not reckon, however, on being made the fall guy. Though an integral part of the *cordon sanitaire,* he was unaware of its workings, and he broke the rules by which it existed. He had to go. Dayan and Gibli applied the ancient army practice of SOP (Standard Operating Procedure) regarding the submission of incorrect reports: Motke was transferred from his post. To make this more palatable, Gibli explained to Motke that it was better that *he* be transferred to Staff College (an award of distinction, in itself) than that the *two* of them be court-martialed.

Thinking of his family as well as the army, Motke took the transfer gladly. Gibli was protecting him. The *cordon sanitaire* was back in business.

Dayan was still determined to force Lavon to either accept responsibility for ordering the action or deny it. He had at hand Gibli's conspiratorial account and the knowledge that Motke was disavowing his own factual report.[3] At Dayan's insistence Gibli delivered a full briefing to the general staff on Lavon's two orders. With this presentation to some ten to fourteen generals, high-ranking officers and aides, Lavon was officially saddled with having ordered the sabotage.

When the general staff gave him the meeting minutes, Lavon said, "No one among them wanted to probe into the matter directly." However, Lavon did not lash out in his own defense. Assuming that Dayan was being forced to take the step because of his position as general and chief of staff, he quietly went about getting at the truth. Not for a second did Lavon suspect that Dayan had involved himself in Gibli's lies.

Gibli still had no written proof that Lavon had given him the orders; so he entrusted his secretary, Dalia Carmel (only later would she realize that she had aided a conspiracy), with the task of helping Motke retype various documents certifying his version of the actions in Egypt.

The most important paper undergoing alteration was the carbon of the letter that Gibli had relayed to Dayan in the United States. The final sentence of the letter was changed from "In the wake of the conversations we (Gibli and Dayan) had, the fellows were put into action" to "According to orders by Lavon, the fellows were put into action." (Dayan, as he would testify, had destroyed his copy of the original, leaving only Gibli's altered carbon as testimony.)

Forgery experts from Department 8 were given the task of altering

---

3. In January, before the Olshan-Dori panel, Motke would explain his about-face by saying that he had pirated international newspaper accounts of the ring's actions and absorbed them into his unit reports to general headquarters to embellish his unit's activities. He continued to uphold the conspiracy against Lavon.

documents to prove Gibli's story beyond any doubt. Assigned to the documents piecemeal (to keep them ignorant), they changed an operational order to indicate that on July 17 a message was transmitted to Egypt advising me to ready the ring for action and stating that, on the nineteenth, I was supposed to have received the order to initiate action.

All loose ends were tied together. Gibli stood ready to defend against any Lavon countercharge. However, Lavon was not yet prepared to accuse or defend. He believed that Dayan was working to sift out the truth and that if he did not counter Gibli's assertions, the situation would stabilize.

In mid-December he informed Dayan and Gibli to expect questions either before the Foreign Relations Committee or the prime minister's cabinet. Trying to keep things in perspective, he suggested to them they should state that no orders for action had been given by him, only orders for planning.

However, Dayan and Gibli saw this as Lavon's move to extricate himself. If Lavon escaped responsibility, then the burden fell on them. Dayan was to say regarding Lavon's directive: "I kept quiet like a corpse during the time Lavon suggested the formula which he had already sold to the prime minister. I told Gibli that I was accepting the order only in its negative aspect, but not in the positive one. We will not refute the formula, and on the other hand, we will also not support it."

Realizing now that it was either his neck or Gibli's, Lavon took the offensive. He had to prove Gibli a liar. Fearing to make a frontal attack on Dayan's credibility, he stated for the first time that Gibli was falsely accusing him. Lavon had researched the July 15 and 16 *tête-à-têtes* and discovered, as Gibli knew, that both conversations had been witnessed but not overheard. Only *he* knew that he had never given an action order to Gibli.

The plan Lavon came up with was dishonest, but, backed against the wall, he felt that he had to fight fire with fire. Lavon recalled a staff meeting at his flat on July 31; he would claim that Gibli had issued an action order that day, retroactively, *after* (as Gibli claimed) the single sabotage action on the twenty-second. The story, though full of holes, nevertheless attacked Gibli's credibility. Lavon was in a hurry and under great pressure; he was to appear before the committee of five ministers with the presentation of his investigation.

Lavon got a letter from Gibli stating that Colonel Eshet had been present at the July 15 staff meeting. It wasn't much evidence to prove his case. As Lavon knew, Colonel Eshet had been present at the July 31 staff meeting only; at the July 15 meeting, Eshet had been in Europe. This served as a further attack on Gibli's credibility.

Lavon felt that he had a semblance of a case if he could solidify an additional point. He asked Gibli why the office of defense minister had not been apprised of the debacle in Egypt until August 8, when Gibli knew about it on July 24. Gibli's reply was that he was almost certain that the detailed information had been submitted to Lavon's office prior to August 8. Remembering no such report, Lavon summoned Gibli and accused him officially of trying to frame him by eliciting the action order on July 31, after the fact.

Now Lavon jubilantly informed Dayan of the evidence against Gibli. Dayan, on the surface, was forced to consider Lavon's request that Gibli be dismissed from his post; but he knew he could not ally himself with Lavon and bring Gibli and himself to loggerheads.

The next move was Gibli's, and he had already taken it when he suggested to Lavon that he was "almost certain" the defense minister's office had been apprised of the debacle prior to August 8. After his meeting with Lavon on December 28, at which the defense minister formally accused him of conspiracy, the transcribed minutes of their meeting were conveyed to the chief clerk in Lavon's office. According to his story, the chief clerk, Hayim Israeli, on reading the transcript, understood finally what the furor was about. He then conveniently remembered a certain document that had escaped both Lavon and Gibli's memory, even though it had been the direct basis of their confrontation.

Late in the afternoon, when most of the office employees had left for the day, Hayim Israeli came up with the handwritten memo from Gibli to Lavon, dated July 26, which notified the defense minister of the collapse of the spy cell. Lavon's initials, embossed on the "forgotten" memo, were a forgery, the handiwork of Department 8.

Gibli now answered Lavon's demand. That no other copy of the memo was on file at Modiin headquarters or at the chief of staff's office was of no concern. Gibli now had proof that Lavon knew of the debacle five days before the staff meeting at his flat on July 31, and that Gibli could not have elicited an action order retroactively on that day. Lavon had built his case around July 31. His house of cards collapsed. He was defenseless. To the Olshan-Dori panel, he would describe his next step. "I took a very uncommon path. I decided to suggest to the prime minister the appointment of an inquiry committee. This is the first time that such a thing is done with us. . . ."

In 1960, before the Committee for Foreign and Security Affairs, ex–Prime Minister Sharet described what happened then: " . . . the defense minister came to me and said, 'I investigated the matter and I am convinced that a criminal act has been committed. An order which I had not given is attributed to me.' Then the defense minister suggested I should appoint a two- or three-man (board) before whom he would bring all the proof."

By this action Lavon gained the time he needed to restore his shattered case. He had but one avenue left: He demanded my return to Israel.

I came after receiving Motke's letter. Smuggled into the country (since Gibli was instructed by Lavon not to have any contact with me until the latter interrogated me), with the help of Gibli, Motke, and Dar, I rewrote my field reports to coincide with Gibli's case against the defense minister. Lavon's only chance of getting at the truth was lost when he failed to break me.

Then the Olshan-Dori Court of Inquiry met before Lavon could piece together a defense. He went before the two-man panel as accuser and victim, and in a desperate attempt to extricate himself, he further enmeshed himself in his own web of lies and counterlies. Escape was impossible.

Though the panel brought forward no solid decision, Lavon was left with the stigma of guilt. It was enough to bring about his resignation in February 1955. David Ben-Gurion resumed control of the defense ministry. By November he would again hold both the prime minister and defense minister portfolios.

The *cordon sanitaire* was now full circle, complete. The rottenness was contained within. Israel slept, unaware.

Chapter 19

On January 28, 1955, European newspapers headlined the verdict of the "Zionist spy trial" in Cairo. Though the proceedings had concluded on the fifth, the intervening silence gave the world hope for leniency.

But Israel had little faith in Egyptian mercy. Only two months earlier Nasser had hanged six members of the Egyptian Moslem Brotherhood for similar crimes. How could he not hang Jews?

Nasser lived up to our worst expectations with his group verdict:

Dr. Moussa Lieto Marzouk—death.

Shmuel Azar—death.

Maj. Avraham Dar, alias John Darling—death, verdict in absentia.

Paul Frank—death, verdict in absentia.

Philip Nathanson—life at hard labor.

Victor Levy—life at hard labor.

Reuben Dassa—15 years.

Victorine Marcel Ninio—15 years.

Mayer Zafran—7 years.

Meir Meyouchas—5 years.

Eli Jacob Naim—acquitted.

Joseph Cesar Cohen—acquitted.

Eleventh-hour pleas failed. On January 31, Marzouk mounted the gallows. Azar followed him. Eyewitnesses at Bab El Halek Prison in Cairo saw Marzouk, shackled in chains, die stoically, requesting only that he be buried near his father. Azar, also shackled, was tearful and terrified and died as I had known him, persecuted by indecision.

The world's Jewry, totally ignorant of the facts behind the "heinous anti-Semitism" (Israel emphatically denied all involvement) rose up in self-righteous indignation at the new wave of nazism by proxy. Jews had four martyred deaths to mourn: Marzouk. Azar. Max Benet, death by suicide. Moshe Cremona, death by torture.

Simultaneously, with the executions and in contradiction to Israel's wails of innocence, Egypt published a pamphlet, *The Story of Zionist Espionage in Egypt*. It sought to demonstrate that the incendiary bomb attacks were meant to create the impression of an anti-West attitude in Egypt, with the aim of undermining military and economic negotiations.

The Lebanese newspaper *L'Orient* best summed up the sentencing: "We know that, be it Dreyfus, Rosenberg, or Marzouk, . . it was less a matter of answering the question 'Are they guilty and do they deserve such punishment?' than the question 'Do their lives or their deaths serve the state?' "

Still more brutally, *L'Orient* quoted an Egyptian official: "What do they want? We have hanged the [Moslem] Brothers. We cannot be indulgent towards these people."

Israel had gone black in mourning.

I grieved for all of them, even Azar. As an operative I had come to expect death if caught. Like a deep-sea diver, I had descended inexorably into the depths of my element; I had purged myself of the phantoms of death.

Marzouk's death was understandable because he was a Tunisian, a French national under French passport.

Azar's fate, however, genuinely puzzled me. Unlike the others, he was a native Egyptian, who had, in the past, served his country. His conflict was the rivalry of Jewish blood and heritage, and Egyptian loyalty. Though he had acquiesced in the sabotage, at no time did he plant an incendiary. He had kept lookout for Dassa. In the last action against the theaters, he had probably defused the incendiaries (they had not ignited) and dropped them on the floor under the seats, as demonstrated by the police. He had not been responsible for the ring's collapse. Like dominoes in line, as one fell, so fell the others. The accidental ignition of the incendiary in Philip Nathanson's pocket and his instant arrest outside the theater was the result of only one of many weak links. Once he and Levy were in Egyptian hands, Azar had merely shortened the process by confiding in someone at the Jewish Community Center who acted as intermediary to the police, probably to show the good faith of the Jewish population. But Dassa, however, was not logically one of the dominoes. Only Azar knew that he was returning from Cairo by train. Thus Dassa's stepping into the waiting arms of the police was Azar's handiwork, via the intermediary. Why?

Azar, learning of Nathanson's arrest, panicked. Revealing his activities to his Jewish confidant, he must have remained anonymous until he made his decision not to run for it; otherwise the police would have followed him to me. Only at the end did he step forward and agree to lead them to me. To cover the deal the police announced that Dassa had been arrested at his home instead of at the station; Azar's tipping them to Dassa explained how he could report his arrest to me so speedily.

Azar had also failed to dump the equipment into the sea. His refusal to escape—his flimsy excuse of not wanting to leave his mother—meant that he had resolved to help trap me. I suspected that Azar had cooperated with the police in return for special consideration or immunity. The police used his naivete, and the prosecutors perpetuated the charade.

In court Azar was the most cooperative of the accused and, quite rightly, like the others, tried to extricate himself by blaming Paul Frank. His sentencing had been the next to last shock of his life. His hanging was the last.

My assessment of Azar hit my conscience hard. He was dead, unable to defend himself, and already a martyred hero in Israel.[1] But when one deals with human beings, I had learned the hard way, one can always expect the unexpected. How does inner conflict become the symbol for hero status?

While the debacle in Egypt took its toll in human misery and lives, the conspiracy in Israel was greedily claiming its own victims.

Motke was the first casualty. Driven from Modiin by his factual report to Dayan, he was attending the Staff and Command College. Dependent on Gibli to protect him from further retribution, Motke would remain content to serve as Gibli and Dayan's scapegoat.

On February 17, disillusioned and vilified in governmental and military circles, Pinhas Lavon resigned as minister of defense, his political career shattered. Publicly he resigned because his suggestions for change within the ministry and Zahal were unacceptable. But Lavon did not roll over and play dead. He chose to head the Histadrut, Israel's powerful labor federation and his staunchest political supporter. From this seat of power, he would continue to command tremendous influence on government policy.

It was in his personal life that his disgrace did its greatest damage. Though it meant his health, Lavon continued a low-profile campaign to clear his name and to rid Israel of the corruption in some of its officer corps. His opportunity would arise in January 1960. Then, again, he would confront a powerful opponent, David Ben-Gurion.

---

1. Various public facilities would eventually commemorate Azar and Marzouk's names to perpetuity.

Appointed by Prime Minister Sharet to the ministry of defense the day Lavon quit, David Ben-Gurion returned to the one seat in government he coveted as his divine right. Another winner was Moshe Dayan, who, with his benefactor now back in power, had Zahal's direction completely in his grip.

I was already back in Europe, in my naivete assuming that I had seen the curtain drop on the conspiracy that had snuffed out the threat to Zahal—just another episode of sure expediency in Israel's short history. Pragmatic actions in the past had all been directed outward. This was the first in which we had attacked ourselves. (I had yet to realize how deeply the conspiracy would eat into our flesh, though I was to begin witnessing its viciousness.) I resumed my work in establishing the firm in Munich.

In Paris on business, I saw my friend Lt. Col. Uzi Narkiss. Uzi shocked my complacency by confiding to me that Gibli, as well as Motke, suddenly had become a victim of the conspiracy. Col. Jehosaphat "Fatti" Harkabi was about to succeed him as Modiin director. Wanting answers, I followed Uzi's advice and went to see Fatti, Gibli's former deputy on study leave at the Sorbonne.

While Uzi looked on, we discussed conditions at home in the wake of eight turbulent months. Then, dumbfounded, I listened as he accurately outlined the details of the conspiracy. He didn't know why it had happened, but Fatti knew the truth!

Immediately I wrote Gibli, who shot back a two-page reply. He wrote that he wasn't at all surprised at Fatti's ability, and eagerness, to piece together the conspiracy. Gibli claimed that, above all else, Fatti wanted the Modiin directorship. I had heard Motke expound on the grudge between the two—the real reason Fatti was on leave.

Though confused by Gibli's casualness, I dismissed my forebodings. If Gibli wasn't worried, why should I be?

By March, Engineer Paul Frank Import-Export was swinging into high gear. Posing as the firm's sole owner, I had an impressive office. Hugo Krug now had security clearance and full cognizance of the firm's raison d'être. I opened an account with one of Germany's most discriminating private banks, and its cool politeness changed markedly when our credit check was completed. The figure of deposit was impressive indeed.

Suddenly the doorman was rushing to the curb to hold the door of my new Mercedes Benz 300 limousine, a status symbol during Germany's struggle for normalcy in the early 1950s.

But my shaky relationship with the Mossad had deteriorated further. I took this in stride, certain that the resumption of discord was merely Isser Harel's way of applying pressure, now that Gibli was hanging on to Modiin by only a thumbnail. And pressure was what his Mossad people ap-

214

plied! On the personal level all was friendly, but in business I found them amazingly unavailable. They discouraged my undertakings, made recommendations they knew would fail, and initiated ideas of mine without apprising me. But worse, they monitored the mail, and they spied on me.

A low point was reached when Poldi summoned me to Cologne. "You have to leave Germany," he told me urgently. "The authorities are inquiring about you and the firm. There's no time to lose!"

According to Poldi an official letter of inquiry had been sent to our purchasing mission in Cologne by the office of the governor of the State of North Rhineland and Westphalia requesting information on Avraham Dar—*Avraham Dar!*—and me. I demanded to see the letter; Poldi promised to deliver it. In the meantime I learned that in reality the letter had asked for information on *Baruch* Dar, top man in Israel's armament industry.

I confronted Poldi with his deception, then I relayed the episode to headquarters as a warning to Jossi Harel (no relation to Isser Harel), who had succeeded Motke as head of Unit 131. Modiin was rapidly being absorbed into the Mossad's broad organization, and I doubted that Jossi fully appreciated the significance of that. I liked his open honesty but not his personal leanings toward Isser's Mossad.

Yet Jossi Harel had gained his place in the sun as the commander of the famous immigration ship *Exodus*. After our War of Independence, he had gone to the United States to study shipbuilding. Marrying, he remained until he was hastily summoned home to take over the unit. Jossi was clearly a good man, wrongly posted.

Shula and my son, now seven years old, were staying in Vienna until I could make arrangements for their move to Munich. My plan was to fit them into my Paul Frank cover story: I was in love with the widow of a wartime friend of mine. Shula was to be "Lore Landshut" (her maiden name) and Harel, her son, "Harry." However, since he was too young to have been born during the war, I amended the story. Lore's husband, instead of dying in the war, had been captured by the Russians; after his return home, he had died of a pulmonary disease.

In Vienna Shula and Harel would become fluent in the language. Our charade had every chance of success. The only factor that bothered me was that we had to teach my son to lie.

Endless business activity moved spring to the end of summer. I was criss-crossing Europe, charging from one negotiation to another. Flying to Frankfurt to meet Hugo Krug one day (we were asking a Dutch financial consortium a loan of five-million deutsche marks) I bumped into an old acquaintance, one I was not anxious to see.

Gerhard Mertens, architect of Egypt's paratroop corps, weapons trafficker and confidant of the military elite, had met with Theo Bechtold-sheim and me several months before, when he was in Germany on a parachute-buying mission.

Spotting me deplaning, Mertens said, "Oh ho! The master spy! What's new in the spy business these days?"

"I don't believe, Gerhard, you're one to pay attention to everything you hear."

His laughter changed quickly to seriousness. "No, but some of my friends do exactly that. In fact, a close friend of mine has just been appointed head of military intelligence. He's interested in you, and I promised him I'd see you." He grinned sardonically. "As my luck would have it, here you are!"

I went along with Mertens as we got our luggage, concluding that the Egyptians still thought I was a German mercenary. He had told his friend that I would most definitely not be working for the Jews, but probably for a European intelligence group. As had many others who had alternately worked for the West German BND, the CIA, and even Israel (disguised as a NATO organization), Mertens could be taken at face value; his efforts on behalf of Egypt were solely for his own benefit; he was not concerned with my loyalties. He left with my promise to call him.

To be on the safe side with the Mossad, since I was under scrutiny, I informed Ghandi, resident Mossad director in Cologne, of my intention to follow up. Intrigued, Ghandi furnished me with a mini-tape recorder and, much to my relief, said I was on my own.

Long aware of the value in numbers, I decided to take Bob Jansen with me to Hanover, where Mertens had a home. I needed a witness to counter any claims the Mossad might make. Bob was the logical choice; he knew Mertens from Egypt. A further precaution was a Luger tucked into my shoulder holster. Mertens, reluctant to talk in front of Bob, broke off the discussion by asking us to drive him to the airport in Bremen; he was going to Yugoslavia for a few days.

Bob drove, as the recorder in my briefcase taped our conversation, which was mostly about money, naturally. That's what mercenary meant.

"By the way," I asked, "have you seen Colonel Nouri?" Osman Nouri had been deputy director of Egyptian military intelligence at the time of my escape from Egypt; Merten's answer surprised me.

"He has been appointed military attaché in Bonn."

At the airport he said, "If we don't meet again, I'll take the matter up with my friend. He will probably be in touch with you. I knew you were one of us."

Listening to the tape while Bob headed us back to Cologne, I was distressed to find that certain parts were nearly inaudible. However, I knew that the Mossad, with its sophisticated equipment, could rectify that. A week after I'd given Ghandi the tape, I inquired. He replied that there was nothing on the tapes, that, by mistake, I must have erased the conversation!

I was astonished by the blatant lie. I had heard it, and Poldi had later referred to details that he could only have learned from the tape. I immediately reported to headquarters. Jaschka Janiv, one of Jossi Harel's deputies in Unit 131, shot back a reply: "I warned you to stay away from them [Mossad]."

Col. Jehosaphat "Fatti" Harkabi, so far the sole (and innocent) benefactor of the conspiracy, replaced Gibli as Modiin director. Lavon, Motke, now Gibli. Who stood next in line—me?

Gibli had been powerless to stop his own removal. Ben-Gurion, screened by Dayan, could demand Gibli's ouster now that he was minister of defense.

Ben-Gurion later explained it thus in his book, *Things As They Are:*

"I knew very well, as well as respected very much, these two personalities [Olshan and Dori], and because they didn't probe into the whole truth, I decided in my heart not to deal with this 'affair.'

"To Pinhas Lavon, I had to grant the benefit of the doubt, and I continued my relationship with him as a friend to a friend. With regard to Gibli, I saw need to be severe, because of the doubt. He was an officer in an institution that demands a lot of trust, and I decided to transfer him to another post. I spoke about it with [Dayan] . . . This was also the prime minister's [Sharet] opinion. And after I dwelled again in the matters of the defense ministry, I transferred Gibli to another assignment."

This was Ben-Gurion's *official* statement, but it didn't reflect the conspirator's reasoning. Leaving Gibli as head of Modiin would have raised many dangerous questions. Neither Ben-Gurion nor the conspiracy could tolerate Isser Harel's relentless probing, backed by Ben-Gurion's opponents. Mossad had to be placated. At the same time, Ben-Gurion had appeased Gibli by assigning him to command the prestigious Golani Brigade. Moreover, Gibli, who aspired to return as head of Modiin, was immediately available as a threat to keep Fatti in line. But most important, Gibli had to be appeased because he held a sword over Dayan's head: He always had the option of telling the truth.

Everything was running smoothly with the firm when—with no warning—a letter from Jossi Harel stunned me. My operation was to be terminated; I was being recalled.

No reasons were given, but I knew it was an Isser Harel edict. Jossi finally admitted that the Mossad chief had *declared me a security risk.* Though the charge was not spelled out, I felt certain the basis for it was the possibility that I was vulnerable to capture by the Egyptians. I *did* have a lot of information that could have been crippling to our overseas security operations, but so did a lot of other people. Still, I did not associate the charge with the conspiracy.

At this time the negotiations between our purchasing mission in Cologne and Germany's Mercedes-Benz had reached a point of decision. The negotiations had evolved from a chance encounter on a train with my friend Brig. Gen. Amos Horev, head of Zahal's Ordnance Corps. General Horev had suggested that I ask Mercedes-Benz about the possibility of Israel's purchasing and developing diesel engines for our tanks. Even more important was Israel's need for marine engines for torpedo boats. Through Hans Schneider I went directly to the top people. Decisions had come fast, and not to my liking. Since Germany was not permitted by the Allied Control Commission to export marine engines, which were considered war matériel, the talks had stalemated. (Earlier, Israel had attempted to secure the engines via a false French firm. The Mercedes-Benz negotiators saw through the ruse and broke off the talks. Herr Schaffer, Mercedes-Benz export manager, later told me, "The scheme was so amateurish as to insult our intelligence.")

With our cards on the table, Hugo Krug and I presented our firm as the buyer, since Mercedes-Benz objected to being the exporter to Israel. Now Israel was also interested in the UNIMOG, an all-purpose vehicle also built by Mercedes-Benz, plus other small power units not banned by the war-matériel embargo.

Negotiations deepened, and at the breakthrough, Avigdor Dagan, deputy head of our purchasing mission, proposed that Mercedes-Benz send a team to Israel to study the feasibility of their building a plant to assemble the power units. Dagan's suggestion went to its board of directors.

Our fingers were tightly crossed. We were at this stage when I received word to close down the firm. Persuading Jossi was not easy, but he gave me two months.

The last round of talks was attended by Hugo, Avigdor Dagan, and myself. Schaffer, the export manager, stated the decision. Mercedes-Benz wanted a monopoly on the commodities produced and assembled in Israel. After five years Mercedes-Benz would give Israel a license to produce a line of engines, with the right of exportation. The deal would be contracted with Solel Boneh, our largest industrial complex. The company wanted me, as owner of Engineer Paul Frank Import-Export, the firm that was to intercede in case of Arab complaints, to accompany its director, a man named Papas, to Israel.

To send me to Israel as German Paul Frank was almost a sick joke. Exposure of my real identity would bring down the curtain on the impending deal. Everyone knowledgeable was well aware of it; but everyone knew that Israel desperately needed to shore up its sagging economy. The deal with Mercedes-Benz would be the first of its kind.

I had to forestall the disbanding of the firm, and I had to have permission to return home as Paul Frank.

I found Jossi Harel on a cool, rainy night on the Montmartre, that part of the boulevard known as the Street of Whores. I got permission for both, and more.

Modiin's arrangements for safeguarding my identity in Israel were top priority. One mistake in the presence of the sharp-eyed Mercedes-Benz director would not only jeopardize the whole venture, it would also implicate our Cologne-based purchasing mission in activity contrary to reparations agreements. It was up to Modiin to keep the true purpose of my trip home totally secret.

Chapter 20

Late on an August afternoon, shortly before the national elections in which Ben-Gurion would resume the prime ministership from Moshe Sharet, the KLM flight carrying Papas and myself set down at Lod Airport outside Tel Aviv.

Three officials from Solel Boneh, prepared to negotiate for the partnership with Mercedes-Benz, and a representative of the minister of finance took Papas and me to the Dan Hotel on the beachfront. It was, to say the least, unsettling to touch home soil swathed in German identity. I was fearful that some grief-stricken Jew, still suffering from Hitler's insanities, might take a shot at me. The welcoming committee hated me right down to the stiff suit, hat, and cigar—the image I projected was just short of heel-clicking. Our common language, English, I steeped in heavy, guttural German. Papas, however, being of Greek parentage, even allowed himself the sincerity of a *Shalom*.

After a briefing Jossi Harel explained to me that the Solel Boneh negotiators were ignorant of my role; I would have to play it all the way. To ward off encounters with any who might know me, Maj. Jonny Mannerheim of Zahal's Field Security Service would accompany me. He would also be my bodyguard.

Solel Boneh, anxious to get down to business, hustled Papas and me to the hotel's conference room early next morning to meet its representatives. I had already been introduced when I spotted Aron Remes, Israel's first chief of the air force, who knew me from my days in the parachute unit.

Frantically I searched for Jonny Mannerheim as Aron Remes stood ready to grip my hand. Remes looked at me, then beyond! I passed on. Remes had merely seen a hated image. He had blocked out Avri, a Jew. As a stiff German entrepreneur, I was completely outside his realm of association. This interesting discovery about human response gave me a certain freedom in my role.

We were only a few minutes into the talks when one of the men was called outside. When he returned, his face ablaze with sheer joy, he announced in booming Hebrew: "Oil has been found in the Northern Negev!"[1] The negotiators whooped and yelled like rambunctious schoolboys, but since I supposedly didn't understand Hebrew, I joined Papas in his perplexity. Someone explained, and after a thousand *Mazel Tov*'s the meeting came back to order.

"Now," someone said proudly, "we shall be no more a mere dot on the map!"

Because Papas and I presumably didn't know the language, much of what might have been discussed privately by the Solel Boneh members became hurried whispers across the table. As a result I was able to formulate my inquiries to them in a disturbingly penetrating manner, so much so that Aron Remes, clearly agitated by my astuteness, passed in front of me a cigarette box on which he had scribbled a note to his colleague.

The message, in Hebrew, said: "Beware the *goy*. He seems to understand."

I smiled.

"What's so funny, Mr. Frank?" Remes asked, alarmed. "Do you understand what I've written?"

Now I laughed openly. "No, no! It's the way you write, from right to left."

My humorous explanation cleared the sudden tension. Everybody chuckled. Remes countered: "That's because Moses was left-handed."

The next day began the grand tour of the country, our German-speaking guide filled with the need to impress us that the bloody Jews can do anything. When we drove from Tel Aviv to Jerusalem, on the road where, in 1948, during the siege of the city, I had had charge of traffic security, he glorified more than one fact. With a well-placed question or two, which Jonny Mannerheim enjoyed immensely, I brought our guide back to earth. He wanted to know how I was so well versed in Israeli history.

"Quite simple," I replied. "I made a thorough study of your country before I came." I smiled in his face. "German efficiency, I think it is called."

---

1. The Heletz-Bror-Kohav area became Israel's one yielding oil field, producing 14.4 million barrels. By 1973 exploitable oil was down to 1.6 million barrels reserve.

The last evening in Haifa, after five days of touring, Papas was in conference; so I decided to visit friends. Jonny Mannerheim was leaving the hotel with me when I realized I'd forgotten my wallet. While my shadow waited in the lobby, I raced up the stairs and was at my door when I detected movement inside. Easing the door open, I caught a man rifling through my things while his partner photographed my papers. They whirled about, ready to bolt; then the bald one recognized me.

"Avri! What in hell are you doing here? Get out and forget you ever saw us. Please, quick!"

I almost laughed in his face. Internal security (Shin-Beth) was checking Paul Frank's possessions, not knowing that I was Paul Frank. Another case of one hand not knowing what the other was doing. Astounding!

With an understanding wink, I went downstairs, chuckling. I told Jonny; laughing, we left the Shin-Beth with their exercise.

On the day of our departure a final meeting was held at the Zion Hotel in Haifa. Papas told me that he was extremely impressed, and I felt that it was just a matter of his presentation to the Mercedes-Benz board of directors for Solel Boneh to become a partner with the powerful German automotive empire.

Suddenly the Solel Boneh bargainers delivered a radical about-face that compromised everything. They wanted a license to produce and assemble the power products without having to wait the agreed-upon five-year period. Papas, taken aback by the new sledgehammer line of bargaining, stalled.

He left for Germany that night. I remained behind with his blessings, hoping I could persuade Solel Boneh to reverse its position. I was to fail, and by the time I would get to Germany, her biggest automotive company would have already backed out of the deal. Regretfully, Israel missed a chance she desperately needed for her defense and her industry-hungry economy.

It more than slightly rocked me. The deal would definitely have kept the Paul Frank firm in business, regardless of the Mossad. But even more staggering was the fact that Israel, with its flaunting reversal, had insulted one of the most powerful and respected manufacturers in the world. The reason escaped me.

Taking the opportunity while I was home to plead a case for Engineer Paul Frank Import-Export's continuance, I met with Col. Fatti Harkabi, Modiin director; his deputy, Juval Naaman; Mordechai Almog; Jossi Harel, Motke's successor; and others. The subject of the firm's existence had been bandied about rather cavalierly, I thought, and, when my own performance came under fire, Fatti said, "Explain, Avri," antagonism creeping into his voice.

Instead I put a direct question to the group. "Are there any complaints about my work, about lack of results?" The response, to the contrary, made it clear that my recall was the handiwork of Isser Harel and that Jossi, who was my superior, was fast proving himself the Mossad's man in Modiin.

Fighting for my future as well as the firm's, I summed up our achievements in terms of pounds returned for pounds spent, the invaluable connections with German industry, and other benefits to Modiin. The firm was now a tool that would operate without me in another ten months.

"To close it down now, as Jossi has ordered, will be sheer stupidity!" I had no qualms about confronting Jossi when I saw that Fatti was swayed by my arguments. "If I thought Isser right about my being a security risk," I added, "I wouldn't question the wisdom of the order. But the Egyptians wouldn't still be trying to buy my services if they had an idea in the world that I am who I am!" I paused, thoroughly annoyed. "There's a grudge somewhere that I don't know about. To claim that I'm a security risk is blatant hypocrisy. Every Mossad man I deal with is an overt operative, openly employed or connected to our semiofficial or official organizations, all well known to the local security agencies *and* to the Arabs. If anybody is a security risk, they are!"

Jossi was seething, but I didn't care. I was determined to have my say. Admittedly my outspokenness had got me in trouble more than a few times in my life.

"What's behind Isser's charge? I've done nothing but try to cooperate with the Mossad." I then recounted all the obstacles Mossad had thrown in my path. Three years of it, right up to the lie Poldi had told me and the erasure of the tape. I made no concessions in my charge that Isser Harel was trying to get rid of me and the firm for reasons of his own.

"Without Isser's cooperation," I said, in conclusion, "there's no sense in my going back to Germany. His people will simply make it too difficult to operate."

Fatti, agitated over the aspersions I'd cast on his authority, exploded, "Who is Isser! You are going back to Germany and continue your work." When Jossi tried to interject, Fatti cut him down to size. "Let Isser be my worry. Avri is going back!"

Fatti brought up the subject of my former rank. He admitted originally having committed himself to its restoration. However, it seemed that Dayan wanted me returned to Zahal only as a captain.

The decision hurt. "Fatti, I was a major, on the eve of promotion to lieutenant colonel."

"Moshe knows that. Gibli had recommended you for promotion, but in view of what happened, Moshe couldn't follow his recommendation. He's willing to give you captaincy." He visibly tried to brighten the atmosphere. "Above that, though, he wants to award you the Mention in Dispatches.[2] It's only the fifth one awarded so far."

The Mention in Dispatches had been introduced into Zahal during my time in Egypt, and at the time of this meeting was the only notice of any kind given for service to Israel. It signified gallantry and bravery.

"It's not a medal, Avri, it's a parchment scroll which cites your deed." He paused, and I sensed that the award I didn't give a damn about—since my rank was being withheld from me—was conditional.

The condition was: Because my deeds were secret, the awarding of my honor would also be kept secret.

"The award should certainly ease your disappointment in not getting your full rank back," Fatti said.

But Fatti didn't know how deeply my disappointment ran. My guts burned from it. Calmly, bitterly, I said, "I can do without the rank, Fatti, and I can also relinquish the honor of being mentioned in praise in secret." I took a deep breath. "And Moshe Dayan can take the award and stick it up his bloody ass! I don't need it!"

Shock filled the room. Mordechai Almog said, "How dare you express yourself like that about the chief of staff!"

My anger was not to be subverted. "If I am not good enough to have my rank back, I certainly am not good enough for the award. I didn't go out on this mission for it, and I sure as hell don't want it!"

With my outburst, the meeting ended. Fatti decided that I would leave for Munich whenever ready. Despite his boast that he would deal personally with the Mossad chief, I still doubted his backbone. Fatti was an intellectual; Isser was a bedrock of ambition. Therefore I saw no sense in going out again without getting the green light from Isser himself. Jossi said he'd set up a meeting.

A day passed before I had the Mossad chief's answer.

"Isser won't see you," Jossi announced with a somewhat less than convincing tone of ruefulness in his voice. "I couldn't persuade him otherwise."

Hours before I was to fly out, I went to Mossad headquarters and was informed by the guard: "Isser said if you want to see him, you have to go through the proper channels."

Burning mad, I left, already having tried the proper channels through Jossi. By late evening I was airborne, going through the usual envelope of material from headquarters. Inserted was a warning from Jaschka Janiv,

---

2. As of the 1970s, Zahal increased its awards with decorations in three categories, in descending order: Heroism, Bravery, and Mention in Dispatches.

deputy head of my unit: "For your sake and mine, avoid any contact with Isser's men if possible." He'd said it again, this time on paper.

The message sickened me. Jaschka's caution came from experience; he had formerly been in the Mossad. But how was I supposed to avoid the Mossad when my only channels of communication were via the Mossad?

Was everyone blind to the fact that Isser Harel had strangled the very life out of Modiin? Isser seemed hell-bent to emerge the master of all our security services. Once more I vowed silently to avoid Mossad people like the plague.

It was November, and Hugo Krug and I began converting the firm from Engineer Paul Frank Import-Export to a corporation under a permanent name. Hugo's participation had already paid off handsomely; he had led us to conclude our first business deal with an Eastern bloc country. We were prospering beyond all expectations, and for the past two or three months I had enjoyed something of a moratorium on my troubles with the Mossad. Was Fatti actually seeing eye to eye with Isser?

I received a call from Col. Osman Nouri one day. The voice of the former deputy head of Egyptian intelligence startled me. I had thought him too proud to confront me after my duping him when he told me that he was chasing the leader of the ring. But I had underestimated Osman Nouri, an impressive Egyptian soldier if I had ever met one. I did not reveal that I knew he was military attaché in Bonn.

"Mr. Frank, I have regards for you from a mutual acquaintance. Major Mertens told me he'd spoken to you."

I recalled vividly Gerhard Mertens and the tape erasure.

"Are you visiting Germany, Colonel Nouri? I would consider it an honor if you could visit me whenever you get to Munich."

Nouri chuckled. "I'm now accredited to the German government as military attaché, as I believe Major Mertens informed you. Actually I wanted to invite you to visit me here in Bonn. I have a business proposition which might interest you, Mr. Frank."

"Could you be more specific?" I wanted him to broach the subject, especially since he'd just seen through my pretended ignorance.

"No offense meant, but I would rather we discuss it here, say in eight to ten days."

"I do have to be in the north within a fortnight," I lied. "I'll stop over if you're there."

"Just give me a day's notice and I'll see you at the embassy."

We rang off. For a fleeting moment I debated my acceptance of Nouri's invitation. But only for a moment. Damn it! Mossad had gotten to Modiin, and they were insidiously getting to me as well. Nouri was definitely courting me. But what about headquarters? And Jossi Harel?

Back to the old routine, I was forced to go to Ghandi for the minifon tape recorder. However, it would not be available for a few days. Ghandi cautioned me against entering the Egyptian embassy (my sentiments exactly!) and advised that I set up the rendezvous at a coffeehouse where his Mossad people could cover me.

Ten days later the recorder was still out in the field. To gain time I sent Bob Jansen to Nouri to explain that I was temporarily out of the country. Nouri, as I'd hoped, asked Bob about my activities, and Bob replied as I had briefed him.

Another week and no recorder. I finally bypassed Ghandi and met Nouri in Bonn at a coffee garden near the railway terminal. I went armed, my Luger shoulder-holstered.

One thing I wanted to find out, if possible, was whom he had meant when he told me in Egypt that his opposite number was lending him a hand in apprehending the ringleader.

Nouri, a handsome man, looked considerably less menacing in a business suit. Had he known of my true involvement in Egypt, I would be as dead as Marzouk and Azar. Yet because I had evaded him, we sat here now, chatting pleasantly. There must, I thought, be an explanation for this kind of human insanity. He came to the point.

"Mr. Frank, I once tried to hire your services—" he smiled knowingly, I returned it—"and now I speak to you of it again. You are, as you well know, especially valuable to us with your connections. . . ."

At length I explained my personal satisfaction with my business, especially with Israel's purchasing mission.

"The Jew's money doesn't smell," I said. "I make plenty by dealing with them, believe me."

Nouri understood the language of a mercenary. "You are a businessman, Mr. Frank, and I would think that any businessman would sell to the highest bidder. With respect to money, we will do better than the Jews."

"You have a point. Everybody has his price." I had to stall him. "But I have to think about it, Colonel Nouri."

Nouri smiled. "That's why I mentioned the highest bidder."

We parted with the understanding that he would hear from me. However, I hadn't had time to inform headquarters before I had a distraught call to rush to Vienna. Shula was undergoing emergency surgery.

The city was bathed in Yuletide decorations as I waited for her to get well, and I no sooner had got her home from the hospital when I received word to proceed to Cologne. Jossi Harel wanted to see me urgently.

Jossi's Christmas gift to businessman Paul Frank was demoralizing, even if not altogether unexpected. The Mossad chief had bulldozed Fatti. I was being recalled. "You know too much," Jossi said with a shrug. "You could easily become a prize catch for enemy agents."

I countered Jossi's feeble explanation by briefing him on Osman Nouri's offer of no more than a week or so ago. But Jossi, in his typical indecision and inexperience, suggested we discuss it with Ghandi. As expected that meeting became an evening full of rebuke. Ghandi demanded to know why I'd gone to Nouri without advising him, and, to compound his audacity, he claimed I should have obtained his approval!

I was even more infuriated by Jossi and Ghandi's cohesiveness. I exploded, making it clear that he had stalled me almost a month with the tape recorder. "I operate on orders out of Unit 131 and I don't have to get your approval for a damned thing!"

"But you should have informed *me*," Jossi injected.

"Listen, Jossi," I said, unable to hide my sarcasm, "if you had taken the time to study the old correspondence in my file, you would see I have free rein to initiate this kind of contact, and that previous approaches by the Egyptians led to this last one. It didn't come right out of the blue!

"Now, I only want to know whether I continue the contact with Osman Nouri or not? Bear in mind, be warned: Whatever your decision, this opportunity may never come again."

Jossi and Ghandi's *tête-à-tête* in the kitchen of Ghandi's flat left them undecided. Jossi wanted to discuss the matter in Paris (with Avner, head of Mossad in Europe, I imagined); meanwhile I was not to contact Nouri.

"Then do me one favor," I said, still angry. "Get the decision to me fast. I'm committed to another call to Nouri."

He assured me that I would know within four days, and the discussion led to my handing over the firm to Hugo Krug, who would forego all intelligence activity. And I, it was decided, would return home in January.

Hugo seemed genuinely saddened about my leaving. Though happy that he could continue with the firm, he was adamant about his suspicions of the Mossad.

"There's one thing you can count on, Avri," he said. "I don't plan to sit still until they come and tell me to get out. I plan to use my connections not only for the firm, but for myself as well. You didn't, and look what you wind up with. It's only because of you that I'm where I am; so whatever I can do, half of it is yours."

Since Hugo had come into the picture, he and others who helped get the firm going had urged me to make outside deals for myself, but my fingers still ached from being burned in the refrigerator episode.

Shula came to Munich, after recuperating from her operation, and we prepared for our return home. Ghandi then informed me that further contact with Osman Nouri was ruled out. Missing the opportunity of entrenching me as a double agent seemed nearly as shortsighted as when Motke had removed me from my role as a German businessman and installed me as head of the sabotage plan. How many agents in the world ever had *two* chances! And now it looked as if I would never learn the identity of Colonel Nouri's opposite number. Within three weeks the firm was incorporated under another name and transferred to Hugo. Shula had already gone to Israel with our son.

Late in January 1956, I flew home, ready for reassignment. One long year had elapsed since the sabotage; the framing of Lavon; the findings of the Olshan-Dori Court of Inquiry; Lavon's ouster; and the hanging of Marzouk and Azar. Four dead, one disgraced. Gibli and Motke transferred, safe from further consequences.

Had the conspiracy sated itself on victims? I was aware that someone was spreading word about my being a security problem.

Still I was happy to be home. I would return to officer status in Zahal, to my family, and to our beautiful flat up on the Carmel mountainside overlooking lower Haifa. No more pretending, no more guarding against every slip day and night. No more Mossad. No more Isser Harel. My son no longer having to lie and call me "Uncle Paul." Above all I would walk hand in hand with Shula.

Unit 131, now in the confusion of moving to its new headquarters building, was staffed mostly with unfamiliar faces. There were few left who knew of its humble beginnings, with Motke and a single secretary, in the old Arab building in Jaffa. A distinctive difference that chilled me was the obvious presence of Mossad people: Isser Harel was winning the power struggle. Not only was Jossi Harel a Mossad "leaner," but one of his close subordinates, Jaschka Janiv, was formerly Mossad. The addition that really angered me was Benni Magen, the Mossad operative who had once reported me to Motke for a breach of silence. It seemed evident from his appointment as head of the Unit 131 training department that I was being shoved aside. Jossi had offered me that job when I was in Europe. I took the matter to him.

"You have lots to do for the time being," he said. "First, straighten out all your firm's financial accounts with the unit. Then write a summary of all your experiences and conclusions, all your operational ideas and suggestions. They're valuable to us."

I agreed to write a summary but wondered about the firm's financial accounts. What straightening out? I had been painfully meticulous. Nevertheless, after working on it for five days, I submitted the accounting. The response: I owed Modiin more than five thousand Israeli pounds!

When I requested proof of their bookkeeping, Jaschka Janiv found an error in the unit's books: For almost fifteen months the paymaster had credited me with a higher salary than I'd received. The final accounting proved that Modiin was in debt to me for seven thousand pounds!

But before I could be paid, I had to activate a clause in my contract stating that, in a financial dispute, a third party would serve as arbiter.

That done, I began my summary of the past three years. From a room in Tel Aviv, with Shlomo Millet's assistance, the details rolled into countless pages of notes. I realized that the report was going to be more of an operations manual than a summary, for my meticulous field reports had been aptly named "El-Ad Sarchi's volumes."

Headquarters had now decided that I would remain in Israel; so I requested the return of all my personal things that had accumulated in Modiin's archives since I had gone out as a fledgling operative just before Christmas 1952. One day I went to headquarters, to the office of Etka Jiftach, administrative officer in Modiin and the wife of an officer friend of mine. We chatted as she handed me three bulky envelopes. "Check through it and see if it's all there," Etka said. "We're moving, and everything is being thrown into cabinets and boxes."

I held up several rolls of negatives to the light and then rifled through the papers, letters, hundreds of snapshots, dozens of film strips, fifteen or twenty rolls of 35mm negatives, and other stuff long forgotten.

"Got everything?"

"I think so, except for a photo album."

Handing the three envelopes back to Etka for Jossi Harel's approval of their return to me, I left. Two days later, on my thirtieth birthday, Etka gave me the envelopes and I signed the receipt. In an outer room I sat looking back through three years of memories—hundreds of pictures. Then I happened on some negatives I knew weren't mine: a legal report of Max Benet's defense in Egypt before his suicide. Since it was hardly more than confidential material, I didn't concern myself with it.

But what confusion could account for the *other* negatives? In my hand, I held copies of some of the rocket blueprints I had taken out of Egypt with Willi Kubie's help. Was this the way Modiin regarded material for which men had risked their lives? I assumed the negatives were not the only copies of the blueprints extant in Modiin, *but still!*

Shlomo, who had recently been appointed to head Modiin's archive and documentary department, was incredulous.

"You'd better give it back," he said, "and let somebody catch hell."

"I will," I said, "at the proper time."

I had an idea. Why not rechannel these rocket blueprints back to the

Egyptian authorities? We could probably get rid of certain German scientists currently in Egyptian employ.

My report was finished by the end of February. Because of its security sensitivity, I made only three copies, one of which I gave to Fatti Harkabi. Jossi suggested I give the other to Dayan.

"Fine," I agreed. "I'll give it to him personally." I had not seen Dayan since just before I suggested what he could do with the Mention in Dispatches; he had since refused to see me, according to Fatti.

At my return home two months ago, I had questioned Fatti about a future assignment; he had hedged; that puzzled me, until he confessed that *Dayan didn't want me in Modiin any longer!* Then, having finished my financial report—fighting all the while my horizontal push into the tank corps—duty about which I knew nothing and cared less—I had decided to go back to Fatti. Dayan's refusal to see me only drove me harder.

Thwarted and angered, I decided to take my case to Ben-Gurion. There was also my report, which contained a number of proposals of importance to the security of the State.

Without informing my superiors and without prior arrangements, I arrived in Jerusalem. I was unconcerned about whether I would see the Old Man right away: I knew his military adjutant, Nachemia Argov. Ben-Gurion did not show up at his office; so I left. The following day Fatti summoned me.

"Why did you have to run to Nachemia? Do you think he can make Dayan see you?"

"I didn't go there for that reason," I said. "I went to see the Old Man to find out once and for all what is wrong with me. I want to know why I'm not wanted in Modiin."

"Nothing is wrong with you, Avri. Moshe simply thinks it would be better if you transferred to another branch of Zahal." Fatti shrugged helplessly. "You can ask him yourself. He'll see you in a few days."

Suddenly Dayan was willing to see me. Why? I couldn't figure it, unless he was afraid of my talking to Ben-Gurion. Whatever the reason, though Dayan and I would look at each other from behind closed masks, I could talk straight to him.

Sadly the interview was not as I expected. Besides a cold greeting from him, I saw that he had insured himself against my mentioning the past by having Colonel Bar-On with him.

"Why do you want to see me?" Dayan demanded abruptly. Dayan's agitation was reflected in his every movement, his hostility blatant.

"I understand from Fatti that it was your decision I would not remain in Modiin," I said.

"Who said it was my decision?" Dayan barked. "Ask again the one who told you that!"

End of discussion. The buck was passed, and so was I. Typically, Dayan wanted the blame elsewhere. Thinking back, I now realized how right Gibli had been; Dayan was smart as a fox. With oriental guile, he had carved out for himself a reputation for directness, one that had him spitting in the devil's eye, and saying, "I did it! So what!"

Yet the real Moshe Dayan was quite the opposite. In my opinion he was as oriental in mentality as the Arab. He gave the impression of saying one thing when he was in fact saying something quite different. He had all the adaptability of the chameleon. No wonder the Arab had such respect for him. No wonder they feared him.

I could only stare at him now, wondering if Fatti had lied to me. But I knew that Dayan was in the camouflage of deception.

I handed Dayan a copy of the summary I had written, pointing out a number of conclusions I hoped could be put to immediate use. Dayan's relief was visible; encouraged, I brought up the subject of my reinstatement into the regular army. I suggested that I participate in the general staff course to update my qualifications.

"A sound idea," Dayan said thoughtfully. "Why don't you talk to Fatti about it. Two places in the course have been allotted to Modiin, but Fatti decides who gets them."

Fatti promised me a place in the course commencing in early fall. I ignored the discrepancy between what Fatti and Dayan had said about my remaining in Modiin. Since Fatti had given one of the two coveted places to me, I could only assume that it was not he who had lied. Fatti also gave me paid leave. I settled down to wait for orders.

In April a letter from Olga informed me that my father, who had never been sick a day in his life, was ill. Another, two weeks later, warned that he was in the hospital. Olga wanted me to come to Vienna. She was no alarmist. I had to go.

Alerting Jossi Harel, I asked him to arrange my leave with Fatti. Three days passed. Jossi informed me that Fatti had refused my request, saying that I had lied about my father's sickness. Dumbfounded I stared at Jossi and my old friend, Lt. Col. Uzi Narkiss, now Fatti's deputy. Uzi, who had met my father, explained that Fatti had contacted Chanan Barel, Mossad station-chief in Vienna, and Barel's report was that my father was in good health.

I couldn't believe my ears! Fury rose up in me. I looked Uzi squarely in the eyes:

"If my father should die and I'm not at his bedside, I will put a bullet in

Fatti's head! Tell him that, and tell him I want his answer in forty-eight hours!''

Another cable to Chanan Barel brought confirmation of my father's hospitalization (earlier Barel had received erroneous information from an acquaintance of father's). I was given permission to fly to Vienna and, since the arbiter of my financial dispute with Modiin had ruled that the unit owed me seven thousand pounds, the unit provided my ticket.

I was concerned over the safety of certain materials I had in my possession—Fatti had startled me by insisting that I sign an agreement stating that I would not go to Germany. In short he was saying my "security problem" label had deepened to "security risk." I had swallowed enormous pride when I signed the document, but this was no time for haggling.

With Shlomo, the safest hands I knew, I left my attaché case containing materials that at all costs had to remain with me. Included were my personal papers returned to me by Etka, and the all-important materials related to the conspiracy: the fake diary, the page of revisions in Gibli's handwriting, and Gibli's letter to me about Fatti. Additionally there were the Egyptian blueprints, which I had yet to return to the archives.

On boarding the plane for Vienna, I felt as much an outcast as I had after my court-martial, but I soon forgot my own troubles. Olga, forever blessed in my heart for what she had given to my father, crumbled into tears on my arrival. Her family had disappeared in the holocaust, and now she faced losing her husband.

Professor Popper, a renowned specialist in blood diseases, wouldn't commit himself yet on a diagnosis of leukemia, but he prepared me confidentially for the worst. Father failed to hide his pain. His spirits were good, but he was incredibly bent. As I held his hand at the hospital, I realized that we'd been apart most of our lives. As I left he whispered to me, "Don't worry. I'm not kicking the bucket yet."

The endless days of watching took the wind out of all of us. I was exhausted, having given as much blood as Professor Popper would allow. Meanwhile, Olga had taken another flat, and we drove Father to his new home. Then came the prognosis: no hope of recovery. It might be weeks, months, perhaps even a year.

Soon Father improved, and after three months, I decided that it was time to head home. Earlier, Hugo Krug had come to Vienna to report on the firm's prosperity. He told me confidentially of his decision to sever his connections with Modiin, and he reiterated his pledge that whatever he did on the side, half the profits were mine. I had a thousand dollars coming to me on a deal he'd consummated. I debated over taking the money until

Hugo assured me that it was completely independent of the firm's business. He still felt, he said, that he owed me everything.

Two weeks later, on the last of July, I boarded ship in Naples. Everything behind me looked good. Conversely, everything ahead lay cloaked in doubt.

Chapter 21

Throughout the summer and fall of 1956, political bombs from the Middle East exploded in the world's eye, sharpening its image fearfully: a blowtorch trained on a powder keg. Once you have been a participant in a pattern of events, you can no longer be an innocent bystander. You are involved as surely as smoke seeps beneath a door. I stood in the other room as the smoke boiled around me and throughout the Middle East.

JUNE 24. Nasser is elected president of Egypt.

JULY 19. The last of the eighty-thousand-man British contingent leaves Suez, reflecting final failure of Israel's ambitions to halt the evacuation and precipitating the events that follow.

JULY 19, 20. U.S. and England withdraw financial aid for the Aswan Dam, Nasser's glorious vision.

JULY 26. Nasser, in retaliation, nationalizes Suez Canal.

JULY 26-31. U.S., England, and France, counterretaliating, place embargoes against Egypt.

AUGUST-OCTOBER. Nasser rejects international control of the canal, proclaims Egyptian sovereignty.

OCTOBER 25. Syria, Jordan, and Egypt establish a unified military command.

OCTOBER 29. Israel strikes across the Sinai Desert.

NOVEMBER 5. The 100-Hours War ends.

In these five months, major powers were roughly polarized into two camps, and the antagonists themselves settled few if any problems. In the end the one hundred hours only presaged further conflict.

At the beginning the July 1954 sabotage scheme proved to be one of Israel's greatest tactical misjudgments. After that, Nasser became president, assuming total control. Actually his days of compromise had ended before he became president, and two men quite aware of it were John Foster Dulles, U.S. secretary of state, and Sir Anthony Eden, prime minister of England. For Nasser not only refused to lead the other Moslem countries into the Baghdad Pact, he did all he could to wreck the pact. Dulles and Eden promptly withdrew financial aid for the huge Aswan Dam project. Nasser nationalized the Suez Canal, thus fulfilling Israel's worst predictions (and Motke's warning to me at our June 1954 meeting in Paris).

Israel and Syria, after blasting away at each other by plane and artillery and supporting hand-to-hand skirmishes atop Mt. Hermon for almost 116 days, finally disengaged their troops. Jordan questing for Palestine could be dealt with after the Syrians came to terms.

When France, England, and the U.S. placed embargoes on Egypt in July of 1956, Nasser responded by rejecting all attempts at international control of the waterway. Stirred by the intensity of their own propaganda, France and England, calling Nasser a tin colonel and making allusions to Hitler's resurrection, entered into secret war negotiations with Israel.

Ben-Gurion was delighted. Nasser had been receiving arms from the Communist bloc since the first of the year; Ben-Gurion wanted a preemptive strike against them, and France's willingness to supply him with offensive weapons furnished him the capability. His only concern was how much he could count on his European allies once the shooting began.

On the move Nasser took Syria and Jordan under his wing, forming a unified military command; four days later, Israeli forces struck across the Sinai Desert, followed by British and French air strikes on Egyptian airfields.

Six days later, on November 5, with American and Russian threats becoming strident, the one hundred hours ended. Egypt was crushed, but Nasser still reigned.

On my arrival in Israel prior to the fighting, I was still on paid leave and awaiting assignment to the staff college. Completion of the course would prepare me for a raise in rank. One day Jossi Harel requested that I participate in an exchange of ideas with key Mossad personnel. I gladly agreed; perhaps I could help bring a closer working bond between our two foreign-intelligence arms. However, I couldn't forget that the Mossad had callously, and without evidence, branded me a security problem—or was it security risk?

Unfortunately, early in the discussion they began leveling unfair criticism against Motke (already a year and a half out of Modiin). They also attacked past Modiin operations, especially the abortive sabotage operation. I lashed out in defense of both.

I was the only Modiin man present, except for Jossi Harel. I found myself resorting to calling those who were present "pencil pushers" who operated mostly on neutral territory.

"It's easy to be a wise guy after the fact," I charged, "but when Egyptian security breathes down your neck, you move according to the prevailing circumstances. Anybody can sit behind a cup of coffee in Europe and be clever."

Jossi Harel was my superior. Though I hid my anger at him for siding with them, I vented it on the Mossad and its crippling history of competitiveness. Jossi had certainly earned his laurels before the State was a fact, but neither he, nor any of the others, had ever operated behind enemy lines.

Burning from the discussion, I had a chance encounter some time later with Maj. Avraham Dar. I wanted from him the answer to a question I had never had the opportunity to ask Gibli.

"What would have been done if I had not agreed to testify against Lavon the way you, Motke, and Gibli wanted?" I asked him.

With a cavalier, cynical grin, Dar gave me the answer—one that flashed like fire through my body.

"We would have claimed that you carried out the sabotage action on your own, without orders from us—even without our knowledge. But we knew you could be trusted."

I realized that Gibli had really given me no choice but to go along with the framing, even had I known the true motives behind it. And it made sense, from the conspiratorial point of view. With Lavon never having issued an order and with Motke, Gibli, and Dayan denying having set the sabotage in motion, they were free to place the sole responsibility for its initiation on me. Nathanson, Levy, and the rest were safely in Egyptian hands. It would be stupid at this point to even ponder the might-have-beens; there were none.

I was not among those summoned for the general staff and command course commencing in late August.

I carried my angry disappointment straight to Fatti. He explained that he could not afford to offer me one of the two Modiin allocations to the course because I was leaving Modiin anyway.

Refusing to accept the decision, I recruited my friend Gen. Yitzhak Rabin, commander of the Northern Region, to intervene, but Yitzhak came back from Fatti empty-handed. In desperation I suggested that Gibli, who was serving now as Yitzhak's deputy, place me under him, but he refused. It seemed the only assignment available to me was the Tank Corps. The walls seemed to be closing in on another victim of the conspiracy. It was only a question of when.

One particular struggle during my time in military limbo propelled me toward leaving the army. I had gone to see Shimon Peres, who had been director-general of the defense ministry under Ben-Gurion, Lavon, and again Ben-Gurion. He was an old acquaintance from school, the kibbutz, and meetings abroad. Shimon was an acquiescing witness to the conspiracy; so he was somewhat aware of the forces against me. I asked his help in getting me to Ben-Gurion. Shimon sent me to Israel Baer, Ben-Gurion's military adviser.

I had known Israel Baer since the 1940s, and I found his ear friendly. I had brought a copy of my intelligence report, hoping that its critical conclusions would serve my case. Even though Baer did not put me before Ben-Gurion, his response on reading the report was hopeful.

"It's excellent, Avri, but instead of laying it in the Old Man's hands, I think you should deal with the Mossad on this. Has Isser Harel seen it?"

"No. You know he considers me something of a security problem, or worse!"

"I've heard that. Nevertheless, without his consent, nothing can be done. He has absolute veto power. Take the report to him."

When I revealed my earlier attempts to see him, Baer said, "OK, I'll take it to him. I believe it's of the utmost importance."

A week later Israel Baer handed the report back to me.

"You're right about one thing," he said. "Isser hates your guts. At least that was my impression. It has something to do with your appearance before the Olshan-Dori inquiry."

"What about the report?" I asked.

Pain swept Baer's face. "He wouldn't even read it, Avri. I'm sorry."

Nothing could have shocked me more. What in hell did Isser's opinion of me have to do with the report! It seemed so out of proportion as to be funny. But actually it was gruesomely dangerous, a reflection of the egomania that characterized our total security apparatus.

This last rejection made me resolve to quit Zahal. But being daily at general headquarters, I postponed my final decision; all of us now had war nerves; we weren't listening to news of anything else.

I was deeply disturbed in those early October days leading up to the Sinai Campaign. Unique to Israel, everybody was slowly and unobtrusively disappearing from the streets, especially from the usual places of military consort. An old feeling of isolation and shame, one I'd known well as a court-martialed outcast five years before, began creeping back into my gut. My country was going to war, and nobody would accept my help.

As our forces struck across the Sinai Desert on the morning of October 29, 1956, I had, in my agony, one consolation. I knew that they would be striking territory and defenses already known to them from the intelligence data I had fed headquarters.

In the middle of the war came a cable from Olga: "Father hospitalized again. His condition grave. Please come."

I hurried to Tel Aviv, hoping to gain exit at the first sign that the war was ending; but Jaschka Janiv, Jossi Harel's subordinate, intercepted me.

"I was sending a car to Haifa for you," he said at headquarters. A rescue team of seven or so parachutists was being hurriedly organized to drop into Egypt near the Sudan border, where it had been reported that Nathanson, Levy, and the rest of our people had been transferred. The team would land near the remote desert prison, make the rescue, then work its way to the Red Sea, where either boat or helicopter pickup would be waiting.

"Will you lead the team, Avri? We see no other man commanding except you."

With his request, I suddenly discovered that a strange thing had happened to me. Earlier my reactions would have been immediate. Now I was torn between my dying father, who had lived his life, and the lives of my former charges, who most certainly would not live long if we left them where they were. It never crossed my mind that if I were captured and identified as Paul Frank, I would be summarily executed. I felt a great debt to the prisoners; the most horrible place in the world right then for an Israeli was in Egyptian hands. Father would understand. I would go.

"You realize the plan is crude," Jaschka said. "Nothing is definite. I came to you first to lead."

I remained in Tel Aviv as preparations began. And then the 100-Hours War ended on November 5, before the raid could get under way. Our forces occupied the Sinai Desert and were facing Egypt across the canal. As it turned out, our raid would have failed. Intelligence data had been in error: The prisoners had been kept in Toura Prison in Cairo.

I boarded a flight for Vienna, the only male on the plane. Within a week, my father's crisis lifted, but I had already decided to remain with him in Vienna. I informed the unit and pressed for the balance of the seven thousand pounds still owed me.

I had already notified Shula to sell the car, rent the flat, and come prepared to stay. However, when she came, she brought unsettling news. My friend, and Fatti's deputy in Modiin, Col. Uzi Narkiss, had said to Shula on her departure, "Avri knows too much. We don't like him being abroad." Though the remark cut deep, I knew that Uzi was merely parroting policy. For me, it seemed, unconfirmed rumor had become fact in the eyes of many.

During these endless days of watching over Father while Olga maintained her job, I met often with Chanan Barel and even rendered him small services. Even though Barel was the Mossad station chief in Vienna, I'd always found him fair. He even apologized for his inaccurate report on Father's health. Once, the subject of Osman Nouri's attempt to recruit me for Egyptian intelligence came up. Barel remarked, "It would be interesting to know if Nouri still wanted your services after all this time."

1957 came. Four years had elapsed since I had first left Israel as a novice spy. Watching my father's condition fluctuate, it seemed a lifetime. Leukemia was a little-understood disease, and seeing the inevitable was painful. I had read an article on bone-marrow diseases by a Nobel Prize winner, a doctor in Germany, and I decided to make the trip to Germany even though it meant breaking my pledge to Fatti.

Staying with Hugo Krug in Dusseldorf, where he had relocated the firm, I made contact with the specialist. He explained that his findings were only experimental; no cure was possible.

Down in spirits, I remained with Hugo a few days. Considering the directive ordering him to avoid contact with me, his reception was not too unlike our old, open relationship. I was astonished by the firm's growth, partly a result of strategic materials supplied to Israel during the war. It made me proud. . . .

Bob Jansen lived in Krefeld, a small town nearby, and I visited him at the service station he had leased. He remarked casually that he was going to Bonn, and asked, "Wouldn't it be proper for me to give your regards to Osman Nouri?"

"Yes," I said, "and be sure to ask him if he's still favorable to making contact with Wagner." Bob's puzzlement was understandable; he had no way of knowing that "Wagner" was the code Nouri and I had agreed to use once.

Several days later, ready to return to Vienna, I dropped in on Bob to say goodbye and learned that Nouri had been out of town; Bob had left my message with an assistant. I had regretted my impulse in sending Bob to Nouri; so I was greatly relieved. There was little chance that the contact would go undetected by our people; the Egyptian embassy was full of holes.

"Shall I follow it up?"

"Forget it," I said. "I think this is one business deal I won't involve myself in further."

In March a letter from headquarters reached me in Vienna. I was being reinstated to my former rank of major; also, Dayan had taken my Modiin years into account, making me eligible for advancement. The happy end of a long, ugly nightmare I thought.

At last I had regained everything I'd lost in 1952: my rank, my seniority, my family, everything. But I had other problems: Being now on unpaid leave of absence, my funds were critically short and Father's prognosis was indefinite. A friend of his offered me a place in the newly created Austrian army; I still held dual citizenship. But when I informed headquarters of the offer, I asked instead to be located with any of Israel's organizations in Vienna. Then I was summoned to Stuttgart by my unit commander.

Jossi Harel was accompanied by a friend of mine, Gen. Amos Horav, Zahal's head of ordnance. They had come to convince me to return to Israel. According to Jossi certain people felt that I had left home for good, angered by my denial of a seat in the staff and command course. Once more I made a futile attempt to convince Jossi that I was in Vienna indefinitely because of my father.

"Is your father really as sick as you say?" Jossi asked.

I was infuriated and baffled. Almost a year of Father's sickness, and this question was still being raised. Between clenched teeth I invited Jossi and the entire Mossad organization to visit Vienna and have a talk with my father's physician. If the Mossad couldn't verify the sickness of a public man, I said the whole security apparatus should be disbanded.

Apparently satisfied, Jossi brought up my return to Zahal. He and General Horav did their best to glorify the Tank Corps.

"Not to the tanks, Jossi. I won't go to them." The topic made me weary.

"And the alternative?"

"I'll leave the army and go into business here in Europe."

I simply had to have a future. If not in Zahal, then it lay here, just for the asking: Hugo Krug and I had kept alive our contacts with Herr Backhaus, a German manufacturer of tank treads and light vehicles who was still highly receptive to the manufacture of his products in Israel. Israel's cheap labor market and a woefully short life for tank treads made the venture potentially lucrative—it could make a rich man of me. General Horav, an ordnance man right down to his shoe soles, was hooked by the prospect of manufacturing tank treads in Israel and began to prod me into reopening negotiations with Backhaus. He even offered an army site for the factory.

Jossi left, promising that I would be advised within two weeks of my next military posting, and that, if I didn't accept the assignment, I was free to pursue any private venture I wished.

His message arrived. I was assigned to participate in the tank commanders course to commence in a fortnight. I didn't even bother to respond, I was so sick with disgust.

Now psychologically out of Zahal, I was still stymied by one detail of the Backhaus project: In Vienna, I was Avri Seidenwerg and, in Germany, Paul Frank. To continue my business life in Germany, I either remained Paul Frank, or all past business connections, including the negotiations with Herr Backhaus, could be forgotten. Unfortunately I had given headquarters all my Paul Frank credentials.

Without informing them, I drove to Germany via Salzburg, where I told the police I had lost my passport. I was allowed to cross into Germany, and I went straight to Munich. Registering my address as a friend's house, I applied for another Paul Frank passport, received it promptly, and returned to Vienna.

My money was nearly gone. Rent from the flat in Haifa helped, but I was forced to inquire again about the balance of the seven thousand pounds owed me. My request was answered by Joske Yariv; Jossi Harel had left Modiin to go into private business. When I wrote back, telling him that I was being forced to accept work in Vienna, he came to see me. He seemed curious about our meager furnishings, as though he had expected something more elaborate.

Three days of marathon talks produced mixed news. Modiin would pay me what it owed, 4000 pounds. But headquarters was still worried about my future.

"There are rumors that you have left Israel for good," Joske said one evening when we went nightclubbing. "The rumors say it's because you have something to hide in regard to your activity in Egypt."

I responded angrily, again explaining my intention to return home at my father's death, a few more months at best.

"But are you really coming home? Can I have your word on it?"

"It has nothing to do with my word," I said, feeling suddenly definite about the resolve I had been slowly exploring: I was growing less and less inclined to hide what had gone on in Lavon's framing. "The moment Father's suffering is over, I'm coming home." I looked into Joske Yariv's slightly tipsy face, wondering how much he knew about the three-year-old conspiracy. "You can count on it."

We shook hands.

"And there's something else you can count on," I said, dropping a bomb on Joske's head. "When I come home, I'm going to make a clean table of what happened in the past. There are some things Israel needs to know."

Joske's eyes were riveted on me. "What do you mean?"

"I'm going to tell all, I think." My trailing "I think" was meant to add to his uncertainty.

Joske left Vienna to report home, and I waited for the explosion. If I decided to cross the Rubicon now, there would be no turning back. But I could not cross without the truth from Gibli. If not Gibli, then Motke.

In July, headquarters arranged a job for me at El-Al's midtown office, and Modiin made its final payment.

On a warm August day, seated on the patio of the Burggarten with a cup of coffee, I spotted an unorthodox sight for Vienna, an attractive blonde chatting cozily with an Arab—an Egyptian, unless I missed my guess. A week or so later Chanan Barel's ears shot up; my description of the man fitted the new Egyptian intelligence station-chief for Vienna, whose whereabouts the Mossad had been trying to determine.

"Why didn't you call me sooner?" he demanded almost angrily.

"How did I know you were looking for him?" I laughed. "Besides I was more interested in the blonde."

Some time later I was awaiting a friend for lunch at the Europa Coffee House when Arab-accented English sent a chill up my spine.

"Is this seat occupied?"

I glanced up at the Egyptian intelligence officer. Aware that the chair was about the only vacant seat in the room, I indicated for him to sit, explaining that he could stay until my lunch partner arrived.

We began the lies. He said that he was in Vienna to buy electrical appliances, and I dealt out my Paul Frank story, baiting him with my connections with electrical firms. We had arranged to meet here the following day, when my friend Jackie Schaufer arrived. "Until tomorrow," the Egyptian said.

Though I would have liked not to reveal the situation to Jackie, in the light of those parting words I had to. From now on I wanted everything out in the open.

Chanan Barel was ecstatic. He suggested a particular table for our meeting so that we could be photographed from the street.

"We'll have the place covered," Chanan told me. "Your job is to get his address and anything else helpful to us."

That night, as I told Shula of the incident, she became furious.

"Haven't you had enough? Nobody is going to thank you. Let the Mossad do their own dirty work!"

But I welcomed the opportunity to match wits with the Egyptians again. A half-hour early, I was stationed at the table. Among the customers I recognized one of Chanan's aides, an Israeli studying medicine in Vienna. I wondered how many others were present.

Punctually the Egyptian arrived, trailed by Chanan. He launched into tales of Vienna's night life. When we came down to personal things, I told him that I stayed with a lady friend whenever I was in Vienna.

"I, too, live with a woman," he admitted proudly, then suggested that we get together for an evening. He gave me her phone number and an address in the remotest part of the city.

Chanan urged me to move quickly. But doubts began to crop up in my mind; when I asked Chanan to get permission from his superiors to use me, he was told that I was to be avoided.

Modiin had ceased to exist as I had known it. It had been such a long, tiresome struggle that I didn't really care. I was simply waiting for my father's death to go back to Israel and reveal the blight the conspiracy had placed on my country's conscience.

Chanan Barel and I still met often. Once he mentioned an Egyptian general who was in town; the Mossad simply could not locate him. One day at the El-Al office, I dialed a phone number (not really knowing whether I'd connect, because the telephone system was undergoing a major overhaul) and discovered I'd tapped into someone's line. Two physicians, a male and female, were gossiping about movie stars they had met at a party. Enjoying their chatter, I motioned for a female co-worker to pick up the phone. Soon the woman physician changed the subject.

"You know who called me today?" she said.

"I should know?"

"You remember the Egyptian general with the particular ailment?"

"Oh, that one!"

The woman physician continued. "He's staying on there for another cure." She tittered uncomfortably. "He invited me to dinner."

"Be sure to wear your track shoes. Where is he staying this time?"

"At the Hitzinger Park Hotel."

I'd heard enough. I called Chanan. He doubted the source of my information until the girl in the office confirmed it. He found his general.

The odds against such an incident occurring would require a master computer to calculate. That's luck, pure and simple. Chanan's, not mine. My luck seemed to have run out. It was the last service I ever paid to either Modiin or Mossad.

Father's battle for life reached an alarming low in early October. Though he never complained, his clenched fists and pressed lips betrayed the agony of this uniquely brave man.

The secrecy of the Lavon affair was dying with my father, and my resolve to lay it bare was final. I was going home to clear up the sickness that had destroyed something pure in Israel, just as cancer was destroying my father. I wrote Motke informing him of my plans.

Motke replied in a quick, long letter. To warn me without exposing himself to Israel's postal censors, he drew on a parable:

"Let me tell you a story I read recently in the newspaper. Then draw your own conclusions.

"The president of the Spanish Olympic Committee was invited to the

Soviet Union to participate in an Olympic festivity in Moscow. The president politely rejected the offer. When questioned by friends as to why he had done so [for rarely was such an honor bestowed upon citizens of Franco's Spain], the president replied, 'Everything you say is true. They have promised me the best hotel in the city, they have promised me free movement wherever I want to go, they indicated all the cultural events were open to me, they even sent me a first-class ticket on their airlines. . . .'

"His friends chimed in, 'So why did you reject the invitation?' The president replied caustically, 'Because the ticket was for only one way.' "

But Motke's meaning was not clear, nor was his motive. Was he saying that *I was getting a one-way ticket,* or was he attempting to protect himself? Or both? Motke had been let down easy in the aftermath of the conspiracy. After attending the general staff course (the one denied to me), he went into Zahal. At this point the scandal was history for him. Unless I spilled out the conspiracy. There are no statutes of limitation on our kind of moral deception. Three years or a hundred, all the same.

Shortly I received another warning from a former Mossad secretary, a friend of Shula's and mine who had just visited us and who wrote from Israel: "There are many ships coming to Israel. You don't have to take the first one." What did she know from inside?

Though my decision was firm, these warnings for my safety made me dig deep into the entire imbroglio. Had I missed something? (I was not aware of the rumor charging me with being a double agent and with having turned in my own people to Nasser in Egypt for four thousand pounds British sterling.) Was Motke only trying to save *his* skin, or Israel's—as he'd claimed to be doing when we framed Lavon? Israel, I now realized, could never be protected by a perpetuation of the lie. Motke was simply trying to protect himself, just as Gibli, Dayan, and all the rest would when they learned of my intentions.

Yet I was certain that something big was in the offing; something dangerous. But I no longer cared. I began to feel that what should concern us most about the past is the breed of men who have been cast in its mold. The profession of secrecy, which I had once loved so well and that was new to us, had bred men I did not like. I myself had epitomized their kind of pragmatism. Because there could not have been a conspiracy without my cooperation, even though I'd been duped into it, and because I still supported the lie, I envisioned myself *primus inter pares* among the conspirators—first among equals. Somehow I had slipped beyond the confines of my own identity.

Siegmund Seidenwerg, whose Jewishness was incidental to his life, died on October 29, 1957, after having personally arranged for his own cremation and burial.

I watched the final placing of his ashes in a cemetery in the western district of Vienna, a spot overlooking the beautiful Lainzer Hills of the famous Vienna Woods. There I marveled at the hundreds who had attended the nonsecular service and who were filing past now. They were from all walks of life, many from Austria's powerful bureaucracy. I was proud for my father that they honored him not as a Jew, but as a man, a man who had remained in the forefront of rising socialism in Austria at a time when it was dangerous to be Jewish *or* Socialist. Father had been both.

His mourners had known him well; most carried bouquets of red carnations, Father's favorite and the flower of the Austrian Socialist Labor Party. These were his compatriots, his friends, his followers. For them and their children, he had fought since the 1920s to make a better world in Austria than it had known in its monarchial past. Loyalty, integrity, spiritual adherence to goal and idea were his unwavering values. Loyalty to friends, self-sacrifice, and struggle were everyday deeds.

When had I become aware that Father was involved in some kind of forbidden activity? Ten years of age? Younger? Was it during a game of soccer with Czechoslovakia, when I noticed that he did not speak to his friends whenever the police happened by?

I remember vividly waiting for him on his birthday in 1934: A neighbor came and whispered something to my mother. Switching on the radio, we heard the announcer report street fighting between the Socialist Defense League and the police. Without being told, I read my father's participation in the anarchy on my mother's face. He didn't come home for his surprise party, nor for days afterward. Meanwhile mother sealed the lips of my sister Ruth and me, as the detectives came making the usual threats about my father's political activity.

Then I was made his confidant, running secret errands for him and attending secret meetings at night, learning all the rules of conspiracy. Another time the police came to our flat searching for evidence; my task was to flush whatever was in the house down the toilet. I remember well the times Father was taken from home by the police, the days of silence, my mother's tears, our fear.

Then came the arrest in which he was charged with high treason and sentenced to five years' imprisonment and hard labor in the notorious Stein A.D. Donau. He handed me the mantle of adulthood as they took him away. My young heart surged with pride as he told me I would one day understand that sometimes imprisonment can be the highest award bestowed on a man. "It is like giving a soldier the great medal of the state." I looked at him through the steel mesh, my eyes glued to his face, my ears only for him.

Now, over twenty years later, I listened as a minister of the Socialist government spoke.

"By taking upon himself the responsibility, those of us on trial with Mundl Seidenwerg were made free to leave and continue our fight. Mundl was a true Socialist, a brave and courageous man."

But it was the eulogy of the editor of the *Workers Daily*, a member of parliament, that spoke to me most profoundly. Oscar Pollak brought the Jewish aspect into focus.

"Being a true revolutionary Socialist did not cause him to deny his creed. If there ever was an upright Jew, it was our Mundl. And being such, he knew that a state that does not give to the individual the full justice to which he is entitled, has violated its own basic right to existence. . . ."

I closed my eyes, for suddenly Jacob Dori's words were ringing in my ears, words he had spoken in the hotel room after my testimony before the Olshan-Dori panel. It was Dori's last appeal for me to tell the truth. "In a democratic nation, it cannot be that a few, by avoiding the democratic process of decision, are making policy on their own, involving other people's lives."

Anguished, I realized that I had failed my father and my country. I had placed personal loyalty before the basic values of life. Only *I* was responsible for my crimes, no one else. Not even Motke and Gibli, who had lied to me.

Justice had to prevail for Pinhas Lavon. I owed it to him, to my father's memory, to Israel. And, most of all, I owed it to myself.

Book 4

Chapter 22

Siegmund Seidenwerg was gone, but his vision of human justice was very alive to me. It was driving me home to unearth the full truth behind Pinhas Lavon's framing.

But there was more at stake than clearing Lavon: fairness, justice, Jewish concepts that had burned in the souls of my people for millennia. Corruption of either precedes the ruin of a person or a state. Yesterday it had been Lavon. Tomorrow, who would be the victim?

My sense of impending calamity was ever with me. But so was my anger. To hell with having been stupid and worse. To hell with having allowed my narrow self-righteousness to make a willing tool of me. I was sick of what I'd done, and I was sick of the consequences. Now that I knew most of what had gone on, I wanted to know the rest. And I wanted Israel to know.

Three weeks after my father's death in October, I left a forewarned and frightened Shula in Vienna with Olga and my son, and I returned to Israel.[1]

My traveling companion by car to Istanbul was Moshe Medzini, a renowned Israeli journalist who had served with our delegation to the United Nations and was on his way home. His running commentary on

---

1. Author's note. I recount my return to Israel only to refute internationally published versions that I was "run to earth" by our intelligence people and forcibly brought back as one of Israel's celebrated "trunk" cases.

Zionist history, as we passed into Turkey in Chanan Barel's Vauxhall, proved an elixir for my worries. For a while I was on an odyssey, forgetting what was behind me and oblivious of what lay ahead.

Medzini and I parted in Istanbul. As arranged, I dropped off Chanan Barel's car at our consulate, and I found myself confronted with reality. An old acquaintance, now serving as first secretary to the consul, recruited me to deliver the diplomatic mail to Tel Aviv. I thought it humorous and damned inconsistent, since I bore the stigma of security risk, or worse.

Receiving a receipt for the mail at Lod Airport, I took a Sherut taxi directly to the flat in Haifa, where I spent a sleepless night. At the crack of day I headed for Tel Aviv with three objectives in mind:

Before I revealed Lavon's purging to any nonconspirator, I had to learn from Motke and Gibli the full truth; I wanted to know once and for all my official status with Zahal; and I demanded to know what was behind the rumor that I was a security problem.

Anticipating shock waves, I decided to gather all evidence relative to the conspiracy and hold it close. I took from Shlomo Millet, still head of Modiin's archives, my attaché case containing materials that proved that the conspiracy existed and tied Gibli undeniably to it. If Motke and Gibli would not cooperate with me, I didn't want it to be just my word against theirs.

Shlomo alerted me to rumors that Gibli, trading on his success as a field commander in the Sinai Campaign of a year ago, was maneuvering to regain his former post as director of Modiin; this meant Fatti Harkabi would lose out and Isser Harel's most implacable adversary would be in control. But if I exposed the conspiracy, Gibli would be ruined. How cooperative would he be, I wondered, as I ambled through Tel Aviv's streets, waiting for nightfall.

Under the cover of darkness, I headed for Motke's house in Zahala, Tel Aviv's suburb of ranking officers. Motke wouldn't be back until the next day; so I left the car and walked to Gibli's nearby. On seeing me walk into his parlor, the blood drained from his face.

"What are you doing here?" he exclaimed.

I told him, fully aware that Motke had already apprised him of my intentions, "To know why we did what we did to Lavon."

Gibli's panic was undisguised. He grabbed up his beret. "I can't talk right now, Avri, I have to rush out. Besides, I'm too tense to go into it."

My "Why have I been warned not to come back?" halted his headlong rush to the door. He whirled on me, ready to strike. "Because 'the little one'[2] is warming up the porridge again." Gibli glared at me. "We know

---

2. Isser Harel was known as "the little one."

what that means, don't we? Come and see me another time!" He shot out the door.

In Haifa over the weekend, I stewed in confusion. Was Isser's reopening of the conspiracy sparked by my hints that I planned to speak out, or was he simply trying to stop Gibli? Was Gibli more afraid of Isser or of me? What I said to Gibli should have stopped him cold.

Pushing things, I arranged a meeting in Tel Aviv with Col. Uzi Narkiss, still deputy to Fatti Harkabi. I told him of my brief encounter with Gibli and asked him point-blank what my future was in Zahal.

Uzi didn't hesitate. "You have no place at all in the army, Avri."

I had accepted Shlomo's invitation to spend the night. His only comment about Uzi's prediction was, "Maybe he knows what he's talking about."

The next day I caught up with Motke. When I questioned him about his cryptic message warning me not to return, his answer was equally involuted.

"Didn't Gibli explain that 'the little one' is rewarming the soup?" he asked.

"What about Fatti, now that Gibli wants his old job back?"

"Fatti is hand in fist with Isser to keep Gibli out of Modiin."

I asked Motke to set up a meeting of the three of us. "I plan to make a clean breast of what went on, Motke." My longtime friend looked at me long and searchingly.

"If that's the way you want it, Avri," he said. "But understand one thing: You will gain nothing."

Laughing inwardly, I pressed him with direct questions concerning the testimony in the January 1955 Olshan-Dori investigation. Motke wouldn't admit anything.

"Nothing has changed the reasons for what we did to Lavon," he said.

Motke was not going to help a man who could bury him. But I couldn't wait until we met with Gibli; I had to find out what to expect, where help lay. I floundered, going from one to another, asking, always asking.

From Martin Hauser, who had been close to me since my enlistment into Modiin: "I knew you would come back! I told them so. I knew you had nothing to hide. Thank God!"

From Pinhas Sapir, minister of finance, with whom I had hoped to discuss my potential German Backhaus deal: "Are you OK with the security people?"

A Zahal colonel: "You have no one to talk to. Running around asking questions will only harm you. Listen to me. Stop it!"

A Modiin major: "You belong to Gibli's people. Fatti doesn't like to see you around."

From others: "Mind your own business!" "Leave well enough alone!" "Let the past lay; nobody will gain from it."

Nobody? Was Motke right?

Gibli was not to be cornered; neither was Motke, not again. Why avoid me? I thought. It was only a matter of time before their fear of my talking would force them to seek me out. It wouldn't take long, if I knew Gibli. The only factor that held me back was knowing that if I spoke out without being armed with *all* the facts, Gibli and Motke might deny everything.

I retreated to Haifa, hoping to think through the maze while I helped Shula's sister prepare for her move to Australia, where she was to marry. Then I decided to prepare for my return to Europe just in case I embarked on the Backhaus deal. This would mean that Shula and I would be in Vienna for another four to six months. I packed a small wooden crate with the few valuable household items that remained. Hidden in the crate was the revised field diary that had aided in the purging of Lavon. The real diary Motke had taken for safekeeping. How I ached for it now.

Peter Landesman, former police sergeant and a friend associated with the Globus travel business, had made arrangements for my sister-in-law. I turned over my crate to him for shipment.

A few days later Hugo Krug arrived to discuss the Backhaus proposal and the merits of my immediate return. Hugo went back to Tel Aviv. That same evening, December 15, I received the following cable from Jossi Harel, now more than a year out of Modiin: "*Urgent.* Be in Tel Aviv tomorrow. Café Batya. 10:00 A.M. sharp."

I couldn't imagine what Jossi Harel wanted, but since it was the first sign of life out of anybody, I responded. I was glad that he had set an early time, because Hugo and I planned to talk further around noon.

Café Batya, a popular hangout for officers of the general staff, was quiet. I chatted with an officer I knew until Jossi Harel pulled to the curb and honked. He had an air of anticipation as I took a seat in the gray Willis Jeepster. He sailed out for army general headquarters, where somebody awaited me.

"Who are we seeing?" I asked.

"An old acquaintance of yours."

Jossi led the way to GHQ compound and delivered me to Col. Jacob Hafez, head of Zahal's Field Security Service.

"Avri," Hafez said as I seated myself, "I have some questions to ask you, and I beg you to answer them candidly." He paused. A sense of urgency gripped me. "Avri, have you ever done anything to harm the interest of the State?"

Since Vienna I had been preparing myself for something like this. Here we go, I thought. I answered in the negative.

"Might you have erred without any ill intention?" Hafez pressed. "Take your time, and consider the question carefully. Try to remember."

"I don't have to remember! I am certain I've done nothing, intentionally or otherwise, that can be interpreted as being harmful to the interest of the State."

Hafez sighed heavily. "If that's your answer, then you leave me no choice but to hand you over to our interrogator."

I barely had time to think, *What the hell is this?*

Instantly two men entered the room. Hafez gave his chair to the taller of the two, a lean, hawkeyed man with a graying crew cut. I was sorting him out in my memory while he introduced himself as a Modiin investigator who had been assigned to question me. "I hope you are going to answer truthfully," he said.

I cut him short. "If you are looking for the truth, then let's start with it. I know who you are." Zvi Aharoni was one of the Shin-Beth's[3] chief investigators. He also held the rank of major in the Shin-Beth's executive arm, which was an integral part of the police.

Aharoni looked at Colonel Hafez and Jossi Harel who, all of a sudden, found it very difficult to meet my eye. Then Aharoni asked, "Where did we meet?"

"We haven't met. But I know who you are," I said with a grin. "In Department 8 a few times, I overheard you talking . . . without regard for security regulations, if I remember correctly." As soon as I'd said it, I realized I'd shot my mouth off. Exposing his laxness to men to whom security was a way of life was a mistake.

Aharoni turned to his partner from the Shin-Beth, who had been taking notes. "This has nothing to do with the subject matter. Strike it." He came back to my grin. "Let's get to cases. Are you willing to answer my questions?"

"I have nothing to hide."

"Have you ever harmed the security of the State?"

"Never!"

Aharoni's voice pitched dramatically. "Well, I am telling you that you have been *traitorous!*"

Fury seized me completely. For the space of a second I was blinded by an urge to grab his puny throat and choke him lifeless. By sheer willpower I kept myself seated. "If it were not for this forum," I said raggedly, "I'd kill you with my bare hands—and feel no conscience for it." On the periphery of my fury I was aware of Jossi Harel saying uncomfortably that

---

3. Department of Internal Security. Equatable to the FBI.

he had to attend traffic court. *Traffic court!* I almost laughed at the disparity of it.

Colonel Hafez rose to calm me, but I was already calmed. Jossi's ridiculous excuse to escape the room had done it. "We are here to help you," Hafez said. "It's just that we are responsible for checking out certain information." He and Jossi left.

Undaunted, Aharoni continued, probing my friendship with Bob Jansen. Very quickly I realized that the questions teetered dangerously close to the conspiracy against Lavon. My hedging was obvious. Goddamn Gibli and Motke for avoiding me!

"Where is your German passport?" I told him that I had returned it to headquarters. "I mean the additional German passport you got on your own," Aharoni barked, becoming the professional interrogator he was.

My thoughts raced into high gear. Accused of being a traitor, my attempt to explain the passport would only tighten Aharoni's resolve. Also the passport was at the flat in Haifa. Finally I told him that I would explain the passport in writing to Fatti Harkabi, as head of Modiin. Aharoni had been trained in the interrogation method of "sublatey," meaning that whatever I said, the opposite must be true, and I wanted to have as little to do with him as possible.

I was led through an office where there were two secretaries. One of them, Bracha, had once been in my unit. Stepping over and inquiring how things were going, I whispered to her, "Tell Motke that I am here." Bracha didn't blink as she nodded and turned away.

In an hour, I had written out my explanation and handed the sealed explanation to Colonel Hafez, who gave it to Aharoni. It was lunchtime, too late to meet Hugo Krug; so I had lunch with Hafez at his suggestion.

He attempted to put me at ease by saying that he didn't personally believe any of the suspicions against me. He apologized for Aharoni's "traitor" epithet. "Zvi Aharoni is the best interrogator around," he said. I had to agree. The first real hint that today was not a onetime thing was when Hafez suggested that I stay in Tel Aviv overnight, or until the quizzing was finished. I told him that I would cooperate fully, provided I could return to Haifa briefly to take care of a few things at the flat.

What I really wanted was to remove a few items in case there should be callers during the night. Everything I had that proved the existence of the conspiracy, and linked Gibli to it, was in my attaché case in the bedroom. There was also the matter of the negatives of the Egyptian rocket blueprints; I felt it best not to have them found.

Resuming my parry-and-thrust session, I soon realized that Zvi Aharoni was the boss, not Colonel Hafez. This time Aharoni and his colleague came at me with the soft approach: "Everybody makes mistakes once in a while." Obviously they had read my long note to Fatti Harkabi, because they pressed harder into my association with Bob Jansen. Then they leaped to Mohammed Ibrahim, the Egyptian businessman I had befriended in Vienna for Mossad's Chanan Barel. I referred them to Barel.

One thing became clear to me right away: Aharoni was not on a fishing expedition. He had definite areas to probe. The day grew uglier, his attitude grew more hostile, and I'd had enough.

I rose. "I don't like what's going on here. I don't intend to continue this with *you*!"

Aharoni was perplexed. He summoned Colonel Hafez who chewed me out for failing to cooperate as I'd promised at lunch.

"It seems," I said, "that I'm branded a liar, whatever I say. I'm not willing to answer any more of his questions."

Hafez, put off by my anger, asked Aharoni to leave, then pleaded with me to understand that they were only doing a job.

"It's not the questions, it's his attitude," I said. "If a lie detector test would convince you, I'm ready for it." As long as they stayed away from the heart of the conspiracy, I was on safe ground. Hafez scheduled a polygraph test for later in the evening.

"I have to go to Haifa, as I told you," I said. "I have to see to the flat."

"Yes, we've arranged for someone to accompany you." My bewilderment must have showed. "Avri, you're not under arrest. But I hope you'll cooperate."

Suddenly I understood that the polygraph test was merely another step in a process that was getting more involved by the hour.

Eli Prager, a captain under Hafez in the Field Security Service, was brought in as my watchdog. In silence he drove us to Haifa. Once there, I made a big show of my pretext for coming: the opened windows and the carpet exposed to rain. Saying that I wanted to take a few things, I left Eli in the parlor while I went to the bedroom and hurriedly emptied the critical contents of my attaché case into a small blue suitcase. My P.38, my passport, and a few notes I left in the attaché case, along with some toilet articles. Into the blue suitcase I put the critical materials: a page in Gibli's handwriting of the revision, from the night we altered my field reports; Gibli's letter telling me that Fatti Harkabi had an accurate master table of the conspiracy; several letters from Motke; and the negatives of the Egyptian rocket blueprints. Gibli's handwriting proved beyond any doubt his involvement in the conspiracy against Lavon. Without it, I probably could prove nothing. Though the rocket negatives were of no importance now, I could always say that Shlomo Millet had known about them since I'd reacquired the film accidentally on February 19, 1956, my birthday two years ago.

Wanting to guarantee that the blue suitcase remained safe and available, I decided to use the friendship of a neighbor to see that it got into the right hands. On the pretext of getting her to look after the flat, I crossed the street under Eli Prager's watchful eye and went to the door of Hadassah Nagler, the beautiful daughter of a wealthy mill owner. I was certain I could trust her.

"Call my friend Peter Landesman, and tell him to take the small blue suitcase from my flat and keep it for me. Then call Col. Benjamin Gibli, *tonight;* tell him that I'm in the Little One's hands and that he should act to secure my release. I gave her the necessary phone numbers and the key to my flat.

"Is something wrong, Avri?" Hadassah asked.

"Nothing to worry about, but please keep this between us."

Hadassah promised to follow my instructions.

Upstairs at the Sadans' I handed over my German passport for safekeeping. The lady of the house was very friendly with Shula and had an inkling of my past activities; so she did not question me.

On the way back to Tel Aviv I convinced Eli that it would be wise for me to see my sister, Ruth, for a moment; otherwise she would start asking questions, knowing I'd just returned from Vienna and Father's funeral. (I hadn't seen Ruth for a year, on the last day of the war.) At Ruth's flat, Eli remained in the Jeep. Unable to explain fully, I simply asked Ruth to inform Gibli and Motke that I was in Colonel Hafez's hands. She asked no questions.

At general headquarters everything was ready for the polygraph test. In Hafez's office the tester, Chayim Victor Cohen, Aharoni's Shin-Beth teammate, was presented to me as a doctor—a fact that I doubted; I proved to be right. After describing the machine, he gave me a simple test to ascertain, so he said afterward, whether I was a pathological liar. When I had passed, we agreed on twenty-one questions for the true test of my veracity.

Twice we ran through the set of questions, and I could see that my doctor wasn't getting the results he sought. While he conferred in the adjacent office, I disconnected myself from the machine and eavesdropped at the door: He was telling Colonel Hafez and Aharoni, "There's nothing definite to show that he's lying."

When he returned, I was plugged to the machine. He disconnected me while answering my questions as to my performance.

"Something is not clear," he said sternly. "You haven't told the entire truth. You're holding something back."

Little did they know! Some of the questions had come dangerously close to leading to the conspiracy. *Yet I had passed the test regarding my allegiance to my country.* I asked Hafez what happened next.

"We have a hotel room for you. Eli Prager will stay with you until tomorrow morning." I started to protest, but Hafez stopped me with a wave. "Avri, Eli has no idea what this is all about. He's a good chap; so don't make it hard on him."

All that night at the Yarcon Hotel Eli treated me as if I were planning to escape at any moment. After breakfast, back to Hafez's office. Bracha, the secretary who'd taken my message to Motke, whispered to me that my brother-in-law, Zvi Swet, was at the compound entrance. I started down, but Hafez and Eli blocked my path.

"You can't go out!" they exclaimed almost in unison. I pushed them aside. Harried and uncertain, they trailed me to the gate where my brother-in-law waited in the taxi he drove. To my utter relief Motke stood alongside. I hurried to him, with Hafez and Eli at my heels, and caught his furtive "Everything will be all right" as he jumped to Hafez's curt order to follow him upstairs. My arrest had scared the pants off him. *Good!* Some reaction out of him, finally.

Eli Prager took over. "What's going on here?"

From behind the steering wheel, Zvi Swet looked at him coldly. "I forced Motke to bring me here"—and, for me—"after Gibli played evasive about Avri and why he's being held here. I just want to know one thing. Is Avri under arrest?"

Zvi, even without his legs, commanded respect. As a British commando during the war, he had lost his legs in Italy; he was a Stern member in our fight for independence. Zvi was not a man to be trifled with. His huge shoulders filled the front seat of his taxi, and his hot eyes burned. Eli made it clear that I was not under arrest.

I confirmed it because, technically, I was free. I reassured Zvi that, now that Motke was on the scene, "Everything will be all right."

Back upstairs I felt pounds lighter knowing that Motke had finally moved his ass. And that undoubtedly he and Gibli would devise some plan to contact me. I *had* to talk to them. Aharoni was getting hot on the trail of the conspiracy, and I had long since decided not to talk about that until I had discussed it with them.

For another day and a half Aharoni accused me of disclosing unspecified information to the enemy. Infuriated, I referred him to my field reports. Then he came at me with a shocker.

"And I tell you that you're hiding something in regard to your contacts with this Col. Osman Nouri," Aharoni accused. "And please never mind that he's now the military attaché. He is *still* Egyptian intelligence!"

Good God! Osman Nouri. I'd completely forgotten sending Bob Jansen to Bonn with a message for him. That Bob hadn't been able to meet him was beside the point; so, too, was the fact that Chanan Barel had wondered if Nouri were still interested in my services. I started to lash out but again decided against explaining to Aharoni. This was Modiin business, and if Fatti Harkabi wanted to give it out, it was OK with me. I insisted on writing the explanation to Modiin's director.

In an outer office I completed the detailed briefing of the only unauthorized *effort* to contact—or *actual* contact with—the enemy that had not been included in my field report. At that time I wrote, I was still operating under carte blanche from Motke. My sin was going to Germany when I'd been ordered not to. I made an addendum to Fatti, requesting that he put a halt to this farce. I was no damned collaborator, and he damned well knew it.

When I handed the sealed briefing to Hafez, he stung me with the announcement that I would not be allowed to leave the country for a while, and that I should summon Shula home. Despite my protests, an overseas call was put in to Vienna. "Tell her to come at first opportunity," Hafez said, handing me the phone.

Shula came on the line. I explained that "due to certain developments" she should prepare to return home. I would have to find a way to warn her later.

Afterward I was told that I was not under arrest if I consented to remain with them of my own free will. I had no choice.

This drove home to me the seriousness of the situation. Either they believed I had in fact collaborated with the Egyptians, or somebody was complicating my life, to keep me from speaking out on the conspiracy. I was sinking into the mire, and I had to bide my time until Motke and Gibli made a move.

The next day, at the hotel with Eli Prager, I decided to hand over my P.38. Without warning I took it from my attaché case and laid it in his hand. Eli had spent three nights with me as my jailer; he was stunned. I was still laughing to myself on the following morning, when under blackened welder's goggles, I was taken to an isolated former Arab home on the outskirts of Tel Aviv.

My room, of impregnable stone and steel, was part of a walled compound that had to be a secret Shin-Beth jail. Out the tiny barred window of the steel door I could see two muftied guards lounging in the adjacent room and two Uzi submachine guns hanging on the bare walls.

Isolation. The oldest tactic in the book to break a man's will. But one very important trait in my character had been overlooked: I function best when alone. I've always been my own best company. Still, I would show on my face the pain they expected to see.

I was definitely out of reach. How in hell could Motke or Gibli get to me? I wanted no legal advice, primarily because I was still prepared to believe that Aharoni, Hafez, Fatti, and all were sincerely trying to clear up the question of my guilt.

On the other hand there were strong signs that there was more to my detention than I could assess at this stage. All I could do was remain calm and keep a firm grip on my wits. And never, above all, must I lose my sense of irony. To do so was to roll into the grave. But as the weeks of intense interrogation spilled over into 1958, maintaining my control was the most difficult chore I'd ever faced. The questioning of my loyalty to Israel seemed the most incredible thing I could imagine.

Life is filled with strange paradoxes. It had been exactly three years before that Lavon had faced false accusations he was powerless to refute; now I faced a not dissimilar situation. Here was where I drew on my sense of irony to quell the anger raging in my head, lurking there to destroy my reasoning.

Aharoni and Chayim were grindingly effective as one day of questioning rolled into the next. I was enduring my incarceration, but I was worried. With all my Modiin field reports (El-Ad Sarchi's volumes) at their disposal, my interrogators were well versed in my past activities. In the bond of silence about the sabotage-conspiracy entanglement, I could not shake them off my tail. The discrepancies, the hedging, were burying me deeper in suspicion. To clarify certain points I would have to reveal all. Then came questions so on target that I had to refuse to answer. "I have nothing to hide," I kept claiming, even though I had everything to hide—Israel's most dangerous scandal. "To talk about those times, I need specific orders releasing me from silence."

The days of questioning seemed endless. Aharoni and Chayim never let up, alternately attacking and retreating, playing enemy then friend, relentlessly trying to confuse me. At one point, because I wanted desperately to find out if Peter Landesman had gotten my blue suitcase containing the critical letters, papers, and negatives, I suggested to Aharoni that I could clarify our impasse if I had certain notes from my flat.

Equally important was mailing a letter I had written to Shula. I wanted to smuggle it to Peter for posting in Europe. Censors would unquestionably be monitoring all her mail.

Eli, again my watchdog, accompanied me to Haifa. After a quick stop at my flat, I convinced him to let me visit Peter and his wife, Mala. Under the pretense of having to use the bathroom, I had the opportunity to verify, with Mala, Peter's possession of my suitcase, while hiding a note in his bathrobe asking him to post the letter abroad.

On another trip to Haifa with Eli Prager a few days later, I had hidden in my shirt a letter for Shlomo Millet that also explained my situation. I followed the same routine in hiding it. I also hid another note to Peter, cautioning him not to hand over my suitcase to anyone without written instructions from me. I was as emphatic as possible when I wrote: "The proof of my innocence is entrusted in your hands."

Before I left with Eli, I had whispered to Peter to stop the shipping of the crate of household goods (containing the fake field diary) to Vienna. I couldn't explain what was going on, for obvious reasons. Unless he had read the previous letter to Shula, Peter was still in the dark as to my sudden appearances and departures with Eli, whom I had introduced as my bodyguard. However, since he appeared to be fully supportive of my furtive behavior, I assumed he was responding solely out of our friendship.

Shula's return to Israel became a point of contention. Why they wanted her safe in Israel I was not to know until later, but, for now, their eagerness led them to offer to pay for her and Harel's air fare. Their generosity was touching. Hafez and Aharoni decided that I should call her, sticking strictly to their script.

"I'm personally going to supervise this call of yours," Aharoni said. He wagged a finger commandingly. "Any diversion from the written text will result in a cutoff."

I nodded obediently (which should have put him on guard automatically; I had obeyed so seldom). There hadn't been time for my letter to reach Shula; so I was plotting in the back of my mind a way to warn her not to come, without having the connection broken. I had a minute or two to reread the script before the call was placed.

"Keep to the contents," Aharoni warned, leaving the room to monitor the call from another office.

The script was geared to do one thing: Entice Shula back to Israel. When she had seemingly been convinced to return because everything was all right with me, I said, "Tell Olga that the Woellersdorf family is well, and they send their best to her. Don't forget to tell her; she asked me to check on them. They have a sparsely furnished little room, but they are making the best of everything they have at their disposal."

Ringing off, I was returned to my cell. Almost two hours later, Aharoni, red-faced and eyes burning in anger, came in. Saliva foamed at the corners of his mouth as he shouted, "We have checked! There is no such name as Woellersdorf in the register. There is no family by that name. Why?"

I smirked at him, enjoying immensely my minor coup. A man can enjoy the smallest things, I'd grown to realize. What was important was that Shula would not return.

"You really want to know, Zvi?" I said, dragging out an explanation that was going to cut him like a knife. "Woellersdorf was an Austrian political prison which once had the pleasure of keeping my father as a guest for some years. Olga is well acquainted with it, and Shula will be, too, when she gives Olga my regards from the Woellersdorf family."

"I trusted you, and you misused my trust!" he hissed.

I couldn't restrain a laugh. "If you trusted me, then it's the first time!"

"I will pay you back, rest assured of that!"

I knew then that I had made an enemy of Zvi Aharoni. Over the coming months, I was to learn just how much of an enemy.

Day after day, six- to eight-hour stretches, the interrogation continued. The loneliness of my cell and the tension of the sessions were so horrible that I began to dread the simple state of wakefulness. More and more the questions centered on the sabotage and the aftermath between Gibli and Lavon. I stuck to my guns. "I cannot talk about it until I'm released from secrecy." I held on to the premise that I was bound to secrecy by my pledge before the Olshan-Dori inquiry.

Then came the day that I was given a handwritten note from Fatti Harkabi allowing me to tell all. I laughed in my interrogators' faces. Of course he wanted me to talk! Talking would bury Gibli and take away the threat he posed to Fatti's position. *In due time,* I thought to myself, *and never to men who'd spent endless weeks trying to tear me apart.*

"You'll have to get a release from Moshe Sharet. He was prime minister at the time. I'm bound to secrecy by his order."

Stalled on this, Aharoni and Chayim suddenly came back to my contacts with the Eygptians in Europe, and especially to Osman Nouri in Bonn. Aharoni wanted to know whether I cared if they questioned Bob Jansen about his attempt to contact Nouri. I did not, and I even wrote a note to Bob telling him to speak the entire truth. To authenticate the note I added a personal remark in the upper corner: "Fornicating is quite a problem here"—a condition we had always laughed at regarding Jewish girls.

Later I learned that Bob had corroborated everything I had said, and, in telling what he knew of me, revealed his ignorance of my true role. He thought I was a German ex-Abwehr officer who worked for the Gehlen Organization, the West German intelligence group, and that what I did for Israel was by the way. However, Aharoni was to lie during my trial, when he claimed that he had not taken a statement from Bob Jansen, explaining that after the Woellersdorf trick, he learned that the personal remark about fornication on my note was another code.

On Aharoni's return, the mood of the sessions changed radically, if hostility and antagonism can get worse.

It was now claimed that Aharoni's findings in Europe pointed to the fact that I had been a double agent, responsible for the quick collapse of the network in Egypt. The final proof of their assertion was that I continued to withhold details concerning that period.

I countered by claiming that I could prove my innocence when the time came; I backed it up by saying that I had written material with which to substantiate my position (the blue suitcase). I demanded another lie detector test with a more sophisticated machine and a more expert tester. A newer machine was brought, and again Chayim played the expert. After the reading, Aharoni demanded that I confess. "There are other means available to extract the truth," he threatened, looking every bit the archenemy. And I believed him.

On a Friday, a day before the Sabbath, I reached the limits of my tolerance. I began to think about escape. However, there was no way to break out without hurting my guards. I couldn't do this. They were old men. But I *could* give Aharoni something to think about. That night I paced to and fro, like a caged animal under the watchful eye of his trainers. I refused breakfast and almost more important to me, my morning shave. At noon I requested paper and two envelopes and asked my guards if they would witness what I wrote. They glanced cautiously at one another, saying that they would have to ask for permission. I urged them to do so, hinting that I would have to do what I had to do anyway.

I dragged out the writing of the notes, one to Motke, the other to Shlomo Millet, to whom I explained my inability to withstand this disbelief of my loyalty any longer. I also asked that he clarify things to Shula and, when my son became of age, to make sure he understood what I had to do. In essence the notes bore the earmarks of a last will and testament. That evening Chayim came demanding to know what was going on.

"You've got four more days to release me from this farce," I said.

"And if not?"

"Then I shall have to take certain measures."

Chayim's eyes roved between the mask of resolve on my face and the two sealed envelopes on the table. "Don't do anything rash." Solicitude had crept into his voice.

"You give me no choice. It's entirely up to you."

After whispering to my guards, he left. I fell asleep, appeased by the success of my minidrama.

Waking me later, Aharoni and Chayim took the envelopes against my feeble protest. They ordered me to give them my shoelaces and belt; then they searched my cell, removing everything a man might use to hurt himself.

"Why all this?" I asked innocently.

"Because you're acting foolish," Aharoni barked. But, like Chayim, he was worried.

I told them I would do nothing for a week, provided they would come to a final decision regarding my fate. Next day my stuff was handed back. Certain they were deep in debate, I had a reasonably peaceful few days.

I was listening to the three o'clock afternoon news on the radio when Jacob and his companion guard clanged open the steel-plate door.

"Get ready to go," Jacob said, his voice hard with unfamiliar coldness. The slash of it pulled me to my feet.

"Go where?" I asked.

"Don't ask questions!" the other guard snapped, his fleshy round face stiff, his eyes, like Jacob's, avoiding mine.

"You're being transferred," Jacob volunteered.

I crossed to the radio and snapped it off. I took my time emptying my pipe. Use every fleeting moment. I had known a thousand such.

Apparently my maneuver to rouse my keepers from their complacency had scored. Something was up. A glance at my guards' official Shin-Beth faces, easily the coldest facades in Israel, made me sure I was right. Why was I being transferred? Where? Certainly they were not exposing me to the world or to the press. Censorship had the press firmly under its thumb. Nobody wanted accusations flying around that the Shin-Beth was using Nazi tactics; my detention was officially chargeless, therefore illegal.

"Transferred to where, Jacob?"

"It's not for you to know," the other one said. The man's pettiness sickened me. He shared a common weakness with the lion's share of men; he held eager dominion over my helplessness.

I smiled. "Won't I be coming back, Jacob? Even to see you?" The man who had often spoken of his grandchildren to me shifted his short, rotund body, a body more suited to hoisting a child than the Uzi submachine gun. Jacob was a man wishing to be elsewhere. So was I. Yet as much as I dreaded facing more interrogation, I figured that the sooner it was done with, the sooner I would be released.

"Whenever you're ready," Jacob's companion said impatiently. I smiled again at men who were proud of making their contribution to the State. Their pride was justified; they'd done a good job of guarding me.

But I had expected more from them. More respect, perhaps. But why? They didn't know that my penetration of the Egyptians had helped make our 1956 victory a Sunday stroll. My contributions over the past four years were the most secret in all Israel.

Outside the sun burned in my eyes. Eli Prager stood by. We were getting to be a habit. I greeted him with a slightly mocking grin. *"Shalom, Eli."*

Eli whispered to my guards. Jacob locked handcuffs on my wrists.

"What is this?" I demanded. I snapped my wrists apart, testing with malice the strength of the steel.

Roughly wedged between them, I was led through the courtyard to a waiting car and shoved into the back seat. The engine came to life. A hood was pulled down over my head. Aharoni got into the front, and we pulled away. My heart missed a beat; I could hardly breathe. Don't panic, I told myself. Calm down.

"Hey! Can't you hear? Or have you already suffocated?" It was the voice of the guard next to me. "Hold out. We are almost here."

I tried to answer, but my voice failed me. Why did he say "already?" Had Azar, the member of my network in Cairo, felt likewise when he'd been hooded and dragged to the gallows?

At one point the car swung left, pancaking the three of us in the back seat. I reached out to right myself. My manacled hands touched the windowsill—and curtains. Curtains! Not only couldn't I see, I couldn't be seen. Fear flooded over me in a wave, real fear this time.

As abruptly as the ride began, it ended.

"Back up to the door!" someone commanded.

The driver followed directions. The door flew open, and the man to my left vacated his seat. A strong hand on my arm pulled me out on gravel footing.

"He's all yours," Aharoni said to someone.

The fear had stilled my brain. A hand piloted me upstairs into a cool, echo-filled corridor. Hands on each side stopped me at a door.

A voice heavy with a German accent said, "Lower your head or you'll chop it off. Lift your feet." A steel door opened in front of me. The one I had come through closed. "Come on. This is no hotel. Move it!"

I was annoyed; didn't they know that blindness caused hesitation? Calloused fingers removed the handcuffs. "You are bleeding." Then the goggles. I stood facing a gruff-voiced sergeant major and a captain. "Get undressed," the Germanic sergeant major ordered, "you are going to be body searched."

I tried not to admit to myself where I was, but there was no denying it. I was in Ramla prison, Israel's answer to America's Alcatraz.

When they finally left me locked in a small cell within a larger cell, I realized that all the games—theirs and mine—were over. For the first time since I had met my interrogators, I was chilled to the marrow of my bones. Three steel doors, four padlocks, and two bolt locks do not make a man feel large. Unless, of course, one gauges his worth by the amount of steel containing him.

Chapter 23

My mind closed to the enormity of what was happening. It registered only sensory things—feeling, touch, smell. I was locked in a cage inside a large cell. I leaned my back against the barred door, barely aware of how much of a cage it really was. It was a bit over seven feet long, a little over four feet wide. Three steps carried me to its depth. My shoulder never left the wall beside me, my thigh never left the edge of the iron bunk. When I stood on tiptoes, my head brushed the ceiling. I turned, retracing the three short steps. It *was* a cage. Stone and iron isolation.

I slumped on the narrow bunk. Tomorrow, the day after, would have to wait. Somehow this minute was very important, as my mind grasped enough of raw reality to spin backward. It had all begun in Ramla, with Dr. Rudi, who wanted to know if I masturbated. Now to see him again in these circumstances; now let him ask me about masturbation!

Resigned, as night drew near I lay back and stared at the mottled walls. Fresh paint barely obscured the previous tenant's graffiti. In the dying light it looked like prehistoric scribbling, challenging interpretation. Tomorrow, maybe, I would feel up to deciphering it.

Funny how history repeats itself, I thought. My father had gone to Woellersdorf Prison in the 1930s, as a political prisoner in *his* thirties. Now it was 1958, and my thirty-third birthday had come three weeks ago. Had I known it would be a year and a half before the opening of my trial, and that this solitary Dantean hell would be forced on me most of that time, I'm certain I would have been totally stricken. Even knowing nothing at all took its toll.

My mind tormented by injustice, my body fettered by my cage, I lay for days, neither asleep nor awake. In my despair I fantasized grimacing monsters, constantly taunting me but never advancing. My isolation with the demons of my imagination was absolute, until an order came for me to dress in clothes brought from my flat.

Quickly obeying, hopeful of miraculous rescue, I stepped into the corridor only to confront handcuffs. Maddened by the sight, I refused. The guard's brief but futile struggle with me sent him scurrying for the deputy warden.

"I'll go nowhere with those things on!" I said to him. By this time several of the staff were milling around. I felt almost euphoric; I had something to battle besides the demon of despair.

"These are our regulations," he said. "You have to accept them."

"And you will carry me out on a stretcher." I braced myself, ready to take on the entire prison force, if necessary. No more blindfolding, no more handcuffs. Hesitantly the deputy warden proposed a compromise: The handcuffs would be removed in the car that was waiting outside. Again I refused. When he ordered his men to use force, I grabbed an iron bar used to secure the main hall door at night.

"Don't take a step," I warned through clenched teeth.

The deputy warden headed for the warden's office. In a moment he was back with Eli Prager.

"Are you prepared to give your word you won't try to escape?" Eli knew my threat was no bluff.

"I gave it once, and you have it again; I have absolutely no intention of trying to escape!"

They led me outside to a car that would take Chayim, Eli, and me to Jerusalem. Two Shin-Beth guards accompanied us. En route to the capital, I saw the burned-out wrecks of the vehicles that commemorated the struggle we'd had in our War of Independence to open the corridor to the Arab-strangled city. Scores of men and machines had died in the process. "I know your part in all this history," Chayim said, reading my thoughts. "See where you've landed." His words cut deeply, as intended. I was proud of the deeds to which he referred. Friends had fallen, a country was made, history fashioned, and I had given much to it.

At Russian Square in Jerusalem we entered a complex of buildings housing the district and supreme court and met Aharoni. Then I was taken to police headquarters and jailed until my court appearance. I had a chance to read my first newspaper in some time; nothing in it indicated that Israel's most damaging political scandal was in the making.

Returning to the district court building under armed guard (each policeman bore an Uzi submachine gun), I was vaguely amused by Aharoni's attempt to convince the judge that a most dangerous criminal was being brought before him. Outside the courtroom Ezra Hadaya, the chief district prosecutor, handed me a single-page document listing possible charges against me. "It will be amended with time," he added. "What you're reading is only to prove to the judge that we have sufficient evidence to hold you." The document stated that I was being charged with contacting enemy (Egyptian) agents with the intent of causing harm to the State. With no time to digest the accusation, I was ushered into the judge's chamber, where he warily appraised me over the rims of his glasses.

"Do you understand the charges brought against you and the State's request to hold you confined until you are brought to trial?" he asked.

"I know what they're claiming, Your Honor, but I reject it. I am innocent."

"This is not a trial to determine your guilt," he said sternly, "only to consider the request to hold you imprisoned. Do you have anything against being held?"

"No," I said bitterly, disdaining a useless argument.

"If you haven't a lawyer, I suggest you get one. I don't think you appreciate the gravity of the situation."

Back at Ramla, under a temporary order of arrest until such time as I was represented by counsel, I checked out healthy in the prison doctor's examination. On my medical chart I noticed a curious omission: There was no name, only an X4. Again I glimpsed the designation when the prison quartermaster came for my clothes. It struck me that I had neither name nor identity. I was X4, an unknown factor. As my missions were buried in secrecy, so was I. Why?

In the first weeks solitary confinement was broken by three to four hours of daily interrogation. Gradually Aharoni dropped out and Chayim became my relentless adversary. When not matching wits with him and his partner, Kipnes, I fought hourly the humiliation forced on me by the primitiveness of Ramla and the special treatment accorded us on X-row. I wanted desperately for my keepers to feel the hell they had wrapped around me. I fought against undressing under the eyes of my guards, against using the stinking bombsight toilet in full view of anyone who cared to watch, against food pitched to me like a pig. I refused to act the role of stoic; I complained about everything, even the conditions of my twenty-minute exercise period. To prevent my identification, the corridors were emptied on the way to and from the yard, which was little more than a long cell without a roof. Yet I waited eagerly for those minutes in the sun. Even outside, I was alone, but the few steps I took then were better than the three in my cage.

Except for interrogation and exercise, I was allowed out of my cage only when I washed and shaved in the morning. I soon knew the cage intimately; I could shut my eyes and envision every ripple in the cement floor, every scar on the walls. I gauged the hours by the physical anguish of my cramped muscles. Three steps forward, three steps back, a spinning turn on my toes so as not to squander a precious inch of space. An old Eastern adage kept popping into my mind: "May I never experience all that is humanly possible to get accustomed to."

Then, by my third month in solitary, I slowly gained more time in the larger cell. The days had become routine. As conditions improved slightly, I eased off. I had come to a stark realization: If I planned to survive this hell of humiliation, I would have to accept it as another mission. I had to survive, not only in mind, but in health. I began to eat every scrap of food on my plate, I took daily calisthenics, and I began to sleep. The better I controlled my emotions, the more determined I became to survive.

From the imbecilic literature handed me at the beginning, I had read heavily into the pathetically stocked prison library. All my life, I had only skimmed the surface of what I had read; now I wanted to expand my mind in depth as well as breadth.

Terror, I realized, had been a factor in my failure to yield to my keepers: the open hostility among some of the guards toward those on my tier; the screams in the night as Jews called Jews "Nazis" and "Gestapo"; the fettering by chains of Motke Kedar in the next cell. (Kedar had chipped a tiny hole in the wall between our cells one day after we had communicated by Morse code. Since then, we had been playing chess, announcing our moves in code.) "Don't let them drag you down!" he tapped. "If you let them demoralize you, you're a broken man." Convinced, I was determined to make this a working philosophy.

Thus my fight came to be more philosophical than physical. I fought to repair my battered pride. What few rights I had left, I had to protect at all costs in this shrunken, insane existence. If I failed to fight, I would be lost. Sealed off from the world, family, and friends, I would be dead.

Chayim questioned me almost daily. I had to agree that my unwillingness to talk about my actions in Egypt justified the suspicions against me. Even so I still had to confer with Gibli or Motke. Only their cooperation would undo all that had happened.

Chayim was adamant. "We'll spend all the money necessary to find out the truth. We can buy *any* Egyptian, even your friend Osman Nouri." I was dead sure that *no* amount of money could buy Osman Nouri, one of the most honest persons I had ever encountered in Egypt. But I began to have doubts about the wisdom of my silence on the activity in Egypt. Had Gibli and Motke abandoned me? Or were they unable to contact me? I had to find out. I asked to see them. Meeting them, I hinted, might result in a reversal of my position. Even though my request was denied, I was determined to make contact.

On a routine day of quizzing I entered the interrogation room to find my brother-in-law, Zvi Swet, with one of Chayim's men. Guardedly, Zvi related his and Ruth's efforts to meet with the proper people on my behalf. In his dominant, irritating manner Zvi then half-cautioned, half-reprimanded me for covering up for others. Annoyed with him, I said angrily, "I am not guilty of anything."

"I know you're not guilty of what they're saying. But they tell me you're covering up for others and that you have documents to prove it. Where are these documents?"

Calming myself (Zvi had the remarkable ability to anger me), I regarded my paraplegic brother-in-law, the maimed warrior, the virulent Sternist, the anti-Ben-Gurionist. Zvi had been completely taken in by the Shin-Beth. Yet I could understand his motives. "Security of the State" was Holy Writ; few had the courage to question the acts committed by the State in its name.

What I didn't know was that overwhelming pressure had been brought to bear on Zvi and Ruth. The Shin-Beth had badgered them unceasingly, and Isser Harel, whose identity as Mossad head and chairman of the combined directors of security was almost a State secret, had even visited their home to convince them of my guilt and to advise them to abandon me. He warned Ruth that he would do all in his power to "put me in the refrigerator for as long as possible."

My sister, an incredibly strong-minded woman whose will matched Zvi's, believed every word she uttered when she replied, "If my brother is guilty, he should hang. But at least he is entitled to prove his innocence, and we are going to fight for it." According to Ruth, Isser Harel was seemingly filled with hatred for me; she, and even Zvi, were alarmed by his behavior. But, cleverly manipulated, they had cooperated closely with the Shin-Beth and Aharoni, believing that they were legitimately pursuing the truth that I refused to reveal. At this meeting with Zvi, however, I had not known these facts.

I returned to my cell, deeply disturbed by lingering doubts about Gibli's efforts to secure my release or even to contact me. The gnawing in my gut affected my mood, and Chayim used it shrewdly. His false sympathy, and his pointed insinuations that I had been abandoned, contributed to my decision to find out where Gibli stood.

I asked to see my brother-in-law again. A few days later in the interrogation room, I pressed two notes into Zvi's hands. The one intended for Benjamin Gibli stated: "Until now, I have kept my mouth shut; but they have put a knife to my throat. I am even blamed for the fall of the network in Egypt. This is hard to swallow. I don't know what to do. I can clarify the entire situation but will not do so without your consent. Please let me know your position. My brother-in-law will convey your answer to me."

The second note outlined a method for Zvi to communicate Gibli's response to me. At a certain hour he was to pass by the prison and honk his horn five times if Gibli's answer was positive.

Having no watch, I monitored the time by small signs in prison routine. Perhaps because I was so anxiety-ridden, perhaps because I sensed that the end was near, I dozed off. I was awakened by the honking of a car horn. Was it Zvi? Had I heard five honks? I had counted only three or four. I couldn't sleep the whole night.

Early next morning I was in Morse code communication through the wall to Kedar, my chess partner. Had he heard a car horn? *Yes.* How many times? *Not sure.*

At the morning's interrogation I asked for my brother-in-law. "I see no reason for it!" Chayim retorted. I refused to talk at all if he didn't produce Zvi Swet.

Zvi was at the prison the next day. Left with him and one of Chayim's men, eagerness almost overcame my caution as I asked him indirectly if he had passed outside the prison a couple of days ago and blown his horn.

Zvi mumbled something to the effect that he "was around." Matching my impatience, he added, "I already told you, *you can talk.*"

Was he saying that Gibli had OKed my request to tell all that I knew? I wanted to believe it. Zvi would not deceive me; Gibli had said I could speak freely. As if a giant hand had reached down and taken the burden from my shoulders, I sagged in relief. I was ready to unload the burden I'd been carrying since 1955. Mine was a spirit finally unfettered, despite the stone and iron engulfing me.

I could hardly wait for Chayim to begin. There was so much I wanted to spill out. Thank God it was he who would hear it first. Damn Aharoni. Chayim and I were now equals. He would see it. No longer would I be a traitor in the eyes of my colleagues.

"Are you satisfied now?" Chayim asked, entering after Zvi had gone.

"I have a surprise for you, Chayim," I said. "I'm willing to tell you everything. All you have to do is ask."

I began dictating to Chayim, and the truth gushed out for three days. It was all down on paper, all out in the open. *Now I would be able to go home.*

Chayim, skeptical, said little throughout. I could see that the truth was accommodating neither his nor Aharoni's theme. At the end he wanted me to repeat my story before a board of inquiry; I agreed, on the condition that it be a Zahal board of inquiry. I was taken to the Foreign Office, Liaison Department, near the general headquarters compound in Tel Aviv. In my mind it was all formality from here on.

Col. Ariel Amiad, an acquaintance of mine from school and the army, headed the panel. He introduced Lieutenant Colonel Shamgar, the chief army prosecutor. The third man on the panel needed no introduction: Aharoni. The female stenographer also had a familiar face: Isser Harel's private secretary.

I protested Aharoni's presence and demanded to see the board's letter of appointment. Seeing it authorized and signed by Isser Harel was a slap in the face. I refused to utter a word to the panel until it was made official by the general chief of staff, Chayim Laskov, Moshe Dayan's successor. Two days later, he did so. Isser Harel's secretary had been replaced by a tape recorder. Aharoni, however, still sat on the panel. Again voicing my opposition to him, I was swayed by Colonel Amiad. Knowing the panel chairman's integrity, I conceded reluctantly.

The panel launched its investigation. Not strangely, they were uninterested in the accusations of traitor that Aharoni and company had been lodging against me for so long. I related to them the facts from my recruitment to my meeting with Motke in Paris in June of 1954, at which time he ordered me to take command of the sabotage in Egypt and prepare for political assassinations. I spoke in detail of the awful conditions in the so-called Zionist network in Egypt, what happened in the collapse, and the conspiracy in which I allowed myself to become involved with Motke and Gibli.

Because my version of the facts did not coincide with Aharoni's, he sniped at me with questions that boldly implied that my statement was neatly tailored to offset my suspicious behavior as commander of the group in Egypt. Tempers flared, and I refused to continue. Colonel Amiad, in a private talk, assured me that Aharoni would in no way prejudice them. "Aharoni is a necessary evil that we will have to put up with," he said. The session adjourned.

Instead of being returned to Ramla, I was whisked to the police prison in Jaffa, as gloomy and dirty as any hole in Israel. The place reeked of urine and vomit, the bedclothing smelled worse, the food was unswallowable. Expecting to be interned only one night, I made the best of it, but, taken back to the inquiry, unshaven and rumpled, I complained. More punishment! I had already vowed to accept no more of Aharoni's dominion.

What had caused the rift in the session was Aharoni's objection to my reconstruction of the events in Egypt as documented in the field diary I had kept as a German businessman—the diary that Gibli had taken from me, the diary Motke had kept for safekeeping. I said that I had not seen the diary since that night in early January 1955. Colonel Amiad replied that he would try to retrieve it from Motke.

In the following session he announced that *Motke claimed I had taken it back that same night, and that there was only one diary!*

Why was Motke denying the existence of the two diaries? If I was telling everything with his blessings, why keep the diaries hidden?

"Where is the diary you claim to be the fake?" Aharoni asked.

I looked at him hard. "In safe hands, where only I can get it."

Colonel Amiad cut in. "Would you tell us where, so we can see it?"

"Yes, provided I can be present when it's taken from the container." I related to the panel how I had crated the fake diary among the household goods that were being held by a shipping agent in Haifa.

"What is the agent's name?" Aharoni demanded.

"That you will know when you take me to Haifa, not before!" Ignoring Aharoni, I addressed the chairman. "I will cooperate, but those are my terms."

Aharoni called for my attention, his look that of a man with something up his sleeve. "Tell me, Avri," he said, "is this the genuine or the fake diary?"

From his attaché case, *he produced the fake diary,* the one I had secured in the shipping crate.

"How did you get it?"

"We have our ways."

His ways meant that either Eli Prager, at Peter Landesman's flat, had overhead my whispered instructions to stop the shipping of the crate, or Peter had cooperated with them. I trusted Peter.

Aharoni held up the diary. "Can you identify it? Is this yours?"

"It looks like it, yes."

"Are you certain this is the *fake* diary?" he said sarcastically.

He refused my request to check the entries to determine it exactly, and an argument ensued that broke up the session.

In the following days (in which Aharoni adopted a more pleasant position, thanks to Colonel Amiad) I covered the entire Egyptian episode, the blueprint for perjury to frame Lavon, the establishing of the firm in Munich, and the incidents with the Egyptians in Europe. The impact of my testimony was staggering. The panel tried in vain to shake my story. It scandalized Amiad and Shamgar, who, like Israel's populace, could not believe that such a lethal conspiracy could occur in our defense establishment. And I could see open fear over what I had said regarding Moshe

Dayan's place in all this. Yet not one of them pursued it. The subject of Dayan was taboo.

On another day I sensed that something was up as I entered the inquiry room. They were hastily conferring. Colonel Amiad opened up the mystery.

"Avri," he said, "what you have revealed to us casts heavy shadows on your former superiors. And we think it only fair that we hear what they have to say to your testimony."

They had Motke waiting outside. Not only did I want to see him after my ordeal, but I welcomed, with every fiber in my being, his confirmation of my revelations. It seemed that only his and Gibli's corroboration would crack the wall of skepticism. "Yes, yes!" I could have shouted. "Bring him!"

Motke, pale as a ghost, hardly looked in my direction as he took a chair. *He then denied everything I had said about the false action report in Egypt and the conspiracy against Lavon.*

The panel's eyes flickered back and forth, to Motke, to me. In the deathly quiet I could only stare incredulously at Motke.

"Are you saying, Lt. Col. Ben Zur," Colonel Amiad pressed, "that Avri has not stated the truth?"

"What a liar!" Motke could not look at me as he continued. "It's all sucked from his finger. No truth whatsoever!"

"Then this whole story about altering his field reports and your getting together against Pinhas Lavon is all a lie? Everything Avri said?"

"I can't imagine where he cooked all that up from. . . ."

"But why would he lie, or involve you?" Colonel Shamgar cut in. "You, yourself, have already said that the two of you are close friends."

"Ask him," Motke shot back. "Maybe Avri has something to hide."

The truth broke on me like a collapsing dam: *I've been tricked!* Motke did not know I was going to talk. Neither did Gibli. In my eagerness to tell, to escape from the hell I was living, I had fallen into a trap. Aharoni's trap, my brother-in-law's trap. Frightened by what I had done and by the realization that Motke and Gibli were throwing me to the wolves, I felt a moment of sheer panic. It was them or me. I could not still the surge of futility that clawed at my gut. I stood. Desperately I said, "Motke, we have walked the same path for a long time, now we have parted. You know very well what I have said is the truth, and for reasons everyone in this room can understand, you are denying it." I stared coldly at Aharoni, the only man in the room with a smile in his eyes. "But, Motke, I can prove what I've said."

Motke sneered at me and, trying to draw support from the panel, said, "How can you do it? Tell me, I'd like to know."

I said slowly, for effect, "I have material, in Gibli's handwriting, that proves what I've said about the past."

Motke was stunned. Undoubtedly Gibli had told him about the letter he wrote to me in Paris, his acknowledgment to my warning that Fatti Harkabi had pieced together the conspiracy. But Motke did not know, nor did anyone else, that I had kept a page of the conspiratorial revisions of my field reports. The page, matching the revisions, was in Gibli's own handwriting. The panel saw Motke's reaction. Aharoni had gone deadpan.

"Avri, where are these documents?" Colonel Amiad asked, suddenly confused by the shape of things. Consenting to a private conference with me, he released Motke. I watched him go, feeling the pain of an ugly ending. Motke and I were finished forever.

I told Colonel Amiad I would have to talk with my sister. Though I knew that Ruth was privy to my brother-in-law's betrayal of my confidence, I believed that she would understand this. I wanted her to get my suitcase from Peter Landesman. I believed that Peter had served my cause faithfully, and I did not want to involve him for having held my documents, nor for having mailed the letters I'd sent to Shula and Shlomo Millet. I had no choice but to trust Ruth.

Ruth was brought to a room at the Jaffa police jail. Certain the room was bugged, I slipped a note to her: "Tell Peter Landesman to give you my blue suitcase. I must have it to prove my innocence. Remove all the pictures and film negatives and preserve them well. *All* the other material, bring to me. *Give to no one but me."*

By the next session, I waited in vain for Ruth's return with the all-important papers. I was alone with Chayim and, reading my troubled mind, he said, "Your blue suitcase is in our hands, but not the material you claim is inside."

Startled by both statements, I said, "What do you mean?"

"Your friend, Peter Landesman, said he burned it. Only certain nonflammable negatives survived."

"Burned it!" I was foreseeing a catastrophe. "Why in God's name would he burn it? He was supposed to protect it with his life!"

Chayim shrugged and opened a file in front of me. "We're questioning him. Now try to recall every single item you had in the suitcase, every piece of paper."

All I was able to think of was that Peter, having burned the contents of my suitcase, had doomed Lavon's purging to fate of eternal suspicion, unless someone else spoke out. Without the evidence contained in my suitcase, I couldn't bind Gibli to the conspiracy.

Desperate now to salvage what I could of my credibility, I itemized all I remembered transferring from my attaché case to the blue suitcase—except for the negatives of the Egyptian rocket blueprints; Aharoni's suspicions would only deepen if he knew. Watching Chayim as I called off the items, a curious thing struck me. Leaning forward, I got an upside-down view of the page in his hand. It was an exact list of what was in my suitcase! Either Peter had *not* burned the contents of my suitcase, or he had related the contents from memory. But that was impossible. Yet he *had* remembered. Apparently.

I didn't close my eyes that night. During all these months I had felt confident that, at the exposure of the material binding Gibli to the conspiracy, my claims of innocence would be verified. Yet now I sensed that this was futile.

At the next interrogation Chayim's usual cordiality was replaced by harshness, as he warned that whatever I said could be used against me in court. "There's nothing more to disclose," I said hotly, signing a paper stating I had been duly warned.

Chayim began with questions about the negatives confiscated from Peter Landesman. Some were personal film with no bearing on anything; others were negatives of the rocket blueprints that, I explained in detail, had been mistakenly given to me by Modiin people with the return of my personal things. It was clear that Chayim had no interest in the rocket negatives. Bigger things were on his mind.

"Take a look at these," he said, and handed me three rolls of negatives, which I held up to the light. They were microfilms of some typewritten pages and diagrams.

"These are not mine. I never had them."

"Then why were they in your suitcase?"

"They were never in my suitcase. Not while I had it, in any event. What are these films, anyway?"

"They're from the Violet File. . . ." Chayim's voice trailed off.

A chill swept over me. The Violet File was the most sensitive file in Modiin Unit 131. Top secret. I was numbed; all I could think of was the gravity of even an *implication* that I had taken them. Suddenly my entire credibility seemed untenable; even a denial was an effort for me. I needed time to think.

They gave me two endless days of grilling such as I had not imagined possible. According to Chayim I had photographed the top secret Modiin Violet File. I attempted to make them see that I had neither the equipment to photograph such documents nor the access to it. "We don't know how you did it, but you did it," they said time and again.

Their story was that I had planned to hand over the file to Osman Nouri. The motive: money. They more than hinted that I was a willing tool in my wife's hands, that she used my love for her as leverage to acquire material advantages. "Even your sister says that if you are guilty, it is only because of your wife," they said.

I wasn't prepared for their attack on Shula. If Ruth had said it, I wasn't surprised; her hatred for Shula was morbid. But since attacks on Shula had opened, I prepared myself for more.

Though conditions had improved slightly at the Jaffa police prison, my temper got the best of me one day, and Police Sergeant Levy became the victim. I was seated on my bunk as he entered with two of his goons and, since he offered no word of greeting, I ignored him. Angered by what he must have viewed as impertinence, he shouted at me, then grabbed my ankle and yanked, almost throwing me onto the cement floor. "Next time I'll break your leg if you don't hop down when I enter your cell!" Defiantly I warned him not to try it, which brought his fist up, poised to strike; just then another policeman stepped between us. After searching my cell for God knows what, they left an embittered man behind. I decided to repay Sergeant Levy.

I connected a metal spring from the bunk to the steel door of my cell. Using the blanket as an insulator, I attached the spring to open electrical wires in a circular hole in the wall. Then I called for permission to visit the toilet, knowing full well that Sergeant Levy was the only one who could open my door. Half an hour later I heard his footsteps approaching. I quickly connected a circuit to the door and waited for Levy to make contact with the 220-volt direct current lock. The jingling of keys and a muffled cry preceded a loud thud in the hall. Sergeant Levy had made contact. Quickly I disassembled my apparatus and sat back on my bunk.

Half an hour after they had carted the prostrate sergeant to the infirmary, two NCOs made a brief inquiry as to what had gone on.

"All I want to do is go to the toilet," I said.

Certainly Chayim was aware of the electrocution incident as he introduced me to a new team of interrogators. Their purpose was immediately apparent: to exploit the breach between Gibli and Motke, and myself, and to investigate the grave charges I had launched against them. But their theories were farfetched in many respects, and I refused to respond.

Passewitz exploded. "Why are you covering up for them? Do you still think they are friends you can trust? Let me tell you something, Avri, while you were out there risking your life for the State, for its security, your *friends* were busy sleeping with your wife. . . ."

I didn't hear the rest of it as I recoiled under the hammerblow attack on Shula. I stepped to the window overlooking the small courtyard. Outside it was pitch dark. Only the high wall and the stars in the black night were visible as I forced myself to separate emotions from logic. They knew that

Shula was a weak point with me. If their claims were true, I had only myself to blame. Though I loved Shula very much, I had neglected her terribly over the years; I was too busy being a soldier to be a husband. A soldier for the State!

"Even if what you say is true," I said, speaking deliberately, "it changes nothing. I'm to blame. I left a young, vital woman alone much too much, for too many years. She has done nothing more than what I've done." I sat. "Now if you have questions on the case, ask them."

The game continued. Finally I offered to submit to another polygraph test, but a test administered by an expert.

The attack on Shula was not over, as I saw after the session. I was alone in the interrogation room when the door opened and my sister came in, crying and shouting that I was "defending a whore who had ruined my life and my name." There was no reasoning with her. If this was her belief, I resolved never to see Ruth again.

Within twenty-four hours Shula's mother came from Jerusalem to heap guilt on my shoulders. As she would on two future visits—I saw all this as an effort by my jailers to keep me under emotional strain—she hurled accusations that I had destroyed her daughter's life. It almost worked. I almost began to believe that I had destroyed Shula herself.

The third polygraph test was conducted at the beginning of April, and again I was incredibly frustrated by not being believed. This led to almost an obsession to get even with my interrogators—and I had the perfect opportunity.

Passover, a holy night in the Jewish faith, fell in the second week of April. I had been held for four months. Weeks earlier I had decided that if I was to spend Passover alone, then somebody would suffer with me. All day prior to Seder night, I paced the floor under the tight scrutiny of the guards. Late in the afternoon I demanded to see Aharoni. "Tell him it's his only chance. And tell him to bring a bottle of cognac and a tape recorder."

I knew Aharoni. In his eagerness to bury me, he would assume that I was ready to spill my guts on this holy night, and that, being of weak character, I would need the alcohol to open up.

But I had another reason for the cognac. Statements taken under the influence of alcohol are void in court. Especially if it is supplied by the interrogators.

At seven in the evening the prison captain came, inquiring if I really had something to say and wouldn't it keep until tomorrow.

"If Aharoni doesn't want to hear what I've got to say," I said, appearing unconcerned, "then to hell with him. Tell him this is his chance."

Less than an hour later I joined Aharoni and Chayim in the prison interrogation room. Both were in festive attire, both had dragged themselves from their families. I couldn't have been happier. Aharoni had the tape recorder ready to go. On the table was the bottle of cognac (the brand I'd specified) and silver goblets from his Seder table. He poured each of us a goblet and we raised them in toast.

"To the truth!" they chimed.

Accepting another goblet, I stated that I was ready to begin. Aharoni started the recorder, giving my name, the date, place, and hour. "Are you, Avri Seidenwerg, telling us, of your own free will, the following statement?"

"Yes. This is at my own request. By the way, thanks for bringing the cognac."

Aharoni and Chayim exchanged glances. I requested another goblet of the hot spirits, prepared to embellish whatever they might have expected.

"What I am going to say isn't easy. I have come to the conclusion that it is better to be called a liar than a traitor. I understand that, because of all the inaccuracies, everything I said has a suspicious ring, and consequently, a distorted picture of my character . . ." I rehashed all the Egyptian activity, and tossed them a lollipop when I lied, stating that I had never met President Naguib and I had never written Nasser a letter and delivered it to him with Bob Jansen. After twenty minutes of this the farce came to an end. Aharoni exploded.

"We know all this. Get to the revelations!"

"What revelations?" I said innocently. "You always claimed I never told the truth; so now I'm saying what you want to hear . . . because I'd rather be known as a liar than a traitor."

Aharoni leaped up, his chair crashing against the wall. "This is all old trash! Get on with it!"

"There is nothing *but* old trash," I said, grinning over the goblet.

Aharoni was seething with rage. "You had the audacity to call us away from our Seder tables, our family, our children, to listen to your lies? If you have something to say, say it!"

It was my turn to be explicit. "It is not my fault that I'm not able to be with *my* family at the Seder table. Remember, Aharoni, I promised you I would not spend Passover alone. Well, I have *not* spent it alone."

"I won't forget this," Aharoni seethed. As if the hounds of hell were laughing at him, he fled, with Chayim in his wake.

After a final, short briefing by Col. Ariel Amiad, in which he apprised me that the inquiry would take all the time it needed to make its assessment of my testimony, he said that he personally intended to do all in his power to break the collusion of Gibli and Motke.

I was returned to Ramla. After the weeks at the Jaffa police prison, Ramla was like coming home to a grand hotel. To a man with nothing to cling to except himself, the simple gift of comfort is a pleasure.

Chapter 24

It was nearly inconceivable to me how *any* occurrence in my years of dedication to Israel's security could be even remotely construed as traitorous; yet now I faced charges based on that very premise. The original rage that my helplessness had engendered turned to numbness; I had hesitated to acquire legal counsel, even though my sister and her husband badgered me constantly about it. Though I now gave in, I was animal-wary of anyone consenting to defend me. Perhaps I'd begun to believe, as Isser Harel and his underlings would have it, that I was unworthy. But I only became depressed as I pondered the problem of who *would* defend me. Israeli lawyers had no stomach for security affairs involving one of their own. All Israel, lawyers and judges included, revered patriotism.

To represent an Israeli Arab or a foreigner charged with spying was one thing; to stand up for a Jew accused of betraying the paramount security of the State was something else. Chauvinism! We were blinded by it.

Responding to Ruth and Zvi's pleadings, Shlomo Tussia-Cohen—an experienced Jerusalem lawyer, a former district judge, and a legal brain reputed to be among the best in jurisprudence—visited me at Ramla. I still held doggedly to the illusion that my freedom could be gained without a trial. Nevertheless I secretly welcomed this man. His bearing was more that of an undertaker than a lawyer. In his early forties, tall, formal, and stiff, Tussia-Cohen had black, slick hair and a black mustache to match his eyebrows. He was so soft-spoken that he amplified my worst doubts.

Could he stand up to an establishment whose eleventh commandment was to bring down the heavens on one and all suspected of anti-Israelism?

He had as many doubts about me. He declared his position simply: "Your story depends on its credibility. In such cases I make my decision the following way. If the client claims his innocence, I will try to verify it before taking his defense. Convinced he's stated the truth, I will go all the way with him. Should I be convinced of his guilt, I'll advise him to admit it, then I will use every letter in the law to get the most lenient sentence possible. However, should a guilty client remain adamant about his innocence, I usually advise him to seek other counsel. I cannot convince a court my client is innocent when I don't believe it myself."

I accepted his premise but cautioned him to expect unusual problems in his quest for the truth of my case. He smiled serenely. He had his sources, he said. I believed him. There wasn't a hint of magniloquence about the man.

I anticipated word from Tussia-Cohen within ten days, yet it was six long, anxious weeks until he reappeared. Explaining his absence, he said that the difficulties were much greater than he'd expected.

"I don't mind telling you," he said, "I had serious doubts about you when I left. What finally convinced me to accept your defense was none other than Isser Harel himself."

"Isser?" I exclaimed.

He read my mind accurately. "I'm well aware, *very well aware,* that the Mossad chief is no friend of yours. Quite the contrary! And because of that fact, I'm here."

As a result of his inquiries to the Shin-Beth for my testimony, which had been taken in interrogation and introduced before Zahal's board of inquiry, Tussia-Cohen had been summoned to the office of the Mossad director. Isser Harel had stepped far beyond the ethics of his authority in trying to convince him of my guilt; he attempted to prejudice him with the fact that I was a traitor, hence undeserving of representation. However, Tussia-Cohen had studied the records and noted remarkable inconsistencies between what appeared to him to be the truth, and what he was hearing. In questioning some of Isser's assertions, he had indicated that he could demonstrate a binding connection between the Egyptian sabotage, the Lavon imbroglio, and my incarceration. Isser had then put on the pressure, warning Tussia-Cohen that if the connection was employed in my defense, he would see me behind bars for a long time to come, the same brand of intimidation Isser had used on my sister and brother-in-law.

As a last resort, Isser had intimated that defending me might reflect adversely on his personal future. "It was here that Isser Harel made his biggest mistake," Tussia-Cohen said somberly. "I am not a man to be bulldozed. I have no fear of Isser Harel's power."

Early, Tussia-Cohen brought in his young associate, Jigal Arnon, an aggressive dynamo. Together they proved to be an excellent team: Arnon, the wily interrogator; Tussia-Cohen, the analytical tactician. They restored my sagging faith. Since there were only bare indications of the charges being brought against me, we began to construct a defense based on the emphasis of the interrogation. One thing that impressed me greatly about Tussia-Cohen was his sense of fairness. He gave freely—to Motke, Gibli, Chayim, Aharoni, Isser Harel, and the rest—the benefit of his doubts.

"But when they are on the witness stand," he said, "we shall see how honest they are."

Clothed in the security of legal counsel, my mind wandered beyond the walls of my own predicament to that of my family, now in the midst of a terrible plight of their own. Shula had answered none of the few letters I'd written, but I attributed this to Aharoni's withholding them, further evidence of his vindictive nature. All I knew of their situation—financial worries, concern for me, and the very real doubt that I *might* be guilty of something—forced me into a wretched state of guilt for having brought this burden on them. I had heard that Shula and my son were in Berlin with her relatives, but I did not know definitely.

After six months prison conditions had improved slightly. The days now had some routine, marked mainly by my one-hour morning toilet in the outer cell, two twenty-minute exercise periods, and meals. It was as if I'd been forgotten except by Chayim and Kipnes, who now grilled me only once weekly. In my loneliness, in my constant attention to the construction of my defense, I slowly achieved a mental capacity that, at its full awareness, amazed me. I had observed the virtuosity of a man's memory when it is honed by absolute isolation from outside impressions. One begins to remember everything with fantastic clarity, even conversations, expressions, subtle nuances. Suddenly I wanted to recall everything.

One development worried me. I saw it around me and in me. Despair seeks its own environment, and a false serenity had evolved from my chronic despair. I feared that I was becoming so accustomed to my lot that the world beyond my cell would cease to have meaning for me. Something of my attitude must have bothered someone else; one day I was transferred from X-row to the general prison wing. After the long months of isolation to which I had made an animal-like adjustment, I was forced to shift to the environment of a five-man cell.

My cell mates were easy company, and it was with them that I experienced my first interlude of social sanity in the false world of confinement. Nowhere do men become acquainted faster than in prison. It strips away all facades. Our shared fear of the future and sense of outrage bind us in moods that fluctuate between Homeric mirth and Dantesque depression. Once set into motion, our feelings are difficult to restrain. After I'd adjusted to my companions, the clock began to move, life to have meaning. My awareness fluttered and creaked into motion.

I came to know my fellow cell mates, though unfortunately, I wasn't supposed to identify myself, nor talk about my past. I had three convicted murderers in with me and also Seev Avni, who was probably the most important security prisoner in Israel at the time. Soon, I fear, my case eclipsed the notoriety of his.

Seev Avni, born Wolf Goldstein in Switzerland of Jewish parents steeped in Russian communism, was indoctrinated early. When Lenin sought asylum in Switzerland before the great 1918 revolution, he had lived with the Goldsteins for a period. From the beginning Seev was recruited and trained by Russian intelligence, later to be planted in Israel during our 1948 War of Independence. A virulent disciple of Lenin-Marxism, Seev disdained his Jewish heritage and sought a platform from which to report to the Kremlin.

Knowing of Israel's lack of manpower to staff its fledgling foreign ministry, Seev—highly intelligent, educated in economics, fluent in several languages—crept, via connections, into the commercial attaché post to the Benelux countries. Significant posts followed in other European states after he had participated in Israel's 1952 negotiations with West Germany on the reparations agreement. Quickly recruited by the Mossad hierarchy, he was soon able to identify all overt and covert Mossad agents, through his function as "letter box." This disaster was considered a personal failure for Isser Harel. It was extremely interesting to note that Seev Avni's exposure coincided with the beginnings of my own troubles. I could not but think that Isser Harel had become so paranoid as a result of this blunder that he was lashing out at anybody causing him worry. That Isser Harel was out to get me, there was no doubt.

For reasons demonstrated to me later, I was given this prison opportunity to know Seev Avni quite well. I was cautious of his probing but returned it in kind. It was then that he revealed his knowledge, while functioning as a Russian spy, of our network in Egypt, its setup, and the names of those involved.

This introduced me to totally new lines of thought. It was only my direct contact with headquarters, through Faust and Stollberg in Frankfurt, that kept my name and penetration of Egypt away from the Russians. And, as a consequence, from the Egyptians.

After a couple of weeks with my cell mates, I was escorted to the deputy warden's office one evening after lockup. This was unusual, since roll call was the last head count and final order of the day. However, I was told that a high-ranking officer awaited me.

Col. Ariel Amiad, chairman of the Zahal board of inquiry, before which I had testified only weeks ago, had brought good—and bad—news.

"I promised I'd advise you of the board's findings," he said. "I also promised I was going to find out the truth of your claims regarding Gibli and Motke. Well, I broke Motke; he verified everything you said, even the plot against Lavon." Colonel Amiad's smile of obvious pleasure quickly faded. "However, Motke warned me that if I quote him before any kind of forum, he will deny everything."

Grabbing at anything to get Colonel Amiad's revelation into some perspective, I said, "But even if he does deny it, he still told you!"

"True, but it's his word against mine."

"So what do we do, wait until he's confronted with it?"

"Yes, wait," he nodded.

"And what happens to Motke then?"

"It's not up to the board to decide, but he'll certainly have to bear the consequences. You don't have to feel sorry for him; he's a liar."

"What happens to me?"

"You'll face trial for the documents they found on you. You might get a year or two."

"A year or two!" I echoed.

"It's unavoidable, Avri. But if you approach the president for his grace, you'll undoubtedly be out in a jiffy."

I was flabbergasted by the impossibility of his logic. "You've already found me guilty, sentenced me, and decided what I'll have to do to get out! How do *you* know I'll be pardoned?"

Colonel Amiad lifted his eyebrows. "You know quite well that we (the army) have something to say about it."

Escorted back to the cell after the colonel's disconcerting revelation, I could tell that the duty officer was stalling my return. Once locked in I sensed an underlying tension among my cell mates. Late at night, while the prison slept, one whispered to me what had gone on in my absence. Each had been questioned by Aharoni for anything I might have spilled during my stay with them. They had also been warned not to let on.

Another damned Aharoni witchhunt! I had spilled my guts to Chayim in interrogation, to Zahal's inquiry board (the board now knew of Motke's admission), and still that bastard Aharoni was chasing ghosts. The man was driven by his assurance of my guilt; it had become personal. Recognizing this quirk in him, I began to doubt that justice would ever be meted out to me.

Predictably I was tossed back into my X-row cell. But I was no longer a "greener." Better versed in my basic rights, I refused to be locked overnight in the inner cage of the cell. Losing this battle to the warden did not lose the war; I presented to the Supreme Court my first attempt at legalistics on my behalf. The *Order Nisi* requested that the prison authority show cause why it locked me in the inner cage at night. Meantime, another sudden development resulted from a prison inspection by Minister of Police Bachor Shitrith. Arriving at my cell, Shitrith looked quizzically at me.

"Haven't we met before?" he asked.

I nodded. "I've been in your home a few times. Your daughter and I were good friends." I said no more about the olive-skinned beauty who had been the Palmach's first female physical instructor.

Studiedly he said, "So you are the one."

Responding to his query about complaints, I pointed out my months in solitary confinement. "If I could share my cell, it might make the time easier," I said.

Unannounced, Seev Avni, my former Russian-spy cell mate, was moved in with me despite my vigorous efforts to keep him out.

Seev Avni was no ordinary stool pigeon. I had inadvertently discovered that he was acting as Aharoni's ears, which explained my previous move to his cell and his coy bartering of background information. I had traded with him but had given him nothing Aharoni wanted. Now I was force-fed Seev's inquisition.

Aharoni had chosen this particular time to honor my request for company because my preliminary hearing was scheduled. Apprising Tussia-Cohen of the rat in my cell, I said I feared that Seev Avni might put words in my mouth to verify Aharoni's theories of my treason. His testimony might influence the court.

When I confronted Seev Avni, surprisingly he admitted his role. Further, he told me of the home visits Aharoni had rewarded him with. His game was up with me, but he continued to play it with Aharoni for a while before returning to the general wing on the excuse that I was sticking to my silence.

In October 1958, ten months after my arrest, my preliminary hearing commenced in Jerusalem before District Court Judge Edan. District Prosecutor Ezra Hadaya, in his opening statement, attributed to me more than a half-dozen security violations, from photographing top secret Modiin documents to making unauthorized contacts with the enemy.

"Don't worry about the charges," Tussia-Cohen whispered. "They try to cover all the grounds. Some of them will be dropped."

I couldn't share my counsel's optimism. Prosecution received an *in camera* hearing on the basis that this was a critical case involving some of "the highest, most closely guarded secrets in the land."

Prosecutor Hadaya spun an intriguing tale of how my unauthorized contact with Osman Nouri had been accidentally discovered by the Mossad in a recruiting approach to Bob Jansen; how, after that, they had watched my every move, while my Modiin superiors began coaxing me home during my father's illness; how I had compounded my guilt by additional contacts with Egyptians in Vienna; and how, on coming home, I had refused to reveal anything of my shady past in Egypt. He told of discovering the incriminating Violet File negatives that had been held by Peter Landesman, documents *never* before officially photographed. And prosecution would, he announced, prove that my intent was to hand this secret material over to the enemy. My motive: greed.

Tussia-Cohen and Arnon failed to soothe my rage. My divorce from Shula had been partly on account of a lack of money, due to low army pay; I had lived for a while, during my training, on one pound a day; I had survived in Germany, for a while, on a deutsche mark a day; I had received one dollar danger pay for my work in Egypt. Tens of thousands of dollars I'd handled as head of the firm in Munich and not a single dollar misspent. *Greed?*

My thirty-fourth birthday would arrive in three months, and I had literally nothing to show for the twenty years I'd given to my country.

During the week of hearing I was kept in the police prison near the Jerusalem district court building. A two-day recess had been called, when my sister paid me a frenetic visit; the Shin-Beth had convinced her to fly to Austria and Germany to collect any materials I might have stashed with Olga and Shula. I tried to assure Ruth that her mission was a wild goose chase; the Mossad, on Isser Harel's orders, had already attempted to burglarize Olga's flat in Vienna. Now they were giving it the front door approach.

But why should I deny her a trip to Europe? She needed the vacation, and I wanted firsthand news of my family. My last consideration, in writing notes to Shula and Olga requesting that they hand over all materials, was that it might help to prove to both Ruth and Aharoni that I had nothing more to hide, that my speaking out spelled the end to all my secrets.

Ruth had departed when Judge Edan ruled that, since I was accused of severe offenses carrying a minimum of ten years' imprisonment, the defense was allowed to cross-examine preliminary witnesses. The issue had arisen out of a new law, and Prosecutor Hadaya, in the name of the attorney general of the State, appealed to the Supreme Court.

Waiting in my X-row cell in Ramla, I was surprised by my sister's swift return from Europe with her meager booty: an old calendar (useful only to me), some pictures, and letters. She did bring the news that Shula and my son were staying with relatives in Berlin. In addition she told of Tussia-Cohen's eloquent defense before the Supreme Court.

Tussia-Cohen couldn't explain the delay in the court's decision; on his advice I submitted a letter asking for speed on the basis of my long ordeal. In early December Tussia-Cohen won a sound legal victory; the hearing resumed.

To show why I should stand trial for the multiple charges, prosecution had to establish that I had "acquired and photographed," three and a half years ago, Unit 131's top secret Violet File and that I planned to pass it to the enemy.

I had not as yet allowed myself to believe that the Violet file negatives had been a plant. Yet Modiin claimed that the file had *never* been photographed. But if Modiin hadn't photographed it, who had? And how had the negatives come to be among my things?

Etka Jiftach, administrative officer in Unit 131, was late in her pregnancy. Prosecutor Hadaya struck out when Etka denied that I'd had access to the safe containing Unit 131's secret materials.

But, as Etka had helped me, she also hurt me. She denied that it was she who had finally given me back my things from the archives—thus denying responsibility for accidentally passing the secret Egyptian rocket blueprints to me. Unfortunately the receipt bore only my signature. Etka wanted no part of the responsibility of having mishandled either the rocket negatives or the Violet File. In fact Etka said that she had never seen such a film.

Tussia-Cohen wanted badly to rip into her testimony, but I stopped him. We had a past I couldn't forget: I had brought back the body of her boyfriend, mutilated by Arabs in the village of Jasur in the War of Independence. I was present at the first meeting with her husband, Jiftach. I remembered her being thrown from a jeep and taken to the hospital; later, her rejoicing with me as she sent me the official letter restoring my former rank.

My counsel reproached me sharply. "Don't be such a sentimental fool! She's lying and you know it. There are millions of pregnant women, but it's your future on the line."

Maybe, but she wasn't lying to hurt me, only to protect herself.

Peter Landesman and I had an unpleasant past I shouldn't have forgotten, but when I entrusted him with my suitcase, I considered him a confidant. As he took the stand, I pondered hard the dividing line between dubious friendship and survival. I could allow no replays of Etka's testimony.

Would Peter's story hold up? That, on seeing the contents of my suitcase, he had realized his involvement in an explosive situation? That he panicked, burning all the flammable papers and negatives while hiding all the nonflammable negatives of the Violet File until he turned them over to the Shin-Beth?

There was a flaw in Peter's version that only I saw. According to him, he realized the importance of the suitcase's contents *only* on opening it. This was impossible!

Peter, ignorant of my arrest at the time, could have made no sense at all of the suitcase's contents unless he had opened and read the two letters I'd given him for forwarding, one to Shula and the other to Shlomo. Peter had already stated that I had *never* left any letters with him.

I knew that Peter was playing Aharoni's dupe, but how could I prove it?

Judge Edan ruled that "on first sight" there was sufficient evidence to bring me to trial.

An unexplained six-month postponement preceded the opening of my trial on July 29, 1959, on the following charges: unlawful gathering of secret documents, unlawful photographing of secret documents, unlawful possession of secret documents, unlawful contact with enemy agents, preparation to carry out offenses against State security.

The secret documents involved only the Violet File negatives; no importance was attached to Egyptian rocket blueprints or other films. My contact with enemy agents concerned Osman Nouri in Bonn and others in Vienna.

Equally impressive was prosecution's witness list. Col. Benjamin Gibli's absence from the list was no surprise; prosecution seemed determined to sever all connection between my arrest and the action in Egypt. To prove my intent to harm Israel, Hayada had to isolate me from all my previous operations. He had one hell of a job in front of him.

My juryless trial would be heard by a panel of three judges. In accordance with Israeli procedure, there would be no court recorder; the transcript would be a subjective summation of the judges' interpretations, written by them as the trial proceeded.

My judges were Dr. Benjamin Halevi, president of the Jerusalem District Court; M. Golan; and Y. Cohen. Tussia-Cohen made an unnerving comment about Judge Halevi, the presiding panelist: "With him, everything is either black or white. In some ways he's an extremist on security cases." My counsel's opinions on the other panelists were mixed, but my Ramla inmates agreed on several points: M. Golan was a blind chauvinist who heeded only the prosecution, as if the State's case were Holy Writ; Y. Cohen they praised for warmth and understanding; Dr. Halevi they feared. My attorneys declined to comment on the inmates' opinions, but later, when the going got rough, they admitted their accuracy.

By this time I had ceased feeling sorry for myself. No longer was I the martyr, shamed by the charges that boiled down to "traitor." In Israel no sin surpassed treason. But I knew my innocence. I also knew the courtroom was the battlefield—them or us. I came prepared to fight.

The room was large, but pressure closed the walls in on me. The focal point was the dais and the wall behind, which cloaked in the State's emblem, the seven-armed Menorah. My place, the prisoner's dock, was to the left of the judges' dais, the witness stand to the right.

That first morning was the worst. Early, armed guards took me from the nearby Jerusalem police prison to the great stone building. The long, empty corridors were still chilled from last night's cold. By the time my attorneys arrived, the building was coming to life, but I'd yet to accustom myself to the stares of passersby.

Things warmed up as Prosecutor Hadaya and his entourage entered. Brandishing my blue suitcase, he smiled as if to say, "I trust you know who this belongs to!"

Chanan Barel, brought from Vienna by the prosecution, stood in the corridor. He stared at me, then mouthed: "What can I do?" I knew what he could do: Tell the truth; embellish nothing. I mentioned to my counsel that Barel would probably be the first witness.

Prosecutor Hadaya overheard my remark and said, "Quite right, you are. He will tell us about your meeting with the Egyptians in Vienna." By his tone, I wondered if he hadn't gotten some distorted information about my meetings with Mohammed Ibrahim in Vienna. My brief friendship with the Egyptian intelligence officer was strictly a Chanan Barel—therefore Mossad—brainchild. Barel had nothing more to testify to.

Prosecutor Hadaya surprised Tussia-Cohen by whipping out a picture of an Egyptian who, he said, was the intelligence officer I had met. Curious, I glanced over their shoulders.

In utter surprise I blurted out, "That's not the fellow!" Tussia-Cohen jabbed me in the ribs. "Be quiet!"

But the damage was done. Prosecutor Hadaya had overheard our exchange. "What do you mean? You don't know the man in the picture?" He read mine and Tussia-Cohen's faces. "This is not the Egyptian agent you met in Café Europa in Vienna?"

Perturbed, Hadaya hurriedly conferred with Aharoni and Chayim, then went to Chanan Barel. Presently he came over and said to Tussia-Cohen and Arnon, "Strike out that point in the indictment (meeting with an enemy agent in Vienna)."

"So quickly?" Tussia-Cohen jested. "Let's go through all your evidence; maybe we can spare everyone the burden of a trial."

Hadaya was rattled but determined. "Don't worry! We have evidence enough against your client."

Chanan Barel was hastily returned to Vienna for fear we would subpoena him as a defense witness.

The court came alert at the bailiff's cry. With racing heart I watched the judges take their seats on the dais. As expected presiding Judge Halevi commanded attention with his severe countenance, looking critically out over the courtroom. His glance at me was a practiced evaluation of the man in the dock. I wondered if he was nearly so piously orthodox as his *yarmulke* indicated. Immediately to his right was Judge Golan, whom I intuitively labeled the Gray Ghost for his unbroken mottle of gray skin. He didn't look as if he relished the job on hand. Judge Cohen, in stark contrast to his peers, was tall, heavy, bald, with rosy cheeks. I took him to be every bit the man my fellow inmates had described.

For a moment it seemed inconceivable that these three men who had risen from bed this morning and had had done the same routine things I'd done, were to determine my fate. Why was I obeying the rules of a game that could put me away merely at the turn of a phrase, rules that seemed stacked intransigently against me? Why didn't I leap up and cry out at the injustice of it all? In my pain, why did I not bellow out the folly, the pettiness that was turning travesty into tragedy, the degradation heaped upon my soul by puling, lying philistines?

I said nothing, stilled by the discipline my life had demanded of me. I watched it all as if I were a stranger. Was I actually "the accused"? I couldn't be sure. And then it began.

Having announced my innocence of the charges, I came alive in anticipation of Prosecutor Hadaya's opening statement. He disappointed no one, declaring that I had obtained Modiin's secret documents on dates unknown, photographed them, and stored the negatives. Announcing that he would prove that my intent was to turn them over to the enemy, Hadaya grandiloquently embarked on motive. His theme revealed my deterioration from a "loyal soldier of the State of Israel" to a man who was driven by financial stress and whose only outlet was to sell his services and knowledge. Hadaya paused. "The prosecution will also show that the accused is not the self-proclaimed idealist, as he asserts—but a liar!"

Unable to restrain myself further, I shot out of my seat. "Thank you for the compliment. It means I have the facility necessary for becoming a prosecutor!"

Sharply rebuked by Judge Halevi, warned by Tussia-Cohen, and restrained by a guard's hand on my arm, I sat. As Prosecutor Hadaya resumed, I was damned pleased to see that my interruption had considerably deflated his glibness. With the morning's victory—dismissal of the charge of meeting with enemy agents in Vienna—fresh in my mind, I heard him call his first witness.

Hadassah Nagler, my beautiful neighbor, had been brought from abroad to testify. To suggest that her testimony was prejudiced, Prosecutor Hadaya hinted that Hadassah, as he called her, and I were more than friends. She stated the facts, with one very important omission: my request that she call Gibli and tell him of my arrest. I pointed this out to Tussia-Cohen, and when it came to cross-examination, Hadassah told him, "Avri said to inform Colonel Gibli that he was 'in the Little One's hands' and that Colonel Gibli should act."

"What was Colonel Gibli's reaction?"

"He made me identify myself, then he wanted to know all the details."

Hadassah's revelation was a bombshell to the prosecution. This was the first (and only) verified link between me and Gibli. His involvement showed the futility of the prosecution's attempt to isolate the Egyptian sabotage–Lavon issue from the charges against me.

Prosecutor Hadaya hastily conferred with Aharoni and Chayim (who remained in court throughout, despite the fact that they were scheduled to testify later). On reexamining his witness, Prosecutor Hadaya dropped his informal, first-name approach.

"Tell me, Miss Nagler," he said, obviously annoyed, " why haven't you told me this before?"

Hadassah was as innocent as her reaction. "Because you told me to answer only what you asked. This I did!" The court smiled; the witness was excused.

The next witness was Capt. Eli Prager, my "guardian." Prosecutor Hadaya used Eli's testimony to establish the fact that I had maneuvered to remove the incriminating evidence from my Haifa flat by having Hadassah alert Peter Landesman. But Tussia-Cohen made a better point with the same testimony: that I'd had more than sufficient opportunity on the first visit to my flat with Eli to destroy any incriminating evidence. Eli also admitted that I'd had opportunities to destroy the negatives on the visits to Peter Landesman's. "Does a guilty man not destroy the very evidence that condemns him?" Tussia-Cohen asked the court.

The prosecution followed with a host of police and technical people, who attested the meticulousness with which the search, seizure, and impounding of evidence had been conducted. But Tussia-Cohen pounced on some of the obvious untruths and made it clear that various statutes had been badly compromised, or disregarded, in that very process. Captain Kammer of the Haifa police conceded that he and his partner had acted solely under the guidance of Aharoni and Chayim. This strengthened our contention that the police followed Shin-Beth dictates.

After Etka Jiftach repeated what she had said in the preliminary hearing, two secretaries from Modiin headquarters corroborated her testimony. They, like Etka, were certain that Modiin's safe had never been open to me; neither had they any idea how I'd gotten hold of negatives from the Violet File, when it had never been photographed in the first place.

Next, two of my former Modiin unit commanders came to the stand: Lt.

Col. Jossi Harel and Lt. Col. Joske Yariv. In general, Jossi confirmed the details of my European activities as put forward in my defense. Yariv, in full dress uniform, described his trip to Vienna and the long talks we had had about my financial plight. Supporting prosecution's contention that I'd reached financial destitution, Yariv quoted Shula: "Avri knows too much that is worth money," implying that if the unit didn't aid me financially, I had the means to help myself by selling out to the enemy.

Two things were wrong about Yariv's testimony. He refused to admit his inebriation the night Shula made the alleged threat; and he answered only "I don't know" and "It could be" to Tussia-Cohen's attempt to demonstrate his misquoting her. Shula had alluded to a remark by Lt. Col. Uzi Narkiss, who had said that I was something of a liability if the Egyptians decided to capture me and make me talk. His statement had been: "Avri knows too much, and therefore he constitutes a risk."

Early in the trial, a problem arose out of the transcribing of Judge Halevi's handwritten record of the daily proceedings. Prosecutor Hadaya had volunteered the facilities of his office for the typing of the formal transcript. Despite our protests (the prosecutor's office and the Shin-Beth used a common personnel pool), this method was adopted by the court.

How in God's name, I asked, could this be fair and impartial? The bias of a judge's subjective interpretations were bad enough, but *Aharoni and Chayim were to physically handle Judge Halevi's notes*. And *notes* they were, notes of his *impressions* of all that was said and done.

Immediately we found discrepancies between Tussia-Cohen's notations of statements and impressions and those of Judge Halevi in the typed transcript. Such discrepancies were to be ironed out prior to the day's proceedings, but as Tussia-Cohen's protests swelled, Judge Halevi's impatience grew. "Don't you trust the understanding of the court?" he asked. Before we decided to fall back, for fear of antagonizing the judges irreparably, there were heated debates over the value of a single word. I could only reflect that Aharoni's partner, Chayim, not only had daily access to the original record but was responsible for making the copies. Who was to know that forgery experts in Department 8 weren't altering Judge Halevi's original record, the one that he referred to in each morning's instance of contestation? Moreover, prosecution's having access to the original record permitted it to change its strategy according to Judge Halevi's written impressions. In my eyes this whole arrangement precluded a fair and impartial trial. But these were the rules under the laws of Israel.

The pace of my trial was established. On the days when court was in session, they jailed me in Jerusalem at the police prison; otherwise I was kept in Ramla.

One result of the many delays was the breather it gave us for assessing our progress. So far, it seemed to us that—even though confronting a determined prosecution supported by perjuries—we were more than holding our own.

We decided not to subpoena Gibli as a witness. (He had proved much tougher than Motke.) A year before, Tussia-Cohen had talked to him, trying to confirm the existence of the Egyptian-Lavon affair, Gibli had said that it was a tale I'd concocted, and he had not budged from his position (nor has he since). We let him slide by, for we were fearful that his portrayal in court of an innocent and lauded battlefield commander in the 1956 Sinai Campaign, beset by a desperate character like myself, would offset the gains we'd made.

And prosecution avoided his testimony for fear of opening up a fatal can of worms. It was clear that they were adhering to Isser Harel's position that, as he had threatened Tussia-Cohen, if we tried to connect the Lavon affair with my case, he would see me "in jail for a long, long time." Behind that resolve was Gibli's strongest motivation—self-preservation. Conveniently, during my interrogation Ben-Gurion had suddenly appointed him military attaché to England and the Scandinavian countries, leaving Isser free to maneuver the State's evidence as he saw fit. *Having no opportunity to open Gibli up without the cooperation of the prosecution, we watched the central figure in Israel's most dangerous internecine scandal go unaccosted in court.* Such is the nature of trials.

In the fourth month a written affidavit was accepted for the record: K[1], a Mossad operative, acting in the guise of a NATO organizer, had tried to recruit Bob Jansen to make contact with the Egyptians and learned that he had already been involved with them on the continent: "One of your best men is a close friend of mine: Paul Frank. I worked for him." Thinking all along that I was working for Germany's BND, or NATO, or both. Bob revealed to K his attempt to contact Osman Nouri on my behalf.

It seemed clear to me that the Mossad had already learned this and was making an investigation, because I knew that Bob had already worked for the Mossad under NATO cover.

Whatever K's motive, his affidavit had the effect of pinning me to an unauthorized contact with the enemy and set the stage for proving that I conspired to sell top secret information to them because of financial destitution.

The trend soon became all too clear: I was being presented as an unreliable, weak character whose greed knew few, if any, bounds. Only I knew the extent to which the Shin-Beth had twisted the facts, and I was convinced that there was no way I could win my freedom.

---

1. Name omitted for security reasons.

Outright lying occurred in the testimony of Chayim Victor Cohen, Aharoni's interrogation partner. There was a debate as to whether my replies in interrogation could be entered as evidence, Chayim claiming that all the notes he had brought to court were taken after I'd been duly warned. Tussia-Cohen made mincemeat of him. Half the notes were cleanly spaced, with my initials at the bottom and the warning typed boldly at the top; the other half were notes that Chayim had told me were only to be used as memoranda. A nearly illegible warning had been penned in above the text. His lie was obvious.

Chayim also tried to submit, as a confession, an utterance of mine spoken in a moment of despair. When he had gloatingly informed me that my blue suitcase was in his hands, I had muttered, "In this constellation, everything is lost!" Actually I had been expressing a sudden feeling of futility in trying to defend myself without the documents.

All in all we were pleased with the strong defense we seemed to have formulated.

Zvi Aharoni swore an oath I knew he did not consider binding in the least. He was a professional witness, a professional liar. He told of the Woellersdorf trick and a few other small coups I had pulled on him, Judge Halevi came to my rescue: "By doing this, has the accused violated any law? If this were the case, I assume you would have charged him accordingly. The struggle between you and him seems to me to have been a legitimate war of brains and he got the upper hand."

Aharoni looked crestfallen, but Prosecutor Hadaya leaped to his defense, declaring, "The prosecution will show that cunning is an understatement in describing the accused."

After two days, Aharoni was given to Tussia-Cohen, who demanded to see the records of the first day's interrogation; he sought to show that Aharoni's abrupt epithet of "traitor" had fixed my attitude toward my interrogators.

Aharoni claimed that he'd only used the term at the end of the first interrogation, after I had already denied the charges. "Anyway," he said, "There's no record of that day."

Questioned further, however, he admitted that this part of my interrogation had been recorded.

When the court demanded that he produce the tapes, Aharoni hedged, saying it might take a day or two. I expressed my fear that the tapes would be altered, but Tussia-Cohen, in his indefatigable patience, said, "There's nothing we, or the court, can do about it. We'll just have to wait and see what they submit."

Two weeks later the tapes and a transcript were entered as evidence. Not unexpectedly, Aharoni's version was proved by the transcript. But, in altering the tapes, Aharoni had forgotten one thing: Jossi Harel, who had left to attend to a traffic ticket after the traitorous label, had already contradicted Aharoni in his testimony. On the tapes Aharoni had Jossi leaving at the end of that session, when he had actually left at the beginning. Realizing that the Shin-Beth would illegally doctor the tapes to prove a relatively minor point, I knew that there were no limits to the determination to see me buried in prison.

Aharoni reluctantly testified to the Seder night confessions with the cognac and tape recorder. Only now did he understand the true significance of my opening statement: "I prefer being considered a liar than a traitor." Countering, Aharoni pressed the point that in many ways I was actually anti-Jewish. To substantiate this, a surprise witness appeared.

Aviva Sten, a free-lance journalist, saw me in the hallway prior to her testimony. She cried, saying, "They made me testify." I said nothing; I had the ammunition to destroy her. I had ceased being the gentleman.

In court Prosecutor Hadaya pressed her to recapitulate an article she had written about me months ago, after my arrest. In it, Aviva had portrayed me as insensitive to the Jews by relating a story about ultraorthodox Jewry that I had told one evening in Vienna when Aviva had gotten quite drunk. Tussia-Cohen's colleague, Jigal Arnon, questioned her:

ARNON: "Tell me, was Avri's home in Vienna well known as the house of an Israeli?"

AVIVA: "Very much so."

ARNON: "Does he have children?"

AVIVA: "A very beautiful son."

ARNON: "Do you know his name, and whether he speaks Hebrew?"

AVIVA: "The son is named Harel, and he speaks Hebrew fluently."

ARNON: "Do you know what school the boy attends?"

AVIVA: "Oh, yes. He goes to a Hebrew school."

ARNON: "Are there many such schools in Vienna?"

AVIVA: "No, there's only one Hebrew school in Vienna."

ARNON: "Can you tell us how far is the school from Avri's home, and how long it took for his little boy to get there?"

AVIVA: "The school is maybe twenty miles from Avri's home. I'd say it probably takes an hour to get there."

ARNON: "Why would Avri enroll his son in the Hebrew school? Could he not enroll him in a German-speaking school? Does the boy speak German?"

AVIVA: "I don't know why Avri sent the boy to the school. Because he's an Israeli and wants the boy in a Hebrew school, I imagine. The boy could go to a German-speaking school; he speaks fluent German."

294

Arnon was coiled for the strike. Hadaya realized it and lost his objection on relevancy. Only Aviva failed to see what was coming. I felt sad as the point of her article unraveled before her eyes.

ARNON: "Now tell me . . . do you have a daughter? And how old is she?"
AVIVA: "My daughter is about the same age as Avri's son."
ARNON: "What school do you send her to in Vienna?"

Suddenly Aviva burst into tears. Judge Halevi prompted her sternly to answer.

AVIVA: "She goes to a local school."
ARNON: "Is it not true that this school is a *Catholic* school?"

Our point was brutally made; by all outward signs, *she* was anti-Jewish, not I. Judge Halevi angrily dismissed the witness and reprimanded the prosecution for wasting the court's time.

Tussia-Cohen's main point of contention with Aharoni had been over the handling of the evidence (Violet File negatives) after it was confiscated from Peter Landesman. Aharoni had taken the top-secret, incriminating negatives to his sister's house and hid them under the bed for the night. The chilling fact was that Aharoni's sister lived only a few doors from Isser Harel.

"I reported to the Mossad chief that same night but did not show him the evidence," Aharoni said.

Was the court capable of understanding that I had never seen the negatives of the top secret Violet File? By now I had accepted the fact that someone had planted those negatives *after* the suitcase had left my possession.

The Shin-Beth had not been able to prove that I had dealt with the enemy; so someone had decided to make sure that I was punished for it anyway. It was a frightening realization, and there was no escaping it. I was being framed.

Chapter 25

Delays dragged my trial into the winter months. Tussia-Cohen and Arnon would soon have been on my defense all of 1959, reimbursed only by the five thousand pounds I'd paid them near the outset. (The funds were part of the lease deposit returned to me when I surrendered my flat.)

Shula had no money; she was barely eking out her existence as domestics supervisor in Hugo Krug's small hotel in Hamburg. Neither had my sister; she and Zvi had all they could do to manage the support of their five children. Hugo Krug appeared to be the only one to whom I could turn.

Unfortunately, Hugo was suspect. In the spring Joske Jariv had hinted that Hugo's personal prosperity had been achieved at Unit 131's expense. Later, Joske had fired my old anger by seeking my help in determining how Hugo could offer to buy the firm from the unit. So now I elected to ride out the financial pinch, since neither attorney was pressing me.

Peter Landesman was well rehearsed. Under Prosecutor Hadaya's guidance, he repeated his version of the Shin-Beth's recovery of the Violet File negatives that I had allegedly entrusted to him.

Two lies supported Peter's story: his denial of any knowledge of my two letters to Shula and Shlomo Millet and of having made a deal with Aharoni and the Shin-Beth in the pending felony case against him for smuggling foreign currency out of the country. In pleading ignorance of my two letters, Peter lied *to* Aharoni, and he lied *with* Aharoni. His logic was simple.

On taking possession of my suitcase, Peter had been ignorant both of my arrest and of the significance of its contents. Only on reading Shula's letter did he understand anything at all. Still considerably in the dark, he recruited a seaman friend of his to post the letter in Europe, which incriminated his friend. Posting letters abroad to circumvent censorship was a very serious offense. Thus Peter was now forced to lie *to* Aharoni for fear of involving his friend, as well as of complicating the smuggling case. On reading my letter to Shlomo, Peter realized what the situation was. He decided to hand over Shlomo's letter and tell them about my suitcase—his opportunity to rid himself of the smuggling charge.

In testimony Peter lied *with* Aharoni by denying any knowledge of the letter to Shlomo. (But Shlomo's later testimony would tie him directly to it.) Peter's denying knowledge of the letter served to squelch accusations that he might be lying in return for Aharoni's killing the smuggling charge. Since Peter had not read the letters, how could he have made a deal?

More importantly, though, Peter's cooperation with Aharoni was an absolute necessity. If the Violet File negatives had been planted in my suitcase *after* it left Peter's hands, then he must not be able to identify in court *exactly* what negatives the suitcase had held. He would have to plead ignorance.

As expected Peter's statement was that, on opening my suitcase, he had realized the implications of the contents. He had panicked. At his father's farm he had burned everything that would burn. However, the negatives were on nonflammable film. (In our examination at my hearing, none of the negatives Peter had exposed to flame bore any sign of scorching or crumbling.) Peter had then stored the negatives on the farm.

Two things were wrong with Peter's story. Being a former police sergeant, he would have neither panicked nor given the negatives only a cursory glance; he would have inspected them with a fine-tooth comb. He further stated that he recalled only the negatives that had "Warhead" written on them. These were the rocket blueprint negatives, of no importance in the trial. He could not testify as to whether Violet File negatives were there. Like me, Peter Landesman had cooperated in a conspiracy because he had been fed a bit of truth with a pound of lies.

Flinching at Tussia-Cohen's drilling, Peter's contradictions became so blatant that Judge Halevi warned him of the consequences of perjury. I soon realized that Peter Landesman had been coerced. Later he was to take heavily to the bottle; a serious illness followed his divorce. As the years passed, friends told me that Peter lived in terror of me. A few months after my release from prison, Peter was found burned to death in his bed. After an evening of heavy drinking, he had dropped off to sleep with a lighted cigarette.

Prosecution witness Col. Ariel Amiad, chairman of the Zahal board of inquiry whose findings stated that I had told the truth about the Egyptian-Lavon affair, gave his testimony in two appearances before and following Motke's testimony. After he stepped down the first time, Tussia-Cohen and he agreed that if Motke denied on the stand what he had confessed in private, Colonel Amiad would then tell the court all he knew.

As if fate had willed it, I was in the corridor when Lt. Col. Mordechai "Motke" Ben Zur arrived. Though he had testified in front of me at Zahal's inquiry, we had not passed a private word since my arrest almost two years ago. (Over eight years would pass before our next encounter, when he would say, "Don't trust anybody! All of them are whores!" He meant that everybody in Zahal was interested only in his own future.) Now, in the corridor, we met again. "I covered you with my hat, Avri," Motke now said with great bitterness in his voice, "and I see now where it got me."

Besides wanting to give me the impression that he believed I was guilty, Motke was mortified by what he felt was my deceit in spilling out the truth of the conspiracy. I realized the futility of trying to make him understand that I had been tricked by Isser Harel and Aharoni.

"Motke, I'm not guilty of these things I'm charged with; so your faith in me is as valid now as it ever was. The charges against me are trumped up. Believe me."

He moved on.

Prosecutor Hadaya led Motke gently through my two years of Modiin duty under his command, but none of these questions touched on the sabotage operation or the Lavon frame-up. Prosecution still sought to separate that period from my subsequent activities in Europe, thus avoiding our contention that revenge might be a reason for the case against me.

Motke's first lie under cross-examination was stupid, for it only served to denigrate my role in our War of Independence. When asked what my function had been, he answered, "I think he was a driver for headquarters or the transportation unit." Tussia-Cohen asked if I hadn't actually been in command of heaquarters company and acting logistics officer for the brigade, but Motke answered with an emphatic "No!"

Tussia-Cohen stared Motke dead in the eye. "And what would you say if the commander of the brigade at the time, Gen. Yitzhak Rabin, stated that Avri fulfilled those functions? Would you *still* say it was not so?"

No response from the witness box, but we could see wheels churning frantically in Motke's head. But we weren't bluffing. He admitted his error. Motke's purposeless lie was the first of many. *He stuck doggedly to the conspiratorial version of the sabotage, denying that he'd given me operational orders in Paris, that Mordechai Almog had delivered his letter to me in Paris, that he had met me at the airport or Gibli's house prior to my interrogation by Lavon* (these lies would be exposed by direct testimony). *He also denied all knowledge of a fake diary or Pierre Report and of any conspiracy leveled at Lavon.*

But one lie hung Motke in the court's eyes: He denied ever having warned me not to come home when I wrote him that I was returning to make a clean breast of the conspiracy. Tussia-Cohen had Motke in his web. "And what would you say, Colonel Ben Zur," he said, "if I told you that we are in possession of a letter you wrote to Avri in which you told him indirectly not to come to Israel, by using the story that the president of the Spanish Olympic team received an invitation from the Russians, an invitation that the president refused on the basis that the plane ticket was a one-way passage?"

Motke hesitated, then said, "I don't recall clearly if I wrote such a letter." Tussia-Cohen made a production of rifling through his briefcase for the letter while Motke eyed him furtively, shifting his lumbrous body from side to side. Suddenly he blurted his recall of writing a letter "something like that."

Smiling, his hand empty, Tussia-Cohen turned to Motke. "Can you explain to the court *why* you wrote it?"

Judge Halevi interrupted, demanding to know the significance of the letter, and then asked Motke if the letter contained what my defense asserted, and, if so, what purpose it was meant to serve.

Fidgeting like a worm in hot ashes, Motke said, "I probably had a reason at the time . . . but I forget what it was."

Judge Halevi, annoyed, concluded: "The parable has only one meaning: *Don't come home!"*

Though I was angry and disappointed in Motke, I nevertheless felt sympathy for him. The picture of his desperation was compounded by the fact that he was totally unaware that the fly on his trousers was open for the court to see.

One charge against me, the photographing of the Violet File, had been driving me crazy. All Modiin personnel who had testified had stated that the documents had never been photographed. I'd never seen the documents or the negatives; so, who had photographed them? Suddenly when Motke took the stand I remembered something from a long time ago: *Major E. Alroy!*

The Violet File had in fact been photographed by the former Modiin staffer. With Motke nearing the conclusion of his testimony, Tussia-Cohen showed him several enlarged photostats of documents from the file and asked:

TUSSIA-COHEN: "Do you happen to know whether this file of documents was ever photographed during your tenure as head of Unit 131?"

MOTKE: "Not during my time, that I'm sure."

TUSSIA-COHEN: "You said 'not during my time' with great conviction. Does that imply that, at *other* times, the documents might have been photographed?"

MOTKE: "I don't know about *other* times. I know only of *one* time when my predecessor tried to establish a microfilm library, and he photographed most of the unit's documents. The Violet File was among those photographed."

TUSSIA-COHEN: "Do you know what happened to those negatives?"

MOTKE: "Upon taking command of the unit, I discontinued Major Alroy's undertaking; whatever material I found, I stored away in the unit's safe."

TUSSIA-COHEN: "When you say 'whatever materials,' do you mean the negatives of the Violet File?"

MOTKE: "That, among other negatives."

With no prompting, Prosecutor Hadaya announced that the State was dropping a second charge against me: the photographing of Modiin's top secret Violet File.

Motke had been caught in a veritable cross fire, and then Colonel Amiad followed on his heels and contradicted Motke's entire testimony. Colonel Amiad revealed that Motke had confessed to him during the army inquiry that the conspiracy against Lavon had in fact existed, but that he would deny it if it ever came before any forum. Motke had carried out his threat in denying it to the court, and in one fell swoop, Motke was demolished as a witness.

Maj. Shlomo Millet followed. If he would speak out, he could damn Motke after the burial. To have a quick word with him prior to his testimony, I lingered in the corridor during the short recess. My old friend did not disappoint me. His response to my cynical remark about loyalty was: "I'm going to prove to you there is really such a thing as friendship, and that everybody is not out to protect his own hide. I'm telling the truth, Avri, and nothing else."

Only minutes into his testimony, it became obvious that Shlomo, though prosecution's witness, was not helping its case. His testimony was so damaging, in fact, that Prosecutor Hadaya asked the court to declare him a hostile witness. Shlomo retorted angrily: "If my answers, which are the truth as I know it, don't fit into your scheme, that's your problem! It's true, Avri is a friend of mine; it's also true that I don't believe he's guilty of the charges. But I wouldn't lie for him. I believe that justice is best served by telling the truth . . . and God knows we have little enough of that!"

The court reprimanded him, but it refused prosecution's request. In the cross-examination, Shlomo further substantiated the existence of the Lavon conspiracy by revealing that the Modiin operational file on the sabotage in Egypt had undergone remarkable changes.

"I started the file while I was Avri's supervising case officer," Shlomo said; then he went on to explain that Motke had assumed personal control. "Now I see that the file's binding has been changed, the index of its contents is missing, and certain communication copies have been removed."

This revelation pointed the finger of criminal perjury directly at Motke: He had removed or modified relevant materials in the file to make it coincide with the conspiratorial version of the events in Egypt.

"For example," Shlomo said, "I personally hand-carried to the radio station the taped order to commence the second sabotage action in Egypt. It is no longer in the file."

Shlomo also put to rest the mystery of my letter to him, the one Peter Landesman had denied all knowledge of. Shlomo had been summoned to Field Security Headquarters, where Colonel Hafez showed him my letter and demanded to know if other notes had passed between us. Shlomo exploded and, in turn, demanded an explanation for the interception of his mail. Colonel Hafez would say only that " . . . this is a security matter and we have every right."

Two final points made by Shlomo disproved, we thought, my intent to harm State security. He verified that I had left my attaché case (containing all the materials) with him for the entire year that I was in Vienna at my father's bedside. ("Would he have entrusted *stolen* intelligence materials with me? Why hadn't he taken the material to Europe, where he could have passed it to the enemy?") Shlomo also revealed that I had told him of the rocket blueprint negatives the day after they had been mistakenly given to me at Modiin's archives. ("If the rocket blueprints had been so carelessly passed around, why wasn't it possible that the Violet File negatives were part of the batch of film?") He further stated that I had utilized the rocket blueprints in the secret report on my past experiences in the field. ("If he had stolen the Violet File negatives, would he have connected himself to *any* secret Modiin material?")

A revealing development stemmed from testimony surrounding the report I'd written when I left the firm in early 1956, almost four years before. When Judge Halevi asked to be told the importance of "this report everybody is talking about," Tussia-Cohen leaped at the opportunity, for it supported many of his claims. The judge ordered prosecution to produce the special report.

At the following session Prosecutor Hadaya handed the court a signed order from Prime and Defense Minister Ben-Gurion, which sheltered my report from the court. Judge Halevi exploded, "The prosecutor and his staff know what the report is all about, the accused *certainly* knows—he wrote it!—and it stands to reason that the defense attorney and his aide also know. But only *we*, the judges, who decide the accused's guilt or innocence, are not allowed to see if the report is relevant to the case! I am going to summon the defense minister to the witness stand and let him explain why this report is to be held secret from the court."

Prosecutor Hadaya went white in the face of Judge Halevi's fury. During an hour's recess, I imagined that the telephone wires to Ben-Gurion's office were red-hot. Then the prosecutor offered an acceptable compromise to the court: Only certain agreed-upon parts of the report would go into the record. Still, it helped.

Prosecution's list of witnesses neared an end. Since the State's case had been badly damaged, the prosecutor had to employ his heaviest piece of artillery in a final attempt to shift the court's opinion in his favor. He called Isser Harel to the stand.

At the creation of the State in May 1948, Isser Harel was appointed head of the Shin-Beth (Department of Internal Security) and soon began to seek broader responsibilities. In 1953, shortly after I became a fledgling Modiin operative, Ben-Gurion appointed Isser to the coveted post of director of the Mossad. Recognizing a man of his own mold, Ben-Gurion also created a new title for his protégé: chief executive of the Secret Services. Isser thus became the "Memune," the all-powerful head of a state within a state, answering *only* to the prime minister. Having brought Modiin's intelligence-gathering role abroad under the Mossad's umbrella, Isser Harel took the stand at my trial with no equal except Ben-Gurion. (It would be Isser's power climb into the area of policy that would bring about his political demise by the very man who had elevated him.)

I'd set eyes only once on the man whose thirst for supremacy had made difficult my life in Modiin, and whose later branding me a security case had made it impossible.

A few minutes before court reconvened, I was returning from the rest room with my guardians, when I saw in the corridor the man known variously as "little Isser" or "the little one."

As diminutive as Napoleon, Isser clutched a small, mirrored, powder compact, into which he stared at his gargoyle features. I passed by into the courtroom; impressed by his molelike ugliness, I realized that the balding, gray-suited, stocky figure was nothing like the Machiavellian monster I'd conjured up.

Isser Harel was greeted deferentially by prosecution and almost reverently by the judges. Isser seemed to revel in the weight his testimony would carry and, from prosecution's first question, he threw the full authority of his lofty position into the arena. He rejected vigorously the idea that the State's case was a vendetta; I had become a security case only after his men had discovered my contact with Osman Nouri. He claimed that I'd blown my cover and, endangering his operatives, I was ordered home. He was convinced that I was "crazy for intelligence work"—in other words, "an intelligence maniac."

Isser was permitted to exaggerate so obviously and to lie so freely that I became concerned about the court's impartiality. He denied knowing I had operated in Egypt, that I had testified to the Olshan-Dori court of inquiry, and that I had commanded the sabotage. He also rejected the insinuation that I was being framed as "infamy."

From the outset, the cross-examination was a battle of giants. Mutual animosity reached a crescendo as Tussia-Cohen asked Isser for his theory as to how the Violet File negatives came to be in my possession when several prosecution witnesses had stated they had not been handed to me by mistake, nor had I had access to the safe in which they were stored. The implication of a framing slapped Isser in the face.

Isser exploded, his pugnacious, beady eyes wide, his jaws clenched. "How dare you suggest such a thing! I find it disgraceful that a lawyer of your standing would callously insinuate that our secret service, a true servant of the State, would do such infamy! I find it below my dignity to reply to such a question!"

Tussia-Cohen was having none of Isser's holier-than-thouism. "Maybe outside this courtroom, I have to answer to you; but here on this floor, you answer me!"

Judge Halevi corrected Isser. Fuming, Isser categorically denied any possibility of a frame-up, but he had no explanation for finding the negatives among my things. Shortly, Tussia-Cohen brought up Isser's threat to us, if we utilized the connection between the Egyptian-Lavon episode and my arrest.

"The security services," Isser declared, "have never put anybody on trial if we were not convinced of his guilt." Then he added smugly, "And up to now everyone we have put on trial has been found guilty. And convicted." Prosecution rested its case.

It was now our turn. Originally we had planned to call several character witnesses, but because things were going so well we limited these to five, including me.

Two of prosecution's charges had already been thrown out: meeting with enemy agents in Vienna and unlawfully photographing the Violet File. We were reasonably sure that we had disposed of the other charges as well. Only one, "possession of top secret documents," perplexed us. How to prove that I had never seen the top secret Violet File negatives? That the negatives had never been in my possession? That some person or persons had planted them on me?

But first we wanted to show that, beyond all doubt, Motke had lied about the past and to push my claim that this past was directly connected to this case. We brought in the one-armed security man to prove that Motke had met me that night at the airport. Then we put Col. Mordechai Almog on the stand to refute Motke's denial of having ever sent a letter to me in Paris (via Almog), to plead for my cooperation in the plan to frame Lavon.

Hoping to demonstrate a further vengeance-is-mine attitude on the part of Isser Harel and Aharoni, we summoned my sister and her husband. Strangely there was an unexpected air of hostility between Zvi Swet and Judge Halevi. Unable to stand on his wooden legs throughout the questioning, Zvi's request for a chair was met at first with Judge Halevi's "You will stand like all the other witnesses!"—ignoring the fact that he had offered Isser Harel the opportunity to sit. Only at Tussia-Cohen's plea did he grudgingly consent.

Zvi solidified several of our contentions. He verified our complaints that the Shin-Beth and Isser Harel had attempted to elicit his and Ruth's cooperation through deception and threats. He then explained his and Ruth's part in the deception that led to my exposing the conspiracy. "At first," he said, "we were told and convinced Avri was covering for higher-ups. We were convinced that justice would best be served if all the truth came out."

Ruth brought out one other circumstantial bit of evidence that the conspiracy did in fact exist and that Motke was tied to it. After the Shin-Beth had searched my flat, Motke came asking for the key, saying that he wanted to make sure I had no important Modiin papers hidden away. It was transparent; Motke was searching for anything relative to the Lavon conspiracy.

I was the last witness, and eagerly I seized the opportunity. It had been two long, painful, humiliating years since I had returned to Israel from my father's graveside and met my arrest as a treason suspect. For two days my defense led me in intricate detail from my Modiin recruitment in late 1952 to my arrest and interrogation in late 1957. For three days I caustically countered prosecution's attempt to shake the foundations of truth. From the first, Prosecutor Hadaya and I clashed sharply. I felt exhilaration now, because I could finally defend myself directly. I was not in the least disturbed by Judge Halevi's repeated warnings to curb my contempt for the arena in which I had stood muted for six months. Then it was finished. Nothing remained but the final pleadings.

Prosecutor Hadaya's opening statement stunned me. "A hero of the State is sitting on the bench of the accused. . . ."

"What in hell is going on?" I whispered to Tussia-Cohen. "Has he had a change of heart?"

My attorney gave me one of his rare smiles. "The higher he praises you, the deeper he wants to bury you."

In his closing Prosecutor Hadaya gave me one more generous accolade before he began the condemnation. "Yes, in many eyes, Avri Seidenwerg is considered a hero," he said grandiloquently, "even though a dark cloud hovers over his head. . . ." Then he depicted me as a man motivated by two insidious forces eating inside me: I was incapable of accepting the decisions of my betters (the Mossad), and when asked to abandon my work in Europe (the firm), I became embittered; I had been unable to adjust to a lower standard of living after my Modiin-financed years in Europe, and my financial condition drove me to desperation. After obtaining the top-secret Modiin documents by (unknown) contrivance, I took the opportunity of my father's illness to sell out to the enemy.

The State's case was purely circumstantial, except for the Violet File negatives. They had been found in my possession. My attempt to involve a fictitious conspiracy was merely a way of confusing the issues.

Great stress was placed on Isser Harel's appearance. "And if the court has any doubts," Prosecutor Hadaya declared, "the testimony of the man heading all of Israel's security—the top expert in the field—should dispel any doubts whatsoever as to the guilt of the accused." Prosecution asked the court to find me guilty and punish me according to the Laws of Israel.

Tussia-Cohen, in his final statement in my defense, set the record straight insofar as the most dangerous indictment was concerned. The prosecution had not and could not prove that I had obtained the Violet File negatives in an unlawful manner; the *only* alternative worth taking into consideration was that the negatives had been planted on me.

Tussia-Cohen concluded his pleading. "This man has been willing to sacrifice his life for the security of the State, the State which has been a giant part of his life since his coming to this land. This man finds himself accused of having acted against what has been closest to his heart. One of the witnesses of the prosecution has stated that in this particular area of intelligence work, only extremists are to be found. This witness also said that the accused was the most extreme he has ever encountered. Therefore, believing in justice, the accused expects the court to give him back his freedom, and his pride, for he has done nothing that would warrant his conviction."

Suddenly it was over; 1960 had rolled up on the calendar.

I shared with my attorneys the confidence that the State's case had dissolved before Prosecutor Hadaya's eyes. The only charge remotely intact, in our opinions, was my alleged possession of the Violet File negatives. But to convict me was to discredit me. To discredit me was to keep covered Lavon's framing. To vindicate me was to open the scandalous wound. Was Israel prepared for it?

Were any of my judges open to the possibility that the guardian of the land, the Shin-Beth, or any of Israel's intelligence services, would resort to a framing to prove their accusations? No, not in Israel, not in these times.

Tussia-Cohen's prediction for my future was based on solid supposition. He felt that at worst I would be found guilty of the single charge and sentenced to the length of my stay in prison; and at best I would be exonerated. From his words I drew the courage to return to Ramla to await the verdict that would come in a month or two.

At first Tussia-Cohen teased my mother-in-law, telling her that she should prepare a place for me for a well-deserved rest. However, with no explanation, the month or two stretched into an agonizing six. In the midst of summer's heat, I was unable to cope with the tension any longer and, at Tussia-Cohen's prompting, I wrote a plea to Judge Halevi, stating that I'd already served a thirty-one-month incarceration, eighteen in solitary confinement, and that I felt that a swift conclusion to my tormenting vigil was justified.

I was escorted to Jerusalem in August for the reading of the verdict. I was angered by the timing; Tussia-Cohen was in Europe on a business trip. Arnon and I met, flanked by my two guardians, in the cold, early-morning silence of the stone court building. My sister and a friend recently released from Ramla were the only others there to give me comfort. My stomach churned.

Behind closed doors with Arnon and the prosecution, I watched my three blank-faced judges take their seats. Judge Halevi commenced to read the eighty-page verdict. Slowly the bitter taste of defeat began to disappear. I felt myself growing light in disbelief at the positive flavor of his words when, thirty minutes into the reading, Judge Halevi abruptly called a recess. In the corridor Ruth came over to me.

"How does it go?" she asked anxiously.

I smiled; I couldn't help it. "Until now, very good. Things are looking up."

Frustration and anger contorted Ruth's face.

"They are going to throw the book at you!"

My heart went out to her; she hadn't heard what had been presented to us by Judge Halevi. She was torn between her allegiance to her brother and her patriotism. If I was guilty, where did that leave her trust in the integrity of her own flesh and blood? If I was being railroaded, where did that leave her faith in the dream of Israel?

"They are going to throw the book at you!" she repeated.

I listened to her description of what had transpired only minutes earlier. Ruth and my friend had been seated near the hall telephone, unseen by Chayim, my old interrogator, as he rushed from Judge Halevi's chamber and called the prosecutor's office. To someone there he said, "Everything is all right. They are announcing him guilty."

In numbed acceptance I returned to hear Judge Halevi's anticlimactic pronouncement of my guilt, protected from shock by my belief in Tussia-Cohen's educated guess that my sentence might be only the length of my stay in prison.

Later, at Ramla, I would study the document containing the court's findings. The panel had agreed unanimously, despite the barrage of lies, evasions, distortions, and omissions fed to them. That Peter Landesman had been upended time and again in conflicting testimony, that Motke had been proved a wholesale liar, apparently did not faze them; Motke was not even recommended for a charge of perjury!

The document made clear distinctions. Regarding the security mishap in Egypt and the subsequent Lavon conspiracy, I had spoken the truth. Yet in my fight against the charges, I had cleverly lied, trying to force higher-ups (Gibli) to come to my aid. Judge Halevi did state that the allegations I'd made against Motke and Gibli *should* be brought to the minister of defense's attention. This, I thought bitterly, was a futile gesture; Ben-Gurion wasn't about to open up a political scandal that was partly of his own making.

Riding back to Ramla in the prison vehicle, we passed along the road where we had fought our 1948 duel with the Arabs. I thought back on all the misgivings I'd had about the impartiality of my trial. Now those concerns had been forged into facts. Had political corruption also penetrated our courts? If our courts hadn't integrity, what had we? I couldn't remember who said it, but it came to me unbidden: "Corruption of justice is the first step in the ruin of a state." Yet, low in spirits as I was, I told myself that the verdict was not the end of the road.

In Ramla I awaited my sentencing through two postponements. I ascribed the delay to circumstances edging toward eruption: The Lavon affair, as the whole imbroglio of Egyptian sabotage and Lavon conspiracy would come to be known, stood at the precipice of becoming a public issue.

I also learned something else: Judge Benjamin Halevi had met with

Isser Harel in Europe. Coincidentally. And it was known that Judge Halevi had a history of meeting with key witnesses of the prosecution; a minor scandal of this kind had once arisen out of the military inquiry into the Kafar Kassem massacre. In that incident his offer to resign had been refused by Ben-Gurion. Knowing these things, the possible severity of my sentence frightened me.

(Months later I smuggled a letter to Israel's best-known weekly. The letter, printed in full, stated that Judge Halevi had in fact met with the Mossad chief prior to my sentencing and that the meeting with the man who was responsible for my incarceration had a decided effect on my sentencing. My letter was meant to smoke out Judge Halevi, but he disdained to comment. His silence spoke for itself.

The day of my sentencing came on November 20, 1960, three years after my arrest. An armed police detail transported me from Ramla to a secret place outside Jerusalem. I was told that the court was convening in a compound for advance intelligence schooling in an effort to avoid probe by local and foreign journalists, who were demanding more details about the secret trial of "the Third Man," as I was known to the public. Because of censorship, neither my name nor picture would appear in any Israeli publication until 1972. Only parties to the court were allowed inside the area by the Uzi-carrying policemen and their leashed dogs. My sister and her husband were grudgingly admitted only after Ruth had threatened to lead foreign journalists to the area.

Judge Halevi allowed counsel a final statement. With his usual dramatics Prosecutor Hadaya expressed first his patriotic regret in seeing me in the dock, then demanded that my sentence be extended to the fullest of the law. No mercy in his presentation.

Tussia-Cohen asked the court to take all my past deeds in service to the country into consideration. He explained why he had not called character witnesses to the stand. "The accused has already had the best character witnesses in the appearance of prosecution's witnesses. All, save three, have praised him."

On my refusal to make a final statement, court recessed for lunch. Oddly, all parties to the court ate simultaneously in the canteen: the judges at one table, prosecution at another, defense at still another. Answering my question of how long the deliberating would take, Tussia-Cohen said that he felt we still had a few hours. However, after I had been led back to a waiting room, I was quickly summoned to the court hall.

Judge Halevi ordered me to rise. "The court has found you guilty. Taking into account your lawyer's pleas for consideration of your past deeds, we hereby sentence you to twelve years' imprisonment, commencing the day of your arrest."

Tussia-Cohen's stunned "This is contempt of the justice of Israel!" was the only real thing in this bad tragi-farce.

I put my arm around his shoulder. "Don't take it to heart, Tussia. You did all you could, and more." He looked curiously at me and answered out of a defeat that was his as well, "Isn't it the lawyer's place to do the comforting?"

A loud fracas in the corridor drew our attention. Tussia-Cohen close on my heels, I ran out to see my brother-in-law raging at Judge Halevi, who, wielding his cape of authority, threatened Zvi with expulsion " . . . from this courthouse if you don't hold your tongue!"

"Courthouse!" Zvi shouted. "This is a restaurant! You have been sitting there over a plate of meat and spinach deciding to give him twelve years! Or has it been decided *for* you!"

Judge Halevi was so intimidated by Zvi's threatening demeanor that he rushed out of the building still garbed in his black robe, only to rush back in to hurriedly sign the order remanding me to prison. Not once did he raise his eyes to any of us.

They took me back to Ramla, where for a few days I was celebrated among the prison population as a man seemingly unaffected by my fate. But then the enormity of the sentence hit me. I went away into myself, deeply depressed, shunning everybody. When I came out of it, I realized that I had not lost quite everything; my feelings were crystallized in a letter I wrote to Olga in Vienna. Olga's opinions were then, as they are today, very important to me.

November 24, 1960

Dear Olga,

As you know by now, the little snowball we once spoke of has become an avalanche. My case became a State affair. Over the past year, it has been smoldering beneath the surface; and now that a twelve-year sentence has been passed on me, *all hell is breaking loose outside.* Everybody has been waiting for the conclusion of my trial. I can only watch from inside.

The first phase of a flagrant violation of justice has reached an end. We will see if it will correct itself in my appeal. However, the twelve years, thought by some to be sufficient to silence my voice and thus withhold the truth from the people, will not break my determination to prove that I was railroaded into prison. I have no intention of spending these next years behind walls to benefit Ben-Gurion and his fair-haired boys.

It is still too early to analyze the fundamental reasons for my conviction; there is always a danger in oversimplifying intricate issues.

In spite of all, my spirit is high, and I'm convinced that the whole truth will emerge—even if eventually.

Living in Hamburg where she still directed domestics in Hugo Krug's small hotel, Shula had not complained about the tediousness of her social and financial plight, and I had not complained to her. We'd held up stoic fronts to each other, and I now felt the time had come to confront the realities that governed our lives. I wrote that I no longer expected her to wait for my release:

"You have suffered enough, and I cannot, in any conscience, even hope for your loyalty as a wife. However, it isn't too late for you to build yourself a new life in a new family. You should have the happiness everyone deserves. As for Harel, he needs a father, as any boy of ten years does, and not a father who sits indefinitely behind bars. From now on, Shula, you are free. I will do everything in my power to make this step as easy as possible for you . . . ."

Shula's answer was terse: "Forget you have written this letter. I will wait for you as long as it takes. We are finally together, in good and bad."

Tears welled in my eyes for the first time in three years. What good had I given her, for God's sake?

Bolstered by my family's faith in me and my faith that Israeli justice would right itself, I had a good perspective on things as Tussia-Cohen put my appeal to the Supreme Court.

But with the reading of my verdict, the Lavon affair erupted, unleashing a storm outside.

Chapter 26

In September 1960, less than a month after my verdict was announced, Israel's greatest scandal, the Lavon affair, went *qualifiedly* public. Censorship worked overtime during the implosion of the Lavon affair. I leave to Israel the painful burden of rooting out the tentacles of its cancer and to the historians the task of putting into perspective its impact on Israel and its influence on international affairs. For now, I offer developments as I monitored them from behind Ramla's prison walls.

Sadly, the full truths behind the affair—the framing of Pinhas Lavon, its cover-up, and the *raison d'être*, the Egyptian operation—remained confined to the conspirators, to secret military inquiries, to my *in camera* trial, and to whispered military and political dialogues. Only the affair's broadest aspects emerged. Continuing her policy of denying to the world community any responsibility for the Egyptian operation, and concealing from her own public the truths of the scandal, Israel blanketed the entire matter beneath national security.

The surface eruption did break out between David Ben-Gurion, who was determined to hide the affair forever, and Pinhas Lavon, who was determined to vindicate his name, overwhelming an unsuspecting and unprepared Israeli public, a nation of idealists rocked by claims and counterclaims of frame-ups, purges, and cover-ups. To Israel, and to Jews still in the Diaspora, such pragmatic treachery belonged in a cruel Germany, a decadent Europe, a Communist Russia, not to Israel, hewed from an ancient Jewish conviction that no Jew need fear for his justice from a brother Jew. Israel *was* the land of justice.

But Israel was to learn that "All for one and one for all" was the dream, not the reality. It was a brutal, ugly confrontation; none wanted to believe it. Most didn't. More than twenty years after its onset, the scandal is still unresolved.

How did the Lavon affair emerge out of secrecy? I would have to go back to the last half of 1959, the time of my trial, to bring into sequence the hidden events that led to Pinhas Lavon's cryptic announcement to Israel's press in September 1960, that the public should prepare itself for "unpleasant disclosures that will try our strength as a nation." At this first hint that something was amiss in the Israeli ideal, the battle lines of a war between the chief adversaries, Lavon and Ben-Gurion, were being drawn.

The single reason that nothing of the scandal had become known prior to Lavon's warning was that my verdict was sub judice: Any publicity might have prejudiced the outcome of my trial.

Thus, Lavon had less than a year—from the beginning of 1960, the end of my trial, to September, just after my verdict—to prepare his case. While he waited to launch his attack against Ben-Gurion, I awaited my fate.

The inexorable path toward exposure of the affair began with the opening of my trial, and it was the machinations of Isser Harel, the Gray Eminence himself, that led to the exposure. As the *Memune,* chief executive of the Secret Services, it was his responsibility to keep Ben-Gurion briefed on the progress of my trial; but he clandestinely kept Pinhas Lavon informed as well.

Why was Isser playing the arsonist in the fire brigade? Ambition. Isser wanted the conspiracy exposed to the extent that its scandal would sweep away three men who threatened his ambitions: Moshe Dayan, currently minister of agriculture in Ben-Gurion's government; Shimon Peres, still director of the defense ministry; and Gibli, shuffled off to London as military attaché.

Though he knew that Gibli was expendable, Isser could not chance a frontal attack on the credibility of Dayan and Peres without risking Ben-Gurion's wrath. If he hoped to rise and, at the same time, rid his path of his primary adversaries, then he had to find another way to expose the framing and the cover-up without exposing himself as the informer. Isser knew that when sub judice was no longer a danger, Lavon would come out after Ben-Gurion with guns blazing; he was determined not to be caught in the cross fire.

Isser turned to Pinhas Sapir, then minister of commerce and industry. Sapir reached all the way to Ethiopia, where Jossi Harel, long relieved as head of Modiin Unit 131, was engaged in private business. Sapir convinced Jossi to reveal to Lavon what he knew of the past. Jossi had no choice; his business was a government concession from Sapir's ministry of commerce and industry.

On February 4, 1960, just after my trial ended, Jossi visited Pinhas Lavon, who for five years had kept the fires of his own exoneration burning furiously in his brain. This fever—even though he had been secretary-general of the powerful Histadrut labor federation since his resignation as minister of defense—had stripped him of his health. Ephraim "Eppie" Evron, Lavon's former aide and faithful supporter, took down the substance of this fateful meeting.

According to Evron's notes,[1] Jossi Harel, as a young naval officer in Israel's fledgling defense forces, left for the United States in 1950 to study shipbuilding. Four years later he received an urgent cable from General Chief of Staff Dayan demanding his immediate return to Israel. Upon his arrival in the fall of 1954, he was handed the reins of Unit 131. Only later did he learn that he was replacing Motke, after his blunderous report to Dayan in which he had failed to implicate Lavon as having given the order for the Egyptian operation.

Shaken by this unexpected command and never having been involved in intelligence work of this sort, he was forced to rely on the advice and experience of others to guide him. Jossi was warned not to concern himself with what had happened in Egypt. Reuben Schiloach, former head of the intelligence community and special adviser to Ben-Gurion, hinted that it would be wise for him to delve only into the technical errors of the operation. Shortly thereafter Col. Jehosaphat "Fatti" Harkabi replaced Gibli as director of Modiin. Despite the warnings Jossi slowly—and to his dismay—began to realize that Israel's military-political hierarchy had a mistaken impression of the events in Egypt. But his education in the Haganah had taught him to accept the authority of his superiors and not to involve himself.

Jossi's information had come mostly from a good friend of his, a well-known public figure, Gen. Ya'acov Dori (of the Olshan-Dori military inquiry), and from his superior, Fatti Harkabi. He had learned, for example, of the disappearance from the unit's archives of the orders to carry out sabotage actions. Then he was told by a member of Department 8 that other materials had been submitted for alteration directly to the experts—not to the department head, as was customary.

Fatti Harkabi refused to tell him further details, for fear of giving the impression of undermining Gibli because of personal animosity. At one point Jossi was told by Col. Ariel Amiad (who had conducted the secret

---

1. The original typed notes have been translated by the author.

military inquiry prior to my trial) that he was expected to testify. But the call never came.

Finally Jossi told Lavon that he was willing to appear before an authorized public body and tell all that he knew. He suggested that others be called to testify, as well: Harkabi (by 1960, a general); Colonel Almog; Colonel J. Haifez; Uri and Chayim of Department 8; Dalia Carmel, Gibli's former secretary; A. Har Even, former head of Gibli's office; Motke; Mussa of Department 5; the wireless operators from Unit 131, and their commander, Neri.[2]

If, as he claimed, conscience was his motivation for opening up about the past, why hadn't Jossi gone to Ben-Gurion, or to Gen. Chaim Laskov, successor to Dayan as chief of staff? But Jossi was motivated by pressure; that's why he confessed to Lavon, who had no power to initiate action. Lavon was a totally illogical choice as confessor—unless Isser Harel (through Jossi) was trying to open up the wound of the past by unleashing Lavon on Ben-Gurion, while protecting his own future.

Whether inadvertently or by design, Jossi's visit with Lavon did not escape Ben-Gurion. Afraid of the possible consequences, Ben-Gurion went to see Lavon on the following day, determined to catch the fish before the net. He met only silence.

Chagrined, Ben-Gurion tried another tactic. He invited him to his office to discuss a teachers' dispute, which was Lavon's bailiwick as head of the Histadrut labor union. After a brief exchange, Ben-Gurion asked "Tell me, Pinhas, but tell me the truth. Do you still hold a grudge with regard to the affair?"

Lavon replied, "Why do you speak about a grudge? If you really and seriously want to know, I have evidence to prove my charges." Lavon told him of Jossi's visit and promised to give him Evron's notes. However, he waited a day or two for a propitious moment to do so—in front of witnesses.

Ben-Gurion now faced the most critical ordeal of his momentous career: Jossi's revelations, in the hands of Lavon, pinned him to the wall. On the one hand, he had to investigate the alleged acts of forgery, perjury, and worse; on the other, he was bound to hide from idealistic public fascistic tendencies within the military. He feared incriminating certain of his protégés and bringing to light his own part in the whole affair.

To gain maneuvering time, Ben-Gurion appointed Col. Chayim Ben David, his adjutant, to investigate the allegations of criminal misconduct

---

2. If most of those listed for questioning by Jossi had been called to testify before the January 1955 Olshan-Dori inquiry into the question of "who gave the order" to initiate action in Egypt, then it would have been impossible for the conspiracy against Lavon to have survived detection.

among senior army officers. But in this early part of February, Ben-Gurion had a solid ace in the hole; he knew that so long as my verdict stood sub judice, the matter need not be dealt with.[3] Any publicity would constitute possible grounds for dismissal of my case.

Within five days Ben-Gurion's adjutant delivered his first report on discussions with Jossi Harel and other key army officers. However, using the fact that a certain key witness was serving in France, Ben-Gurion decided that Col. Ben David would wait until their forthcoming trip to Europe to interrogate this witness. This postponement of a month was later attributed to a desire to economize.

On July 15, Col. Ben David delivered his conclusion. It was terse: "Indeed, alterations of documents were carried out in the Army Intelligence Department."

Eppie Evron knew of the conclusion beforehand and was already en route to Switzerland, where Lavon was recuperating from heart trouble. Overjoyed that he could finally clear the stigma from his name but aware of the pending verdict in my trial, Lavon waited. And, sweltering in Jerusalem's summer heat, Ben-Gurion sat still. The next move appeared to be Lavon's.

Instead, on August 21, the day of the verdict, it was Isser Harel who swung into action. He had finished me off with a framing; now he was going after bigger game. The following day he submitted to Chief of Staff Laskov excerpts of my eighty-page verdict. Following through, General Laskov wrote a letter to Ben-Gurion, asking what investigative steps he, as chief of staff, should take. The day this letter arrived, Isser advised Ben-Gurion to appoint a military board to investigate charges of criminal corruption against Gibli and Motke—but not the question of "Who gave the order." His reasoning was inescapable:

1. Dealing only with Gibli and Motke would finally destroy any chance of Gibli's comeback to Modiin.
2. Advising against investigating "Who gave the order" avoided a confrontation with Ben-Gurion and Dayan.
3. *Not* investigating "Who gave the order" would bring Lavon to loggerheads with Ben-Gurion.

Divide and rule was the basic concept of Isser's machination.

Unsuspecting, Ben-Gurion ordered General Laskov to appoint a board of inquiry that included a man of jurisprudence. By mid-September the three-man committee, presided over by Justice Chaim Cohn of the

---

3. It was only later that I realized the probable reason for the eight-month delay in the announcement of the verdict.

Supreme Court, was seated and ordered to investigate only the following points from the 1955 Olshan-Dori inquiry:

1. Were steps taken by Gibli, Motke, and other officers to suborn witnesses in general and the Third Man[4] in particular to commit perjury before the Olshan-Dori inquiry, as well as to the chief of staff (Dayan) and the minister of defense (Lavon)?
2. Were alterations made on documents relating to the investigation, and, if so, who performed the alterations and by whose order?

The Cohn Committee was *not* charged with determining "Who gave the order." Isser had triumphed again.

Eppie Evron returned to Switzerland and, within a week, was back, explaining to the prime minister Lavon's objections to the inquiry. They were twofold: First, there was no need for the panel to study these points because the district court, in my trial, had already declared that alteration of documents and subornation of witnesses had indeed occurred; and second, Justice Cohn had no place on the panel. Once, while holding ministerial portfolio, Lavon had demanded Cohn's dismissal as state attorney general. Furthermore, Cohn's colleague, the president of the Supreme Court, was Justice Yitzak Olshan of the Olshan-Dori inquiry; he might prejudice Cohn.

Ben-Gurion rejected Lavon's protest, stating bluntly that it was none of his business. Angered and disappointed, Lavon flew to Israel on September 25. At Lod Airport he issued his warning that in the near future he would have to speak "some unpleasant truths."

The Lavon affair broke into the open. Ben-Gurion and Lavon thrashed each other daily in public forums. Both were determined to win: Ben-Gurion to hide the affair, Lavon to clear his name and to absolve Israel of its worst sin. In the glare of battle between Israel's two most powerful men, I was forgotten. I waited, my sentencing ahead of me, hoping desperately that the furor would in some way correct the injustice that had been dealt me.

On September 26, a day after Lavon's arrival, he went to Jerusalem where he and Ben-Gurion had a "summit meeting." It has been written in *The Jerusalem Post* that Lavon "possesses a gentle almost rabbinical manner. His straight hair, nearly white, is accentuated by dark, arching eyebrows that seem to register surprise. The other parts of his face register

---

4. From my arrest in late 1957 until March 1971, Israel's censorship would never allow my name, picture, or background to appear in any publication within their control. I would be referred to as "the Third Man."

resignation, a lazy hound-dog expression. Behind this facade is an imperious and vengeful nature when crossed."

It is not difficult to imagine the animosity that must have risen between him and his former mentor as they parried the issue that meant destruction for the loser. However, as yet the swords were not drawn. It was still relatively congenial between Lavon, the idealist of brilliant oratory, and Ben-Gurion, a soldier of the mind, a man who understood the uses of pragmatism.

Still hearing both Ben-Gurion's rejection of his protest about the Cohn Committee and his refusal to take steps to clear his name, Lavon departed, furious, vowing that he would boycott the inquiry. Things turned hot.

A clamor arose for clarification, and opposing factions in parliament demanded to be informed about the real circumstances that had led to Lavon's February, 1955, resignation from the ministry of defense. The Foreign Affairs and Security Committee was summoned into extraordinary session on October 2 to hear Ben-Gurion.

Asked who had ordered the debacle in Egypt, Ben-Gurion replied that the task of examining the guilt or innocence was a matter for a judicial forum. His position made it clear that the Cohn inquiry should look into the security mishap in Egypt and not Lavon's subsequent resignation. But Ben-Gurion's rigid interpretation did not distract everyone. The clamor forced him to make a lengthy statement the following day. Speaking as prime minister, he told of his September 26 meeting with Lavon:

> I had nothing to do with what is called "the Lavon affair." I had no reason to blame Mr. Lavon for anything done by him during his term of office as minister of defense, and as I told him . . . I see no need or obligation to exonerate him: (a) because I did not censure him, and (b) if anyone did censure him or try to do so, it is not within my authority to exonerate him. I am not an investigator or a judge.
>
> Through misinformation or bad faith, several newspapers are confusing two separate matters: 1) An unfortunate incident on which an inquiry committee [Olshan-Dori] appointed by the prime minister [Sharet] at the end of 1954 at the request of the then minister of defense, Mr. Lavon, reached no conclusions; 2) The resignation from the government of Mr. Lavon.

It was clear why he wanted the two issues separated. As long as he could control the investigation, he could contain the scandal; if he lost control, then the scandal would slip beyond his grasp.

Lavon retorted in a statement to the press, declaring that the circumstances leading to his resignation, as presented by Ben-Gurion, were not factual but political. He stated that the matter demanded a political inquiry by the cabinet or parliament. Lavon explained that he had kept silent for almost six years because critical security matters were involved and because the reputation of Zahal was dear to him.

"Rumors are being spread," he said, "to create the impression that there is no connection between the facts that have come to light and the affair which occurred shortly before my resignation. I take full responsibility for saying that the new facts are all connected with the affair and nothing else."

Lavon then went before the parliament's Foreign Affairs and Security Committee at its request and demanded a full probe of the circumstances leading to his resignation.

Ben-Gurion was confident that the committee would not proceed without his blessing. But a pebble out of control became an avalanche, as opposition parties demanded full disclosure and the inquiry began.

Lavon; former prime minister Sharet; Dayan; Shimon Peres; and others appeared, and the testimony, which leaked to the press, added to the breach between Ben-Gurion and Lavon. Lavon literally declared war on Ben-Gurion. He stated: "I am now more convinced than ever that Ben-Gurion is a party to this matter. . . ."

Meanwhile the Cohn probe had been conducting secret sessions for almost five weeks. Even Lavon, ignoring his boycott threat, testified before it. Gibli was secretly brought to Israel as the last witness. For obvious reasons I was not called. I had been framed and found guilty and awaited my sentencing. No one was about to listen to me.

Referred to in the press only as the "senior officer," Gibli was reported to have been warned by Ben-Gurion not to talk to anyone. But what the press did not report about Gibli's October 11 arrival in Israel was that only the evening before he had met with Moshe Dayan in Athens. (When their meeting surfaced later, Dayan explained that he and Gibli had only exchanged words of greeting.) Dayan had already testified before the inquiry; the scenario of their clandestine rendezvous would not be difficult to write.

But there was more to Dayan's travels. In mid-September, before Lavon's return from Switzerland, Ben-Gurion had to dismantle Lavon's evidence: Jossi Harel's February 4 confession. He dispatched Dayan, as minister of agriculture, to Ethiopia to confer with Haile Selassie. There Dayan met Jossi Harel in Asmara. Had Dayan gone there to twist Jossi's arm, trying to convince him to retract his confession to Lavon? (On February 12, 1961, one year and eight days after his revelations, Jossi would use the pretext of something Lavon had said to the Maariv newspaper to refute his confession, in a scorching letter of threat and retribution.)

On October 11 Gibli was grilled for more than two hours by the Cohn Committee. That same day an article by Dayan appeared in Israel's English-language newspaper, *The Jerusalem Post*. I had come to believe that no man is lost as long as he maintains his sense of irony; but at my reading of Dayan's words, I must admit I had to muster all my resources. Dayan was feeling supremely confident:

Under no circumstances whatever can one condone forgery or the manipulation of facts, and if anyone has been guilty of such things, he must be dealt with according to the full force of the law. Severe measures must be taken not only against those who actually commit such crimes, but also against anyone (if there were such persons) indirectly connected either by having encouraged such actions or by closing their eyes to them. Moreover, any commander in the Israeli Army who was aware of such acts and did not immediately take all steps open to him to investigate the case and punish those guilty should be considered an accomplice, and the full force of the law should be invoked against him also.

By now everybody had gotten into the act, taking verbal potshots at the issues, at Ben-Gurion, or at Lavon, who was suffering the cruelest attack. I saw shades of our 1954 conspiracy against him in the way he was being flailed for his "political comeback." But he did not retreat. The ghosts of the past were too firmly fixed in his mind for him to falter now.

On October 15, after six weeks, the Cohn inquiry submitted its report to Ben-Gurion, who kept it to himself, on the premise that it contained highly secret security documents. To back up his stand he sent the findings to State Attorney General Gideon Hausner, asking him to determine if criminal proceedings were justified.

Only Ben-Gurion knew that the Cohn inquiry had exonerated Lavon of blame in ordering the sabotage and that Gibli and Motke had been implicated as being guilty of perjury and subornation. Shortly after Gibli testified, he met with Ben-Gurion and Dayan. Ben-Gurion probably advised him to demand a trial before a court of law, which was what Ben-Gurion had wanted all along—but *only* if he had to investigate the Lavon affair. Ben-Gurion realized the safety in the investigative limitations of a courtroom trial. Gibli hired counsel and wrote a letter to Chief of Staff Laskov demanding just such a legal inquiry into "Who gave the order." He created a diversion that confused the issues further: more cover-up.

While Attorney General Hausner studied the Cohn findings, Ben-Gurion reported them to his cabinet. He also submitted Gibli's letter to the minister of justice, who postponed a decision until the last of the month, a week away.

There was no question that I was witnessing the greatest political crisis in my country's short history. I saw in each party's house organ a bristling sense of outrage, confusion, and shock. The Mapai (Labor) party—Lavon and Ben-Gurion's party, which held a slim majority in the coalition government—had already met to discuss the dissension created by the affair and by Lavon himself, a member of its secretariat. His staunchest supporters, apparently taken aback by his willingness to let the party suffer for his own ends, began attacking him.

Fearing that the status quo would be upset, they had yet to grasp the seriousness of the past, or of the moment. But as the opposition parties joined in the attack, worsening the crisis by demanding a full disclosure of the affair, Levi Eshkol, minister of finance, was handed the thorny task of arbitrating interparty peace.

With his Labor party abandoning Lavon, Ben-Gurion announced his doubts that the full truth of the affair would ever be understood because the Olshan-Dori inquiry had reached no conclusion; and that no evidence was sufficient in his eyes to leave Lavon free of blame. Former Prime Minister Sharet, appeased, stated in an article in *Devar* that the criminal aspect of the affair was a matter for the courts; the political-security aspect, for the Foreign Affairs and Security Committee; and the fact of Lavon's resignation, for the historians.

Others were not quite so gentle. Poet and author Natan Alterman in his seventh column in the *Devar* accused Lavon of having "cast an ominous shadow on the integrity of Israel's entire defense organization," adding that Lavon's charges had made it "not too dissimilar from an underworld of extortion, fear, and lies." Alterman added, however, that if Lavon was right, he should be commended.

Sraya Shapiro, in *The Jerusalem Post,* threw a protective blanket around the image of the military and revived the reputation Lavon had been saddled with as minister of defense: a nonsoldier without experience in security matters; a thinker, a peruser, not subject to decisive, unstudied moves. This image contrasted markedly with those of Ben-Gurion, a militarist and a warrior, and with Dayan, an impulsive soldier of action in the most democratic army in the world.

Shapiro wrote: "Good soldiers do not seek to usurp civilian authority, unless the civilians, forgetting their duty to provide sound government, lose themselves in futile political games; but there is little which is more likely to exasperate the military expert than a civilian giving orders in matters the soldier believes he does not understand."

On October 24 I read Hausner's report on the Cohn findings. Ben-Gurion had not liked what the attorney general had found. The report read, in part, as follows:

A. At the onset, it must be stated that the evidence given during the Cohn Committee inquiry is not admissible as trial evidence except insofar as anyone may be charged with testifying falsely before it. I have therefore understood your [Ben-Gurion] request to mean: Do I find in the findings of the Cohn Committee and in the evidence given before it sufficient grounds for launching an investigation, as a result of which there might be room to bring anyone to trial?

B. Following are the pertinent factual findings: . . .

1) [Motke Ben Zur][5] sent a letter to the Third Man through [Lt. Col. Mordechai Almog] to persuade him to testify in a particular way before the Olshan Committee. This was done with the knowledge of [Gibli]. [Motke] also tried to persuade the Third Man to do so . . . when they met at the airport.

2) The contact with the Third Man . . . took place contrary to the instructions to the Chief of Staff [Dayan]. During this contact, [Motke] "warned" the Third Man to ignore a suggestion that he testify about having received certain instructions.

3) The "warning" . . . was the same as the one given him in connection with his conversation with [Dayan] and the minister of defense [Lavon].

4) [Gibli] and [Motke] both knew that what they were trying to do was subornation.

5) It has not been proved that anyone other than the Third Man has been suborned to testify falsely before the Olshan Committee.

6) [Motke] swore falsely both before the District Court in the trial of the Third Man and before the Cohn Committee, but the committee is inclined to think that he had done so out of stupidity and not criminal intent.

7) [Gibli] knew and remembered more than he has been willing to testify. He did not give the sincere and full testimony that the committee had expected of him, shrugging off responsibility for the acts of his subordinates which, without doubt, had been committed in coordination with him, if not at his express orders.

C. There is no ground for bringing [Motke] to trial on charges of suborning the Third Man to swear falsely. . . .

1) [Some of the] violations are misdemeanors which expired three years after they were committed, so that no criminal charges can be brought against them.

---

5. Names in the attorney general's published report were coded to obscure the principal figures.

2) [Motke's] testimony in the Jerusalem District Court in the Third Man's trial was false on three counts. First, [Motke] did not remember that he had given [Almog] a letter for the Third Man. . . . [Motke] retracted his testimony when he appeared before the Cohn Committee. At first, he did so with hesitation, saying "I may have written," then frankly, "I sent him the letter."

Secondly, [Motke] testified in the Third Man's trial that he had not met him in Israel before the latter appeared before the Olshan Committee. . . . Before the Cohn Committee . . . [Motke] said that he "may well have" met the Third Man at the airport.

Thirdly, in the trial, [Motke] denied having given the Third Man certain instructions on a certain day. The Cohn Committee established for a fact that such instructions had been given. . . .

[But the three points on which Motke testified falsely in the district court had no connection whatsoever with the matter for which my trial was held. His testimony therefore was not perjury.]

D. According to the Cohn Committee, [Gibli] had planned with [Motke] to suborn the Third Man to lie before the Olshan Committee, but what was stated in C(1) above, in reference to [Motke], also applies to [Gibli].

The Cohn Committee has not established that [Gibli] has not told it the truth. But his denial of any connection with [Motke's] actions is not acceptable. This is not enough, however, to make him liable to criminal action. He did not testify in the Third Man's trial. The appropriate bodies will have to consider whether to retain his service in the regular army. . . .

E. 1) The Cohn Committee dealt at length with the charges of forged documents and with suspicions that were raised as a result of and in connection with the [Egyptian operation]. . . . It concluded that it had no data which could lead it to assume that documents concerning the affair had been forged. . . .

2) Certain persons abroad whose names had been mentioned as possible witnesses in connection with the forgery were not interrogated by the Cohn Committee. In my opinion, the clarification of this matter should be concluded with the interrogation of those persons by an authorized body . . . so that a final conclusion may be reached.

The State was reeling under the blows: Suddenly the Israeli Dream was crumbling down around the fallen image of the military, and neither the institutions of government nor its elected leaders were free of the suspicion of taint. It seemed that the very bindings of Israel's democracy were coming apart. There was genuine fright in everyone's heart, and it was no less so among the Ramla Prison population. A rash of public statements filled Israel's dailies and her party organs.

Lavon, in his typically quiet but forceful voice, answered Israel: He considered the affair closed from the moral and public points of view. "I had just one demand . . . to establish, on the basis of new data, that I bear no responsibility (for ordering the Egyptian operation)."

Former Prime Minister Sharet announced: "I am convinced that, had the facts now brought to light by the Cohn Committee been known then (1955), they would have served as weighty evidence that the charges leveled against Pinhas Lavon at that time, accusing him of direct responsibility for a certain event, were false."

The press, finally appreciating the humiliation Lavon had suffered, asked him to comment on the branding of the affair as a "Dreyfusad."[6] Lavon said simply: "I have repeatedly said that I was not referring to the army, but to certain staff members of the Defense Ministry—who also include an officer or two. On the contrary, I have stressed all the while that I do not accuse the army—which is busy doing its own job, and I do not consider the army a party to any part of this affair."

Not everyone was satisfied that the Lavon affair had reached its conclusion. The Mapam, Haboker (Zionist), and Herut parties shot barbs straight at the heart of Ben-Gurion; this reflected rampant disillusionment in the country. Stunned by the Cohn Report, Ben-Guron did not help matters. There were instances when the very mention of Lavon's name sent him reeling into paroxysms of rage. Privately he threatened to quit. Then he insisted on the creation of a special judicial commission to establish the "real" facts.

The end of October neared.

Gibli's demand for a legal inquiry into "Who gave the order" had been postponed. Despite Ben-Gurion's strong opposition—"The cabinet cannot set itself up as a judge!"—his coalition cabinet, on October 31, elected a parliament ministerial committee, the Committee of Seven. It was approved by all the cabinet except Ben-Gurion, who was absent, and Dayan, who abstained. Again the pattern. However, it would not call witnesses but rely on documentation.

One of its first pieces of business was to send Attorney General Hausner to Europe to interview four people pertinent to the study: Dalia, Gibli's secretary, who made the crucial changes in a document that fortified the conspiracy; Gen. Fatti Harkabi; a man from Department 8; and Shamay Cahana, who was former Prime Minister Sharet's secretary in 1954–55.

---

6. Alfred Dreyfus, the French artillery officer who was sent to Devil's Island on the basis of forged papers. He was later pardoned.

Burned by the question of "juntaism," Ben-Gurion told parliament that he had asked the attorney general if there were grounds for libel action against persons making statements degrading to the army and the personnel of the defense ministry—a gun aimed at Lavon.

He also submitted to the Committee of Seven a letter from Avraham Dar that asserted that he knew Lavon had "given the order" in 1954. Dar's letter was a total lie.

On November 20, 1960, my twelve-year sentence was handed down. Contrary to all my hopes, the cover-up was simply too strong, the *cordon sanitaire* too tight.

Following my appeal to the Supreme Court, Hausner returned home after five weeks in Europe and handed his evidence to the committee. At about the same time, tired of Ben-Gurion's sniping, Lavon warned the country against etatism.[7] As expected, his inflammatory remark was leaped upon by his own Labor party.

Ben-Gurion, certain that only one of them could survive the conflagration, revealed that he would disclose hitherto unknown evidence of misconduct by Lavon, but parliament censured him for hiding whatever he may have kept back.

It was a vicious circle of charge and countercharge, which was only dispelled when the Committee of Seven, on December 21, made public its findings. It unanimously adopted several conclusions.

1. Lavon did not give the direct order for the 1954 action.
2. This committee sees no need for further inquiry.
3. No one except Gibli and Motke bears any responsibility for the mishap.

One of the more curious aspects of the cover-up occurred in the interrogation of Dalia, Gibli's former secretary. She was an innocent participant in the conspiracy, but her contribution had closed the noose around Lavon's neck while protecting Gibli and, thus, Dayan. In Gibli's letter to Dayan, she had changed the sentence " . . . following the conversation we had had, the boys were activated" to read: "Upon Lavon's instructions we have activated ——'s men." Dayan had destroyed the original for "security purposes." When she admitted her role in the alteration, Hausner promised her amnesty.

Now the strange part began. Dalia returned to Israel and faced interrogation by the police. However, she had lost her powers of recollection. Suddenly uncertain that the document she had altered was the letter in

---

7. The frame of mind that is willing to sacrifice the individual to the need of the State.

question, Dalia had sudden help. The military police reported that the suspicion of alteration was completely groundless.[8]

For a second time in as many months, Lavon announced that he was satisfied with a committee's report.

As Christian pilgrims poured into Israel to celebrate the birth of their Savior, the Committee of Seven's findings went to the cabinet, which recommended that the affair be closed.

Ben-Gurion, stunned and angered, again threatened to resign: He would not be a party to a miscarriage of justice, discrimination, and half-truths. Now it was the cabinet's turn for anger and shock. Golda Meir, then foreign minister, drew up her resignation, but withheld it until Ben-Gurion's intentions were clear. Under his blackmail, the party urged him not to resign, and the public clamored for peace. Never had the word *Shalom* meant so much.

The Intellectuals' Manifesto, a plea by fifty leading educators, writers, and philosophers, stated: "A crisis of confidence is sweeping Israeli society. With public opinion what it is, there is a great danger to the future of the State of Israel." Israel suddenly understood that the Lavon affair was not a political crisis but a moral one.

On the first day of 1961, Gibli withdrew his demand for a legal inquiry into "Who gave the order." His diversionary tactic had failed.

Ben-Gurion, away on vacation, with Levi Eshkol as acting prime minister, executed another thrust. He threatened to resign on the following day, January 7. The Old Man, now seventy-four, his craggy face a block of grizzled granite, knew that his career was finished if he did not triumph over Lavon. He lashed out in every direction, including Diasporic Jews, historically one of his pet hates. (He had said, "Whoever dwells outside the land of Israel is considered to have no God.") He demanded a legal inquiry. Why all of this?

Exoneration—a whitewashing for himself, his protégés, the army, Israel. And control—absolute authority over the government and all its institutions.

But Ben-Gurion had shaken his cabinet by attacking the probity of the Committee of Seven. With Golda Meir's continuation as foreign minister in question, Minister of Justice Pinhas Rosen not only offered his resignation but recommended the dissolution of the government.

The opposition parties were scathing in their condemnation of Ben-

---

8. In 1972, interviewed by the author about her part in the alteration of the critical letter, Dalia, then working in New York, said: "It was so absurd! I told them I typed the alteration in Gibli's letter to Dayan. They said, 'No.' I pointed out exactly what I did, but the police expert still said, 'No.' If the truth didn't fit into what they were doing, then what sense was there for me to try to convince them otherwise?"

Gurion, and Lavon, sobered by the furor, and feeling abandoned, told a thousand high school students: "Democracy is not merely a matter of laws or forms of rules; it depends on the awareness of each and every individual that it is his duty to be a free man." There was booing in Israel's movie houses whenever Ben-Gurion appeared.

By the third week of January, public faith in the body politic had ebbed so dangerously that the cabinet hastily determined that "the government crisis is over" and, therefore, that it should "proceed with the agenda."

Lavon, abandoning all restraint in a stormy party session with Ben-Gurion, lost all support. Still under heavy attack, Ben-Gurion tendered his resignation. Labor leadership, in shock, officially notified Lavon of his dismissal as the Histadrut secretary-general four days later, on February 4— exactly one year to the day since he had reopened the affair.

Pinhas Lavon had won a moral victory, but he had lost the political battle. I wondered if he believed his words: "I am not leaving my post as a defeated man." A final, empty cry to the victor. Lavon's resignation was a major victory for Ben-Gurion. Abandoning his petulance, he made it known that he welcomed returning to the government. (He did return and was reelected.) Ben-Gurion and Lavon had fought so doggedly and bitterly because they were so alike. Both were energetic, adamant, brilliant, and possessed of leadership. Both had tremendous capacities for imperious and vengeful behavior. The essential difference between them was that Ben-Gurion was a pragmatist, and Lavon was an ideologue. Theirs had been a clash of giants.

Staggered by too many internal blows, a reeling Israel was suddenly alerted to the capture of the most hated survivor of Hitler's Third Reich: Adolph Eichmann. With the world closely watching his trial, the Lavon affair had dwindled to a minor issue by the spring of 1961.

But after his withdrawal from public office in June 1963, Ben-Gurion turned his attention to the affair once more. Concerned, like all politicians, with the historians (there could be no second-guessing on their part), he decided to write a book. He engaged Amnon Dror, a conscientious journalist and deputy editor for the *La-Merchav* newspaper, to compile voluminous documentation into a readable volume. Deep into his investigation of my part in the affair, Amnon realized that something was very wrong. Apparently his doubts became known; one day, without warning, he was dismissed.

Another journalist, Jigal Lev, was entrusted with the job. But after the meeting with Tussia-Cohen and my sister and brother-in-law, Jigal resigned. Both journalists eventually became good friends and ardent supporters of my fight for freedom. It was to their credit that my public image eventually changed for the better.

Finally Ben-Gurion found the man he was looking for, a loyalist by the name of Chaggai Eshed (formerly Chaggi Edelmann) from the staff of *Devar,* the Labor party's newspaper. He dissected me with unexpected fervor—but his enthusiasm resulted in such libel that the censor disallowed the publishing of certain parts of his work.

During the writing, Ben-Gurion had employed two lawyers to consider the legal aspects of the affair. On October 22, 1964, he took the results of their investigation to the minister of justice, Dr. Dov Joseph, who proposed that Ben-Gurion submit the dossier of some five hundred pages to the attorney general.

The attorney general's opinion was presented to the cabinet of Levi Eshkol, Ben-Gurion's successor, on December 8; it was released to the public six days later. Eshkol was adamant that neither he nor his cabinet was prepared to reopen the Lavon affair, and, when the Labor party's central committee refused to set up a judicial committee, Ben-Gurion and his protégés, Dayan and Shimon Peres, formed the breakaway Rafi party. The three did not return to the fold until two years later. Only after the publication of his own veiled version of the scandal, *Things As They Are,* did he grudgingly abandon the political scene, retiring to his house in kibbutz Ste Boker in the Negev Desert.

As for Lavon, he and his own breakaway group, Min Hayessod ("from the foundation"), stayed out of the Labor party until shortly before the Six Day War in June 1967. Lavon died after a long illness in January, 1976, still hoping for final exoneration.

Chapter 27

Beyond Ramla's walls, I was generally believed to be a sellout, a merce-nary, a traitor. Inside, because convicts are usually anti-authority, I rose in their esteem. I was recognized as the Third Man in the Lavon affair and the mystery man in Israel's even more mysterious security case. To them I had been instrumental in toppling the government, and the severity of my sentence was more proof of my importance. I couldn't enjoy their esteem, however, for I suffered a chronic pain in the pit of my stomach as I watched helplessly the winding down of the furor. The investigations had not aided my cause; the Lavon affair lived on in deceit and cover-up.

Immediately after the sentencing, Tussia-Cohen submitted our appeal to the High Court; he enumerated 104 legal objections to be reviewed. This time, unlike the response to my trial in the district court, the press gave wide coverage to the fact that the number of objections constituted some sort of record in the annals of security trials.

Life in prison had deteriorated. The new warden leaned toward new, psychological trends and unfortunately this was interpreted by some con-victs as a sign of weakness. As a result I witnessed the first outbreak of vio-lence behind the walls.

The instigator was a former neighbor in solitary confinement, a dema-gogue named Joseph Menkens. He had been sentenced to life imprison-ment for having initiated the murder of a Dr. Kastner, who, during World War II, had been head of the Jewish community in Budapest.

At that time I was allowed to join the other inmates at mealtimes, but afterward I was returned to my cell. I preferred this arrangement, for it gave me the privacy I needed to continue my study of journalism. In the courtyard before entering the mess hall one day, I noticed Menkens huddled in a corner with some of the younger convicts. I could see that Menkens had stirred up their fury.

I was fifth in line at the kitchen window when Menkens, in front of me, took the food and threw it on the floor, shouting, "We are not going to eat that shit!" His young followers did likewise, urging everyone to follow suit. There were many inmates who were against this sort of demonstration yet feared to take the first step to show it. I picked up my plate and walked toward my table, announcing loudly, half jokingly, "I don't like the macaroni, but the fruit gelatin I do, and I am not willing to give it up." When Menkens told me that I was breaking the solidarity of the inmates, I replied that I agreed with the complaints but not with his way of handling them. I said that he was jeopardizing the little progress we had made since the new warden's arrival. "We are providing fuel for those who claim that psychology is for the books, not behind bars."

"*Meragel meluchlach*!" Menkens shouted, raising his hand. "Dirty spy" did it. My stored-up anger, frustration, and agony had found an outlet. I hit Menkens squarely in his mouth and, with another blow to his solar plexus, sent him gasping to the floor. The short brawl that ensued was broken up by guards, who came streaming into the dining hall, and after a couple of hours life returned to normal. Although the inmates accepted my assessment of the situation as accurate, repercussion followed, and the guards appeared with sticks again. (One of them had written "psychology" on his and removed it only after I complained to the warden.) Inmates were confined to their cells after working hours, and all plans to improve life behind the walls were canceled.

Shortly after this a violent, mass escape of Arab prisoners occurred in the northern Shatta prison, and two former Ramla guards were killed. The guards had been liked by all the inmates, and we all knew that the resentment of the Jewish convicts toward Arabs in general and security offenders in particular was bound to explode. Led by Menkens, the Jewish convicts of Iraqui and Moroccan origin planned to demonstrate their patriotic fury by executing a massacre during lunch. Iron bars and handmade knives were hidden in the mess hall. Everything was ready for the kill.

Although it was incompatible with my nature to remain passive, I was in a dilemma. On the one hand, I couldn't inform on my fellow inmates, and, on the other, I couldn't abet what certainly would become a slaughter. Moreover there was a likelihood that the attack would be carried over to Jewish security offenders, and that personal scores would be settled in the process. My futile attempts to dissuade the plotters left only one alternative: I had to sabotage the plan in such a way that the eruption would start in the courtyard and not in the mess hall.

One of the hotheads was a fellow by the name of Moshe Dahan, built like an ox and well known in the Israeli underworld. (A musical based on his life has been shown on the screen, *Casablan*.) Being emotional and a user of hashish even behind bars, he was easily influenced. While all the inmates assembled in the courtyard before lunch, I had a few words with him. As a result he attacked one of the Arab inmates, and the whole courtyard became a fighting arena for Arab and Jew, then Jew against Jew. The guards soon stopped it. Questioned by the warden, one inmate revealed the plan, and an immediate search produced all the deadly weapons hidden away in the mess hall.

What followed made me furious as hell, and I smuggled the following note to a well-known Israeli weekly:

"It seems as if the Arab inmates of Ramla Prison were right by complaining about discrimination behind the walls. Never before was the accuracy of their accusations so lucidly demonstrated as it has been today. A few Jewish convicts who kindled a short but fierce outbreak of violence in the prison yard were sent to solitary confinement by the deputy warden. Twelve hours later, all of them were released by the warden's order. Not so the Arab convicts, the targets and victims of this bloody brawl.

"The warden's decision can be termed only as a most flagrant injustice. The troublemakers were rewarded; their victims thrown into the hole.

"In the wake of the warden's decision, a hunger strike was called by the involved Arab inmates, twenty-one of them altogether. Their demand: an official inquiry by members of the Knesset and transfer of the troublemakers to another prison.

"I, for myself, dare say that the Arab inmates, being citizens of Israel, are fully entitled to a correct treatment—whatever their offense might have been. Unjust measures of this kind serve merely to aggravate the constant efforts of striving to bring about a better understanding between the two people, the Arab and the Jews."

This outrage had provoked one of my first attempts toward achieving some form of group justice.

The appeal before the High Court in Jerusalem commenced on May 15, 1961. Both my counsel and I were pleased with the three-man panel. Tussia-Cohen thought them the best in Israel's jurisprudence: Justice Shimon Agranat, flanked by justices Sussman and Berenson, presided.

The day before, I was brought from Ramla to the police prison, where I had been kept during the trial that had begun almost two years ago.

Greeted by the police as an old friend, I was given the best available cell. I shared it with Professor Kurt Sita, considered to be one of the world's top scientists in the field of cosmic rays. I had met him in Ramla, where he had been confined for having spied for the Czechoslovakian Intelligence Service. Being in that room with him is an experience I will treasure all my life; a new world was opened before me. But what stirred me most was the fact that Professor Sita had shared the same block with my father in the Nazi concentration camp in Buchenwald and remembered him well. The earth was growing smaller.

At 8:00 A.M. on May 15, I was taken to the court building and ushered into a small room, bare of everything save a long table for the judges and two smaller ones for the prosecution and defense. Later I learned that the room represented a compromise between Justice Agranat and the Shin-Beth, who wanted my hearing held in even more restrictive quarters.

Waiting for the judges, I passed the time smoking my pipe. Hence the small chamber was filled with the aroma of tobacco when they entered. Justice Agranat stopped short, sniffed once or twice and then, with a curious glance at me, lowered himself into his chair. This reaction of his became almost routine during the eleven days of appeal. When the hearing was over, he asked me, "Tell me now, what brand of tobacco you are using? Being a heavy pipe smoker myself, the aroma of the smoke made me suffer a little bit." I offered him my tobacco pouch; he declined but took time to scribble the brand into his agenda.

From the start I ran headlong into more Shin-Beth tricks; an apprentice lawyer, a Shin-Bethnik, had been assigned as secretary to Justice Sussman. When I told Tussia-Cohen about it, he dismissed my suspicion with, "It is impossible." Unfortunately I was right. We realized later that the Shin-Beth had had access to the judge's inner considerations, as well as to the records as written by the individual justices. I was astonished by the judges' caustic attitude toward the security service; Justice Sussman was especially critical in his remarks.

Before the appeal began, I had given much thought to how I could learn the truth about Peter Landesman's testimony. Although no witnesses could be called, new evidence not at our disposal during the trial could be introduced. Two of my fellow inmates who were to be released shortly, volunteered to kidnap Landesman and record his confession on tape. With my brother-in-law's help, everything was set in motion, but at the last moment Tussia-Cohen rejected the plan, explaining that the tape could not be admitted as evidence because Peter's testimony would have been achieved through coercion. We would gain nothing and might lose all. (I still think that abandoning the plan was a mistake.)

Nevertheless my hopes were running high and were reflected in a letter to Shula: "Despite my recent not-so-sympathetic experience with Goddess Justicia, I can hardly deny that by summing up the High Court's sessions held until now, I have ample reason to believe that the appeal's outcome will be favorable. In other words, I am optimistic again. It reflects the deep truth in the poet's saying: 'Hope springs eternal in the human breast, Man never is, but always to be blest.' "

Taken back to Ramla prison to await the outcome, I replied to Shula's questions about what I intended to do after my release:

"The decision whether to rebuild life in Israel depends chiefly on two factors: (a) the outcome of the appeal; (b) the possibility of rehabilitation.

"Both factors are strongly tied together, and it would be foolish to deny their reciprocal influence. If the High Court repeals the district court's decision and declares my offense a misdemeanor instead of a felony, then rehabilitation will be considerably easier. Only the High Court's decision will do the trick; any other official statement will merely mean a modification of my conviction. My concept of rehabilitation does not necessarily imply being reinstated, but sets the path to being restored to good repute.

"Another factor to be taken into account is the considerations and hesitations of the authorities who—quite understandably—are not very happy over the thought that I am to leave the country. The question *where to*—if at all—is still undecided. Germany is out of the question, for I can't see that I should be able to live there. It is not a question of occupation or in what way I shall earn my livelihood. It is solely a matter of feeling and nothing else. If I were in doubt and vacillating in regard to the German nation, the Eichmann trial convinced me finally that to live among those who committed every crime written in the book against the human race, and especially against us Jews, is impossible.

"Indeed, as you can see, I have some problems at hand. Anyway, there is no other choice than to wait, and meanwhile try to figure things out."

It had been almost a year before, on May 23, 1960, that Ben-Gurion made his dramatic announcement in a parliament filled to the rafters: "A short time ago, one of the greatest of Nazi war criminals, Adolph Eichmann, who was responsible together with the Nazi leaders for what they had called the 'final solution of the Jewish question'—that is, the extermination of six million Jews of Europe—was found. He is already under arrest in Israel and will shortly be put on trial under the Nazi Collaborators Law."

The entire Jewish world was electrified. Being brought to trial was Hitler's SS architect of death, who had dipped his bloody hand into almost every home in Israel; the death's-head leader who pushed millions of my people to a degrading end; the murderer of my mother and other relatives. Despite the disclaimers, every Jewish heart clamored for retribution and even revenge. Justice would have been well served had Eichmann's throat been slit upon his arrival in Israel; but his trial promised to be an example of Israeli justice: more image, more asking the world for acceptance, more laments of martyrdom.

Israel, forced to remember an appalling past, could now think of nothing but Eichmann. I have often wondered if the timing in capturing Eichmann was not in some way influenced by the overhanging shadow of the Lavon affair. While the state rallied behind Ben-Gurion, restoring Israel's cohesiveness, Eichmann's trial restored the faith in the Israeli Dream to Jews in the Diaspora.

As usual prison grapevine was accurate in relaying details as to Eichmann's whereabouts. (At first he was in the same "villa" I had been housed in by the Shin-Beth, later in the police fortress of Galame near Haifa). Grapevine also reported that within ten hours of his arrival in Israel, he had been formally charged and remanded to custody for fifteen days. With regard to Eichmann, I mused, the judicial procedures were followed to the letter. Not so with me, I thought cynically. *Eichmann did more for the Jewish State than I.*

With the nation, I followed the trial and, with my fellow inmates, wagered that he would be sentenced to be hanged. I had ample proof of this. Eichmann would be transferred to Ramla prison; the preparations were obvious. The third floor was remodeled, special guards selected, and extraordinary security measures taken. But what few people knew was that a hanging apparatus was already under construction. I learned of it through a fellow inmate named Silberman, an elderly metallurgist who was serving a long term for having been a Russian agent and who was working as a carpenter. One day he showed me four different blueprints.

"What do you make of it?" he asked.

I glanced at them, but only when the four were viewed together did they make sense. This was a scaffold, there could be no doubt. "Yes," Silberman replied. "It is to be installed on the third floor."

"So why the four different blueprints?" I asked.

"Security and secrecy. So that no one should guess what it is."

Stupidity has many faces, I thought. Convicts' wits were grossly underestimated. I also learned that red cloth had been delivered to the tailor shop. Under British mandate, prisoners condemned to death had been dressed in red, many Jewish underground members among them. I was certain that as soon as this fact became known, there would be a strong protest among the former underground movements. When he arrived, Eichmann was garbed in brown slacks and shirt, the same as we were wearing.

On May 31, 1962, Eichmann exhibited a greater defiance than he had shown during his long trial. At 8:00 P.M., a Reverend Hull, head of the nondenominational Zion Christian Mission in Jerusalem, was ushered into his cell and abruptly dismissed. Eichmann said, "I am not prepared to discuss the Bible. I do not have the time to waste."

While being led toward the execution chamber about twenty-five minutes later, Eichmann stopped suddenly and asked to be allowed to return to his cell for a moment. His guards reluctantly agreed. Back in his cell Eichmann stepped to the table, removed his partial dental plate from his mouth, and said with a ghastly grin, "It might cause me to choke."

Stepping on the trapdoor beneath the beam from which the noose hung, Eichmann requested that the fetters binding his ankles be loosened. "I might lose my balance" was his explanation. He also refused the black hood, and then, turning to the small group of men facing him, he said calmly, "After a short while, gentlemen, we shall meet again. That is the fate of all men." When he had dropped to his death, his body was carried outside the prison and cremated by the man in charge of the prison's boiler room; he himself had lost his family in Hungary during the war.

In the predawn hours of June 1, 1962, Prison Commissioner A. Nir scattered the ashes eight miles out, onto the waters of the Mediterranean Sea. But what not many know is the story of Israel's last act of revenge on Col. Adolph Eichmann. The so-called plain metal urn in which the ashes were collected was in fact a "piss tankard" from the prison hospital.

Meanwhile I was absorbed with my pending High Court decision. The end of 1961 neared, and it had now been eight months since the onset of my hearing—still another record delay in the case of the State *vs.* the Third Man. My patience seemed stretched beyond endurance. I wrote to Justice Agranat asking that my appeal be passed upon, and, four years after my arrest, late on the evening of January 2, 1962, I was ushered into his chambers.

"What's going to happen?" I asked Tussia-Cohen, feeling dread seeping into my spine.

Tussa-Cohen smiled. "Either they will accept our appeal, or they will not."

It was my turn to smile, if nervously. "And if it is the latter?"

"It will mean that three more men have said you are a liar."

Tussia-Cohen realized the distress his attempt at comic relief had caused. He added quickly, "But if they reduce your penalty by so much as one single day, it will imply that someone else is a liar."

A more futile implication I couldn't imagine! It would mean nothing beyond the reduction of my twelve-year sentence. I thought about the wager between my police escort and a fellow from the Shin-Beth, who was certain that my sentence would be reduced by two years. I told Tussia-Cohen about the wager.

"Pay no attention to it," he said, not wanting me to suffer further if the ruling went against me. "He doesn't know any more than you."

But he did know. The three judges, to silence their own consciences, reduced my sentence by two years. I now had a sentence of ten years, four of which I had already served. They had rejected my appeal on the grounds that the credibility that the district court had bestowed upon the prosecution's witnesses could not be questioned.

But there were compensations. Not only had the High Court given me back two years of my life, but it had established the irrevocable fact that the prosecution in my trial had not proven that I had caused any harm to Israel, even though I had been convicted of possessing highly secret documents. Their pointing out my "heroic past" in service to the State, along with the sentence reduction, meant in legal terms that my reputation was restored to me, a reputation that some had calculatedly and systematically sought to destroy.

But my anger was not appeased. I didn't give a damn about their heaping praise upon me while still upholding a framing. I wanted my freedom; nothing else would suffice.

Headlines about the Third Man appeared again in the newspapers, even though the details of my appeal had been kept secret. This was actually a turning point. Until this decision I had not always been optimistic: to be looked upon as the most vicious and treacherous of men was hard to bear. The idea of putting this ordeal of mine to an end had occurred to me quite often. For one thing it would have brought an unbiased public inquiry in its wake. But of what use would a post-mortem rehabilitation of my reputation have been? Those who needed me and believed in me wanted me alive.

It is true that life becomes a habit and goes on (perhaps therein lies salvation?). Until this point, all my letters had ended with some sort of banner flying, however ragged. But there were moments when life seemed to me a void.

When Arye Nir, a former high-ranking police officer, was appointed commissioner of prisons after a mass escape from Shatta, he imposed stringent security measures. We clashed openly. The first collision came when the commissioner, though a pipe smoker himself, banned all pipes from prison cells. Life in Ramla was terrible at best, but without my pipe it would be unbearable. Refusing to bend, I approached the Supreme Court with a writ of mandamus, and the three judges (among them Justice Agranat, the pipe smoker) ruled in my favor.

The next clash regarded both my incoming and outgoing mail, which took three to four weeks to reach its destination because of Shin-Beth censorship. I decided to go the unorthodox route—smuggling. One day, however, a fellow inmate conveyed a warning from Commissioner Nir that steps would be taken to restrain me from further smuggling. In defiance, I wrote the following:

Subject: Mail

Thanks for the fair warning!
Enclosed herewith are all the copies of letters I have sent out through irregular channels.
Please do not interpret this step wrongly. The enclosure of the copies is not a show-off or mockery, but only proof that the term "fairness" is not a stranger to me, and that the trust between us is mutual.
By reading these letters you will convince yourself that their contents do not necessitate circumvention of censorship. The use of unorthodox ways is the result of the long delays and my inability to overcome torture of this sort in the established prison way.

all honour due
(signed)

Two weeks later, through the grapevine, I heard of plans for my transfer to Shatta Prison, notorious for its harsh conditions. At seven in the morning on March 25, 1961, I was given twenty minutes to pack.
Ramla's Warden Jogev, outstanding in the history of Israeli prisons, explained that the commissioner had been blamed by the Shin-Beth for not keeping me isolated from the outside world. But, angry as I was, I fired off another letter to the commissioner:

A few minutes ago I was informed about your decision to transfer me to the Shatta Prison.
I can merely say that it is very painful to me, finding out that those who claimed what they had been claiming about Commissioner Nir, the man, were justified, having proven to my face that my assessment of you was basically wrong.
I believed that a man who is carrying that special insignia on his collar (the insignia of a sword with olive branches given to those who held officer's rank in the underground movement) would know to raise himself above routine things, would show the understanding and tolerance which are integral to the principles of leadership.

Fairness in your mouth, Mr. Nir, was only a phrase, nothing else. And for this I am disappointed.

(signed)

I found Shatta Prison to be a heat box set squarely in the middle of the Yesrael Valley, if possible more primitive than Ramla and without question more degrading. The first thing I did there was to smuggle a letter to Commissioner Nir, informing him that Shatta was even easier in this particular respect. After undergoing dental treatment, which, oddly enough, was superior to that received in Ramla, I was immediately ordered back to Ramla.

I gradually adjusted to prison restrictions. As a result of studying journalism and economics through a British university correspondence course, I became instrumental in making changes both in prison life and in the penal code.

Aided by other inmates, I wrote a few plays, headed the dramatic circle, and acted in the performances. The main reason for this was to gain access to the outside world, especially to journalists. Most of the plays had messages: I wanted to show the public that the convict is not some dread creature, but a man with the same needs and feelings as free men. But the stage also gave me the opportunity to settle some personal accounts and to criticize stupid regulations in a humorous way without really offending anyone. Many obsolete regulations were changed as a result. One of the reviews published by *The Jerusalem Post* read: "It was a show in more ways than one. On the stage was a central figure in the Lavon affair. They made superb actors—witty, natural, and eloquent. In a series of sketches, they made fun of restrictive prison regulations, of the food, and of the resident doctor, who did everything but cure them. . . ."

Thanks to the newly appointed warden, Jogev, prison life gradually improved.

One day I read beneath the headlines in one of the leading dailies:

Charge of Perjury to Be Lodged Against the Reserve Officer

In the wake of the Third Man's decision and a demand that the reserve officer "Motke" should face trial for perjury, the Lavon affair might occupy the public's mind again.

Members of the Third Man's family who had counsel with men of jurisprudence in this matter decided on this step after the verdict of the appeal court—which reduced the penalty to 10 years—was handed down.

337

Members of the family are basing their actions on the judges' findings as well as those of a military inquiry which had been presided over by a justice of the Supreme Court. Both bodies indicated the fact that the Reserve Officer had been suborned to give false testimony in the trial of the Third Man.

In spite of the reply of the chief prosecutor of the State that "It was not in the public's interest to put (Motke) on trial," my sister and her husband ended their campaign only when I demanded that they do so. My decision was due to Motke's appeal: "Why does Avri want me behind bars? Isn't it enough that he's there and his life is destroyed?" Motke was right. One victim *was* enough.

The summer of 1962 passed.

I encountered many more restrictions than did any other inmate, (no leaves of absence, for example), but I did not hold it against the prison authorities; they had their orders. What made life bearable was the relationship between the staff and the inmates that probably can only be found in an Israeli prison; perhaps it can be explained as the Jewish soul and Jewish nature. For instance, when it was learned that the wife of the officer in charge of the security wing had to undergo open-heart surgery, nearly all of the inmates volunteered to donate blood. Two years later the same need arose again; again everybody donated; but Captain Avidan's wife died. The entire ward went silent in mourning.

I was proud of the prison achievements to which I had contributed: Ramla now had excellent basketball and volleyball teams, courses in music and in biblical studies; lectures; a good library; a canteen; three movies a month; and personal appearances by entertainers.

I was especially proud of the Braille shop I had founded. We transcribed scores of books from Hebrew and English, among them the first Braille version of the Bible in Hebrew. For blind children from an institute in Jerusalem, we organized a campaign throughout Israel, collecting about twenty-five thousand Israeli lira. Later in Ramla's new print shop, I began printing the protocols of the parliament on the linotype.

The breakthrough in my relationship with the hard-boiled convicts came when the commissioner tried to convince me to become a narcotics informer. I saw his proposition as an insult. "I am fighting against the use of narcotics in my own way, by bringing the men down to the basketball court, by engaging them in productive activities. An inmate who is occupied and tired," I held, "is most likely to fall on his bunk to sleep, not to look for an escape in narcotic dreams."

Grapevine spread my answer throughout the prison, and one day, when special police were brought in to search for narcotics, I was entrusted with a heavy quantity of hashish. I accepted it only on the condition that I could dispose of it permanently. No narcotics were discovered and I informed the warden that I had destroyed them. No action was taken against me.

During my ten years in prison, there were many such struggles for the basic rights of the convicts. Once I even approached the Supreme Court for a decision on whether a convict was entitled to vote. The answer was *yes*.

But life behind bars, no matter how improved, was unacceptable to me. I wanted a new trial; therefore I had to study the records of my old one. Blocked by the Shin-Beth, I approached the Supreme Court and received a favorable decision. But there were security regulations: The member of the Shin-Beth assigned to sit beside me while I was reading the records was none other than the one who acted as Justice Sussmann's legal secretary during my appeal.

In any event, I lacked financial means to take legal steps, as well as lines of communication with the outside world. Only eight people were allowed to visit me; everyone else had to apply for permission from the Shin-Beth. However, I was nearing the end of two-thirds of my sentence, and I was entitled to parole. That prospect kept me going. Still, I feared that my case would be viewed as exceptional. My appearance before the parole board on August 14, 1964, proved me correct.

A few days before my review, I sneaked a glance at the warden's desk and saw a list of names on his calendar. Mine was crossed out with a red pencil. Warden Turgeman's answers were evasive, so I prepared to do battle.

Deputy-Prosecutor of the State Gabriel Bach, who had assisted in Eichmann's prosecution, was to present the government's case. His presence meant one thing: a guarantee of my continued confinement. When I saw who was to preside—Justice Asulai, a nasty old crank disliked even by his own staff—my last shred of hope disappeared. Asulai and I had once had a sharp encounter following his address to a Ramla audience.

"What do you have to say for yourself?" Justice Asulai wheezed. He remembered me well; it was evident in his glare.

Looking away and biting my tongue so as not to explode, I said softly, "My prison record is known to you. I haven't come to talk, only to listen."

For a moment Justice Asulai was perplexed; then he turned to Gabriel Bach, asking him the opinion of the State. Bach presented his position with enthusiasm: My crime had been severe, and therefore I should serve all my term. "Furthermore," he said, "a man of his vast knowledge about the inner workings of our security system, embittered as he is, constitutes a risk to our national security." When he described me as an acrobat of brains, I shot out of my seat. "Beside you, Mr. Bach, I am a dwarf."

A shouting match ensued, and when it died down I demanded my right to respond. I proclaimed that the board's decision, according to the law ("Don't tell me what the law is!" yelled Justice Asulai) should be based solely on three factors: my past, my prison behavior, and my potential for rehabiliation. Thus the nature of my conviction had nothing whatsoever to do with it. The district court had imposed upon me the term befitting my alleged crime, the High Court of Appeals had concurred, minus two years, and neither had denied my right to parole.

"It is not the duty, nor is it within the jurisdiction of this board, to deal a second time with my conviction. This is not a trial!" I declared. I denigrated as outright idiocy Bach's feeble warning about the danger I represented to security. "Keeping me in prison another three years would definitely not make me less bitter," I said. "I have proven many times over that no prison wall is able to keep me completely isolated; if I really wished to use the knowledge I have to harm our security, I could have done it long ago. It follows that there is only one solution to Mr. Bach's assertion—the grave!"

I reserved my anger and disgust for the last. To a somewhat shocked board, I said, "I know you are only playing the second fiddle, but I appeal to you to marshal the guts to stand up and judge me as you would without adherence to an outside script."

Justice Asulai's face went crimson. I was led outside while they reached their decision. It came quickly. "We have decided to reject your appeal for parole for reasons we will forward to you in writing."

I was no longer angry, just numb. As I explained to Warden Turgeman, "It wouldn't have hurt so much if I had not seen—with my own eyes— three convicted Arab terrorists, who had crossed the border to kill everyone in their path, receiving parole just ahead of me. They have more rights in my country than I."

"What are you going to do?" the warden asked cautiously.

"I am going on a hunger strike."

He looked at me curiously, then smiled. "What good will it do you? Nobody will know about it."

Laying my cards on the table, I answered him. "I am aware that without publicity, the effect will amount to a big fat zero; and because of that, I have made arrangements to keep the public informed."

Warden Turgeman stiffened. "We will take special precautions!"

"This, too, I have taken into account."

On the following morning I informed the officer on duty that I was declaring a hunger strike; I was immediately taken to the dungeon and moved into a special cell with a round-the-clock guard. But communication with other inmates, and through them with the outside world, worked fine. The next day the largest newspaper ran banner headlines: "The Third Man Opens Hunger Strike." The story soon reached the *London Times* and the *New York Times*.

I refused even water. On the fourth day the prison doctor paid a call on a weakened, dizzy rebel. "You're taking this strike in order to live, aren't you?" he said somewhat condescendingly. "That being the case, why deny yourself water? Your kidneys won't last without it."

It was certainly a valid argument, new to me. All the papers in the country were now dealing with my strike; I was kept informed through the grapevine.

After the fifth day I was fed by force. Through a tube, a concoction of eggs, butter, milk, sugar, and vitamins was rushed into my stomach.

On the ninth day I had a visitor. Esrach More was adjutant to the minister of police and an old friend of mine from the Haganah days. With tears in his eyes, he pleaded with me to give up my rebellion. I knew that his position was too sensitive for him to have come without a reason other than friendship. I was right. Late in the evening the warden entered the dungeon and brought with him the barber to have me shaved. In reply to my question, he told me that somebody was coming to see me.

At about 9:00 P.M. I was led to the warden's office. I recognized immediately Shmuel Tamir, a well-known lawyer with high political aspirations and a member of Herut, the right-wing opposition party to Ben-Gurion's Labor. When the warden left the room, Tamir explained to me that Amnon Dror, my journalist friend who had been contracted first to write Ben-Gurion's warped version of the Lavon affair, had persuaded him to take up my battle. I relaxed my vigil. Still there was something screwy about it; Amnon Dror belonged to the ruling Labor party. But I didn't care. I would have welcomed almost anyone joining me in my fight to regain freedom.

Using my sister as leverage, Tamir tried to pry open my mouth. Seeing he was getting nowhere, he upped the ante by telling me that the attorney general's office had told him that my demands would be considered. Tamir further agreed that my idea of a public inquiry was workable, and he promised to see the prime minister, Levi Eshkol, on my behalf. "But first," he said, "you have to terminate your strike."

I considered for only a moment. If things didn't work out, I could always resume it. I consented, and he promised to return the following day. When he had gone, the warden ushered my sister into the room. We embraced. Ruth was crying as I had never seen her cry. When she left, I was taken to the prison hospital and given my first semisolid food. I had lost twenty-two pounds in ten days.

When I had given Tamir the power of attorney so that he could study the secret protocol from my trial, he exclaimed, "My God! It is so clear that Isser Harel lied. Why has nothing been done about it?"

Part of our early strategy to bring about a new trial was to sue Ben-Gurion and his writer, Chaggai Eshed, for libel because they had claimed that I had ordered the sabotage action in Egypt. Tamir called the *Maariv* newspaper and within two hours, it was a front-page headline. I followed up with a letter to Prime Minister Eshkol, stating that I had kept quiet because the security of the State and Zahal were still close to my heart, and requesting that he see either my family or my counsel, who could explain the true circumstances.

Then, for reasons still unclear to me, Tamir began to drag his feet. He lulled me with words of strategy, while delaying the lawsuit. At first he said that financing was the problem. I informed him that as a convict without financial means, I could lodge the suit without having a cent.

His actual reason for stalling became clearer to me later. Lodging the suit would have made the Lavon affair sub judice, and Tamir wanted it aimed at the next Labor convention, to benefit the Herut. He had put his party interests above those of his client; to this day I can find no other reason for his actions. Shmuel Tamir's personal withdrawal from my case was disappointing. He had entered like a tiger and left like a pussycat!

A year before I appealed to the parole board, Isser Harel announced his resignation as the memune. The truth was that Isser was "resigned" by Ben-Gurion, who had at last realized that he was carrying out his own programs behind Ben-Gurion's back. General Meir Amit, whom I had known from the regimental commander course, replaced him. I learned that Aharoni had left along with Isser; but as long as the security service was still infested with Isser's men, I saw no sense in approaching Meir Amit.

At the beginning of 1965, I was visited by Mrs. Rosa Jochmann, member of the Austrian Parliament and chairwoman of the socialistic organization of freedom fighters and Nazi victims. Being an old friend of Father and Olga, she was asked by the latter to inquire, as a member of the International League for Human Rights in Israel, why I had not been granted parole. Although she was an official guest of the State, it took much pressure before she was allowed to visit me. One condition was set: The reason for my detention should not be discussed.

Deeply touched by her visit, I convinced her that I was broken neither in spirit nor in body. We discussed both Father's reaction to imprisonment and hers—under the Fascist Austrian regime and under the Nazis. Her visit was like some sort of other-world greeting from Father. I knew that I had acted behind bars as he would have.

But nothing changed even though, every second week, Tamir sent one of his young lawyers to ask more questions.

It was Seder eve, Passover, 1965. My mood matched the event. I sat down and wrote.

At this very hour, the traditional Seder is being celebrated in every Jewish home throughout the world, commemorating the "passing over" of the houses of Israel, when the Egyptians were smitten with the death of the firstborn. At this very hour, the story of our Exodus is being read from the Haggadah and stress is laid on the passage:

"I am the Lord thy God which brought thee out of the land of Egypt, out of the house of bondage. From slavery to freedom!"

Oh, Irony of Fate! I, who had my own personal Exodus from Egypt—not from ancient Egypt, but from Nasser's—have been deprived of my freedom in the Promised Land. If I had known then what I have learned during the last few years, I would not have fled Nasser's myrimidons by the skin of my teeth. I know for certain what my fate would have been: the gallows. Yet, would it not have been preferable to being tagged as turncoat and branded as traitor? Parks, synagogues, streets, and public places would have been named in my name, in memory of a "knight" who was without fear and reproach.

Instead, those whom I thought my betters have buried me alive. Exaggeration? What else can life without freedom be compared to, if not death? Is a human being without a soul human? I am bitter? If that is the proper term, so I am. I have grown bitter, gradually, step by step, hour after hour, day after day. I have learned what I never thought I was capable of—to hate. To hate with a cold, fierce, raging hate.

"Tell it not in Gad, publish it not in the streets of Ashkalon. Lest the daughters of the Philistines rejoice, lest the daughters of the uncircumcised triumph."

The foe has sentenced me to death!
My people are the executioners!

Justice H. Cohen of the Supreme Court, and the former attorney general, visited the prison and advised me to approach the president of the

State. I explained that, without Shin-Beth consent, the president had nothing to say in my case. Pointing out the change in the chairmanship of the security services, Justice Cohen promised that he would arrange a meeting between me and General Meir Amit.

The commissioner of prisons, now a supporter of my struggle for freedom, also urged me to ask for an interview with the general. So I wrote the following:

Subject: personal interview

The commissioner of prisons has informed me this morning about your willingness to confer with me, and asked me to put in writing the essence of matters I would like to discuss with you. Here, in a few lines, is their nature: the aim of my meeting with you is to find the middle way which shall answer the security requests on the one hand and my goal—namely, my freedom—on the other.

I have learned to know hitherto that publicity is no help in my struggle for freedom, and therefore I am trying to exploit all the other ways which might bring about my release.

It is quite clear to me that first of all I have to find a common language with you, as you are the head of the framework that brought me to this place. I hope that you will receive me as early as possible.

(Signed)

On September 30, 1965, I was visited by Mr. Dagani, who introduced himself as deputy to the head of the Shin-Beth. The conversation boiled down to one thing: The Shin-Beth was still of the opinion that I was withholding details with regard to both the Egyptian debacle and Osman Nouri. What truly aggravated me was his cynical remark: "We have all the time in the world to find out the truth."

A month later my old interrogator Chayim Victor Cohen, asked me to explain to him certain passages in the "forged" diary. I tried my best, but after twelve years it was impossible to recall all the code words. Chayim wanted me to sign the notes he took, and his behavior was that of an inquisitor. To hell with it. Whatever I tried was in vain. I had even lost contact with Tamir, for reasons only he knew.

On January 1, 1966, I renewed my hunger strike, and again the press supported me in my struggle. The following day Uri Avneri introduced an urgent question to the Knesset's agenda concerning my release. On the fourth day of the hunger strike, one of Tamir's aides, a lawyer named Hacohen, came to try his luck. I gave him my only condition. I wanted a date for my release.

The day after, I was informed by Hacohen that within two months I would be told the day of my release. I terminated my strike.

(When I had begun it, my fellow inmates wanted to declare a hunger strike in solidarity with me; I asked them not to. Yet it was good to know that I was not alone.)

A few days later the warden informed me that Uri Avneri had demanded to visit me; as a Knesset member he could not be refused. Hacohen, in the name of Tamir, asked me not to receive him. But Uri Avneri was one of the very few who had stood by my side from the very beginning; he had not been afraid to print my smuggled-out articles and letters in his magazine.

Uri appeared, accompanied by Kipnis, a member of the Shin-Beth, and we discussed steps to be taken. On the same day it became obvious to me that our conversation had been taped: Tamir called the warden, saying that he was pleased with the way I had handled the meeting. Tamir also told me that the interrogation with Chayim would continue. *Interrogation?*

When I next saw Tamir, he informed me about a meeting he had had with a senior official whose name he was unwilling to give me. "They still have their suspicions," he said, adding that Uri Avneri would try to bring my case before the Knesset Committee for Security and Foreign Affairs because the subject could not be dealt with in an open session. He seemed evasive and tired of dealing with my case.

Chayim, on the other hand said that the questioning was only for clarification. I agreed that future meetings should be recorded on tape to speed up the process.

Not long before, I had asked to be returned to Shatta Prison for more dental treatment. My request was denied, I was informed, because Lt. Col. Israel Beer was imprisoned in Shatta. For reasons known only to the security service, we were forbidden to meet; but Beer had sent me a message saying that a meeting was essential. He had said, "If I tell you what I know about your case, we can topple the cabinet a third time." When I informed the commissioner that I would approach the Supreme Court if I did not receive proper dental treatment, I was told that arrangements would be made to bring Beer to Ramla while I was being transferred to Shatta.

One morning I was taken there in the prison's ambulance, a two-hour drive. Two guards accompanied me, and on our way we picked up Dr. Chiya, the head of prison medical service, who had voted against my parole. He seemed rather uncomfortable. Suddenly he turned around and said, "Avraham, don't hold it against me. I belong to a governmental service." Indeed, I understood.

On our arrival I learned that Israel Beer had died early in the morning of a heart attack. It was May 1, 1966. When told that he was being transferred so that we would not meet, he had become upset and collapsed in the guardroom. My trip had been in vain; I never learned what Beer had wanted to tell me. I was given his bunk; maybe someone figured I might also have a heart attack if I slept in his place.

A Mr. Grossmann, attorney-at-law, came to see me; Tamir had asked him to take over my case. I liked him and told him I wanted to proceed with my libel suit against Ben-Gurion. When I asked to be returned to Ramla, it took some persuasion. I faked heart discomfort, knowing that only Ramla had the necessary facilities. When I returned in mid-June of 1966, it was like coming home.

During all the years in prison, I had encountered many provocations, but I was never able to find out what authorities were behind them—until one day a common crook by the name of Dan Israeli, who had been transferred to Ramla, offered himself as a go-between for the French military attaché and me. After several conversations with him, I wrote an urgent note to Chayim Victor.

> *Shalom* Chayim!
>
> Yesterday one of the local lodgers asked me to confer with him in private, telling me that it would be to my advantage. Here is the essence of the story he told me.
>
> In Europe (a relatively short while ago) he was in close contact with certain organizations belonging to a Western power (I surmise these were intelligence organizations), and these bodies were very interested in everything concerning my humble person. The representative of one organization is serving now as military attaché in Israel (name and rank mentioned here) and, according to the inmate, the "Power" would act to regain my freedom if I would be willing to fulfill certain conditions.
>
> In light of the inmate's knowledge with regard to inside details, I found it my duty to inform you about it and ask you how to conduct myself.

I felt it necessary to inform the Shin-Beth. If he was a provocateur, I had to inform them, because not doing so could be labeled an offense. The result, a couple more years behind bars. If the approach was genuine (he *was* of French origin and a newcomer to the country), it was certainly my duty to inform the security services. If he was doing something on his own initiative *for me for his own benefit,* he should certainly learn his lesson *through* me.

346

There was no reply, but through the warden I got a member of the Shin-Beth to come to the prison. I was informed that the fellow was not a provocateur and that they would question him. They never did—but we did. As a result, he got a "blanket parade"; a blanket was thrown over him and he was beaten by a couple of inmates. Immediately after this, he disappeared from prison and, to the best of my knowledge, from the Israeli scene.

Isser Harel had served for a while as adviser on security affairs to Premier Levi Eshkol; soon friction ensued among Isser, the premier, and General Amit—now the head of all intelligence and security services. It was reported in the news media.

At that time I wrote a second letter to the premier, asking the commissioner to forward it directly, not through channels. Instead he promised to deliver it to General Amit. The general, knowing that the letter would otherwise never be delivered, allowed the commissioner to convey it directly to the prime minister.

In public print Ben-Gurion himself had made most of the points that I enumerated in my letter. Using his own words I pointed out to Eskol that a nation that does not give full consideration to justice for every individual is striking at the very foundations of its existence. I then reminded him of the universal rights stated in the declaration scrolls of the United Nations. I went on:

> Any deviation from this principle, the principle of equality and freedom, brings up the question . . . Who is to decide who is less or more worthy than another? . . .
>
> In my case, from the very beginning to the end, one man took upon himself the right to decide my fate, a man who himself should be upright and honest. Because he headed a national framework of supreme importance to the security of the State . . . his testimony in court was accepted without question by the judges. . . .
>
> The attitude of the Mossad's past chairman was, from the very beginning, full of blind hatred. And it was Isser's hatred that prevented my early release from prison, an elementary right that is given to every convict. . . .
>
> The question asked is WHY . . . Was it because of professional jealousy? For even *he* couldn't minimize in court my achievements in the fields in which I had operated. Or is there something else hidden behind this "persecution," something else that could only become known to me through my contacts and movements in enemy land? And true! Twelve years ago I voiced my grave suspicion before my superiors in Zahal, a suspicion which from time to time received more support. How otherwise can one explain the conduct

of the former Memune, who had often declared in front of other people, "I will do all to keep him in the cooler as long as I can"?

Furthermore, men of jurisprudence, renown, and public standing, who have seen the records of the district court, wondered how Isser's testimony was accepted by that court when it is obvious that only lies and falsehood were in his mouth. . . .

After a few more lines, I concluded the letter:

I am well aware that what I have claimed is of a grave and heavy nature. But all I write can stand up to examination and the probe for the truth. It is in your hands to grant me my freedom and allow me to return to my family and to take my place in the nation's framework.

Avri Seidenwerg

The only reply I received was from the prime minister's military aide, who informed me that my letter had been read with deep interest. At the same time I wrote a letter to Yigal Allon, then minister of labor, asking for his help.

At the beginning of 1967 the parole board again rejected my appeal.

I went to the Supreme Court. (I had not done so before, for one simple reason: Rejection would have automatically closed off any other legal move.) Now I claimed discrimination: The parole board had taken upon itself the authority of the court, whereas the High Court of Appeal had considered my case and no *other* body could deal with it again.

I was brought by a police sergeant to the chambers of Justice S. Agranat, who had become the president of the Supreme Court. He was to see if there was legal ground for accepting my request for a writ of mandamus.

"Avri," he said, thoughtfully sucking on his pipe, "you have to look upon your case in a more philosophical way. . . ."

I was flabbergasted; even my guard was stunned. I stammered, "But Honorable President, aren't we a State of law?"

A sad but bemused smile flickered around his mouth, and then he added, "You have to realize, the moment the term 'national security' is introduced, the law has to step aside." It was a hard fact to digest, but Agranat was right. When he promised me that if I were not released at the end of my term I could approach the Supreme Court for "legal support," I withdrew my request for a writ of mandamus.

The international political situation had now become tense, and it seemed evident to me that war was unavoidable. On May 23, 1967, I wrote the following.

> To the Chairmen of the Intelligence and Security Services via the Warden of Ramla Prison.
> *Shalom* to General M. Amit!
> I am well aware of the dangers of the interpretations which may accompany this appeal, yet I do believe that you will not doubt the honesty of my request.
> I will not use many words but only say that at this very hour my place is with one of the combat units. I give you my word that upon ending my service, I will return to the prison.
>
> > Respectfully,
> > (Signed)

I sent a nearly identical note to Yigal Allon, but he received it only after the Six Day War was over.

Within the prison the Arab population became openly patriotic. Fearing that the outbreak of war would bring about violence behind the walls, and knowing that it would take at least five to nine minutes until the guards could come to our aid, I organized the Jewish minority in our ward for self-defense. We had prepared weapons and organized lookouts, and we were ready when the war broke out. The warden asked me to help him put the prison on a war footing. Listening to the radio was one of the hardest things in life I had ever done. I cried silently when I heard the song, "Jerusalem the Golden," after the parachute brigade had broken into the old city and the Israeli flag was raised over the wailing wall. The inmates were, for once, one soul and body, and my appeal for donating blood was answered by everyone, even many Arabs. This was all we could contribute—our blood.

The war was over then, and, learning that we had about five thousand Egyptian prisoners, among them high-ranking officers, I wrote to Yigal Allon begging him that this time no Egyptian soldier should be exchanged if our people (those behind prison walls in Egypt and whom I had commanded) were not freed. And he remained steadfast against heavy pressure from the families of our captured pilots and frogmen. I believe that, thanks to Yigal's stand, Levy, Nathanson, Dassa, and Marcelle Ninio finally reached Israel.

I was not included in the amnesty that followed (it did not cover security offenders), but there were indications that I might be released at the end of my term. My sister and her husband were pessimistic and tried to prepare me for heartbreak, but I had inside information that fortified me. I was certain when I was asked to sign a statement that I would keep silent. I agreed, on one condition—which was added to the statement: I would keep silent as long as no one else published anything about me.

My final days in prison were bristling with activity. We mounted another play that ran for eight evenings before an audience of outside guests. The *Maariv* described my last days at Ramla in a review of *The Three Angels:*

> The Third Man, whose name is not allowed to be published, is going to be released today from the prison. . . .
> The eve of his release was moving to the heart. The tall and handsome man went through the same process so well known to other convicts who have spent a long time behind the bars; the anxiety of what is waiting for them outside. He was ten years in the prison which had become his home and where others provided him with his daily needs. Now, the test of independence and responsibility is awaiting him outside the walls.
> The Third Man was the leading figure and active spirit among the inmates. He was one of those convicts who used his time behind the bars. . . . But his courage, which gave him the respectful position of natural leadership among the inmates, is accompanying him into the outside world.

The following day the warden was forced to use subterfuge to avoid the many reporters gathering outside the gate. The usual hour for release was 11:00 A.M., but I was kept until 3:00 P.M., when I was called to the warden's office. My close friend Yehuda Fried, a major in the reserve and one who had stood beside me all those years, was there to drive me. After an hour I was given the release, and we drove away through the rear exit. Standing there, flowers in hand, were two of my former inmates who had been released in the wake of the amnesty. Reporters could be fooled, but not my friends.

I didn't say goodbye to anyone in the prison, for I had promised to be back in two days for the last time on stage. (Invitations had been sent out before it was known when I would be released.) When the play was over and we parted, we all cried—inmates, guards, and I.

It was past midnight when I drove back to Tel Aviv and my sister's house, but the inmates' shouts coming through the thick concrete walls were still echoing in my ears.

"*Behazlacha*, be blessed, and don't forget us." I never will.

Chapter 28

The outskirts of Tel Aviv, Afeka. My sister's house hummed with activity. From all over the country, friends, relatives, well-wishers had come to congratulate me on being free again. The house swelled at the seams.

The doorbell rang again. I looked across the room. Dalia, a beautiful girl with whom I had struck up a close friendship when she had attended one of our performances in prison, stood at the threshold. I made my way through the crowded room.

"Come with me," she said, drawing me outside.

"Where?" I asked. "Look at all these people. I can't leave."

"You'll be back soon," she said. Smiling, she added, "Don't worry, I'm not kidnapping you. Come on, get in the car."

The night was pitch black; I could hardly make out where we were driving. But this was not just because of darkness: During the last ten years, new roads and new towns had come into existence, making me a stranger.

A slight rain that had started at dusk now pattered steadily against the windshield. In the glow of the dash I watched Dalia expertly handle the car on the slippery road gleaming under the headlights. She was young, but very much a woman. Her letters had helped me through dark periods behind the walls. I felt a renewed surge of appreciation as she brought the car to a sudden stop and turned to me.

"Get out and go down the stairs," she said.

She stayed in the car. At the bottom of the stairs I found myself standing on the sandy beach, the Mediterranean reaching out in front of me.

Then I remembered. In one of her first letters, Dalia had asked what I would like to do first on the day of my release. I had written, "To soak in a bathtub filled to the brim with hot water. And see the sea again. To see the sea. And watch the incoming waves, and hear them breaking against the shore."

Dalia had remembered. Without a word, she had made my second wish come true, to have my fill of the sea.

Through the now gently falling drizzle, the Mediterranean somehow seemed to pick up soft light from the sky. My eyes traveled across it. The sea was quiet, lines of foam advancing on the shore. Far out on the horizon a small light slowly moved south toward Egypt. Probably a boat patrolling our coast, guarding the nation's security.

The nation's security! It had been my life. I suddenly recalled the words of Yigal Allon, then the commander of the Palmach: "Sometimes single fighters are sent out on dangerous missions far away from the controlling eye of headquarters. The question is 'What is there in the routine discipline which commands men to carry out these missions endangering their lives, when they could save themselves by simply evading it?' Who could fault their justifying 'not carrying out the order,' for countless reasons? Now. Is there, *in the formal discipline,* enough to compel men to throw away their lives?"

Yigal knew the answer, and so did all the men in the Palmach. There is nothing, *absolutely nothing,* in the formal discipline that would make a man stand up and give his life if the need arose.

Only discipline that comes from within—the belief, the perception, the adherence to a goal, the tradition of being the first (call it pioneering), and the bonds of fighting men, in short, the heritage of the Palmach—can make a man walk to his death with open eyes. This heritage had guided my deeds and steps in the past, and I was proud of it. Yet somewhere I had failed. I knew now where.

My final guilt was in accepting the saying that the end sanctifies the means. I should have learned the lessons of history. Means have a way of becoming independent and insular, and they become ends in themselves. I should have been aware that for some of those who had reached the peak of power after long struggles, only a single end remained of all those preached and heralded on the way up: to retain power, even by use of the "justifiable" means through which they had achieved it.

My thoughts had made me suddenly cold. Had I become bitter toward my country, or was it the drizzling rain that made me shudder? No, I loved my country too much. My country was much more than Ben-Gurion, Dayan, Isser, Gibli, and all the rest.

It was the road to Jerusalem, the Palmach cemetery in Kiryat Anavim, the man in the streets of Tel Aviv, the memories of my youth, the plowed fields in the south. *This* was my country—not the people who had put me behind bars.

My mind swept back to my coming to Israel. Rejected by the land of my birth, restricted and repressed during those uncritical years of my life, I had found the home for my heart. My heart was free, free to give, to express whatever I chose. Ours was an unabashed love affair—I loved Israel. I had found what my father had fought for all his life, and never found: the closest thing to a true democracy I could envision.

Like all lovers I chose to protect what I loved and to revel in this spirit, this blinding, absorbing emotion. Freedom for one meant freedom for all. Out of the many came one. I chose to protect it, to preserve it.

I joined Zahal—the most democratic, the most unregimented army in the history of the world. We would flourish and survive for the good of Israel.

The glow of the memory engulfed me. I felt warmed despite the drizzling mist, despite the December chill rolling in over the darkened Mediterranean. Remembering what Zahal had meant to us made me feel as powerful as the sea. And yet, in actuality, we had been as vulnerable as the lone coastal boat out there.

My thoughts came and went unmarshaled, making their ambience known and then moving on, replaced by one memory after another. So much had happened. Like the small waves reaching for my feet in the sand and then falling back, so came my thoughts: Zahal—and the good feeling of pride, until Lublini and the abandoned Arab refrigerator. Zahal—a monolith to which I gave tribute with the naivete of youth and the trust of one lost in the joy of brotherhood. Then the court-martial, bringing me down. My euphoria vanished.

The freedom that was now mine was too new, too hard-won to replace the indignity and outrage I had felt in the past ten years. Strangely though, I sensed no impulsive need to act, no sense whatever of exigency.

The recurring, unresisted, unhurried waves of thought continued: My success in Unit 131, easing the disgrace of my court-martial; success all the way to Cairo and Alexandria; then the calamity of our sabotage action.

My pulse quickened and held at the memory. There was no panic now in that pulse; that was a lifetime ago for many of us. But it was not a lifetime ago for Israel. It lived on like a cancer that neither healed nor destroyed.

Places and faces came and went in my mind, outracing the tempo of the incoming waves. From Azar forward, from Azar backward. So many faces. And when they had all come and gone, one face returned and remained: Lavon.

It was suddenly clear to me that the great deceiver had been time. For reality is not history; reality is *now*. For ten years I had been caged, denied access to the community of brotherhood that could have freed my spirit, if not my body. And every day of those years I had fought to retain that last vestige of euphoria that had been *my* Israel. Israel was not a land; it was a spirit. That was the reality then; I could not be certain now. So much had happened; so much ugliness had crept into the Dream.

Lavon. How did he feel now? Did he remember the Dream?

Had I, being in the center of events that crucified him, stolen his adopted birthright? At first I had acted against him unwittingly . . . and, later, knowingly. The fact that I had acted upon a lie apparently mattered not at all, then. I had acted. I had aided and abetted. For the good of Israel—but not really.

Lavon: a spiteful man, an irritable man, a vengeful man, from all accounts. Perhaps. But a brilliant man; heroic, according to his record. For the good of Israel, above all, for the good of Israel—though so many doubted him. Even worse than jailing him, I had helped to crucify him. His torture had not ended; it could not end. He was a sick man, his mind and spirit broken. He was now an old warrior without punch. His time had come, but he had no freedom, nor did Israel, nor I. The reality of the past was now, just as it had been then. . . .

I remembered Dalia waiting in the car. I moved across the beach. The strength in my legs was solid, like that of my being. I breathed deeply. The freedom of my body felt good, almost powerful; but it would not last, I knew, without freedom of spirit.

At the foot of the dune, I turned and looked back at the sea. Under the steady mist was its placid surface. As the sea had communion with the sky and the rain after every turbulence, I realized that I had not lost forever my intimacy with my country. Despite all of the ugly past, I wanted to recapture that spiritual union I had known and lost. I felt a part of it. Israel.

My pace quickened as I walked toward the car.

Index

355

Curriculum vitae, 26
Czechoslovakia, 92, 104, 170, 245
arms deal, 73
intelligence service, 331
Czechs, v, 104

Dachau, 16, 32
Dagan, Avigdor, 171, 218
Dagani, 344
Dalia, P., 351-52, 354
Damascus, 23
Dar, Avraham (alias John Darling), 4-8, 119, 125, 128-29, 168, 172, 179, 182-83, 190, 198, 210-11, 215, 236, 324
Darmstadt, 47, 55
Dassa, Reuben (Rogger), 129-31, 138, 141, 147-48, 151-52, 155-56, 194, 206, 211-13, 349
Dayan, Moshe, 120, 181-83, 185-86, 189, 192-93, 196-99, 201-03, 205-09, 213-14, 217, 223-24, 230-31, 240, 244, 271, 273, 312-13, 316, 318-21, 323-24, 327, 352
De Bouche, Col., 79, 81
Degener, Dr. Albert, 82
De Hass, 72-74, 86-94
De Lavison, Count, 101, 110-13, 127, 141-42, 154, 165
Department Eight, 28, 33, 45, 164-65, 199, 208, 209, 253, 291, 313, 323
Department Five (Mussa), 314
Department of Manpower, 20
Derna, 103
Deutsch Eilau (Germany), 14
Deutsche Reichspartei, 60
Deutsche Soldaten Zeitung, 49
Devar, 320, 327
District Court, 266-67, 321-22, 328, 340
Dolfi, 48, 56
Dori, Jacob (Board of Inquiry), 191, 193-97, 199, 217, 246, 313
Dror, Amnon, 326, 341
Dulles, John Foster, v, vi, vii, 82, 93, 105, 117, 119, 141, 185, 202, 235
Dusseldorf, 113-14, 239

Ebert, Col. (Amer. Military Attache), 143
Edan, Judge, 284-85, 287
Eden, Sir Anthony, 56, 235
Egypt, vii, viii, 13, 17, 23, 30, 47, 54-55, 60, 66, 70, 83, 91, 101, 105, 107, 112, 117, 119, 121, 125, 127, 136, 150, 153, 158, 160-65, 168, 173, 175, 178, 183-84, 186-88, 191-92, 194-95, 198-99, 203-04, 206-09, 212-13,
216, 224, 226, 229, 234-35, 238, 241, 244, 262, 269, 271, 273, 282, 285, 287, 301, 303, 313, 316, 349, 352
Egyptian
army, 26, 50, 56, 105
despot, vi
consulate, 58-59
nationalism, 56
navy, 82, 87
Eichmann, Adolph, 326, 332-34
Eilat, 116, 158
Eisenhower, Dwight D., v, 82
inauguration, vi
administration, vii
El-Ad, 24
El-Ad Sarchi, 24, 28, 42-43, 137-38, 175
volumes, iii, 89, 162, 229, 259
El-Al Airlines, 44, 63, 176
office, 242-43
El Alamein, 94-95
El-Arish, 109
El Gedawy Hassan, 190
El Giza, 71, 148, 159
Eliminations, 120, 125, 129
list, 134-35
Ellison, Captain, 25
Engel, Dr. Rolf, 83, 85, 87, 100-02, 105, 110-14, 128, 134, 141-43, 145, 154, 158
England, vi, 16, 47, 55, 82, 105, 111, 185, 234-35
Enotria, S.S., 66, 69-70, 86, 88
Eshed, Chaggai, 327, 342
Eshet, Col., 208
Eshkol, Levi, 320, 325-26, 341, 347
Ethiopia, 29, 312, 318
Etka, 229, 232
Europa Cafe, 242, 288
Europe, 3, 23, 29, 35, 58, 86, 111, 115, 131, 157, 160, 163, 173, 188, 206, 208, 228, 252, 259, 261, 272, 298, 305, 311, 315, 324
colonialism, vi
Evans, Col. (Amer. Military Attache), 143
Evron, "Eppie" Ephraim, 186-87, 189, 191, 198, 205, 313-16

Fahmi, Rageb (Commodore Egyptian Navy), 104, 111
Fahrmbacher, Gen. Wilhelm, 50, 76, 81, 86, 90, 94-96, 102, 108, 109, 111, 125-26, 134, 137, 142, 157-58, 162, 165
Farida, Princess, 139
Farrag, 74, 82, 101
Farrag, Col., 82, 85

"Paul" (Dr. Moussa Marzouk), 131
Pawelke, Dr. (German Ambassador to Egypt), 70-74, 85-86, 89
Peres, Shimon, 186, 199, 237, 312, 318, 327
Pharonic Engineering Company, 74
Pierre Affair, 161, 181
Pierre (Levi, Victor), 128-29, 134, 149-50
  report, 189, 191, 200, 203, 205, 299
Pohl, Ludwig, 51-52, 60
Poland, 15
Poldi, 90, 113, 115, 165-66, 171, 215, 217, 223
Pollak, Oscar, 246
Polygraph (lie detector), 255, 256, 277
Popper, 232
Port Said, 101-02, 109
Port Taufiq, 108, 158
Prager, Captain Eli, 255-60, 263, 266, 272, 290
Program for the Housewife, 126, 138
Program of Your Choice, 126
Prussian, 35-36

Queen Narriman, 152

Rabbinical Court, 22
Rabin, General Yitzhak, 66, 236, 298
Rachel, 25
Rafi Party, 327
Ramat-David, 13
Ramla Prison, 30, 201, 264-65, 267, 271, 278-79, 291, 306-09, 232, 328, 330-31, 333, 335, 337-38, 345-46, 350
Raphael, Gideon, 170
Ras el Tin, 93
Ras Sudr, 108
Red Sea, 72
Regensburg an der Donau, 104
Regiment Infantry School, 14
Regimental Commander Course, 14, 30
Religion
  law, 11
Remes, Aron, 220-21
Rensburg, 165, 169
Reserve Officer, 337-38
Revolutionary Command Council, 91, 105-06
Rio Movie House, 149, 201
Ritterkreuz, 45
Rivoli Movie House, 147-48
"Robert," 127-28, 131, 134, 138, 149-50, 152-53
Roemisch, Kurt, 76
Roda Island, 106
Roger (Dassa, Reuben), 129, 138
Rome, 62-63, 65, 88, 91, 111-12, 127, 166, 176-77, 181, 205

Rommel, Field Marshall Erwin, 50, 60, 72, 95, 103
Rosen, Pinhas, 325
Roser, Major General SS, 104-05
Rosetta Hotel, 103
Rottem, Benjamin, 88-89, 112, 127, 134, 154, 166
Royal Air Force (WAAF), 15
Rudi, Dr., 30, 32-33, 265
Rushdi, Ahmed, 171
Russia, 82, 104, 117, 235, 311
  intelligence, 282
  spy, 282, 284
Ruth, 256, 269, 274, 276-77, 279, 304, 306-08, 342

Sabotage, 112, 118, 126, 129, 147, 179, 198, 201, 205, 207, 228, 235-36, 261, 271, 280, 290, 298, 307
  action, 178, 191, 200, 203, 342
Sabra, 88
Sabry, Ali, 106
Sachenhausen, 38
Saint Katherina Monastery, 96, 108, 109
Sakara, 75-76
Salem, Major Salah, 106
Samir (transmitter), 131, 135, 150
Sapir, Pinhas, 251, 312-13
Sarafand, 25
Schaffer (Mercedes-Benz V.P. Export), 218
Schaufer, Jacki, 242
Schiloach, Reuben, 313
Schmeisser, 61
Schneider, Hans, 62, 91-92, 127, 136, 145, 218
Schwechat Airfield, 47, 62
Schweizer Hof, 34, 174
Schwilly, Dr. P., 136
Sde Boker, 120, 205, 327
Secret field reports, iii
Security mishap, iii
Segal, Machum, 20
Seidenwerg, Avri (Adolph) El-Ad, iii, 34, 241, 278, 305, 348
Seidenwerg, Cilli (Kober), 16
Seidenwerg, Harel, 4, 15, 21, 63, 89, 161-62
Seidenwerg, Shulamit (Landshut), 14
Seidenwerg, Sigmund, 15, 245, 246, 249
Semiramis Hotel, 76, 86, 139
Shai, 163
Shamgar, Colonel, 271-73
Sharett, Moshe (Prime Minister), 183, 185-86, 191, 193, 196, 201-02, 204-05, 209, 214, 217, 220, 261, 317-20, 323

362